Current Studies in Romance Linguistics

Marta Luján
Fritz Hensey

Editors

Georgetown University Press, Washington, D.C. 20057

Library of Congress Cataloging in Publication Data

Texas Symposium on Romance Linguistics, 4th, University of Texas, 1974.
Current studies in Romance linguistics.

Bibliography: p.
1. Romance languages--Congresses. I. Luján, Marta. II. Hensey, Fritz G. III. Title.
PC11.T4 1974 440 76-897
ISBN 0-87840-041-9

Printed in the United States of America

International Standard Book Number: 0-87840-041-9

CONTENTS

PREFACE

The papers in this volume were presented at the Texas Symposium on Romance Linguistics, which was held at the University of Texas in the spring of 1974. The Texas symposium is the fourth of a series of meetings which constitute the major annual conferences of their kind in the U.S.A. This series of annual conferences on the Romance languages started at the University of Florida in 1971, and were subsequently held at the University of Illinois, and at Indiana University. Their goal has been to bring forth novel contributions to the (synchronic and diachronic) description of the Romance languages in the light of recent developments in linguistic theory. In using the term Romance Linguistics, both in the title of the symposium and in the title of this book, we have departed from the traditional use, as we have broadened its scope to include synchronic studies of the individual Romance languages as well as historical or comparative studies of the Romance family as a whole.

The papers are grouped in two main sections: Phonology, and Syntax and Semantics. In each section, diachronic studies precede synchronic studies, and, wherever it was possible, we clustered the papers according to the topics, rather than according to the individual languages they dealt with. Latin and the four major Romance languages are represented in about the same proportions established in earlier meetings. French and Spanish continue to receive the major emphasis, but Portuguese and Italian show an increase over their representation in previous symposia. Synchronic studies outnumber those of an historical or comparative nature; phonology and syntax dominate the list of topics, but as a reflection of the recent upsurge in semantic studies, the semantic area is far from neglected.

The Texas symposium was sponsored by the Institute of Latin American Studies, the Graduate School, the College of Education, the Division of General and Comparative Studies, the Office of Bilingual Education, the Department of Linguistics, the Department of French and Italian, and the Department of Spanish and Portuguese of the University of Texas at Austin. We are grateful for their support, which made the symposium possible. We are specially indebted to our chairman, Rodolfo Cardona, and to William P. Glade, director of the Institute of Latin American Studies, for their initial support and encouragement. We are also grateful to C. L. Baker, Michael K. Brame, Richard S. Kayne, David M. Perlmutter, Stanley Peters, María-Luisa Rivero, Nicolas Ruwet, Mario Saltarelli, and Dieter Wanner, who integrated the Program Committee, for helping us with the difficult task of selecting the papers for the conference. We finally want to express our gratitude to the many students and colleagues who unstintingly assisted us with the many details of the conference, in particular, our colleagues Lily Litvak and Pablo Beltrán de Heredia. Special thanks go to Professor Yakov Malkiel, who, not having been able to accept our invitation to participate in the symposium due to previous commitments, graciously contributed a paper for this volume.

M. L.
F. H.

Department of Spanish and Portuguese
The University of Texas at Austin

VOWEL-LOWERING AND i-EPENTHESIS IN CLASSICAL LATIN

WAYNE J. REDENBARGER

Harvard University

Synchronic evidence for two key rules of Latin phonology will be offered. These will, in turn, permit a reanalysis of several aspects of Latin noun and verb morphology.

TABLE 1. Second person singular verb forms

Pres. Ind. Act.	laudās	monēs	dūcis	capis	audīs
Pres. Ind. Pas.	laudāris	monēris	dūceris	caperis	audīris
Impf. Sub. Act.	laudārēs	monērēs	dūcerēs	caperēs	audīrēs
Impf. Sub. Pas.	laudārēris	monērēris	dūcerēris	caperēris	audīrēris
Imptv. sg.	laudā	monē	dūc	cape	audī
Imptv. pl.	laudāte	monēte	dūcite	capite	audīte
Infinitive	laudāre	monēre	dūcere	capere	audīre
Fut. Ind. Act.	laudābis	monēbis			
Fut. Ind. Pas.	laudāberis	monēberis			
Fut. Ind. Act.			dūcēs	capiēs	audiēs
Fut. Ind. Pas.			dūcēris	capiēris	audiēris
Impf. Ind. Act.	laudābās	monēbās	dūcēbās	capiēbās	audiēbās
Impf. Ind. Pas.	laudābāris	monēbāris	dūcēbāris	capiēbāris	audiēbāris
Pres. Sub. Act.	laudēs	moneās	dūcās	capiās	audiās
Pres. Sub. Pas.	laudēris	moneāris	dūcāris	capiāris	audiāris
Pres. Ptcpl.	laudāns	monēns	ducēns	capiēns	audiēns

In Table 1, notice the alternation between [e] and [i] in the top seven forms of the fourth column, the *cap-* forms. Although the traditional analysis suggests an underlying theme vowel of short /e/, given the infinitive *capĕre*, the evidence points instead to an underlying /ĭ/. The arguments for this are several and I shall itemize them directly; however, one should first note that this [e]/[i] alternation appears in several other places and in other grammatical categories.

For example, the future marker in the *laud-* and *mon-* forms of the indicative active and passive is [bi] before sibilants, stops, and nasals: 2sg. *monēbis*, *laudābis*; 3sg. *monēbit*, *laudābit*; 1pl. *monēbimus*, *laudābimus*. Likewise, in the passive forms: 3sg. *monēbitur*, *laudābitur*; 1pl. *monēbimur*, *laudābimur*. However, while it happens that the passive third person singular and first person plural forms both begin with the same sound as their active counterparts, the second person singular passive ending is [r] initial and one sees [be] instead of [bi]: *monēberis*, *laudāberis*.

This distribution thus concurs exactly with the top seven *cap-* forms which show [i] before [s] and [t], versus [e] before [r]; in addition, these future forms illustrate the environment before [m] for the sound [i].

Consider also the following neuter nouns of the third declension, *rūs* 'country' (a normal neuter), and *mare* 'sea' (both a neuter and an *i*-stem noun):

nom./acc. sg.	(+∅)	rūs	mare
nom./acc. sg.	(+a)	rūra	maria
gen. pl.	(+um)	rūrum	marium

The difference between the consonant final stem of *rūs* and the vowel final of *mare* is clear, as is the alternation of [e]/[i] in that stem: [e] appears word finally and [i] before vowels.

Referring back to the *cap-* forms listed in Table 1, note that the difference between the 'top 7' and the 'lower 7' is that the top forms have consonant initial affixes plus the affixless imperative, while the lower forms comprise the set of vowel-initial affixes. The *mare*, *maria*, *marium* forms then match exactly this distribution with [e] in final position and [i] before all vowels.

Summarizing the [e]/[i] distribution from these three sources, one finds [i] before sibilants, stops, nasals, and vowels, while [e] is found before [r] and word finally.

A first argument could thus be advanced, based on the formal specification of the rule's environment. Any attempt to posit /e/ as underlying and derive [i] as a variant will be forced to express an environment including vowels, stops, sibilants, and nasals as a natural class. But this is a negative environment, for the upshot of such a 'class' is to say /e/→ [i] everywhere except before [r] and word finally. The basic motivation behind distinctive features is to facilitate the expression of natural classes of sounds; whenever one finds such an environment which encompasses nearly everything and excludes only two segments, the theoretical constraints built into the distinctive feature framework indicate that the correct generalization lies in the reverse direction with /i/→ [e] / ___ $\begin{Bmatrix} [r] \\ \# \end{Bmatrix}$.

A second argument can be based on the unnaturalness of the underlying configurations necessitated by a raising rule instead of my proposed lowering rule. Compare, for example, the ablative singular forms for the two neuter nouns cited earlier: rūre, but marī. If one chooses to lower /i/→[e] in final position, as I am suggesting, the final -[e] ablative marker can be derived from underlying /ĭ/; and, by considering that ablative marker to be underlying /ĭ/, the long [ī] in the i-stem neuter is accomplished by an extremely natural rule /i+i/→[ī], which, as will be seen later, is but a subcase of a rule needed elsewhere in the phonology.

Now, it is not a priori impossible to say the opposite, namely, that the surface ablative [e] of the consonant stems reflects the underlying form and the [ī] in the i-stems nouns is the result of a rule /i+e/→[ī]. This would, however, be a new rule created to handle this case alone, and it is certainly a less desirable alternative than using independently motivated rules.

More importantly, however, there exist forms elsewhere in the phonology which prove that an /i+e/→ [ī] rule is impossible. And, of course, if this can be shown, then my lowering rule will have been demonstrated to be the more plausible alternative.

The forms which show this are the second declension nouns. Their vocative singular ending has the same sort of alternation just seen with the ablative singular of the third declension:

	(normal)	(i-stem)
nom. sg.	amīcus 'friend'	fīlius 'son'
dat. sg.	amīcō	fīliō
voc. sg.	amīce	fīlī

with vocative [e] normally, and [ī] with the i-stem nouns.

Masculine singular adjectives of the second declension generally take the same endings as the noun amīcus and would not normally even require a separate table for their itemization:

nom. sg.	amīcus magnus
dat. sg.	amīcō magnō
voc. sg.	amīce magne

However, when one examines the second declension adjectives having i-stems, like ēgregius 'outstanding', one finds that the vocative singular does not show [ī] but rather [ie].

nom. sg.	fīlius ēgregius
dat. sg.	fīliō ēgregiō

but

voc. sg.	fīlī ēgregie (not *ēgregī)

This example illustrates first that the underlying vocative ending for second declension adjectives must be different from that in nouns, since in the adjective there is no fusion with the /i/ of i-stems to make long [ī]. But more importantly, because of that difference it is clearly impossible to postulate underlying /e/ for nouns in the [i]/[e] vocative affix alternation:

	(assuming a raising rule)
Nouns:	/amīc+e/ ↛
	/fīli+e/→ fīlī (by /i+e/→ [ī])
Adjectives:	/magn+e/ ↛
	/ēgregi+e/→ *ēgregī (by /i+e/→ [i])

Yet if one eliminates the /i+e/→ [ī] rule which is producing the wrong output in i-stem adjectives, there is no way to derive long [ī] in the nouns. In short, since there exist attested examples of [ie] on the surface undisturbed, it is going to be impossible to say that surface [ī] is derived from an /i+e/ sequence.

It might be said that there is something wrong with an analysis requiring a separate set of endings for second declension adjectives when they share all their forms, except one, with the second declension nouns. This is not, however, the only instance of such a paradigm in Latin. Consider the ablative singular desinence in the third declension.

Positive grade participles are i-stems, and thus the ablative singular of amans 'loving' is amantī, just as for any third declension i-stem adjective: ab amantī patre 'by the loving father'. But participles are unusual in that they can be either adjectives or nouns, and when amans is used as in the expression ab amante 'by the lover', it has an ablative singular in [e], not [ī]. Most importantly, this is the only form that changes; all other case forms match exactly.

Note that these forms serve as double examples. They illustrate not only the nature of the difference in underlying forms between adjectives and nouns in nearly identical morphological paradigms, but also that these i-stems (showing a surface alternation of [i]/[e]) comprise yet another case which any analysis based on a raising rule cannot handle. With the lowering process I am suggesting, the final short [e] is seen as the /i/ of the i-stem followed by a -Ø affix, and thus the /i/ is word final and undergoes lowering.

With a raising rule the contrast would have to be a morphologically marked exception. Furthermore, the exception would be a hard one to generalize since it has now been seen that there are unhandleable contrasts between different grammatical categories (adj-noun), in different cases in the same grammatical category (abl. sg. and voc. sg. in i-stem second declension adjectives), and in different declensions (both second and third). Obviously, the alternative solution involving a lowering rule is to be preferred.

Summarizing, the underlying configurations needed for input to a raising rule /e/→[i] in turn necessitate a rule /i+e/→[ī] to explain the ablative singular of third declension nouns and the vocative singular of second declension nouns. This rule is not only ad hoc but it produces erroneous output elsewhere in the phonology and is thus clearly wrong.

It was noted earlier in discussing the /i+i/→ [ī] rule that this was a subcase of a larger process for resolving vocalic hiatus groups. This rule, which I shall refer to as 'Collapsing', can be written:

$$\underset{[\alpha F]}{V(:)}\ \underset{[\alpha F]}{V(:)} \rightarrow \underset{[\alpha F]}{V:}$$

since it produces long vowels from a pair of long vowels: 2sg. imp. ind. act. /monē+ēbā+s/→ [monēbās]; from a short and a long: 3rd dclnsn. dat. sg. /mari-ī/→ [marī]; or from two like short vowels: 3rd dclnsn. abl. sg. /mari+i/→ [marī].

This rule also provides another argument for vowel-lowering over vowel-raising. If it is necessary to postulate an underlying /e/ in the cap- forms to explain the [e]/[i] alternation seen there, the appearance of [i] in the cap- forms with vowel-initial affixes will require a dissimilation rule something like /e/→ [i] / ___ [ē] to explain the fut. ind. act. capiēs, or the impf. ind. act. capiēs, or the impf. ind. act. capiēbās. I think it is generally agreed that an assimilation rule is more natural than a dissimilation rule. Considering also that implementing a dissimilation rule here would directly contradict the highly natural 'Collapsing' rule, it is apparent that in this way too, the underlying /ĕ/, traditionally posited for the third conjugation and necessary for a raising rule, is highly improbable.

My last major argument for /i/→[e] is one which I feel illustrates at its best the superiority of the distinctive feature framework over previous theories. It is a hypothesis of generative phonology that rules should be written as economically as possible and that in so doing, i.e., in always specifying the broadest possible natural class of sounds in defining any phonological change or any phonological environment for a change, one will be directed by the constraints of the theory toward a more correct statement.

In this case, in writing the hypothesized rule:

$$/i/ \rightarrow [e] \; / \; \_\_ \begin{Bmatrix} [r] \\ \# \end{Bmatrix}$$

one is actually abbreviating a distinctive feature matrix by the phonetic symbols:

$$\underset{[-\text{back}]}{V} \rightarrow [-\text{high}] \; / \; \_\_ \left\{ \begin{matrix} \begin{bmatrix} -\text{syl} \\ -\text{obs} \\ -\text{lat} \end{bmatrix} \\ \# \end{matrix} \right\}$$

But no reason has really yet been given for wanting to restrict the operation of the rule to the nonback vowels. And, in fact, the following kind of alternation is found in words like <u>corpus</u>:

	<u>nom./acc. sg.</u>	<u>dat. sg.</u>	<u>nom./acc. pl.</u>
	/corpus+Ø/	/corpus+ī/	/corpus+a/
Rhotacism:	↛	→ corpur ī	→ corpur a
Vowel-lowering:	↛	→ corpor ī	→ corpor a
	[corpus]	[corporī]	[corpora]

where [u] in the stem alternates with [o] in all forms where [u] would have preceded an [r]. The [r] occasioning the change is itself derived from the underlying /s/ seen in the nominative and accusative singular and which, via rhotacism, becomes [r].

Thus, here is a situation where the vowel-lowering process, previously observed in front vowels, is seen to be doing exactly the same thing in back vowels. Whenever an [r] is created by rhotacism, it lowers the high vowel immediately preceding. Although the data might be codified by postulating an underlying /o/ in these cases and adding some rule /o/→[u] / ___ [s] #, notice that this is not only ignoring the symmetry of the vowel-lowering in both front and back vowels, but is also creating a rule of little generality to handle the problem. It was seen in the initial stages of the [e]/[i] alternation arguments, that it was possible to look at the two distributions as being almost complementary; in this case, the modification before final [s] is clearly an unexplanatory subpart of the distribution of [+syl, +high] before sibilants, stops, nasals, and vowels. Since it has already been shown how that distribution is so wide (it describes the panorama of environments with underlying /i/), I submit that it is logical to hypothesize an underlying /u/ here as well.

Thus, this lowering rule is considered to be correct since in its widest expansion it makes correct predictions elsewhere. Its final form reads:

$$[+syl] \rightarrow [-high] \;/\; \underline{\quad} \begin{Bmatrix} [r] \\ \# \end{Bmatrix}$$

A parenthetical comment should be made at this point in order to obviate any confusions caused by [e]/[i] alternations outside the scope of the vowel-lowering rule presented here. Latin has an early iotacism process which converts all short vowels in open syllables to [i], but only in internal syllables. Thus one sees /a/→ [i] in *facio:conficio*; /u/→ [i] in *caput:capitis*; /e/→ [i] in *lego:colligo*, etc. This minor rule, which creates as part of its operation some [e]/[i] alternations, should not be confused with the vowel-lowering rule. That they are separate processes, crucially ordered, (1) iotacism (2) vowel-lowering, is illustrated by the forms *dare:redere*; or *genus:generis*, etc., where the [i] produced by the iotacism rule is lowered to [e] before [r] by the vowel-lowering rule.

The vowel-lowering rule presented above constitutes the key to the entire paradigm of the Latin verb and noun. With the [i]/[e] alternations codified, it is possible to build a straightforward analysis of further rules which are now more discernible. The most important of these is the Epenthesis rule which accounts for the partial similarity of the *dūc-* forms and the *cap-* forms. Referring again to Table 1, notice the same alternation of [e] and [i] in the top *dūc-* forms that is seen in the top *cap-* forms. For reasons argued earlier, it is known that this reflects an underlying /i/, not /e/, in these forms. But notice that in the lower forms, where *cap-* continues to have its underlying /i/ vowel before the vowel-initial affixes, there is no evidence of any theme vowel in the *duc-* forms: where one sees *-iēs* in the *cap-* forms, *dūc-* shows only *-ēs*; *-iās* in the *cap-* forms, but *-ās* in *dūc-*; etc.

Another illustration that the third conjugation in Classical Latin is indeed athematic is furnished by the imperatives. As Meillet notes (1964:236), in Indo-European the imperatives of athematic verbs were formed differently from the imperatives of thematic verbs. For those stems ending in theme vowels, the imperative consisted of only the stem standing alone with no desinence; the athematic verbs, whose stems are consonant-final, formed their imperatives instead by adding to the stem a particle ending in short [i]. This created a situation where all imperatives were vowel final, be they from thematic or athematic stems.

This Indo-European situation is the one found in Old Latin: laudā, monē, audī, /capi/→ cape, and dūce. But in Classical Latin there is an attempt to regularize imperative formation, and one sees the beginnings of the elimination of the final -e in the third conjugation imperatives with (OL) dūce > (CL) dūc; (OL) dice > (CL) dic. This change, which has long been an enigma, makes a great deal of sense when it is seen as the regularization of the morphology of imperative formation (i. e. showing just the stem in the imperatives) and the direction of that change is from a form ending in a vowel to a stem showing no vowel at all.

So, returning to the dūc- and cap- forms in the table, it is clear that the question is not how to get rid of [i] in the lower seven forms without messing up the cap- forms (an impossible task), but rather to ask where the underlying /i/ came from in the top set.

I suggest that the [i] is the result of an epenthesis process, very similar to the one seen in English with the plural affix /+s/ in nouns and the third person singular marker in verbs, and the /+d/ affix in past participles; namely, a vowel is epenthesized between strident segments in the first case and alveolar stops in the second to create more felicitous sequences: /rose+s/→ roses, /bush+s/→ bushes, /fade+d/→ faded. I suggest that Latin has the same general process: [i] is inserted at affix boundaries to break up consonant clusters:

2sg. pres. ind. act.	/dūc+Ø+s/
	→ dūc i s
imperative pl.	/dūc+Ø+te/
	→ dūc i te

No epenthesis is needed with vowel initial affixes since no cluster is created:

2sg. pres. subj. act.	/dūc+Ø+ās/+→
2sg. futr. ind. act.	/dūc+Ø+ēs/+→
3pl. pres. ind. act.	/dūc+Ø+unt/+→
3pl. pres. ind. act.	/capi+Ø+unt/+→

Formalized, the rule is:

$\emptyset \rightarrow [i] \; / \; C \_\_\_ +C$

Note that epenthesis is in a feeding relation to vowel-lowering:

pres. ind. pas.	/dūc+Ø+ris/
	→ dūc i ris (epenthesis)
	→ dūc e ris (vowel-lowering)
infinitive	/dūc+Ø+re/
	→ dūc i re (epenthesis)
	→ dūc e re (vowel-lowering)

Note the necessity to require the plus juncture in order to restrict the rule to operate at affix boundaries only (just like the English rule, incidentally). There are many situations in Latin, as in English, where at the end of a closed syllable preceding another consonant-initial syllable, one finds clusters which do not undergo this epenthesis process: (English) horseshoe ↛ *[horsɨʃuw]; (Latin) mittēs ↛ *[mititēs].

Although I have emphasized the explanatory value of this rule with regard to its ability to solve the taxonomical puzzle which is the third conjugation, let me stress that this is not just an ad hoc rule to solve that problem alone. Consider the future marker as it appears with the laud- forms and the mon-forms:

2sg. futr. ind. act.	laudābis	monēbis
2sg. futr. ind. pas.	laudāberis	monēberis
3sg. futr. ind. act.	laudābit	monēbit

but,

3pl. futr. ind. act.	laudābunt	monēbunt
1sg. futr. ind. act.	laudābō	monēbō

It is clear that an underlying future marker of /bi/ would do the job for only the first three forms; there is trouble with the [i] part of the /bi/ morpheme because it is known that there are forms like capiō with [i] surviving before [ō], thus making it hard to delete in laudābō. Likewise, compare laudabunt and capiunt to show that short [i] does not delete before [u].

Note, however, that if the marker is /b/, the epenthesis rule would correctly predict the occurrence of [i] before [s] and [r]; conversely, it would predict no epenthesized [i] before the vowel-initial affixes.

It is likewise not clear at first glance, given 'Collapsing', why the dat./abl. pl. of i-stems of the third declension have a short [i] just as the regular non-i-stems do: abl. sg. /mari+i/→ marī; dat./abl. pl. /reg+ibus/ ↛ ; dat./abl. pl. /mari+ibus/→ *marībus (correct form maribus). However, if the marker is considered to be /bus/ instead of */ibus/, the noun stems ending in a consonant will be up against a following [b] from the affix and epenthesis will operate: /reg+bus/→ regibus, /mari+bus/+→.

In fact, in codifying these two rules I have totally eliminated many pseudo-problems which were created by the traditional assumption of a third conjugation theme vowel. For instance: (1) when the third conjugation theme vowel is deleted, as in dūcāris (under these rules it was never there); (2) when it changes to [u]: dūcunt (in this analysis the [u] is part of the affix: capiunt and audiunt); (3) when it changes to [i]: dūcis, dūcite (in this analysis this is the underlying quality of the epenthesized vowel); (4) when it changes to [e]: dūcēbās, dūcēris (in this analysis the [e] is part of the affix; the imperfect marker is +/ēbā/+, not +/bā/+); (5) when it just stays [e]: dūcere, dūcerēs, dūceris (by these rules it never 'stays' [e] . . . the [e] is an epenthesized [i] which is in turn lowered before [r]).

It seems especially ironic that the short [e] of the infinitive was for so long used as a taxonomic norm when, if the analysis presented here is correct, the underlying structure has been more obscured in that form than in any other.

Historically, the attempt to force the third conjugation into a thematic mold has obscured the synchronic productivity of the verbal morphology across all the other conjugations as well. To illustrate the immense simplification achieved by adopting vowel-lowering, i-epenthesis, and an athematic third conjugation, I offer the following schema which, together with a few widely accepted rules long recognized in Latin phonology (cf. Appendix), will generate all 315 verb forms based on the present stem, including all details of vowel quality and quantity:

imptv(pl):	Root+TV(+te)	
infntv:	Root+TV+re	
pres. ind.	Root+TV +D	
pres. sub.	Root+TV+ ā +D	(2,3,4)
	Root+ ē +D	(1)
impf. ind.	Root+TV+ēbā+D	
impf. sub.	Root+TV+rē +D	
futr. ind.	Root+TV+ b +D	(1, 2)
	Root+TV+ ē +D	(3, 4)

If I may appeal to an old maxim in science, namely, that 'the right answer is usually a simple one', I submit that the simplicity of this schema--made possible by the rules just presented--argues strongly that this is indeed the correct analysis.

There exist two forms which would appear to be counter-examples to epenthesis; both are only apparent problems. The first of these is the class of 3rd declension nominative singulars which show final clusters like [ks]: dūx 'leader', or [ps]: prīnceps 'chief', where one would have expected the cluster to have been separated by an epenthesized vowel. And indeed, if the situation were that simple, there would be a problem in explaining what happened to the epenthesized [i]. But looking at some i-stem nouns of this same class, one finds the following:

	C-stem	i-stem	
nom. sg.	dūx 'leader'	nox 'night'	urbs 'city'
gen. pl.	dūcum	noctium	urbium
acc. pl.	dūcēs	noctīs	urbīs

Note the -ium genitive plural and the -īs accusative plural which are the sign of i-stem nouns. Yet in the nominative singulars the -i- is missing. Thus it is clear that even if there existed no epenthesis rule, one would still need a rule to delete short [i] in an exceptional class of nominative singulars to explain the behavior of the i-stems. This happens to a special class only, as is shown by the fact that there exist i-stems and consonant stem third declension nouns with their [i] (underlying in the first case and epenthesized in the second) intact:

	C-stems		i-stems	
	'dog'	'youth'	'city'	'fire'
nom. sg.	canis	juvenis	civis	ignis
gen. sg.	canum	juvenum	civium	ignium
acc. sg.	canēs	juvenēs	civīs	ignīs

Thus it is seen that these imparisyllabic nouns like dūx, nox, urbs, etc. are imparisyllabic (i.e. have one fewer syllable in the nominative singular than predicted) because they are marked for a rule [i] → Ø / ___ +[s] #. Since this minor rule deletes both [i]'s from i-stems and [i]'s created by epenthesis, it is clear that the absence of [i] in imparisyllabic nominative singulars does not constitute a counterexample to epenthesis.

The other forms which appear at first glance to be counterexamples to epenthesis are certain perfect passive participles, like ductus, dictus, etc., where the -CC-sequence would appear to be a candidate for epenthesis. Note, however, that this analysis makes the assumption that there is a productive plus boundary separating the [k] and [t], i.e. to consider these as counterexamples is to claim that these fourth-part participles are still productively formed /+tó+/ participles just as they were in Indo-European. I do not think this is the case--especially since it is clear that the only relation these particles have to the present stem is a historical one; note the unpredictable situation in the second conjugation: docēre:doctus, monēre:monitus; the disappearance of the [i] from verbs like faciō, facere:factus; and even the extremely regular first conjugation is not without doublets like fricāre:frictus/fricātus.

I have found it very instructive to examine tables of verb stems to see the immense and arbitrary variation between first and fourth parts of Latin verbs (cf. Bennett 1918:83-94). I do not see how this could be done short of reinstituting the sigmatic aorist and all the other historical apparatus of the Indo-European stem needed to explain the dozens of morphological alternations, reduplications, vowel-lengthenings, vowel-shortenings, ablaut, etc., which would be necessary to derive the present stem, the perfect stem, and the participial stem synchronically in Classical Latin. It seems a very dubious assumption that the Latin participial stem is other than a unitary adjective with no productive plus boundary except at the point where the desinences are attached. Thus, the lack of an epenthesized vowel is no more surprising than its absence in *mititit for mittit.

In summary, six synchronic arguments have been presented for rules of vowel-lowering and i-epenthesis in Classical Latin. These rules form the basis of a new analysis of the Latin conjugational schema that has two types of thematic marker: either (1) a long quantity vowel /ā/, /ē/, or /ī/, or (2) athematic, with no theme vowel at all.

The conjugation previously thought to have a short /e/ theme vowel is seen instead to be athematic; the difference between the regular athematic verbs and the '-iō verbs of the third conjugation' is that, normally, verb stems are consonant-final, but these '-iō' verbs are i-stems. Thus they show their underlying /i/ vowel everywhere, while the [i] created by epenthesis appears only between consonants.

It is a century-old methodological maxim that before doing historical comparative reconstruction, one must first do internal reconstruction. Thus, given this new analysis of the synchronic system of Latin, previous analyses of how Latin developed into the Romance languages must now be reconsidered (cf. Redenbarger (to appear)).

APPENDIX

The widely accepted rules I am assuming are:

(1) $\bar{V} \rightarrow V$ / ___ V 'vocalis ante vocalem corripitur' (cf. Niedermann 1953:83) hence /aud+ī+ē+s/— [audiēs], etc.
(2) $\bar{V} \rightarrow V$ / # C V C ___ # (cf. Meillet-Vendreyes 1968:§ 215 for 'la loi des mots iambes') ordered after vowel-lowering, thus explaining why <u>ubi</u> 'where' or <u>nisi</u> 'if not' are not counter-examples to vowel-lowering (cf. <u>ubīque</u> and <u>sī</u>).
(3) $\bar{V} \rightarrow V$ / ___ C # (cf. Niedermann 1953:59)
[-str] [-strid]
hence <u>laudatur</u>, <u>monet</u>, <u>ducēbam</u>.
(4) and a couple of deletion rules of the type [ā]→ Ø / ___ [ō] for | laud+ā+ō | → [laudō], and $\begin{Bmatrix} a \\ e \end{Bmatrix} \begin{Bmatrix} u \\ e \end{Bmatrix}$ with the second ↓ Ø

as in /laud+ā+unt/→ [laudant], /aud+ī+ēbā+unt/→ [audiebant], /laud+ā+ēbā+s/→ [laudābās].

NOTE

Special thanks are due to Professors James Harris, Jay Jasanoff, and Robert King for their very constructive criticism of the preliminary draft of this paper. Responsibility for errors is, of course, my own.

LATIN k^w, g^w, > RUMANIAN *p*, *b*: AN EXPLANATION

ROBERT L. RANKIN

University of Kansas

The purpose of this paper is twofold. In the first part I propose to explain two sets of facts from Rumanian, which were not generally thought of as being related, as instances of a single process, that of glide strengthening or increment.[1] In the second part I consider a number of other processes active in natural languages (including Rumanian) such as palatalization and assibilation. I claim that these are also instances of glide increment and should be formalized as such. The conclusions drawn here have implications for phonetic and phonological feature systems.

One of the phonological peculiarities most often associated with Rumanian by Romanists who wish to take note of that language's divergent development is the passage of the Latin labiovelars k^w, g^w to bilabial stops *p* and *b*. Typically cited as examples are:

aqua	> apă 'water'
equa	> iapă 'mare'
lingua	> limbă 'tongue'
*quatt(o)ro	> patru 'four'

These are valid examples, and there are numerous others. In point of fact, this change seems only to have occurred before *a*.[2] The labial element was lost with subsequent palatalization of the remaining velar before front vowels: L. *sanguine* > R. *sînge*, L. *quercus* > R. *cer*, L. *quid* > R. *ce*, etc. There are almost no examples of Rumanian reflexes of Latin labiovelars before back rounded vowels. Comparative data, what little of it there is, indicates that labialization had been lost in this environment at an early date, e.g. L. quomodo > F. comme, S. como, R. cum, etc. The restricted nature of the change makes it no less interesting, however.

A similar change is attested in Sardinian, battoro 'four', ebba 'mare', and, in fact, the labiovelar to bilabial shift is fairly popular, occurring also in Welsh and Breton, Oscan-Umbrian, Ancient Greek, Alabama-Koasati, Caddo, and Choctaw-Chickasaw among others.[3]

The relatively high frequency of this change is one of the factors which led linguists to posit a natural phonological class consisting of labials and velars. Acoustic evidence has been adduced (Jakobson, Fant, and Halle 1963: 29f.) in support of a feature GRAVE or PERIPHERAL, which would permit us to make the pertinent generalizations. This apparent velar to labial shift is also the sort of phenomenon that encourages some comparativists to think in terms of instantaneous rather than gradual phonetic change, since in this case a gradual forward shift in point of articulation would, of course, pass through the zones in which č and t are produced, resulting in the mass confusion of all oral stops. A rule assimilating k > p gradually when it precedes w would be an impossibility.[4]

One very interesting but undiscussed aspect of the labiovelar to labial shift is the fact that in all of the aforementioned languages the rule makes labials of velars, never velars of labials. This, combined with the presence of a labial element w in the segments under consideration, narrows down considerably the number and type of hypotheses that one may make in an attempt to explain the phenomenon. As it turns out, the most productive avenue of approach to the problem involves the search for a complementary process, one which makes velars of labials. One finds the complementary process by examining cases of labial stops followed by the other common oral glide y, i.e. palatalized labials, p^y and b^y. The Romance languages, especially Rumanian, provide clear cases of palatovelar reflexes of palatalized labials. Some of them also provide unambiguous explanations of the mechanics of the shift.

In the following examples, drawn from several different languages and dialects, the palatal glide, yod, has, over the years, assumed the manner of articulation of the preceding stop, feature by feature. The process, then, is the familiar one of yod increment or yod obstruentization.

In Italian, yod increment following labial consonants is most common in Lombardy, Liguria, and the Piedmont in the North, and in Apulia, Calabria, Lucania, and Sicily in the South. The yod that undergoes obstruentization may be from a number of different historical sources. The following examples are from Rohlfs (1949: 296-308):

	Tuscan	Northern dialects	
p^y	piazza	pšaša	'plaza'
	pieno	pšen, pčen, čeŋ	'full'
	seppia	sečča	'cuttlefish'
b^y	bianco	bžeŋk bǰeŋk	'white'
	rabbia	rabǰa	'anger'

In Rheto-Romance, as in all of southern Italy and parts of the North, the reflexes of yod have taken on the manner of articulation (occlusive) of the preceding stop. Examples from Surselvan and Engadine dialects of S. E. Switzerland are from Lausberg (1965: 398ff.).

	Latin	Rhetic
p^y	sapiam	sapḱa
b^y	rabia	rabǵa

In modern French the fricative reflexes of yod are preserved, but the preceding labial consonant has been lost (cf. some of the Italian forms, cited previously).

p^y	sapiam	sache [š]
b^y	rubeum	rouge [ž]

Old Provençal preserved some of the intermediate stages lost in French. Lausberg (1965:398f.) has:

p^y	sapiam	sapcha [pč]
b^y	rabia	rauja [wž]

In Portuguese the only yod to undergo the change was a reflex of palatal ʎ. Obstruentization occurred following voiceless labials only.

p^y	plenum	cheio [š] < [č]
	plagam	chaga [š] < [č]

Williams (1962:63) points out that the change is sporadic in Portuguese.

Rumanian dialects, especially those of Moldavia and Northern Transylvania north of the Danube, and the Arumanian dialects of Greece and Macedonia south of the Danube, preserve the various reflexes of yod in different stages of development. As I have discussed the intricacies of the Rumanian data elsewhere (Rankin 1973a), a few examples here will suffice.

	Literary Rumanian		Wallachia	Other dialects
p^y	piept	'breast'	pχ́ept	pḱept, pčept, ḱept, etc.
	piatră	'stone'	pχ́atrə	pḱatrə, pčatrə, ḱatrə, etc.
b^y	biet	'poor'	bɣ́et	bǵet, bǰet, ǵet, etc.
	obiele	'leggings'	obɣ́ele	obǵele, obǰele, ǵele, etc.

I postulate several distinct stages of yod increment in Rumanian. Each is preserved in one or another geographical area.

Stage 1. Yod assimilates the voicing of the preceding labial consonant.

Stage 2. Yod assimilates obstruence of a preceding consonant often becoming a sibilant fricative.

Stage 3. Yod assimilates to the continuance (and often nasality) of the labial.

Stage 4. The preceding labial is lost, leaving only the palatovelar reflex of the yod.

The first stage is preserved at several locations along the Danube in Oltenia and Wallachia, the second and third in parts of northern Transylvania, and the fourth in Rumania and Soviet Moldavia. The fourth stage is the only one preserved in the dialects of the southern Balkans.

The rules for stages 1 through 3 would normally be collapsed in a synchronic phonology, opacity preventing recovery of the earlier versions.

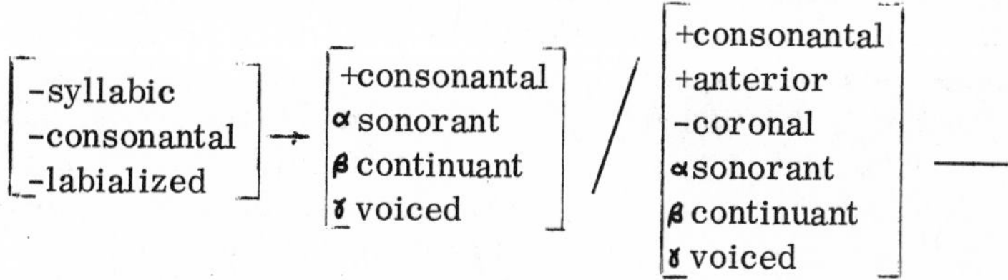

This 'master rule' represents all the various stages of yod increment observable in the Rumanian data. Historically, the variable features were presumably assimilated one or few at a time. Synchronically, different dialects have slightly different versions of the rule, as the isoglosses representing yod after different labial consonants do not entirely overlap, i.e. the typical dialect geography situation.[5]

The Italian examples attested suggest a possible stage in which the reflex of $\underline{y}$ would be a full-fledged fricative, $\underline{\acute{x}}$ or $\underline{\check{s}}$. The apparent progression of yod increment established from the foregoing Romance data and best attested in Rumanian may be summarized as follows:[6]

p^y > $p^{y̥}$ > pχ́ > pḱ > ḱ
b^y > b^y > bɣ́ > bǵ > ǵ

This observed progression suggests a natural and indeed obvious explanation for the apparent passage of k^w and g^w to p and b. If the rules given are written with fewer features specified so that their structural descriptions include w as well as y, and then are applied to k^w and g^w, we derive precisely the desired result. The wau obstruentizes along with the yod:

k^w > $k^{w̥}$ > kɸ > kp > p
g^w > g^w > gβ > gb > b

The following derivations illustrate the operation of the generalized glide obstruentization rules:

	'skin'	'leggings'	'four'	'tongue'
Balkan Romance:	pyele	obyele	kwatru	lingwa
Devoicing rule:	py̥ele	--	*kw̥atru	--
Obstruentization rule:	pχ́ele	obɣ́ele	*kɸatru	*lingβă
Occlusion rule:	pḱele	obǵele	*kpatru	*lingbă
Cluster simplification:	ḱele	oǵele	patru	limbă

Clearly, it is reasonable to assume that the type of glide increment rule, necessary to account for the reflexes of p^y and b^y in most Rumanian dialects, is responsible for the bilabial reflexes of the Latin labiovelars. It is important to note that in no instance has any segment changed point or approximated point of articulation. There has been no actual shift from labial to palatal or from velar to labial articulation, and there is no reason, therefore, to assume that the phonetic process involved was an instantaneous leap. One assumes a similar progression for the other languages which show the labiovelar/ labial correspondence.

In the case of Rumanian, there are one or two important questions of detail that must be dealt with. First, it should be noted that the bilabial reflexes of k^w, g^w, or, more accurately, of w, are found in all Rumanian dialects, both north and south of the Danube.[7] The change must have been completed at a fairly early date, since it spread through all dialects, and intermediate stages, e.g. *kɸ or *gb, are entirely lacking.[8]

It is legitimate to ask whether the glide increment rule responsible for k^w, g^w > p, b is the same one that accounts for the cases of yod increment, or whether glide increment is simply such a common natural process that it was innovated twice, on separate occasions, in early Rumanian. Clearly, the latter is plausible, but I believe that a case can be made for the former also, i.e. it is possible to claim that the two processes were active in the language at the same time.

The passage of y to a palato-velar fricative or stop may have begun somewhat more recently than that of w to a bilabial stop since the change is complete in Arumanian, but only partially complete in Megleno-Rumanian, completely lacking in Istro-Rumanian, and present in Daco-Rumanian dialects to different degrees. It is clear, however (Rankin 1973a), that yod increment following labials had at least begun during the Common Rumanian period before the separation of Arumanian and Daco-Rumanian dialects. Separation was probably complete by the 10th century. The complete generalization of the stop reflexes of w compared with the geographical distribution and variety of the reflexes of yod would seem to argue for an early innovation and spread of wau increment with a somewhat later extension to include yod. If w and y increment began diffusing at the same time, we must explain the lack of dialectal uniformity in the case of y.

Although pḱ, bǵ, etc. might have been caught in process of diffusion by the Slavic invasions and subsequent beginnings of literacy, forms showing yod increment also had a specific, documented sociolinguistic role in Rumanian which may have further affected diffusion, while those showing wau increment had no such role. This role is accorded mention by most Rumanian scholars, but its implications remain largely ignored. It appears that yod increment following labials was a feature of women's speech. The first mention of this fact is in a quotation from the Descriptio Moldaviae (c. 1716) by Prince Dimitrie Cantemir of Moldavia (Meyer-Lübke 1922:14).

> The women of Moldova have a pronunciation different from the men. They change the syllable . . . bi . . . to gi, thus bine: gine . . . (and) pi to ki: pizma: kizma, piatra: kiatra. If a man ever becomes accustomed to this pronunciation, he can almost never free himself of it. . . . Such people are called contemptuously ficior de baba 'mother's boy, sissy' by the common folk.

Meyer Lübke (1922:14) cites information gathered in Wallachia as recently as the early 20th century by one of his students, Vivian Starkey. Starkey also observed that pḱ and bǵ were found 'only in the speech of women'.

The fact that most military and commercial contact was carried on by men explains why the yod increment rule spread more slowly than wau increment. The fact that most of the Rumanian scribes were also men accounts for the lack of written evidence for yod increment in the earliest (16th century) texts. It is frequently claimed that sociological factors play an important role in the diffusion of phonological rules. The observations of Cantemir and Starkey account for early Rumanian philological data and explain why forms showing yod increment and those with yod intact were preserved in the same dialects over a period of several centuries. Sociolinguistic factors played a stabilizing and limiting rather than a catalytic role here.

The attested stages of yod increment following labial consonants help explain the apparent passage of k^w and g^w to p and b, regardless of which phenomenon is historically older.[9] Beyond that, all I can claim to have established is the possibility that there existed a single, generalized glide increment rule in Eastern Latin or Common Rumanian, which failed to spread to a few isolated dialects.[10]

The glide increment rules sketched in this paper represent a perfectly natural development for any oral semivowel in a consonantal environment. So far, I have only examined cases of glide increment following labials and velars, but it is important to note that the rules need contain no reference to labiality or velarity. A glide may assimilate the voicing and consonantality (and often continuance and nasality) of an adjacent consonant, whatever its point or manner of articulation.[11] Thus, for example, yod increment is just as productive following dentals as velars, but its role has been generally overlooked or described incorrectly as 'delayed release', 'palatalization' or 'assibilation'.

The reflexes of such dental and velar 'palatalizations' are typically affricates rather than alveopalatal stops. Thus, in languages which have the process, one normally finds something like the following: t^y or ty, k^y or ky (whether units or clusters) become tš, with slight variation in detail.[12] Voiced or otherwise modified segments or clusters behave analogously.

The two portions of the affricates in question, the stop and the sibilant, are reflexes of separate but interdependent evolution of the two elements within the consonant plus yod clusters. The stop consonant has taken the palatal 'point of articulation' of the following y, while the y has taken the obstruent 'manner of articulation' and voicing of the preceding stop, i.e. it has become a voiced or voiceless fricative instead of an affricate.

Since labial stops do not assimilate to the palatal point of articulation of y, they provide an ideal laboratory in which to observe the evolution of yod following stop consonants generally, without the ambiguity introduced by the competing process of palatalization. Examples of this process have been seen in the Romance data given in this paper.

If the evolution of yod following labial consonants is compared with that of yod following dental and velar consonants, it is seen that the behavior of the semivowel is remarkably similar in all three cases.

Using the rules already observed to operate on yod in Rumanian and Italian dialects and extrapolating for wau increment, one would expect the following. I use voiceless stops as examples for the sake of brevity and clarity, separating the stop and glide so that their separate development is highlighted.

	Wau increment		Yod increment					
	k	w	p	y	t	y	k	y
Devoicing	k	w̥[13]	p	y̥	t́	y̥	t́	y̥[14]
Obstruentization	k	Φ̥	p	x́	t́	x́	t́	x́
Stridency adjustment	k	f	p	š	t́	š	t́	š
Occlusion	k	p	p	ḱ				
Cluster simplification		p		ḱ		š		š

Thus the attested dialectal treatment of labials plus yod in Rumanian provides a model which serves to explain not only the reflexes of Latin labiovelars but also the development of affricates from dental and velar stops in a great variety of the world's languages. This model also permits treatment of both palatalization and subsequent affrication as natural assimilatory processes. Formerly, only palatalization was describable in such terms, while affrication was the product of a nonassimilatory DELAYED RELEASE of the palatalized dental or velar.

The feature DELAYED RELEASE has been systematically misused to describe 'palatalizations'. Chomsky and Halle (1968:420-31) devote about eleven pages to treatment of the dental and velar palatalizations in Slavic and effect affrication by making the vulnerable segments [+coronal, +delrel, +strident, etc.] throughout.

DELREL might be proper for describing (not explaining) affricates when no phonetic glide is present in the structural description of the rule. This might include such cases as German p, t, k > pf, ts, (kx), since this shift does not seem to be amenable to explanation in terms of glide increment,[15] and the release feature is always homorganic to the preceding stop--even in the case of labials.

The developments described in the first part of this paper demonstrate that the process in those cases is not the same as in the German examples. Sound changes such as Germanic *tw > German tsf show that glide increment and delayed release are independent processes, not to be confused with one another. Here, t > ts and w > f.

It is often claimed that the use of certain formal devices such as feature notation lead to improved insight into the mechanisms of language change. I submit that the use of DELAYED RELEASE to describe the process of affrication of dentals and velars is totally inappropriate and, in fact, obscures the operative articulatory processes. Use of DELREL also forces the linguist to make the false claim that the yod which 'causes' affrication undergoes deletion after the affrication has taken place. Rule pairs such as

(a) t, d → t͜š, d͜ž / ___y (etc.), and then
(b) y → ∅ / š, ž ___

or the like, abound in phonological descriptions. There is no reason to think of y as 'absorbed' by š or ž, however. Rule (b) is totally unnecessary when one sees that y in these cases has in fact 'become' š or ž. A single rule of the following form would suffice:

(a′) y → š, ž / t, d___

DELREL, then, is purely classificatory, and although it may permit the linguist to describe phonologically unitary affricates as single underlying segments, it is of limited usefulness in process phonology.

Analysis of the several parallel phenomena discussed in this paper as instances of glide-strengthening has other implications for feature theory and notation. I should like to call into question, as others have, the consistent use in modern phonology of binary features of place, especially GRAVE (or noncoronal) and ANTERIOR.

Features such as DIFFUSE or ANTERIOR which classify labials and dentals together, have always lacked motivation. If ANTERIOR is useful at all, it should be restricted to cases such as θ > f in certain Black and Cockney English dialects, but should not be used just because a given language happens to have labials and dentals.

Similarly, GRAVE should be available for use only in those languages that show significant relationships between labials and velars.[16] Shifts such as x to f might be thought of as applying to GRAVE fricatives; the rules for k^w > p, as has been seen, however, do not require the feature at all. And as I point out at the beginning of this paper, the apparent shift of labiovelars to labials is practically the only evidence that GRAVE ever applies to stop consonants. Features such as GRAVE and ANTERIOR should not be used merely in order to avoid using separate, equipollent features for place of articulation.

In summary, I have shown that several sound changes in Rumanian (and other languages) not previously thought of as related are instances of a single phonetic process, glide increment. This generalized rule must be reconstructed for at least some dialects of Balkan Latin or Common Rumanian.

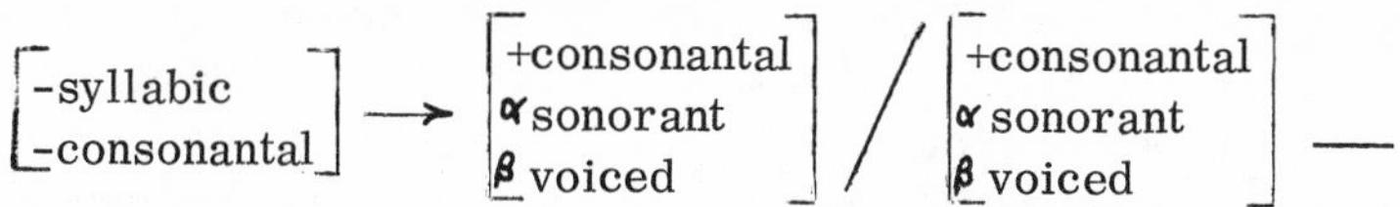

$$\begin{bmatrix} -\text{syllabic} \\ -\text{consonantal} \end{bmatrix} \rightarrow \begin{bmatrix} +\text{consonantal} \\ \alpha\,\text{sonorant} \\ \beta\,\text{voiced} \end{bmatrix} \Big/ \begin{bmatrix} +\text{consonantal} \\ \alpha\,\text{sonorant} \\ \beta\,\text{voiced} \end{bmatrix} \_\_$$

The rule affects either glide (y or w) following labials, dentals, and velars.

Obstruentized glides have become their corresponding stops only if the fricative and preceding stop differed in 'place' of articulation when the rule applied. Homorganic clusters (affricates) appear to be quite stable compared with px́ or kɸ, which undergo the occlusion rule to pḱ and kp

The two primary phenomena discussed in this paper, as well as the extensive velar and dental palatalizations in Romance, Slavic, and many other language families, clearly should be presented as instances of glide increment if the phonetic processes at work are to be accurately formalized.

When rules are written to reflect the phonetic process, it is immediately obvious that a good many types of phonological rules which previously appeared to involve radical shifts in point of articulation actually involve no such shift at all. Although a handful of perplexing cases always remains which would seem to call for out of the ordinary natural classes, it seems to me that any set of universal phonological features must reflect genuinely widespread phenomena.

I believe that when all of the implications of glide-obstruentization are seen and understood, a return to Trubetzkoy's equipollent features for point of articulation may seem more desirable than it has for the past decade. The features LABIAL and VELAR should be used in the phonologies of most languages, with features such as GRAVE, ANTERIOR (and DELAYED RELEASE) relegated to a strictly secondary status and reserved for use in the small number of languages where need for them can be demonstrated on a massive scale.

NOTES

1. I resist the impulse to coin (?) 'fortition' on analogy with

lenition. One linguist has recently borrowed German Verschärfung to fill the terminological gap.

2. Several common interrogative/relative pronouns lost labialization at an early date and are therefore not subject to the change: cît 'how much, many', cînd 'when', care 'which'. Dalmatian and Sardinian show loss of w in the same words.

3. See Solta (1966) for a more comprehensive listing.

4. Many Rumanian scholars have been content simply to point out that Latin qu, gu have bilabial reflexes before a in Rumanian. Rosetti (1932, 1966) and Dimitrescu (1967) propose an epenthesis of p between the k and w elements of the labiovelar, with subsequent w deletion. Densusianu (1901) and Procopovici (1931) propose solutions roughly similar to my own, but without the formal motivation.

5. This rule obstruentizes yod following f, and v and m as well as p and b. This, in fact, occurs but is not treated in this paper. In some Rumanian dialects ḱ and ǵ undergo further evolution to t́, č; d́, ǰ. These changes are discussed in an earlier paper (Rankin 1973b) and, although interesting, have no bearing on the problem at hand.

6. Eric Hamp (personal communication) points out that a similar neat progression is found in Albanian dialects of Yugoslavia from Debar to Skopje. Interestingly, this is an area where many Arumanian speakers are also found.

7. At a similarly early date, Latin w- > v- > Rumanian b- in many instances: L. veteranus > R. bătrîn 'old man', L. vervecem > R. berbece 'ram', L. vocem > Banat R. boace 'voice' (lit. R. voce is a borrowing), etc. Spanish, of course, merges the pair entirely. Siouan languages also show both wau and yod increment in various stages of completion.

8. Wau increment in a slightly different form is still productive in Rumanian. Petrovici (1936:180-81) mentions that in the Banat dialects of western Rumania, words such as (literary) caut 'I search', laud 'I praise', lautǎ 'fiddles', and cheutoare 'button loop' have nonstandard reflexes capt, labd, lawta, cheptoare.

9. Although intermediate stages of wau increment are no longer attested in Rumanian, reflexes of this process are found in a variety of languages, especially at the fricative stage, e.g. German [tsfai] zwei and Russian dva 'two', both from PIE dw-. There is also the standard treatment given loans from Romance in Slavic and Germanic, kw and gw give typically kv or kf and gv, akvavit, coined on aqua vitae, and Russ. gvardeec 'guardsman'. There are hundreds of similar cases. The only stage of wau increment found nowhere is the occlusive stage in combination with the preceding stop, i.e. kp, gb, etc. As noted later, this stage is inherently unstable. Parenthetically, it should be pointed out that the sounds transcribed kp and gb by Africanists probably bear no relation to the clusters under consideration

here; they are usually not clusters at all but velarized labials. Many of the West African languages possessing such sounds also possess a set of labiovelars *k*^{w}, *g*^{w}.

10. Procopovici (1931:417) claims that yod increment did indeed spread to all dialects of Daco-Rumanian. He points out that in those western Transylvanian, Oltenian, and Banat dialects which lack palatal reflexes of the yod, no reflex of *y* is found at all, *piept* > *pept*, etc. He claims that earlier *pḱ* clusters existed, but that the palatal component was lost, i.e. cluster simplification operated on the right-most rather than the leftmost consonant.

11. Spontaneous glide increment, especially syllable initial, is, of course, also very common across languages. This paper, however, is confined to a discussion of increment in assimilatory environments only.

12. I would like to reiterate that the processes discussed in this paper should be looked upon as phonetic. Whether or not a cluster containing an obstruentized glide is treated by the speakers of a language as a unit or a cluster is immaterial. Nor is it necessary for a glide to be phonemic, or to be phonologically present in any sense, in order to be a candidate for such obstruentization. Phonetic glides which appear epenthetically as transitions between a (palatalized) consonant and a following front vowel are equally as susceptible as underlying *y* or *w*.

In point of fact, most affricates (stop plus homorganic fricative) seem to receive the unit interpretation. Interestingly enough, however, the nonhomorganic clusters *pḱ*, *bǵ* from /py/, /by/ in Rumanian are also felt to be units. Procopovici (1931:415) states, '. . . *pḱ* does not represent two phonemes, only one, the labial and palatal occlusions both forming part of its articulatory makeup.' Dialect informants agree with this judgment.

13. Development of parallel clusters such as *pw* and *tw* is not included in this chart as these clusters do not occur in most Romance languages. There is no reason to doubt that they would receive similar treatment.

14. Adjustment in point of articulation may affect reflexes of either the (stop) consonant or yod. The process is not critically ordered in the progression illustrated here. If reflexes of both members of the cluster are lingual, one will take the point of articulation of the other, i.e. the resultant cluster will always be homorganic. The affricate produced, then, will be either entirely palatal, *t́š*, by assimilation of the stop or entirely dental (or alveolar), *ts*, by assimilation of the fricative reflex of the yod. If either member of the cluster is nonlingual, *kɸ*, *kp* or *px́*, *pḱ*, assimilation does not occur.

15. Phonetic aspiration, so common in Germanic, could be analyzed as a glide, of course. Since *h* has no oral point of

articulation, we would expect a resultant fricative to be homorganic to the preceding stop.

16. By 'significant' I mean 'synchronic phonological' but might also include cases in which labials are borrowed as velars and vice versa, e.g. Creek p > Cherokee gw (Dale Nicklas, personal communication), Spanish β > Apache ɣ (Anttila 1972:157). Here the borrowing languages lack the labial series generally. Further evidence for GRAVE is presented by Hyman (1973).

IN SEARCH OF 'PENULTIMATE' CAUSES OF LANGUAGE CHANGE: STUDIES IN THE AVOIDANCE OF /Ž/ IN PROTO-SPANISH

YAKOV MALKIEL

University of California, Berkeley

The highest aim if not always the crowning accomplishment of historical linguistics has at all times been the search for causation. Given the intellectual ambition of theorists and practitioners alike, plus the fact that our discipline developed initially under the aegis of romanticism, it is small wonder that linguists in general, and Romance linguists in particular, have tended to hanker after the discovery of the ultimate causes of change, finding them effortlessly in such forces as substratum or superstratum influence; structural inadequacy of the status quo; striving for heightened expressivity; reshuffling of the socioeducational strata; and whatnot.

To the sober-minded, it would seem advisable in certain situations to refrain from such overextended ambition and to settle, modestly, for the accurate establishment of 'penultimate' causes, provided such a preliminary operation can be carried out with certain guarantees of neatness and, at least, to the analyst's own satisfaction. I am going to illustrate this wisdom of voluntary self-confinement to a reasonable goal by discussing a sorely neglected topic: the aloofness of the speakers of Proto-Spanish from /ž/, without worrying about the ultimate reason for this baffling attitude.

1. The discovery that Old Spanish included in its inventory of sounds the phoneme /ž/--pronounced with or without affrication: [ž], [^{d}ž]--and, obviously, similar to or even identical with phonemes characteristic of practically all other Romance languages--signaled a major triumph of 19th century scholarship. The sources of that

sound--in part Latin, in part Arabic--were before long established; its eventual transmutation into /x/--presumably, via /š/ and /ç/, after merger with its voiceless counterpart--was carefully traced; and its orthographic vicissitudes (specifically, its rendition in medieval texts by g, j, i, etc.) were scrutinized with the traditional machinery of philological erudition. By the middle of the 20th century, a few bits of statistical information on the actual incidence of /ž/ in typical Old Spanish texts at long last became available, but no forceful conclusions were at first drawn from such lacunary data.[1]

The points that I wish to make are: (a) to stress the marked, if not extreme, rarity of /ž/ in Old Spanish--typologically comparable to its striking scarcity in modern English; (b) to emphasize its tendential confinement to certain layers of the lexicon, which can be securely set off through diachronic analysis but may have had synchronic implications as well; and (c) to connect this meager occurrence of the sound with its practically total absence from certain contexts in which it abounds in most, or all, cognate languages. The separate alternative developments that have taken place in these contexts, to the detriment of /ž/, are by now well established, but the plausible link between them and the speaker's aversion to /ž/ seems not to have been clearly grasped as yet.

2. Old Spanish accepted /ž/ word-initially and word-medially (between vowels and after consonants) but practically never word-finally. Where it might have been pushed into that position through the agency of apocope, x /š/ was instantaneously substituted for it: barnage (bernage) ~ barnax 'manly action, heroic deed', from barón (varón).

Genetically, /ž/ occurs in the following categories of words:[2]

(1) Learnèd and partially learnèd words. These may pertain:

(1.1) to the world of pagan antiquity: gigante 'giant', Júpiter 'Jove';

(1.2) to the Biblical tradition and to the long all-important sphere of the Church: Jaob, Jacob, Jafet, Jeremías, Jerusalén, Jhesu, Joan, Job, Judas, Judea, also judío ~ jodío 'Jew'; ángel 'angel', Virge(n), -in 'Virgin', ymagen 'statue, idol', seldom 'portrait, image';

(1.3) to the realm of administration and jurisdiction: judgar 'to judge', júez 'judge', juízio 'judgment', justo 'fair, just' beside justicia, even more tidily marked as learnèd by its telltale suffix;

(1.4) to the domain of abstracts: general (note the lack of syncope), gesto 'bearing, appearance' (observe the absence of a diphthong; but see the following).

(2) Culturally flavored borrowings from cognate languages, chiefly Old French and Old Provençal as purveyors of courtly concepts (these two sources are not always neatly distinguishable;

neither is Old Provençal from Old Catalan), as well as from Arabic:

(2.1) Gallo-Romance: *gemir* 'to sigh, moan', *gentil* 'gentle, elegant', and *genta* (fem.) 'gracious',[3] *girgonça* 'hyacinth', *jamón* 'ham', *juego* 'game, trick, joke, fun', beside *joguete* 'trifle, plaything', *juglar* 'minstrel', *argén* 'silver', *viage* 'voyage', and other derivatives in -*age* < -ĀTICU. In the case of *jamón* (OFr. *jambon*, related to Gr.-Lat. CAMBA 'leg') and in those of *ligero* 'light, fast' (traceable in the last analysis to *LEVIĀRIU) and *vergel* 'flower garden' (descended from VIRIDIĀRIU, suggestive of greenery), the rise of /ž/ occurred in harmony with narrowly local (French), rather than broadly pan-Romanic, tendencies. One may be in doubt whether *gesto* belongs here, or should be pigeonholed under (1.4), or else arose at the point of convergence of two currents. In a case like *joven* 'young' < IUVENE stylistic considerations militate in favor of a learnèd-foreign status, the racy native equivalent having from time immemorial been *moço*.

(2.2) Arabic (and, generally, exotic): *alfaja* 'clothes, adornment, jewels', *alfajeme* 'surgeon, bloodletter', *javalí(n)* '(wild) boar'; *gengibrante* 'ginger'.

This evidence is so unequivocal that where the medieval lexicon exhibits doublets, e.g. *gente* beside *yente* 'people', *ja(más)* 'never' beside *ya* 'now, already', *junta* 'assembly' and *juntar* 'to join' beside *yunta* 'team' and *ayuntar* 'to collect', *jurar* beside *yurar* 'to swear', and the corresponding nouns *jura/yura*, one need not hesitate to credit the /ž/ variant to the learnèd-borrowed stratum.

Finally, there exists a trace of /ž/ in words of old local stock, transmitted by word of mouth, judging from their record, their semantic load, and the phonological conditions involved. Two verbs marked by mutual semantic and grammatical affinity, *mugir* 'to low, bellow' (from MŪGĪRE), and *rugir* 'to roar' (from RUGĪRE), represent this particular strain. Here the source of /ž/ is G preceded by a back vowel and followed by a front vowel. In adjoining Galician-Portuguese, a few nouns and an occasional nominal suffix follow the same direction, cf. Ptg. *mugem* 'striped mullet', Gal. *munge* < MŪGILE and -*ugem* (as in *ferrugem* 'rust') < -ŪGINE. In Spanish dialects and at the periphery of the standard Spanish vocabulary one detects isolated vestiges of this development, e.g. Salm. *amuje* beside Sp. *mujol* 'id.', which seems to have been borrowed from Catalan (cf. Meyer-Lübke 1911:REW^3. § 5717).

3. Up to this juncture, I have been concerned with scattered examples of OSp. /ž/ by and large traceable to the same ancestral sources as this phoneme is in congeneric languages, typically either G$^{e,\,i}$- or prevocalic I- pronounced /j/, aside from Arabic /ǧ/ or

/^{d}ž/. Over against these residual cases of trivially descended /ž/ there evolved, initially inside a small corner of the northern sector of the Peninsula, a /ž/ of an entirely different provenience, namely, a descendant of /λ/--at a time when the product of parental -LL- (and, dialectally, of L-) apparently had not yet reached the /λ/ stage. It is most likely that the development went from /λ/ via /j/ to /ž/, thus exactly paralleling the distinctly later shift /λ/ > /j/ > /ž/ ~ /š/ in modern Platense (cf. the pronunciation of *caballo* 'horse', *calle* 'street' in low-class Porteño). On this score, the Atlantic Coast and the Mediterranean Coast have preserved the original state of affairs: cf. OSp. (sing.) *foja* 'leaf' < FOLIA (plur.) (as against Ptg. *folha*, Cat. *fulla*) and the related cases of *aparejar* 'to fit (out), adapt', *coger* 'to collect, catch', *ojo* 'eye', *ageno* (=mod. *ajeno*) 'alien', *gelo* (mod. *se lo*) 'it to him or to her or to them' (cf. It. *glielo*). Words of non-Latin stock are also marginally represented; cf. Hispano-Gothic *agasajar* 'to shelter, receive kindly, fondle, regale' as against Ptg. *agasalhar*. The chronological relation of this innovative /ž/ nourished by indigenous sources to the /ž/ of Gallicisms, Provençalisms, and Arabisms, remains to be thoroughly investigated.

4. I shall temporarily leave alone the rise and spread of this new /ž/ produced by autochthonous sources as well as the intrusion of the /ž/ lodged in Latinisms and foreignisms and, abruptly changing the perspective, ask in exactly what contexts Castilian shows absence of /ž/, through loss or some other process, while the (near-) consensus of cognate languages prompts one to expect its presence. The advantage of this volteface is obvious: While the case histories of *gesto*, *javalí(n)*, *juglar*, *viaje*, *ymagen*, etc. throw light on trends of lexical borrowing and of correlated sound development in the time segment between the 10th and the 12th century, so vividly reconstructed in Menéndez Pidal's *Orígenes del español* (1926, 1950), the situations to be microscopically examined now will take us back by fully a half-millennium to the period of provincial Latinity.

5. Word-initially Ǵ-, prevocalic I, and related clusters (e.g. the /dj/ of DEO(R)SUM 'below, down'--a cognate of VERTŌ 'I turn'--pronounced /djosu/) yielded in most Romance languages /ž/ or /^{d}ž/, clearly via /j/, and only in a small minority (including Genoese and Friulano) a /z/, aside, of course, from those isolated languages in which G^{e,i} remained a velar stop or changed, without losing its dominant distinctive feature, namely, the occlusive character of /g/ (as when G^{e,i} becomes *b-* in modern Sardinian). By remaining at the /j/ stage, Spanish here discloses a trait of pronounced conservatism and clashes sharply with its closest neighbors, Galician-Portuguese and Catalan. Examples abound: OSp. *yazer* 'to lie' < IACĒRE, *yerno*

'son-in-law' < GENERU, *yelso* < GYPSU and the aforementioned *ya*, *yente*, *yuntar*, *yurar*. Under two conditions the /j/ segment of *ya-*, *ye-*, *yu-* may secondarily disappear: (a) where Cast. *ye-* (and Leon. *ya-*) in unstressed, particularly in pretonic, syllable would give the impression of a misplaced rising diphthong, such diphthongs being restricted to heavily stressed syllables (hence *yermano* 'brother' > *ermano*, mod. *hermano*, from GERMĀNU; **yenero* 'January' > *enero*, from IĒNUĀRIU; OLeon. *azer* 'to lie, stretch out' (by way of reaction against the local diphthong *ia*, as in dial. *pia* 'foot' < PĔDE); and (b) through dissimilatory loss, as in IĀIŪNU 'fast' > *ayuno* (as against the var. IEIŪNU > Ptg. *jejum*; cf. the reverse distribution of the pretonic vowel in Ptg. *janeiro* vs. Sp. *enero*), IUNGERE 'to join' > /d'und'ere/ > OSp. *unzir* 'to yoke' > mod. *uncir* beside dial. *uñir*.[4]

On observing the Spanish speakers' aversion to /ž/ in this particular context, it can be stated, by way of summary, that this reluctance caused them to lag behind their nextdoor neighbors and other cousins by, for once, preserving a stage abandoned by almost everyone. In most other instances, Spanish, conversely, went beyond the Portuguese stage.

6. The development of medial postconsonantal $G^{e,i}$ in Old Spanish--in particular, as found in the clusters -LǴ-, -NǴ-, and -RǴ- -- is one of the most controversial points of Romance phonology, and one especially rich in theoretical implications, as was shown in 1966 and confirmed two years later. Even more dramatically than in the set of circumstances just considered, Old Spanish steered a course entirely at variance with the course favored by its congeners, including its closest neighbors. Essentially, its unique peculiarity consisted in the tendential transmutation of the Ǵ into *z*, i. e. [^{d}z]. The trend is particularly conspicuous in the case of -RǴ- > *-rz-*, as in *arzilla* 'clay' < ARGĪLLA, *erzir* 'to raise', refl. 'to rise' < ER(I)GERE (eventually replaced by analogical *erguir*), *esparzir* 'to stencil, trace the outlines' < EXTERGĒRE 'to wipe, scour, clean'. The evidence for -LǴ- is meager: we have not advanced beyond Menéndez Pidal's etymological equation Ast. *esmucir* < EXMULGĒRE 'to milk'. Conversely, the dossier of -NǴ- is adequate on the quantitative side, but slightly less conclusive, inasmuch as one observes a bifurcation: the outcome is either *-nz-*, as in *enzía* 'gum' < GINGĪVA, or *-ñ-* i. e. [ɲ], with the further possibility of the latter's ultimate reduction to *n* (depalatalization) before *-ie-*, as in *quiñientos* ~ *quinientos* 'five hundred' (masc.) < QUĪNGENTŌS. It will be remembered that the segments *-lg-*, *-ng-*, *-rg-* (with *g* = /ž/) are sporadically encountered in certain categories of Old Spanish words; true, these combinations (as in *ángel*, *vergel*) may have been belatedly reintroduced. Old Portuguese made wide, unrestricted use of /nž/--with the /n/ dissolving more and more in

the preceding vowel, though not quite so rapidly as in French--and, especially, of /rǧ/, cf. jungir 'to join' < IUNGERE and the verbs erger (later erguer), esparger; and Italian resorts to /lǧ/, /nǧ/, /rǧ/ on a sweeping scale, cf. accorgersi 'to notice', bolgia 'pit, ditch, abyss', frangere 'to break', piangere 'to weep', etc.

If one agrees to disregard the older, rambling phase of the discussion, then the hypothesis presented at a 1966 Texas symposium, which is credited with revitalizing the debate, can be capsulized into the following statement. The existence of a tango, tañes, . . . tanga paradigm in the pres. ind. (from TANGERE 'to touch') and the independent existence of a very contagious digo, dizes, . . . diga paradigm (from DĪCERE 'to say'), whose appeal is neatly observable in such imitations as fago, fazes, . . . faga (from FACERE 'to do, make', in lieu of expected *faço . . . *faça, as in Portuguese) and as yago, yazes, . . . yaga (from IACĒRE 'to lie, stretch out', in lieu of *yaço, yazes, . . . *yaça, cf. OPtg. jaço . . . jaça), created a feeling for the affinity of such alternations, within a carefully delimited sector of the verbal paradigm, as -ng- ~ -ñ- and -g- ~ -z-, leading through contamination to -nz-, alongside which -lz- and -rz- also sprouted as a result of the familiar proximity of the outcomes of l, n, and r, as previously observed in several contexts. The concluding evolutionary step might then have been a leap from a morphophonemic alternation to a sound 'law' or 'rule'.

Several critics have disagreed with this analysis,[5] which was never meant to represent the 'last word', and its original proponent modified his views substantially by 1974. Conceivably, the most helpful guidepost is offered by Gallo-Romance, where SURGERE 'to (a)rise, get up' became sourdre and PUNGERE 'to prick, puncture, stab' yielded poindre (tr.) 'to sting', (intr.) 'to dawn, break'; the evolutionary line seems to have run from Gallo-Romance SORǴERE, PONǴERE to /sorjere/ ~ /surdjere/, /ponjere/ ~ /pondjere/, with d acting as an (initially) occasional, optional buffer consonant. In certain varieties of Romance--Portuguese and Italian, for example--the /nj/, /rj/ variants prevailed and, in the process, were allowed to advance to [nž], [rž] or, with the added element of affrication, to [nǧ], [rǧ]. In other provincial varieties, this road was blocked and the further development took its start from the aforementioned /dj/ variants--with French, struck by syncope of the intertonic vowel, settling ultimately for the final segment [dj^{e}re] > [drə] (hence poindre, sourdre, also OFr. espardre < SPARGERE)--, while Old Spanish, less subject to the effects of such compression as a consequence of the amalgam of -ĒRE and -ĔRE infinitives, condensed /dj/ into /z/, in part with help from the numerous and influential -zer/-zir verbs (< -CĒRE, -CĔRE, -CĪRE). In other words, the factor appealed to in 1966-68 as the prime cause of change deserves demotion to the rank of a secondary cause. As for ARGENTEU 'silvery' > OSp. arienço 'small coin' (in lieu of *arzienço), a sort of dissimilatory loss may be involved.

If this revised interpretation is accepted, then the crucial choice before the speakers must have been at a point in time at which the two options were either /j/ potentially conducive to /ž/, or /dj/ potentially conducive to /z/ or /d/. The former option was welcomed by the speakers of Galician-Portuguese, who are remembered from an earlier context as accepting with equal alacrity word-initial /j/ > /ž/; the latter option was agreeable to the speakers of Castilian. The only common denominator between the word-initial and the word-medial developments here examined in close succession was the Castilian speakers' strong recoil from /ž/, or, to use a more cautious formulation, their repugnance to advance toward /ž/.[6]

7. This leaves us with the case of intervocalic -Ǵ-, very closely akin to those of -J-, -GJ-, and -DJ-. Here one discovers a characteristic three-way development: either (a) retention of /j/, which one visualizes as the evolutionary step immediately following upon Ǵ, or (b) disappearance of */j/ thus arrived at, or else, very seldom, (c) full consonantization of /j/ to /ž/.

Retention of /j/ occurs, with regard to -DJ- and -GJ-, between back vowels: cuyo 'whose' < CŪIU(S) (which, in turn, subsequently served as a model for suyo 'his, her, its, theirs'), fuyo 'I flee' < FUGIŌ, moyo 'liquid measure' < MODIU; also between back vowel and any vowel doomed to disappear word-finally: hoy 'today' < HODIĒ; the case of greÿ 'herd' < GRĒGE, leÿ 'law' < LĒGE, and reÿ 'king' < RĒGE is difficult, because the syllabic ÿ might reflect either -Ǵ-, or -E, or both. (The contrast between lee 'he, she, reads' < LEGIT, also eslee 'he elects' < ĒLIGIT, and leÿ 'law' < LĒGE is hard to understand in strictly phonological terms.)

Loss of /j/--except in Navarro-Aragonese, where retention of an archaic feature or its reintroduction may be involved--occurs: (a) between front vowels, either (α) identical: leer 'to read' < LEGERE, or (β) different: reyna 'queen' < RĒGĪNA, veýnte 'twenty' < VĪGINTĪ, suffix -ín < -ĪGINE (sometimes a replacement for -ŪGINE), cf. herrín and orín 'rust', hollín 'soot'; (b) between front and back vowel: navío 'ship' < NĀVIGIU; (c) between central and front vowel: Jud.-Sp. A(y)ifto < AEGYPTU, maestro 'teacher' < MAGISTRU (beside the title maese, more deeply eroded as a result of its pretonic use), ma(i)s 'more, but' < MAGIS, quaraenta (mod. cuarenta) 'forty' < QUADRĀGINTĀ, saeta 'arrow' < SAGITTA, vaýna 'sheath, pod' < VĀGĪNA, and above all the suffix -én < -ĀGINE, as in the phytonym llantén and in sartén 'pan'; (d) between back and front vowel: foir 'to flee' < FUGERE; (e) between front and central vowel: leal 'loyal'

< LĒGĀLE, *real* 'royal' < RĒGĀLE (conceivably under pressure from *ley* and *rey*).

Preservation of Ǵ as /ž/ is characteristic of a handful of verbs (linked by a semantic bond), such as *mugir* and *rugir*, conceivably with some help from sound symbolism. These vernacular verbs must be sharply distinguished from learnèd counterparts, e.g. *elegir*, *proteger*, and *regir*.

In Galician-Portuguese, the brisk advance toward the /ž/ stage has been far more common, hence *hoje* 'today', *fugir* 'to flee', the oft-invoked ichthyonym *mugem* < MŪGILE, plus the locally important suffix -*ugem* < -ŪGINE, which lacks any sharply profiled equivalent in Spanish (either old or new): *ferrugem* 'rust' (beside *ferro*), *penugem* 'down, fuzz, fluff' (beside *pena*). Given the traditionally close ties between -ĀGINE, -ĪGINE, and -ŪGINE (a typical suffixal triad in Latin) and their Romance descendants, one is hardly surprised to see the /ž/ restored (or uninterruptedly preserved?) in -*igem* (*fuligem* 'soot') and, occasionally, in -*agem* (OPtg. *cacragem* 'gristle' < CARTILĀGINE, Ptg. *tanchagem* ~ Gal. *chantagem* < PLANTĀGINE), even though the normal, spontaneous development in the West was clearly -*ã* or -*ãe*, witness *sartã* 'pan' < SARTĀGINE. In fact, there occurred in Portuguese a contamination of native -*agem* from -ĀGINE and the unrelated Gallo-Romance suffix -*age*.[7] Unlike Spanish, Portuguese places no special conditions or 'constraints' on the development of -Ǵ-, -GJ-, -DJ- > /ž/, beyond an appropriate vocalic environment: the words need not belong to a favored form-class, such as verbs; and the /ž/ receives no concomitant support from any onomatopoetic effect.

Once more, the very thin representation of ancestral Ǵ by /ž/ in Old Spanish seems to be traceable to the familiar aversion of speakers to that phoneme, an attitude shared by no other paleo-Romance community. How the difficulties caused by this aloofness were eventually solved is best ascertained through microscopic inspection of the record. It can, for instance, be shown that the functions of the discarded suffix -ŪGINE were, in part, taken over by -ŪMINE, cf. *herrumbre* 'rust' beside *herrín*; there may be a causal relation between this process and the heightened importance of -*umbre* through local merger with *-*dunde* < -TŪDINE, as in *muchedumbre* 'multitude', OSp. *limpiedumbre* 'cleanliness', *suziedumbre* 'dirt(iness)'.[8]

The relative vogue of /ž/ along the Peninsula's Atlantic Coast, as against the wall of resistance to it in the center, produced unexpected repercussions in individual word biographies. Take the especially intricate case of RIGIDUS 'stiff, unbending', where, on account of the hazards besetting both G and D, one must reckon with all sorts of surprises. Although G surrounded by front vowels is normally subject to elimination (cf. *leer*), it was in this unusual instance accorded the same treatment as in cujo, mugem, etc.: rijo. In fact, through an interplay of associations the -j- spread to another adjective, sujo, var. çujo 'dirty' < SŪCIDU, lit. 'juicy, sappy'. In Spanish the two qualifiers descended from RIGIDUS and SŪCIDUS also influenced each other, no doubt for the same reasons; but, given that language's aloofness from /ž/, a different solution was successfully tried out: the /z/ of suzio was allowed to spread to rezio (mod. sucio, recio).[9]

8. In all three contexts so far reexamined, the bulk of Romance dialects--a consensus which Portuguese, for the sake of simplicity, may here be deputized to represent--shows /ž/ where Old Spanish displayed either /j/ (with the further likelihood of eventual loss in certain contexts) or /z/. The aversion of Proto-Spanish to /ž/ is, then, the common denominator under which the three highly idiosyncratic, not to say erratic, cases of (a) yazer, hielo, enero, (b) arzilla, enzía, and (c) cuyo, foir, hoy--to say nothing of ephemeral barnax--can be conveniently subsumed. Portuguese rather characteristically shows the recurrently divergent counterparts with a /ž/: jazer, geio, Janeiro; argila, gengiva; cujo, fugir, hoje; and the suffix -age(m).

From here one can go one step further and argue that the speakers' disinclination to accept /ž/ must have come to an end before, or--at most--in conjunction with, the influx of the numerous 'cultismos' and borrowings from Old Provençal, Old French, and Arabic--also, a fortiori, before the shift of native intervocalic /ʎ/ to /ž/, as in foja 'leave', ojo 'eye' (vis-à-vis Ptg. folha, olho). Consequently, one should speak of an aversion to /ž/ in Proto-Spanish rather than Old Spanish. It is not inconceivable that certain probabilistic conclusions as to the ultimate origin of the process can be drawn from its very chronological boundaries, interpreted in conjunction with its spatial borders. These 'ultimate' causes, however, cannot be here investigated, nor should they be guessed at, since my self-imposed restriction of scope calls for temporary concentration--visibly rewarding--on characteristic 'penultimate' causes of change.

NOTES

1. Tomás Navarro (1946:24,163) furnishes strikingly low figures for the incidence of /x/ in modern Spanish and of /ž/ in Old Spanish, as exemplified by the Cid epic. Since modern 'jota' has absorbed two medieval phonemes, (a) the /ž/ and (b) the /š/ spelled x, it is inexplicable why the frequency of /x/ (0.51) should be lower, by however slight a margin, than that of /ž/ (0.65).

2. I have selected most of my examples from the lexicon of Juan Ruiz, using H. B. Richardson's vocabulary, despite its faults, as my source of information.

3. Apparently *genta* was used only in the feminine, to evoke a stereotype of courtly beauty, cf. the similar restriction on the North American use of Fr. *petite*.

4. For details see Malkiel (1974b), especially Section IIIB.

5. Cf. the original, necessarily tentative, presentation of these ideas in Malkiel (1968, passim).

6. Apart from the criticism voiced from the floor in 1966, there appeared several skeptical reactions to the written version of my paper, by J. R. Craddock and C. P. Otero, plus a mild qualification by M. B. Fontanella de Weinberg; for a digest of this material and a few bits of self-criticism I can now refer to Malkiel (1974a), especially Excursus B (349-51). One gap in my earlier analysis was, I now recognize, my failure to explore the extent of lexical loss as an escape from a phonological difficulty. Thus, OPtg. *merger* < MERGERE 'to dip, plunge, sink' had no equivalent in Old Spanish; rather than experimenting with **merzer* speakers switched to *somorgujar* and its variants (*somormujar*, etc.), derived from MERGULIŌ 'diver' (cf. Ptg. *mergulhar* 'to dip'). Many more similar solutions, so far overlooked, may have been tried out by way of evasion.

Lest I be accused of a naively teleological view, let me remark that a hint of the elimination of /j/ pointing toward a future /ž/, say, here simply means that some of the more enterprising or uninhibited members of the speech community at issue were already using /ž/, ahead of the majority. Thus, a prospect can be sensed by those endowed with sufficient flair and power of observation; the future can be experienced in the present.

7. On sporadic contacts between learnèd -*agen* (as in *imagen*), vernacular -*agem* in the West (as in *cacragem*, *chantagem*), and imported -*a(t)ge*, see Malkiel (1974c).

8. The overlapping, interlocking histories of the three Latin suffixes -ŪGŌ, -ŪMEN, and -(T)ŪDŌ in Luso- and Hispano-Romance remain to be chronicled. There were semantic affinities (the abstract-collective function acted as a common denominator), and there was the dominant role of the same stressed vowel (*u*). Note that CŌ(N)S(U)Ẹ̄TŪDŌ emerges in Portuguese as *costume*, reminiscent of Fr. *coutume* (> E. *custom*), and that Old Leonese transmuted LEGŪMEN into *legunde*, which seems to display metathesized -ŪDINE (cf. OSp. *dezildo* 'say it!' = mod. *decidlo*).

9. S. N. Dworkin's unpublished Berkeley dissertation contains a substantial chapter on Sp. *rezio*, *suzio* ~ Ptg. *rijo*, *sujo*.

PHONOLOGICAL TENSIONS IN FRENCH

YVES-CHARLES MORIN

Université de Montréal

0. Introduction. One of the goals of the notational system set up by generative phonology was the capture of significant generalizations. It soon became apparent that it was unrealistic to expect the formalism to carry the whole burden, and that along with formal explanations there was a need for some functional explanations. In some cases both formal and functional explanations are available. If the two types of explanation are really different, there should be some principled way to decide when we should resort to one, and when we should resort to the other. Kiparsky (1972) gives the bases of a possible empirical distinction between the two types of mechanism, and shows that all known empirical evidence indicates the absence of any justification for formal explanations in a series of phenomena that have been uncovered recently, and in particular in the description of 'conspiracies' (Kisseberth 1970). It should be noted that Kiparsky actually gives two kinds of arguments against formal descriptions in the case of conspiracies: an empirical argument against the need for any formal representation and an argument against derivational constraints as a formal representation for conspiracies. I am concerned here only with the first claim. In this paper I present some new evidence from French showing that Kiparsky's conclusion, based on a limited sample of conspiracies, cannot be maintained. There is no need to underline the importance of evidence of this kind for phonological theory: it points to the need for either a formal device to represent conspiracy or for a drastic change in the formal apparatus currently used, since Kiparsky's arguments against derivational constraints as a formal device for conspiracies still hold. This may be a sign, not of the weakness of the notion of conspiracy, but rather of the current

notational system, or of the distinction between formal and functional explanations.

1. Formal versus functional explanations. When should a formal rather than a functional explanation be invoked to account for some linguistic generalizations? In the consensus that seems to emerge now, formal explanations are for language-specific phenomena, and functional explanations for phenomena which correspond more properly to universal properties. To give a more concrete support to this programmatic distinction between formal and functional explanations, let us examine the cases of assibilation and palatalization in the Romance languages. As early as the second century A.D., there existed an alternation between t and ts (cf. Old French chant:chanson, enfant:enfançon) which could be described as an assibilation of t before yod.

(1) t → ts / ___ y

At the same period, there existed an alternation between k and ts (cf. Old French arc:arçon, tronc:tronçon) which could be described as a palatalization of k before yod.

(2) k → ts / ___ y

There is an obvious similarity between the two rules and they could formally be collapsed into a single rule (3) in the grammar of the language.

(3) $\left\{\begin{matrix} t \\ k \end{matrix}\right\} \rightarrow ts \; / \; \_\_\_ \; y$

The normal implication for a single representation such as (3) is that the two phenomena (1) and (2) actually form a single unit within the grammar. This can be tested empirically. For both (1) and (2) to have the same set of lexical exceptions, or to be subject to similar historical changes, or to be introduced at the same time in the history of the language, would be strong evidence that they behave as a unit in the language.[1] For instance, the fact that in the 12th-13th centuries ts in both rules was reduced to s in French is compatible with an analysis where the two rules came to be analyzed as a single unit. On the other hand, if the historical changes affected only ts when it alternates with k, then there would be very little justification for analyzing (1) and (2) as a single rule.[2] One could still account for the similarity between (1) and (2) on functional grounds: sequences ty and ky being very unstable, rules changing them to tsy are highly natural processes, and as such are frequently found in the languages of the world. It is only natural that some languages should reduce them both, but without necessarily treating them as a single unit within the language.

The same kind of argument can be used to determine how conspiracies should be treated in phonology. I now turn to the conspiracy against clusters of the type Obstruent+Liquid+Glide (henceforth OLG-clusters) in French. Several rules in the grammar are constrained in such a way that they will not apply when it would result in the creation of an OLG-cluster, although all the other conditions for its applicability are met.

The first rule subject to the effect of this tension (I prefer the expression 'tension' to 'derivational constraint' because it can cover both synchronic and diachronic events; for the same reason I use the expression 'relaxation' instead of 'conspiracy') is glide formation, which applies to the initial high vowel in a hiatus. (Following the French tradition, I use the expression 'hiatus' to mean any sequence of two vowels.)

(4a)	(il) scie [si]	(4b)	(il) sciait [syɛ]
	(il) sue [sü]		(il) suait [sẅɛ]
	(il) noue [nu]		(il) nouait [nwɛ]

In the examples (4a), the underlying high vowels, i, ü, u are word-final and syllabic; in the examples (4b) they are followed by the imperfect ending ɛ and are nonsyllabic. When a vowel follows an OL-cluster, however, glide formation is blocked, as shown in (5).[3] When glide formation does not take place, a transitional glide may be observed between the high vowel and the following vowel, as in (5b).

(5a)	(il) trie [tri]	(5b)	(il) triait [triyɛ]
	(ça) flue [flü]		(ça) fluait [flüɛ]
	(il) troue [tru]		(il) trouait [truɛ]

In some dialects, only i is followed by a transitional glide, viz. yod, e.g. in Standard French (henceforth SF). In some other dialects, only i and u are followed by transitional glides, e.g. Belgian French. In still others, all three high vowels are followed by transitional glides, e.g. Québec French. In conformity with my own pronunciation, I shall indicate only transitional yods. The examples (6) show how the verbal endings -ions, and -iez (for the imperfect, subjunctive, and conditional, first and second persons plural) are realized in SF as iyɔ̃, iye after OL-clusters, and as yɔ̃, ye elsewhere.

(6a) (je) monte [mɔ̃t]
(je) montre [mɔ̃tr]

(6b) (nous) montions [mɔ̃tyɔ̃]
(nous) montrions [mɔ̃tryɔ̃]

A formal description of glide formation in the traditional notation requires a context which lists all the possible combinations of segments which can precede a hiatus and would miss some important generalizations; a better representation could be (7) with two contexts, a positive one (before vowel) and a negative one (not after OL-clusters).

(7) $\begin{vmatrix}+\text{syll}\\+\text{high}\end{vmatrix} \rightarrow [-\text{syll}]\ /\ \_\_\_\ \text{V, but not}\ /\ \text{OL}\ \_\_\_$

The second series of rules subject to the same tension are schwa-deletion rules. The precise mechanism of these rules is not completely understood (cf. Morin 1974). I need only describe here one of these rules, viz. the optional deletion of schwa between an obstruent and a liquid, e.g. *pelouse* [pœluz:pluz] 'lawn', *appelez* [apœle:aple] '(you) call', *monterez* [mɔ̃tœre:mɔ̃tre] '(you) will climb'. (In the phonetic representations given here schwas are represented as *œ* as this is their normal phonetic realization in most dialects.) When the liquid consonant is followed by a glide, the deletion of schwa is impossible in SF, e.g. *chapelier* [šapœlye:*šaplye] 'hatter', *appeliez* [apœlye:*aplye] '(you) called', *monteriez* [mɔ̃tœrye:*mɔ̃trye] '(you) would climb'. It must be observed here that glide-formation must take place before schwa-deletion; otherwise one could derive the deviant forms *[šapliye], *[apliye], *[mɔ̃triye], the underlying schwa being deletable in the intermediate forms /šapəlie/, /apəl+ie/, and /mɔ̃t+ə+r+ie/. Note that if schwa-deletion took place before glide-formation, the resulting intermediate forms for *montriez* and *apeliez* would be /mɔ̃tr+ie/ and /apl+ie/, respectively, and should behave identically under glide-formation (cf. also note 5 for a similar minimal opposition between thematic and athematic conditionals). Unlike glide-formation, the formal description of schwa-deletion does not necessarily require a negative context, but could be written as (9) instead of (8), where V has been added to the right context to prevent the segment following the liquid from being a glide.

(8) $\text{ə} \rightarrow \emptyset\ /\ \text{O}\ \_\_\_\ \text{L, but not}\ /\ \_\_\_\ \text{LG}$
(9) $\text{ə} \rightarrow \emptyset\ /\ \text{O}\ \_\_\_\ \text{LV}$

One can account formally for the similarity between the two rules (7) and (8) by limiting their description to their positive contexts and by postulating the existence of a tension (10) inside OLG-clusters blocking the two rules (11) and (12) whenever their application would otherwise create a tense cluster.

(10) tension: OLG

(11) glide-formation: $\begin{bmatrix}+\text{syll}\\+\text{high}\end{bmatrix} \rightarrow [-\text{syll}]\ /\ \_\_\ V$

(12) schwa-deletion: $ə \rightarrow \emptyset\ /\ O\ \_\_\ L$

As in the case of representation (3), the normal interpretation for such a representation is that the tension observed in the mechanism of glide-formation and of schwa-deletion forms a single unit within the grammar. This can also be tested empirically: for example, if it could be shown that changes in the applicability of glide-formation and schwa-deletion at some point in the history of French could be attributed to the development of this tension, or that glide-formation and schwa-deletion had the same set of lexical exceptions for which both rules could apply even though their application results in a tense cluster.

In the next sections I am going to show that this is the case, and that therefore all tensions cannot simply be considered the result of some universal tendencies to avoid some complex configurations which appear independently in several rules of the grammar. Before I show this, I must first examine the effect of this tension on the general development of French.

2. Internal tension and relaxation of OLG-clusters in French. Traditional descriptions of the historical changes that took place in French (e.g. Fouché 1966, Bourciez 1967b) attribute to the emergence of an internal tension within OLG-clusters a series of changes observed between the 13th and 17th centuries. It is argued that there must have been a phonetic change in the nature of glides in this period, making them more constricted and therefore less capable of appearing after an OL-cluster.

There were three main sources for such clusters. First, an early diphthongization of stressed Latin ē, ĕ, ǐ, and the action of a following velar on most vowels, gives the diphthongs ye, we (later wa), ẅi, e.g. brief, ouvrier, trois, croix, fruit. I shall refer to these glides as historic glides. Second, a reduction of the clusters iyV to yV (where the yod is historic) takes place as early as the 12th century in the verbal endings -ions, -iez, e.g. montrions, souffriez. The same reduction appears at the same time in the semi-learned words crêtiien, anciien, where the sequence iyV is not preceded by an OL-cluster. Third, as will be seen later, there is glide-formation.

The relaxation of the tension in OLG-clusters could take four possible forms: (1) vocalization of the glide, (2) loss of the glide,[4] (3) loss of the liquid, and (4) insertion of an epenthetic schwa between the obstruent and the following liquid. All these changes are observed in various dialects with various results. OLy-clusters are always relaxed unless the yod belongs to the verbal endings *-ions*, *-iez*, which in some dialects remain nonsyllabic. Relaxation of OLẅ- and OLw-clusters, where *ẅ* and *w* are historic, is at most marginal in SF, but frequent in many other dialects. Following are some examples of this relaxation (data from Littré 1873, Gilliéron and Edmont 1902-1910, Landreau 1927, Bourulot 1966).

Vocalization of the glide:
(a) vocalization of yod (examples from SF): *ouvrier*, *brièvement*, *montrions*, *souffriez*.
(b) vocalization of *ẅ* and *w* (examples from nonstandard French, this relaxation being unknown in SF, except sometimes in the first of these words): *fluide*, *truie*, *fruit*, *glui*, *croix*, *groin*, *grouiner*.
Loss of the glide:
(a) loss of the yod (examples from SF): *bref*, *grève*, *trève*, *hébreux*, corresponding to former *brief*, *griève*, *trième*, *hébrieux*.
(b) loss of *ẅ* and *w* (example from nonstandard dialects): *fruit*, *pluie*.
Loss of the liquid:
(examples from nonstandard dialects; this relaxation is very frequent in modern colloquial French. I have not listed here the loss of *l* before yod because it happens even without a preceding OL-cluster, e.g. *sanglier* [sãgye], but also *soulier* [suye]): *emploi*, *froid*, *trois*, *crois-tu*, *pluie*, *celui-là* [sẅila].
Epenthetic schwa:
(examples from nonstandard dialects; note that the modern reflexes of earlier schwas may be *e* or *ɛ* in some dialects, particularly before a liquid): *ouvrier* [uvœrye:uverye], *février* [fevœrye:feverye], *sanglier* [sãgœlye], *truie* [tœrẅi].

The phonetic changes described here are all drawn from dialects where the changes are restricted to segments within OLG-clusters. In particular, yod becomes syllabic only within OLG-clusters, and not elsewhere; epenthetic schwas are introduced between an obstruent and a liquid, only when a glide follows, etc. These changes did not create any new alternations in the grammar (except for one alternation *bref*: *brièvement* which resisted several regularization attempts, and a lone variation in bibliothèque [bibliyɔtɛk:bibyɔtɛk]), and left no trace in the grammar of French.[5] If it were not for its action on the rules of the grammar, to which I now turn, the effects of the relaxation would have been completely limited to the lexicon.

3. Effect of the tension on the development of glide formation and schwa-deletion. One observes as early as the 12th century (Fouché 1966:939) that the initial high vowel in a hiatus may become a glide.[6] Glide formation was always more or less optional, with a tendency to become obligatory when the two vowels of the hiatus belong to the same morpheme. Hiatuses that fed glide-formation had three historical sources: (a) loss of an intervocalic consonant, e.g. Lat. vivenda > viande, Lat. scutella > écuelle; (b) various affixations, e.g. be+roue+ette > b(e)rouette, sci+er 'to saw' (the historical development of Lat. secare regularly led to soyer, which was later reanalyzed as sci+er from the stressed form sci+e in the verbal paradigm); and (c) borrowings from Latin after the Carolingian reformation, e.g. diable, affection. It appears that for a time glide-formation was not restricted and could take place even after an OL-cluster. Direct evidence of this chronological order is not available. One still can show that it was the case. We observe in some dialects words where OLG-clusters are relaxed through schwa-epenthesis, even though the glide is historically the initial high vowel of a hiatus, e.g. prier [pœrye:perye], oublier[ubelye], trouer [terwe], truelle [tœrẅɛl] (data from Gilliéron, Landreau, and Bourulot). In these forms the schwa cannot be accounted for unless glide-formation applied first, and the resulting OLG-cluster was subject to tension-relaxation. In most cases (and in particular in SF), however, the initial high vowel of a hiatus after an OL-cluster is now syllabic. This was to be expected: when the effect of the tension began, glide-formation was optional, and therefore every OLG-cluster where the glide is a reflex of an earlier high vowel had a nontense variant with a high vowel instead of the glide. It is only normal that this variant should survive, and that other relaxed versions be exceptional.

Schwa-deletion also began as early as the 12th century, at least as far as schwa-deletion between an obstruent and a liquid is concerned (Fouché 1966:515ff.). The same evidence indicates that it could originally take place before a liquid followed by a yod. One observes in many dialects the forms [drie, driɛr] corresponding to the Old French [dəryɛrə] (in modern SF derrière [dɛryɛr] 'behind') in which the yod is historic, coming from the early diphthongization of e in Latin de retro. These forms are possible only if the schwa of [dəryɛrə] was deleted, giving [dryɛrə], which in turn underwent a relaxation through vocalization of the yod. Generally, however, the relaxation of OLG-clusters resulting from schwa-deletion did not take this form, since they usually had a nontense free variant OəLG, which eventually survived.

We have been able to show that at least in some dialects (and possibly in all dialects) both glide-formation and schwa-deletion had the general form (11) and (12), and were not restricted by any constraints. Subsequently, their application was restricted by the development of a tension in OLG-clusters, which is independently attested by its effects in the phonetic changes that took place in French at the same period. It has also been observed that relaxation was incomplete in SF and did not apply to historical ẅ or w, although always to derived ẅ and w. This is why in SF glide-formation is blocked in the synchronic derivation of words such as trouait /tru+ɛ/ > [truɛ:*trwɛ] and troua /tru+a/ > [trua:*trwa], even though OLw-clusters are found in the language, when w is historic, e.g. trois [trwa].[7] Finally, this kind of phenomenon shows that to account for phonological change (here the change in the applicability of schwa-deletion and glide-formation), one must allow not only the addition of new rules (Kiparsky 1968, 1972; King 1973), but also the addition of new tensions in the grammar of a language.

4. Lexical exceptions to the tension. I mentioned earlier that in all dialects OLy-clusters were relaxed, except possibly when the yod belongs to the verbal endings -ions, -iez. For classificatory purposes I shall distinguish three types of dialects: (1) tense dialects, in which there are no exceptions to the relaxation of OLy-clusters (e.g. SF); (2) lax dialects, in which -ions, -iez can always be exceptions to the relaxation of OLy-clusters (e.g. Belgian French);[8] and (3) semitense dialects, in which -ions, -iez can always be exceptions to the relaxation of Oly-clusters, but never of Ory-clusters (e.g. some forms of French spoken in Paris; cf. Dell 1972, 1973:258, and in Gaspésie, Québec). The different behaviors of these dialects is shown in the following table where the italic forms are exceptions to the relaxation. Observe that in both semitense and lax dialects relaxation is always possible, however, as a variant. In all three dialects, relaxation of OLy-clusters is obligatory for all other yods, e.g. in the nouns encrier [ãkriye:*ãkrye] 'ink-pot', bouclier [bukliye:*buklye] 'shield', chapelier [šapœlye:*šaplye] 'hatter', and in the following verbs, where the underlying i belongs to the stem, and not to the ending: criez /kri+e/ > [kriye:*krye] '(you) shout', plions /pli+ɔ̃/ > [pliyɔ̃:*plyɔ̃] '(we) fold'. To account for the variations in the verbal forms boucliez, encriez in the lax and semitense dialects, one must exceptionally allow glide-formation to apply to the underlying forms /bukl+ie/ and /ãkr+ie/;[9] in the same way, one must postulate an underlying form /apəl+ie/, /ɛd+ə+r+ie/ to account for the variations in the verbal forms appeliez, aideriez, and allow schwa-deletion to apply to the

TABLE 1.

	Forms common to all three dialects	Semitense dialects	Lax dialects
encriez '(you) inked'	ãkriye		ãkrye
aideriez '(you) would help'	ɛdœrye		ɛdrye
boucliez '(you) buckled'	bukliye	buklye	buklye
appeliez '(you) called'	apœlye	aplye	aplye

intermediate forms /apəl+ye/, /ɛd+ə+r+ye/ (if there were no underlying schwa, the behavior of these verbal forms should be identical to the behavior of the verbal forms boucliez, encriez). These two series of exceptions can easily be accounted for by specifying that the endings -ions, -iez are exceptions to the tension in OLG-clusters in the lax dialects, and to the tension in OlG-clusters in the semitense dialects. On the other hand, an analysis in which the tension is assumed to be part of a functional condition which applies independently to glide-formation and schwa-deletion must regard the fact that -ions, -iez in the lax dialects are exceptions to both rules as a mere coincidence; worse, in the semitense dialect it would also be a coincidence that these two morphemes should both be exceptions when it produces Oly-clusters, but not when it would otherwise create Ory-clusters, in exactly the same way for both rules. In other words, if the verbal endings -ions, -iez were exceptions to each of the two rules of the grammar, one would expect nine different types of dialects, instead of the three observed.

5. The status of tension in a grammar. This study reveals that tensions and rules have much more in common than was suspected before. They both have their own synchronic and diachronic identity: they can be added to the grammar of a language at one point in its historical development, interact with the other rules, cause lexical reanalysis, and have their own set of lexical exceptions. The fact that tensions correspond to linguistically complex configurations that tend to be avoided in the languages of the world is actually also a common feature for many rules, e.g. progressive voicing of consonants also corresponds to the elimination of complex sequences, namely, sequences of two consonants with different voicing. The only surprising fact about them is why they have not been observed before. It may simply be because we have not really been looking for them, and because they do not always create a conspiracy. For instance, deletion of schwa between an obstruent and a liquid in

modern French is actually slightly more constrained than I indicated; it will not apply when the obstruent is preceded by another consonant, e.g. the schwa in tourterelle [turtœrɛl], or bordereau [bɔrdœro] is not deletable, although it was in the 12th-14th centuries as shown by the spellings tortrelle and bordrel. Representation (12) corresponds more properly to the rule in the 12th century, whereas its modern version could be (13).

(12) schwa deletion (12th cent.): ə → ∅ /O ___ L
(13) schwa deletion (modern): ə → ∅ /O ___ L, but not /CO ___

This historical change did not affect all morphemes equally, and in particular the thematic schwas in the future and conditional (see note 5) in modern French can still be deleted, even though they are preceded by a CO-cluster. Compare, for instance, (je) garderai [gardœrɛ:gardrɛ] '(I) will keep' vs. garderie [gardœri:*gardri] 'nursery school', (ça) restera [rɛstœra:rɛstra] '(it) will stay' vs. fumisterie [fümistœri:*fümistri] 'nonchalance'. In modern French the thematic schwa would be lexically marked as being an exception to the negative context of rule (13), exactly as the endings -ions, -iez would be marked as being exceptions to the negative contexts of rules (7) and (8), if the existence of a tension in OLG-clusters had not been recognized. It could be that to account for schwa-deletion, one should postulate the existence of a tension in COL-clusters and mark the thematic schwa as an exception to this tension. This tension would have developed sometime after the 15th century; it was not strong enough to lead to the relaxation of primitive CLO-clusters as in perdrix, mercredi[10] but strong enough to eliminate them when they had a COəL variant as in tourterelle and bordereau.

NOTES

I would like to thank John Reighard for his patient criticism of the numerous preliminary versions of this paper.

1. Kiparsky (1968:179-83) uses arguments of this kind to show that two shortening rules in English constitute a unit within the grammar of modern English.

2. Cf. Kaye (1973) for cases of this nature in Algonquian.

3. There are also a number of learned suffixes, e.g. -isme, -iste, -esque, before which glide formation is impossible, e.g. hindouisme [ɛ̃duism:*ɛ̃dwism]. These suffixes would be lexically marked and do not bear directly on this analysis.

4. Fouché (1966:733) gives earlier instances of loss of yod in priembre, criembre, -prient, -crient. In this case, however, it could be a case of paradigmatic regularization from a nondiphthongized

form in the verbal paradigm. The word friente (from Lat. fremita), which does not belong to any verbal paradigm, seems to have kept its yod longer.

5. Except possibly for schwa-epenthesis in some nonstandard dialects. I have observed alternations of the type [gofr:goferye] for gaufre:gaufrier, which, if general in those dialects, would require a rule of schwa (or e) epenthesis in their grammar. On the other hand, alternations such as [pri:pœrye] for prie:prier could be accounted for by postulating a schwa in the underlying forms of the morpheme prie /pəri/. Schwa-deletion would automatically account for the alternations (this solution is not available for gaufre:gaufrier, because a schwa in this position would violate the otherwise general constraint that schwas do not appear in 'stressable' positions). The same analysis accounts for the changes [vudriye] > [vudœrye] for voudriez, and [dœmãdœrye] > [dœmãdriye] for demanderiez. We are here in the presence of a lexical reanalysis. Verbs fall in two classes with respect to future and conditional: thematic and athematic verbs. In the first class a thematic schwa is inserted between the stem and the marker -r-; the thematic schwa is absent from the second class.

	fonder (thematic)	fondre (athematic)
S1, S2, S3, P3	/fɔ̃d+ə+r+ɛ/ [fɔ̃drɛ]	/fɔ̃d+r+ɛ/ [fɔ̃drɛ]
P1	/fɔ̃d+ə+r+iɔ̃/ [fɔ̃dœryɔ̃]	/fɔ̃d+r+iɔ̃/ [fɔ̃driyɔ̃]
P2	/fɔ̃d+ə+r+ie/ [fɔ̃dœrye]	/fɔ̃d+r+ie/ [fɔ̃driye]

As can be observed, in most verbs, the two paradigms are identical, except for the first and second person plural of the conditional. The changes mentioned above and observed by Martinet (1971), Landreau (1927), and Dell (1973) correspond to the reanalysis of a thematic verb as athematic or vice-versa.

6. Fouché (1966:750) analyzes the reduction of iyV to yV as the same phenomenon as glide-formation. When glide-formation was generalized, the yods in -ions, -iez do not share any of the characteristics of the other derived yods, but rather, they behave like historic yods and, in particular, do not undergo diaeresis. It appears that this reduction corresponds simply to the loss of the initial i.

7. Derivational constraints therefore can be very abstract, and not necessarily surface phonetic constraints, as it has sometimes been assumed, e.g. (1) Kisseberth (1970:305) assumes that 'a later rule would necessarily have to apply in order to get admissible phonetic representations' if a rule in the language produced clusters subject to the derivational constraint; (2) Kiparsky (1972:214) refers to them as 'phonotactic conditions on the language'; and (3) Shibatani (1973:92) rules out derivational constraints as ad hoc devices if they are not at the same time surface phonetic constraints.

8. I would like to thank P. Collinge for bringing these dialects to my attention. Note that by Belgian French is meant the Belgian version of SF, and neither the Walloon nor the Picard dialects (although it is very likely that these features have been carried into Belgian French from one of these two dialects).

9. In an alternative solution, one could give to -ions, -iez the underlying forms yɔ̃, ye. In this case we only move the exceptional nature of these endings out of glide-formation into the rules of composition between morphemes, and therefore reach the same conclusions, viz. that the endings -ions, -iez are exceptions to various rules in the grammar.

This solution is not satisfying, however, because it requires a new rule, yod-syllabification to account for the iyɔ̃, iye variants before OL-clusters, which applies to only two morphemes in the grammar. Such a rule might have been independently justified in the past when a difference in behavior could be observed between historical and derived yods, viz. diaeresis being impossible for historical yods. Soon, however, yod formation became obligatory when i was not morpheme-final. Since historical yods are never morpheme-final, diaeresis became a correlate of morpheme boundary and the distinction between historic and derived yods disappeared. This appears to have taken place as early as the 15th century. Before this time, only derived yods had vocalic variants in poetry. In the 15th century, however, we observe that both types of yod could undergo diaeresis in poetry, indicating that diaeresis came to be interpreted as a poetic convention which was extended to historic yods, the phonological basis for a distinction between the two having disappeared.

Another justification for analyzing historical glides as underlying high vowels, even when this violates the tension, is found in the behavior of some SF dialects. I mentioned earlier that historical ẅ and w remained exceptions to the tension against OLG-clusters, whereas all derived ẅ and w are now syllabic after OL-clusters. This is true in what one could describe as conservative dialects of SF. There exists an innovating dialect where former üi hiatuses can also exceptionally undergo glide-formation after OL-clusters, e.g. incongruité /ɛ̃kɔ̃grü+ite/, superfluité /süpɛrflü+ite/, pronounced [ɛ̃kɔ̃grüite], and [süpɛrflüite] in conservative dialects (cf. Dell 1972), but [ɛ̃kɔ̃grẅite] and [süpɛrflẅite] in the innovating ones. Since historic ẅ is always followed by i, this indicates that historical ẅi has been reanalyzed as underlying üi exceptionally undergoing glide-formation after OL-clusters, and that the exceptional character of some underlying üi has been extended to all underlying üi in the innovating dialects. In both conservative and innovating dialects, however, the tension affects all ü followed by any vowel other than i, e.g. truelle [trüɛl: *trẅɛl] in both dialects.

10. One observes in the 17th century (Bourciez 1967b:183) a loss of the first r in rOr-clusters, e.g. abre, mabre, mecredi, for arbre, marbre, mercredi, which might be interpreted as the result of this tension. The facts are obscured, however, by a general tendency in French to lose postvocalic r at various periods in its historical development.

TRUNCATION AND STRESS IN SPANISH

SANFORD A. SCHANE

University of California at San Diego

Generative analyses of Spanish verbs have recognized that all forms of the regular paradigms of the three conjugations contain a theme vowel after the root: cant-a-r 'sing' (I), com-e-r 'eat' (II), viv-i-r 'live' (III). The theme vowel is deleted in the first person singular present indicative (cánt-o, cóm-o, vív-o) and throughout the present subjunctive (cánt-e, cánt-e-s, etc., cóm-a, cóm-a-s, etc., vív-a, vív-a-s, etc.), forms where the theme is followed by a vocalic desinence.

(1) $V_{Th} \rightarrow \emptyset$ / ___ + V

Other verb forms are opaque with respect to truncation rule (1); that is, on the surface the theme vowel is retained although followed by a vowel.

(2a) com-í-a, viv-í-a-s, etc. (all imperfect forms of the II and III conjugations)[1]
(2b) cant-á-is, com-é-is (second person plural present indicative)
(2c) cant-é (<cant+á+i), cant-ó (<cant+á+u), com-í (<com+í+i), viv-i-ó (<viv+í+u) (all first and third person singular preterites)[2]

Note that the theme vowel when it fails to undergo truncation is always stressed. It is natural then to suppose that only unstressed theme vowels can be deleted by (1), an assumption which implies that stress must have been previously assigned. However, those forms undergoing theme deletion show instead that stress assignment has to follow truncation (e.g. *cant+a+o* → *cant+o* → *cánt+o*), for if the stress rule, which assigns penultimate stress, were to apply first, the theme would be stressed (*cant+á+o*) and subsequently could not be deleted. It appears then that the appropriate rule order is 'truncation', 'stress' (Foley 1965, Harris 1969).

Truncation rule (1) must be prevented from applying to the forms cited in (2). For the imperfects (2a), Harris (1969:76) proposes that the imperfect tense marker is *ba*, just as it is in the I conjugation (*cant-á-ba*, *cant-á-ba-s*, etc.). The *b*, intervening between the theme vowel and the vowel of the imperfect, blocks the application of the truncation rule; subsequently, the consonant is deleted when preceded by thematic *i* (e.g. *com+i+ba* (truncation fails) → *com+i+a* (deletion of *b*)).

(3) b → ∅ / i + ___

By having *ba* as the imperfect marker everywhere (instead of two allomorphs--*ba* for I conjugation and *a* for II and III) two main advantages accrue: (1) the truncation rule is not incorrectly applied in II and III conjugations, and (2) 'the "spell-out" rule for the imperfect marker will be simpler if it is the same for all three conjugations' (Harris 1969:77).

(4)
$$\begin{bmatrix} \text{+past} \\ \text{-perf} \\ \text{-subjunc} \end{bmatrix} \rightarrow \text{ba}$$

This 'spell-out' rule is preferred by Harris to one which generates directly both allomorphs of the imperfect marker.

(5)
$$\begin{bmatrix} \text{+past} \\ \text{-perf} \\ \text{-subjunc} \\ \langle\text{+ 1 conj}\rangle \end{bmatrix} \rightarrow \langle\text{b}\rangle\text{a}$$

The initial simplicity of (4) is deceptive, for it must be judged in conjunction with (3). (By adopting (5) one can, of course, entirely dispense with rule (3).) As Harris notes, rule (3) is by no means general; it applies uniquely to the *b* of the imperfect marker when preceded by thematic *i*. In essence it is a morphological ('spell-out') rule--affecting II and III conjugation forms--disguised here as a phonological rule. Together, (3) and (4) state that the imperfect marker has two allomorphs. The logical place for this type of information is in the 'spell-out' rules proper, and not partly there and partly among the phonological rules.[3] The abbreviatory devices utilized in (5) enable one to state whatever generalizations (3) and (4) together capture--namely, that all conjugations have the same imperfect vowel a but that only I conjugation has the initial b. Once one accepts (5) as the correct 'spell-out' rule, one can no longer depend on the b as the device for preventing the truncation rule (1) from applying in II and III conjugations.

In order to explain the nonapplicability of the truncation rule in the second person plural present indicative forms (2b), Harris's (1974) solution is similar to that for the imperfects: there is an intervening consonant. He sets up -dis as the second person plural desinence. The motivation for the d (aside from preventing truncation) comes from the second person plural imperative forms (cantád, coméd, vivíd). To derive both second person plural allomorphs--imperative d and nonimperative is[4]--from underlying -dis requires for imperatives rules of s-deletion (dis → di), lowering (di → de), e-apocope (de → d), and for nonimperatives a rule of d-deletion (dis → is), rules which Harris claims have independent motivation. However, the applicability of each of these rules to second person plural forms is open to question. The rule of s-deletion, specifically, applies to imperatives (both singulars and plurals). Its function is to specify all (for singulars) or part (for plurals) of the shape of the imperative morpheme. Hence, the objections are the same as those for the rule of b-deletion with the imperfects. Essentially, one is dealing here with a type of 'spell-out' rule; there is no compelling need in the first place to 'spell-out' s for imperatives. The rule of lowering must apply to imperatives so that the apocope rule may subsequently apply, but it must not apply to nonimperatives. Harris manages this distinction through a clever use of the + juncture.[5] The only indisputable instance of this rule is the lowering of the unstressed theme vowel in III conjugation present indicative forms: vív+i+s → vív+e+s, etc. (Brame and Bordelois 1973). In his most recent formulation of the rule of e-apocope, Harris (1974) has argued for restricting this rule to nouns and adjectives and he requires a special condition in order to apply it as well to imperatives.[6] Finally, the evidence for a rule of d-deletion is slim, being based on pairs such as incluir 'include', inclusión 'inclusion' (cf. eludir 'elude', elusión 'elusion') (Harris 1969:144). I take the position, then, that both second person plural allomorphs could just as well be generated by 'spell-out' rules.

Finally, we turn to the first and third person singular preterite forms (2c). Here Harris does not resort to an intervening consonant to prevent truncation.[7] Rather he marks first person singular i and third person singular u with a diacritic [-D] and revises the truncation rule so that a theme vowel is not deleted in front of a [-D] vowel.[8] The diacritic, unlike the intervening consonant, provides no explanation at all for why truncation fails, and it is simply a way of marking the vowels i and u as exceptional contexts to the truncation rule. In fact, had Harris recognized allomorphs a for the imperfect and is for the second person plural, he could just as well have marked these with the diacritic [-D]. This maneuver would have been sufficient to account for the nondeletion of the theme vowel before these morphemes.

I assume that the underlying representations of the forms cited in (2) are nearly identical to the surface forms (excluding stress) in the case of (2a) and (2b), whereas the underlying representations for (2c) are the same as those proposed by Harris. In all three cases, then, the theme vowel is directly followed by another vowel and so one needs to explain why it is that the truncation rule has failed to apply. Of course, it is always possible to claim that the morphemes a, is, i, and u provide exceptional contexts to 'truncation' and are marked as such (i.e. Harris's diacritic [-D]).[9] This solution is the least enlightening. It simply says that truncation applies before some morphemes and not before others. Earlier, it was observed that in every case where the truncation rule fails to apply, the theme vowel is the one which receives stress by the stress rule. Hence, one might consider the possibility that stress is the conditioning factor for the nonapplicability of truncation. This would mean that, at least for the forms of (2), stress is assigned prior to application of the truncation rule and that 'truncation' must be reformulated to apply to unstressed theme vowels.

(6) $V_{Th} \rightarrow \emptyset$ / [-stress] + V

A possible solution, one which can be promptly eliminated, is that for the forms in (2) the rules are applied in the order 'stress', 'truncation', whereas for other forms the rules are applied in the opposite order, 'truncation', 'stress'. So far as I can see, this solution is completely ad hoc and says no more than the diacritic approach, with the added disadvantage of variable rule ordering. Let us see whether the stress rule could be revised so that for 'all' verb forms 'stress' could apply before 'truncation'. One cannot apply Harris's (1969) stress rule prior to truncation, for, as has been seen, first person singular present indicative and some of the present subjunctive forms would incorrectly receive stress on the (to be deleted) theme vowel. Any modifications of the stress rule must be such that stress can be assigned to the appropriate vowel independently of the effects of truncation.

Hooper (1973) proposes a morphological analysis for stress assignment in Spanish verbs: past tense forms are stressed on the theme vowel, future and conditional forms on the vowel following the future/conditional marker r, first and second person plural present indicative and subjunctive forms on the vowel preceding the person/number desinence, other present indicative and subjunctive forms on the last root vowel, etc. Morphological stress assignment would allow the correct placement of stress for all forms. Then the truncation rule could delete those theme vowels not receiving stress. However, I am in agreement with Harris's criticism of the morphological approach (cf. Harris 1975). Basically, then, I shall adopt his latest version of the stress rule, making modifications where appropriate.

According to Harris, verbs and nouns (and adjectives) receive antepenultimate stress by different principles. Antepenultimate stress is assigned to verbs whenever the theme vowel is followed by two syllables--first and second person plural imperfect (cant-á-ba-mos, com-í-a-is, etc.), first and second person plural past subjunctives (cant-á-ra-mos, com-ié-ra-is; cant-á-se-mos, com-ié-se-is, etc.), and second person plural preterite (cant-á-steis, etc.).

(7) $V \rightarrow [+\text{ stress}] \;/\; [\,\bar{S}\,]_{\text{ThV}} - S - S\ \#]_{\text{Verb}}$

For nouns it is not always possible to predict antepenultimate or penultimate stress. Harris notes minimal pairs such as sábana 'sheet', sabána 'savanna'. Hence some lexical marking is required. He proposes that vowels having the potential of being unstressed in the penultimate syllable be assigned in the lexicon the diacritic feature [X]. The stress rule is formulated so that stress is assigned to the syllable preceding the diacritic.

(8) $V \rightarrow [+\text{ stress}] \;/\; \bar{S} - (C_o\overset{X}{V}) - S\ \#$

In the lexicon sábana will be listed as /sab$\overset{X}{\text{a}}$n-a/ and sabána as /saban-a/. Certain derivational suffixes such as ic also bear the X diacritic (e.g. telefónico /tele+fon+$\overset{X}{\text{i}}$c-o/).[10] Those verbs and nouns not meeting the conditions for antepenultimate stress assignment receive penultimate stress by the nonparenthesized part of (8).[11]

Rule (7), the two-syllable verb rule, could be completely eliminated if certain inflectional affixes were to be X marked, analogous to the marking on ic. These affixes are the imperfect morpheme -ba (and its allomorph -a), the past subjunctives -ra and -se, and the second person plural preterite -steis. In this way stress would be correctly assigned to the antepenultimate syllable by rule (8): e.g.

cantábamos /cant+a+b$\overset{X}{a}$+mos/. A form such as cantábas /cant+a+b$\overset{X}{a}$+s/ would still receive penultimate stress since the X marked vowel is no longer in the penultimate syllable (the crucial environment for antepenultimate stress). I shall adopt this change. Toward the end of the paper I discuss further my motivation for X marking inflectional affixes and for doing away with the two-syllable verb stress rule.

I turn now to those present indicative and subjunctive forms where truncation is applicable. If stress rule (8) is to precede truncation rule (6), then stress will have to be assigned as follows:

(9)	Present indicative	Present subjunctive
1 sg.	cánt+a+o	cánt+a+e
2 sg.	cánt+a+s	cánt+a+e+s
3 sg.	cánt+a	cánt+a+e
1 pl.	cant+á+mos	cant+a+é+mos
2 pl.	cant+á+is	cant+a+é+is
3 pl.	cánt+a+n	cánt+a+e+n

The critical forms are those receiving antepenultimate stress (first person singular present indicative and first, second, and third person singular, and third person plural present subjunctive). Now, if the theme vowel bore the diacritic X these forms would appropriately receive antepenultimate stress. But then, unfortunately, so should the first and second person plural present indicative. It is necessary, then, to find some context for excluding the latter two forms from the X marking. Note that where one wants the theme vowel to be X marked it is followed by an affix composed of a 'single' vowel (first person singular o or present subjunctive e or a).[12] As Harris (1972) has shown, this environment is significant elsewhere for characterizing a group of verbs which show a consonant augment in the first person singular present indicative and throughout the present subjunctive. An example of such a verb is salir 'leave'.

(10)	Present indicative	Present subjunctive
1 sg.	salgo < sal+i+o	salga < sal+i+a
2 sg.	sales < sal+i+s	salgas < sal+i+a+s
3 sg.	sale < sal+i	salga < sal+i+a
1 pl.	salimos < sal+i+mos	salgamos < sal+i+a+mos
2 pl.	salís < sal+i+is	salgáis < sal+i+a+is
3 pl.	salen < sal+i+n	salgan < sal+i+a+n

It is seen that g is inserted whenever the root is followed by the configuration +V+V+. It is important that this insertion precede truncation; otherwise, the relevant environment for insertion would be destroyed.[13] One could say that in the same context (where the theme vowel is followed by +V+) the X marking is inserted onto the theme vowel. The stress rule will then assign antepenultimate stress in those forms where there is an X marked theme vowel in penultimate position. Some examples follow.

(11)

			X marking	Stress	Truncation
Indic.					
	1 sg.	cant+a+o	cant+$\overset{X}{a}$+o	cánt+$\overset{X}{a}$+o	cánt+o
	2 sg.	cant+a+s	--	cánt+a+s	--
	1 pl.	cant+a+mos	--	cant+á+mos	--
Subjunc.					
	1 sg.	cant+a+e	cant+$\overset{X}{a}$+e	cánt+$\overset{X}{a}$+e	cánt+e
	2 sg.	cant+a+e+s	cant+$\overset{X}{a}$+e+s	cánt+$\overset{X}{a}$+e+s	cánt+e+s
	1 pl.	cant+a+e+mos	cant+$\overset{X}{a}$+e+mos	cant+$\overset{X}{a}$+é+mos	cant+é+mos

However, there is an additional constraint: The X marking must be morphologically restricted to present forms (indicative and subjunctive). Past forms such as the imperfect com+i+a, com+i+a+s, etc. or the preterites cant+a+i (canté), cant+a+u (cantó) cannot have an X marked theme vowel if they are to receive penultimate stress. It is interesting to note that this same morphological constraint needs to be imposed on the insertion of augments (cf. salía, salías, etc.; salí, salió; (*salgía, *salgías, etc.; *salgí, *salgió).

This solution, although it appears to work, is untenable. There are at least two technical flaws, but more importantly, there is an additional set of data for which this analysis, where 'stress' precedes 'truncation', makes wrong predictions. Two immediate disadvantages are: (1) a specialized rule is needed for X marking the theme vowel, whereas other inflectional affixes that are X marked--such as the imperfect <b>a--inherently contain this marking; (2) all and only X marked theme vowels get truncated; hence the claim that lack of stress conditions truncation is weakened. But the coup de grâce comes from some dialectal forms cited by Harris (1974). In certain dialects the first person plural present subjunctive forms have antepenultimate stress (cántemos, cómamos, vívamos). Such forms can be readily accommodated if one assumes that for these dialects the present subjunctive marker, like the imperfect marker and the past subjunctive in the standard dialects, is X marked, but only if stress assignment were a surface phenomenon. However, one cannot account for stress placement in these dialects if stress is assigned when theme vowels are still present (e.g. cant+$\overset{X}{a}$+$\overset{X}{e}$+mos, etc.), for at that level one would have to stress the 'preantepenultimate' vowel and there is no rule for placing stress in this position.[14] At first this would appear to be an argument in favor of assigning stress relatively close to the surface, but we know that this cannot be so, for there are several rules which modify the surface syllable structure but which must apply after stress--e-apocope, gliding (i → y, u → w), and rules affecting first and third person singular preterite forms (á+i → é, á+u → ó, í+i → í, í+u → yó). One is led to conclude that stress placement occurs before these rules but after truncation, which suggests that the original position that 'truncation' precedes 'stress' was all along the correct one. The proposed analysis requires that 'stress' precede 'truncation', yet the peculiar first person plural present subjunctive forms indicate conclusively that 'truncation' precedes 'stress'. But there may be a way out.

It was noted that the rule which X marked the theme vowel does so under two conditions: (1) before +V+ (this prevents the theme vowel from being marked in the present indicative when preceding second person plural is); and (2) in present forms only. It was also noted that an X marked theme vowel is always 'doomed' for truncation, so that the truncation rule could actually refer to an X marked vowel (rather than to an unstressed one). If so, there would be no compelling reason for 'stress' to have to precede 'truncation'; only X marking would need to. What this means is that the set of conditions governing X marking on the theme vowel will be identical to the conditions under which the theme vowel will be deleted, for observe: (1) Theme vowels are X marked in the context ___ +V+; theme vowels are deleted in the context ___ +V+. (2) Theme vowels are not X marked in the past tense; theme vowels are not deleted in the past tense. (3) Theme vowels are X marked prior to stress assignment; (and now to complete the circle) theme vowels are truncated before stress assignment. Consequently, these conditions can be incorporated directly into the truncation rule and there is no need for X marking on theme vowels. (For those inflectional affixes, such as the imperfect (or the present subjunctive in the special dialects), which condition antepenultimate stress, the X marking is an inherent characteristic of the affix.) One is back, then, to two ordered rules, 'truncation', 'stress', but considerably modified from their initial formulations.

(12) Truncation: $V_{Th} \rightarrow \emptyset \;/\; \underline{\quad} \;+V+ \ldots]_{\substack{Verb \\ [-past]}}$

(13) Stress: $V \rightarrow [+\ stress] \;/\; \bar{S} - (C_o\overset{X}{V}) - S\ \#$

The analysis requiring rules (12) and (13) has none of the disadvantages of the earlier proposal and it seems to me to have several advantages over previous formulations of 'truncation' and 'stress'. First, some of the inflectional morphemes are closer to their surface manifestations--second person plural is ~ d(e), imperfect ba ~ a.

Here is a more concrete alternative to Harris's abstract analysis. Second, since allomorphs not derivable by general rules are listed in the lexicon, 'specialized' rules and their extrinsic ordering are eliminated, such as d-deletion, b-deletion, s-deletion, etc. This concrete analysis is possible because the truncation rule has become morphologized: it applies to present forms and only where the vowel following the theme by itself constitutes a morpheme. The rule is transparent as there are no surface forms in conflict with it.

Stress rule (13) (= (8)) merits further justification. It is an adaptation of Harris's 'generalized' stress rule. Furthermore, I have argued that by X marking certain inflectional suffixes--<b>a, -ra, -se, -steis (and subjunctive -e and -a in some dialects)--one can dispense with Harris's two-syllable verb rule (7).

One of the reasons that Harris (1974) has separate rules for assigning antepenultimate stress in nonverbs and verbs is because of pairs such as vómito 'vomit (noun)', vomíto 'I vomit'; práctica 'practice (noun), practical', practíca 'he practices'. Because of the noun (or adjective), stems of these forms in the lexicon require the X diacritic: /vom$\overset{X}{i}$t-o/. According to stress rule (13) antepenultimate stress would be correctly assigned to the noun, but would be incorrectly assigned to the verb (instead of the correct penultimate stress). To circumvent this wrong stress assignment one needs a readjustment rule which removes X markings from the roots of verbs: /vom$\overset{X}{i}$t-o/ → /vomit-o/. With the diacritic gone, the verb will appropriately receive penultimate stress by rule (13). Although Harris does not have such a readjustment rule, he still needs some mechanism for preventing the parenthesized part of (13) from applying to the verb /vom$\overset{X}{i}$t-o/. He complicates the 'generalized' stress rule by restricting the parenthesized part of (13), that which assigns antepenultimate stress, to nonverbs.[15] Consequently, verbs such as /vom$\overset{X}{i}$t-o/, not meeting the conditions of his rule (7) will then undergo the nonparenthesized part of (13) and, accordingly, will receive penultimate stress. The important difference between verb stress and nonverb stress is that in the case of verbs stress is determined uniquely by the particular affixes which follow the root (in my system by the presence or absence of X markings on these affixes) and 'never' by X markings on the root itself as with nonverbs. It seems to me that a readjustment rule which removes X markings from roots of verbs precisely zeroes in on this important difference.

Harris's two-syllable verb rule states a generalization as to when verbs can have antepenultimate stress--namely, just in case the theme vowel is followed by two syllables. Although it is true that the X marking of certain inflectional affixes allows the 'generalized' stress rule (13) to assign the correct stresses, one can legitimately ask why particular morphemes happen to acquire X markings, for, as noted by Harris, X marking (i.e. antepenultimate stress) is the 'marked' stress pattern (at least for nonverbs). It seems to me that the crucial question is not why certain inflectional affixes bear the X diacritic, but rather, why some verb forms have antepenultimate stress in the first place. In fact, if antepenultimate stress is the 'marked' situation, then even within Harris's analysis one wonders why there should be a two-syllable verb rule. Harris has provided an external explanation: columnar stress (i.e. the desire for the same vowel to be stressed throughout the paradigm of a particular tense)--e.g. cant-á-ba, cant-á-ba-s, cant-á-ba, cant-á-ba-mos, cant-á-ba-is, cant-á-ba-n. Although there may indeed be a tendency toward penultimate stress (at least for nonverbs) there is also a tendency toward columnar stress within the verb paradigm and this latter tendency appears to override the one for penultimate stress. So it is not haphazard as to which inflectional affixes are X marked. Columnar stress is found in those forms having a particular surface structure.

(14) Root + Theme + Tense/Mood + (Person/Number)

In verbs exhibiting this structure the Tense/Mood affix has become X marked. On the other hand, where the Theme or the Tense/Mood is lacking on the surface--the present indicative and the present subjunctive--there are no X marked morphemes.

These observations pertaining to X marking are compatible with Harris's historical account of the development of columnar stress. First, only the future subjunctive (which is now obsolete) showed columnar stress, then the imperfect indicative and both past subjunctives. These forms all have the structure exemplified in (14). In those dialects which retract stress in the present subjunctive--e.g. cánt-e-mos--the X marking has been extended to the one remaining Tense/Mood marker, which seems to be a natural enough generalization, given the desire for columnar stress.[16]

Marking a few affixes with the diacritic X is a small price to pay for the elimination of a special two-syllable verb rule; in return, we have a unified treatment of stress for verbs and for nonverbs.

NOTES

Although I was scheduled to appear on the program, a previous commitment prevented me from attending the Texas Symposium on Romance Linguistics. This paper was written after the conference took place. I had the good fortune to have at hand James Harris's (1975) insightful paper on Spanish stress. Because the last half of my paper deals specifically with his proposals, it would be advisable to read his paper before mine. I am grateful to Professor Harris for some written discussion we had concerning some problems raised by my analysis. All interpretations and any errors are of my own creation.

1. In all past tenses and in the present participle II and III conjugation verbs have the same theme vowel--either i or the diphthong ie.

2. I shall accept without further question Harris's underlying representations of preterite forms (1969:79-85). Others (Brame and Bordelois 1973; Hooper 1973) have questioned this analysis. The Harris analysis of preterites is fairly transparent for Portuguese (Mateus 1973; Pardal 1974).

3. Obviously, I am not advocating that all allomorphs be listed in the lexicon. Rather, I see little point in having phonological rules which apply solely to generate the allomorphs of one or two isolated forms.

4. Phonetically the -is allomorph generally appears as [ys]. However, if ys were the underlying form it would be difficult to account for the position of stress in second person plural forms. Underlying -is, on the other hand, allows for normal stress placement on the penultimate vowel. A general gliding rule converts unstressed i to [y] when contiguous to a vowel. Harris (1974) claims that underlying -is presents certain difficulties in regard to a rule which converts ai to e; cf. first person singular preterite cant-á-i → cant-é, a rule which must not apply to I conjugation second person plural present indicative: cant-á-is (*cant-és). Since there are many sequences of ai which are exempt from this rule, the rule, if it exists, is a minor one and those forms to which it applies, such as the first person singular preterite, must be marked to undergo it. In note 2 we observed that the Harris analysis of preterite forms has been questioned. A rule converting ai to e is an essential component of this analysis.

5. Lowering: $V \rightarrow [\text{-high}] \,/\, [\text{-}\overline{\text{stress}}] + C_0]_{\text{Verb}}$

6. The rule of e-apocope deletes a word final e when preceded by a single dental consonant. In nouns and adjectives e shows up in the plural but not in the singular; the underlying e also accounts for the same vowel receiving stress in both the singular and in the plural: e.g. señóres (pl.), señór (sg.) < señóre.

7. Historically, preterite forms (derived from the Latin perfect) had an intervening consonant, just as the imperfect and second person plural forms had--cf. Latin cantāvī, vivēbās, cantātis. Synchronically, however, I maintain that for all three cases there is no strong motivation for the consonant.

8. It seems to me that Harris could just as well have used the phonological feature [-high] instead of the diacritic [-D]. Truncation would then take place before the [-high] vocalic desinences, first person

singular o, subjunctive e and a, but not before the [+high] preterite desinences, first person singular i and third person singular u.

9. The feature specification [-high] to which I referred in the preceding note would work for Harris's analysis, but not where -a and -ba are listed as allomorphs. Truncation does not occur before the imperfect a (viv+i+a → viv-í-a), whereas it does occur before subjunctive a (viv+i+a → vív-a).

10. The morpheme /fon-o/ is also X marked because of teléfono. Hence, telefónico is actually /tele+fon+ic+o/. There is nothing preventing an X marked vowel from receiving stress so long as it is 'not' the penultimate vowel.

11. Stress rule (8) should actually contain another set of parentheses so that monosyllabic words can be stressed on their only vowel.

12. We do not want the theme vowel to be X marked (and hence no antepenultimate stress) before the second person plural desinence -is; the latter is not of the shape +V+.

13. Since the consonant augments only occur with certain II and III conjugation verbs, it is possible to insert the augment in verbs only (after 'truncation') before a [+back] vowel--o or a. Harris (1972) argues for ___VV as the crucial environment to explain the insertion of g in first person singular valg-o 'I value' (<val+e+o) and its absence in the noun val-or 'valor' (*valg-or (<val+or)). By restricting the insertion of the augment to 'verbs' (i.e. the category Verb explicitly is part of the structural description of the rule), the sequence of two vowels becomes no longer imperative. (Brame and Bordelois (1973) have argued that the 'augment' is a segment of the underlying representation of the root and is deleted (after 'truncation') before front vowels.) There is an esthetic gain to inserting the augment while the two vowels are present: The shape of the stem (with or without augment) is determined prior to the application of the phonological rules proper. In Portuguese, the arguments for the importance of the configuration +V+V+ are more compelling: not only are there alternations with stem final consonants, as in Spanish, but there is an interesting harmony between the vowel of the root and the theme vowel (under stress the root vowel has the same height as the theme vowel), but only in those forms (first person singular present indicative and some of the present subjunctive) where the theme vowel will be deleted (Hensey 1972; Mateus 1973; Pardal 1974).

14. If stress assignment precedes truncation, monosyllabic present subjunctive forms--e.g. d-é, d-é-s, etc. 'give'--would be incorrectly stressed on the (to be deleted) theme vowel (*d-á-e, *d-á-e-s).

15. $V \rightarrow [+stress] / \bar{S} - (C_o \overset{X}{V}) - S \#]_{\alpha}$, where α stands for nonverbs.

16. Harris cites an Andalusian dialect where stress retraction occurs in the present subjunctive of II and III conjugations but not in I conjugation: cóm-a-mos, vív-a-mos, but cant-é-mos. In this dialect only subjunctive a is X marked. It is not clear how Harris's analysis would deal with this problem.

VOWEL-LENGTHENING IN FRENCH

GENEVIÈVE ESCURE

University of Minnesota

1. It has been observed in recent papers (Schane 1971; Shibatani 1973; Vennemann 1972) that generative phonologists usually fail to generate accurate phonetic representations which they assign to an undefined block of detail rules relegated at the end of the phonological component.[1] The view has been recently expressed that any successful approach to phonological evaluation needs to proceed from the evaluation of phonetic representations. The problem involved in the nature of Vowel-lengthening in French seems to bear crucially on this issue. Is it a purely phonetic process? Is it to be solely assigned to the phonological component of the grammar? Or is it produced both by phonological and allophonic rules? I argue that an adequate characterization of vowel-length in French must adopt the third interpretation--namely, it must refer to phonological processes as well as to phonetic processes.

This paper proceeds in the following way: first, I specify the constraints observed in phonetic representations; then I show that Vowel-lengthening crucially interacts with various deletion rules, thus establishing a dependency relation between deletion and lengthening.

2.1. Constraints on phonetic representations. Since this discussion is concerned with an accurate account of vowel-length, it is appropriate to specify first the constraints observed in phonetic representations. In the following statement of the distribution of phonetic long vowels I stick closely to the facts described in various discussions of vocalic length in French. Most of these analyses have in common that they usually restrict length to a limited class of vowels--namely, to nasalized vowels and to the high-mid round vowels

[o], [ö], as well as to all vowels when followed by a voiced fricative.

Fouché (1956) is quoted by Schane (1968:53-54). Both agree:

> . . . Accented vowels are long: (i) before single /r z ž v/: rire, rase, neige, neuve. (ii) /o ö a ã ɛ̃ ɔ̃ œ̃/ before all consonants: haute, jeûne, pâte, danse, mince, montre, humble.

Fouché and Schane further claim that vowels are:

> . . . Short otherwise: robe, sud, bague, mais, rue.

2.2. In order to determine the surface phonetic constraints (henceforth SPCs) governing length in French, it is necessary to define the configuration of a word-final syllable. Stress is assigned to the last tense vowel in a word, thus excluding schwa--the only lax vowel in the French vocalic system--from ever bearing stress. Although schwa deletes obligatorily in colloquial Parisian French, it may appear phonetically in poetic style, and in songs, and it never deletes in a number of dialects, in South French in particular. Thus, whether schwa is deleted or not, depending on the dialect considered, the stress falls in any case on the same vowel. The word rouge 'red', underlyingly /ružə/ appears phonetically as either:

[rú:ž] (Parisian French)

or

[rúžə] (South French)

Following Shibatani's formalism, three types of SPCs will be stated: positive constraints (which govern the syllable structure of a word), if-then constraints (which are context-sensitive), and negative constraints (which specify unpermitted sequences).

The SPC governing word-final syllable structure specifies that in Parisian French stress occurs on the last vowel (this follows schwa-deletion):

(1) . . $\acute{V}$ (C_1) #

From SPC (1) follows the distribution of length as a context-sensitive constraint: only a closed syllable can be long, if it is stressed, which is tantamount to saying that stress is a necessary, but not a sufficient condition for length to occur:

(2) If: [+stress] C_1
↓
then: [+long]

SPC (2) necessarily entails a negative SPC (3), stating that no long vowel may occur in stressed open syllable (~ indicates an unpermitted sequence).

(3) $\sim \begin{bmatrix} +\text{stress} \\ +\text{long} \end{bmatrix}$ #

However, if it is established by (3) that *CV:# is not a possible phonetic sequence, the specification of CV:C_1# sequence allowed by (2) requires additional SPCs. In other words, it has been claimed that there are CVC_1# sequences as well as CV:C_1# sequences. I will state the conditions generally assumed for vowel-length in the following SPCs:

(4) If: $\begin{bmatrix} +\text{stress} \\ +\text{nasal} \end{bmatrix}$ as in: [rɔ̃:ž] <u>ronge</u>
↓ [krɛ̃:t] <u>crainte</u>
then: [+long] [mã:bṛ] <u>membre</u>
[mɔ̃:stṛ] <u>monstre</u>

(A nasalized vowel is long before one or more consonants.)

(5) If: $\begin{bmatrix} +\text{stress} \\ -\text{high} \\ +\text{round} \end{bmatrix}$ C_1 as in: [so:t] <u>saute</u>
[krö:z] <u>creuse</u>
↓ [plö:tṛ] <u>pleutre</u>
then: [+long]

(A round high mid vowel /o ö/ is long before one or more consonants.)[2]

(6) If: [+stress] $\begin{bmatrix} +\text{voice} \\ +\text{cont} \end{bmatrix}$ (C_1)
↓
then: [+long]

(Any stressed vowel followed by a voiced fricative and an optional sequence of consonant(s) is long.)

As in: (a) [ti:ž] <u>tige</u> [bi:z] <u>bise</u>
[fɛ:r] <u>fer</u> [inɔ:v] <u>innove</u>

(b) [i:vṛ] *ivre* [ɔrfɛ:vṛ] *orfèvre*
[ku:vṛ] *couvre*
(c) [si:rk] *cirque* [šɛ:rš] *cherche*
[pɛ:rdṛ] *perdre* [ü:rḷ] *hurle*
[pü:zḷ] *puzzle*[3]

Now it appears that SPC (6) does not entail an absolute negative counterpart of the type:

(SPC x . .) [long vowel preceding a stop or a voiceless continuant]

since SPCs (4), (5), and (6) overlap to a certain extent: (4) and (5) state that if a stressed vowel is nasalized or high mid and round, then it is long, irrespective of the following segment. There is, however, a set of vowels which, according to the SPCs given above, are excluded from receiving length. I refer to those vowels which are neither nasalized nor high mid and round, and not followed by a voiced fricative. Such a negative constraint includes so many conditions that it is hardly possible to state it formally. I will therefore only attempt a prose formulation:

(7) If: a stressed vowel is neither nasalized nor high mid and round, nor followed by a voiced continuant
then: it cannot be long.

2.3. Among the seven SPCs specified, it seems that (6) is a universal constraint, physiologically determined, and, therefore, does not need to be stated by a phonological rule. An allophonic rule drawn from the set of universal phonetic constraints will be appropriate in this case: a vowel is lengthened by a following voiced fricative. However, it must be noted that the realization of this phonetic lengthening is subject to the syllable structure of a word (or to stress): it only obtains word-finally, and is thus restricted by two language-specific constraints (1) and (2).

SPCs (1) to (5) are clearly specific to French. SPCs (4) and (5) closely depend on the quality of certain vowels, which are generally assumed to be derived by phonological processes specific to French: (4) crucially depends on the nasalization process which converts oral vowels to nasalized vowels. SPC (5) depends on a process which changes certain sequences to a high mid round vowel. Example (7) is significant inasmuch as it shows that language specific SPCs (4) and (5) take precedence over language-universal constraints like (6). SPC (6) is only true inasmuch as it does not falsify (4) and (5), and, in turn, SPCs (4) and (5) are true only inasmuch as they fit in with

(1), (2), and (3). At this point vowel-length in French seems to be governed by a hierarchical scale of SPCs:

I	(1) (2) (3)	stating the word-final structure of French.
II	(4) (5)	stating segments affected by length in French.
III	(6)	stating a universal phonetic constraint.

2.4. In the foregoing statement of SPCs I have closely followed the various analyses of long vowels given in the literature. Now a fundamental question arises: is the information provided by SPCs (1) through (7) sufficient to derive long vowels in an appropriate manner? This may be doubted when one considers Pierre Delattre's phonetic measurements of vowel duration. He has shown that even in the case of those residual vowels which SPC (7) characterized as short there is a gradation of vocalic duration which is phonetically influenced by the subsequent phoneme. A random sample taken from his analysis will illustrate the complexity of vowel-length, in those very instances where it was considered to be nonexistent. In a paper entitled 'Anticipation in the sequence: Vowel and consonant group' (1966:122-132), Delattre compares the duration of the vowel [ɛ] in various sequences:

p, t, k: 15 f, s, š: 22 b, d, g: 27 rd, rb, rg: 24
dr: 29 vr: 28 br: 32 ž, v: 37 r: 42

In view of these fine phonetic measurements it appears totally arbitrary to draw a sharp line between vowels followed by voiced fricatives and others. Although it may be impossible within any theoretical framework to capture the exact continuum of vowel-duration suggested by Pierre Delattre, the opposite attitude--namely, recognizing only extremes of vowel-length--may lead to gross over-simplifications, such as SPCs (6) and (7), in view of the data provided by Delattre. One of the weak points of generative phonology has been its lack of interest in phonetic detail. But is it possible to give a fairly accurate phonetic account of vowel-length in French, and at the same time benefit from the explanatory power of a phonological interpretation? If it is shown that the information provided by SPCs is not sufficient to derive long vowels in an appropriate manner, then it follows that an analysis of long vowels must have access to deep structure information, and is therefore at least partially a phonological issue.

3.1. The deletion-lengthening correlation. Two crucial points have been generally overlooked in most previous discussions of vowel-length--namely, length is to be explained by reference to deletion, and furthermore, this deletion-length correlation is subjected to constraints on phonetic structure which would yield the following sequences:

$CV_1\#$ $\quad$ $CV{:}C_1\#$

CV phonetic sequences may result either from underlying /CV/ or from underlying /CVC_1/, where the final C has been removed by some deletion rule applying in this environment (Truncation, presumably).

$CV{:}C_1\#$ phonetic sequences result from underlying /CVC_1ə/ sequences to which schwa-deletion and/or some consonant-deletion rule, if a cluster is involved, has been applied. The possible changes from deep to surface structure in final positions are:

(a) /CV#/ → [CV#] (no rule applies): /ami/ → [ami]
(b) /CVC#/ → [CV#] (Truncation applies): /groz/ → [gro]
(c) /CVCə#/ → [CV:C#] (schwa-deletion applies): /ružə/ → [ru:ž]
(d) /CVCCə#/ → [CV:C#] (nasalization and consonant deletion, plus schwa-deletion apply): /grandə/ → [grã:d]

I thus claim that one of the ways in which closed (stressed) syllables are lengthened is by deletion of a neighboring segment. A deletion-lengthening correlation operates in every stressed syllable--but is submitted to the restriction stated by SPCs (2) and (3); only closed syllables are lengthened. One of the most common deletion rules in Parisian French creating a closed final syllable, thereby meeting SPCs (1) and (2) for any vowel, is the general schwa-deletion (henceforth schwa-del).

ə → ∅ / <VC> -- <CV>

(ə deletes anywhere, if it does not create a cluster of three consonants.)

When /ə/ deletes in final position it can be observed that the preceding (stressed) vowel is lengthened.[4] In other words, word-final schwa-deletion is accompanied by a compensatory lengthening of the preceding vowel. But this lengthening does not obtain in medial position since, in French, sentential processes open syllables sentence-medially and transfer length to the only remaining closed syllables; namely, those which occur sentence-finally or pause-finally. The consequence of compensatory lengthening is confirmed by empirical observation:

laque/lakə/	laqué/lake/	
'lacquer'	'lacquered'	
[la:k]	[lake]	
juge/žüžə/	jugea/žüžă/	jugement/žüžəman/
'judge'	'judged'	'trial'
[žü:ž]	[žüža]	[žü$žmã]

(where $ represents a syllable-boundary)

In the phonetic forms, after schwa-del the [a] of laque and the [ü] of juge are clearly longer, respectively, than the [a] of laqué or the [ü] of jugea. This difference is somewhat obscured by the fact stated by SPCs (6) and (7) that [a] before the voiceless stop [k] is relatively less long than [ü] before the voiced fricative [ž]. In any case, lengthening is explained by the fact that laque and juge contain a final /ə/ in closed syllable in their underlying representation, whereas laqué and jugea, as well as jugement [žü$žmã], contain only open syllables. The significant fact is that some sort of lengthening has occurred at the same time as schwa-del, when a closed syllable results. Here is an instance of the overlapping of two types of lengthening: a global type of phonological lengthening which must have access to intermediate representations--namely, to deletions--and a purely phonetic lengthening, caused by voiced fricatives. When phonological and phonetic lengthening coincide, as in [žü:ž], the result is more duration. When they conflict as in [la:k], the result is a reduced duration, but a distinct difference still exists with any open syllable. It must be the case that vowel-lengthening is associated with schwa-del in a dependency relationship since vowel-lengthening takes place in those dialects which have a schwa-del rule (like Parisian French) but does not occur in those dialects where there is no schwa-del (like South French). That is, we get the following phonetic length differentiation considering the two dialects:

	rouge 'red'
Parisian French	[rú:ž] or [rú:ž$]
South French	[rúžə] or [rú$žə]

Notice that the stress falls in any case on the vowel [u]; therefore, stress is not to be uniquely associated with length. Stress and length are not redundant. Stress is a necessary but not sufficient condition for length to occur. SPC (3) says explicitly that a stressed vowel is not long if it is open. This is confirmed by the data from South French.

An analysis incorporating the deletion-lengthening correlation would optimally formulate deletion and lengthening as one single process, thereby capturing more closely the hypothesis that the deletion of /ə/ directly determines the lengthening of the preceding stressed vowel. A combined version of those two rules then expresses the relationship which is felt to exist between them, by stressing that lengthening is due to schwa-del:

Schwa-lengthening:

V	C	ə	# →	1	2	∅	4
1	2	3	4	[+long]			

(When /ə/ deletes, the preceding vowel lengthens.)

3.2. There is further evidence of the importance of length in French phonology: nasalization is another instance in which deletion of a segment cooccurs with vowel-lengthening. Just as a vowel has been shown to be lengthened as a compensation for the loss of /ə/, it can also be shown that a vowel is lengthened as a compensation for the loss of a nasal consonant. This has been mentioned by Schane (1968) and Lightner (1970). The process of nasalization in French is usually characterized as two rules: Vowel-nasalization, conditioned by a following nasal consonant, is paired with Nasal-consonant-deletion, conditioned by a preceding nasalized vowel. Although they may be formulated as two rules intrinsically ordered, I propose here to characterize the process of nasalization as one single rule: N-Del. A one-rule analysis would be as follows:

N-Del:

$$\begin{matrix} V & N & \begin{Bmatrix} C \\ \#\# \end{Bmatrix} & \rightarrow & 1 & \emptyset & 3 \\ 1 & 2 & 3 & & [+nasal] & & \end{matrix}$$

(When the nasal consonant deletes, the preceding vowel is nasalized.)[5]

This rule is illustrated in:

	sang 'blood'	sembla 'seemed'	semble 'seems'	cinq 'five'
Underlying	/san/	/sanbla/	/sanblə/	/sink/
Phonetic	[sã]	[sãbla]	[sã:bl̩]	[sɛ̃:k]

However, different phonetic realizations are represented in the change of /VN/ to [V] or [V:]. This discrepancy corresponds to SPC (1), (2), (3) mentioned previously, namely, that stress is not sufficient to specify length, but that reference must be made to phonotactic constraints on the syllable structure: open syllables must be short, and closed syllables must be long. The hypothesis that nasalization and lengthening are simultaneously triggered by the deletion of the nasal consonant is now captured in one rule, Nasal-lengthening:

Nasal-lengthening:

$$\begin{matrix} V & N & \left\{\begin{matrix} C \\ \#\# \end{matrix}\right\} & \rightarrow & 1 & \emptyset & 3 \\ 1 & 2 & 3 & & \begin{bmatrix} +\text{nasal} \\ +\text{long} \end{bmatrix} & & \end{matrix}$$

(Whenever a nasal consonant deletes, the preceding vowel is nasalized and lengthened.)

Confirming evidence is offered by South French, in which there is correspondingly no nasal consonant-deletion, and no lengthening of the nasalized vowel:

Parisian French	[sã:bl]	
South French	[sãmblə]	(*semble* 'seems' 3 sg.)

Moreover, there are also cases in Standard French in which a vowel is nasalized optionally when it is followed by a sequence of nasal consonant, word-boundary, vowel. In those cases, the nasal consonant does not delete. For example: *on en a* 'we have some of them' becomes optionally:

/on#an#a/ → { [ɔ̃n#ãn#a] / [ɔn#an#a] }

The conditions on lengthening expressed in the foregoing are met at the same time: when deletion does not occur, lengthening is blocked and, correspondingly, the syllable involved is open in the optional nasalization case: [ɔ̃$n#ã$n#a] ~ [ɔ$n#a$n#a].

3.3. A third rule creates lengthening in the same conditions that have been defined earlier. According to Schane (1968:51-52) O-Conversion changes /al/ to [o:] before a consonantal segment. The long [o:] appears phonetically only in closed final syllable. Schane suggests that the two rules involved (a-raising to [o:], and l-deletion) can be stated as one, just as was the case when schwa-deletion and nasal-deletion were involved.

O-Conversion:

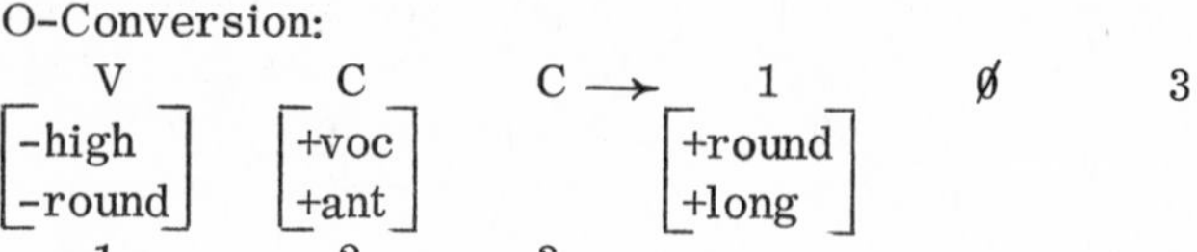

(/1/ deletes before a consonant and the preceding /a/ raises to [o] and lengthens.)[6]

This is shown in:

	cheval 'horse'	chevaux 'horses'	chevauche 'rides a horse'
Underlying	/šəval/	/šəvalz/	/šəvalšə/
Phonetic	[šəval]	[šəvo]	[šəvo:š]

	valent 'be worthy' (3 pl.)	valons (1 pl.)	vaut (3 sg.)
Underlying	/valət/	/valonz/	/valt/
Phonetic	[va:l]	[valɔ̃]	[vo]

Here once more the lengthening process is phonetically realized only in final closed syllable, namely, in chevauche and valent (but not in chevaux), valons and vaut, where the Truncation rule opens the syllable. Schwa-lengthening applies in valent and chevauche, and O-Conversion in chevaux, chevauche, and vaut.

4.1. If my analysis of vowel-length is valid, it can now be established that length in French cannot be explained merely as the result of allophonic rules.

It cannot be denied, however, that a number of detail rules, drawn from the set of universal phonetic rules, do exist: in particular, an allophonic rule lengthening vowels before voiced fricatives, then probably another rule assigning a lower numerical degree of length to vowels followed by voiced stops, and maybe a rule shortening long vowels before voiceless stops.

Besides this phonetic-lengthening, I have hypothesized the existence of a phonological lengthening which follows from various deletion processes. Three deletion rules have been shown to cause lengthening: Schwa-deletion, Nasal-consonant deletion, and O-Conversion (with L-deletion). These deletion rules appear to be all related by their functional unity. In fact, I claim that a generalization would be missed if this deletion-length correlation was not pointed out. Lengthening occurs only when deletion occurs, thus making lengthening a compensatory process with respect to deletion.

This deletion-lengthening correlation is further subordinated to a surface target: namely, that closed syllables be long and open syllables short.

4.2. Synchronic generative phonology (i.e. the Standard Theory, Chomsky and Halle 1968), even if it can capture the relationship between particular deletion and the associated lengthening, can only characterize this relationship as an accidental part of the formulation of each process. The association of lengthening and deletion has been evidenced in the foregoing by incorporating one rule (i.e. lengthening) into another (i.e. deletion) in exactly the same way with respect to all three processes. It now remains to explain why this compensatory lengthening is clearly realized only in closed syllables. Since the deletion rules also apply word-medially, an ad hoc rule of shortening would be required simply to undo the effects of lengthening where a short vowel is required in open syllables.[7]

However, generative phonology has been recently subject to a number of revisions, and it has been claimed that the Markovian mode of rule application of phonological rules required by the 'standard theory' model is too restrictive. It has been argued that instead of being formally limited to one point in the derivation, a rule should be given more scope in certain cases--whence the development of the notions of global rules, output conditions and conspiracies--Kiparsky (1972) and Kisseberth (1970).[8] If a language is found to contain a constraint on phonetic sequences a rule will be blocked if, by applying, it would produce unpermitted sequences. An output condition of this type has been formulated here as SPC (3).

(3) $\sim \begin{bmatrix} +\text{stress} \\ +\text{long} \end{bmatrix} \; \$$

(There are no long stressed vowels in open syllables.)

This output condition is attached to any deletion-lengthening process--namely, Schwa-lengthening, Nasal-lengthening and O-Conversion, and blocks lengthening in open syllables even when a tautosyllabic segment has been deleted. The mechanism of vowel-lengthening in French then involves both 'looking back' and 'looking forward' in the sense of Kiparsky (1973): 'looking back' for deletion--here incorporated in every lengthening rule--'looking forward' for the surface target. But the 'looking back' process is permitted only inasmuch as it does not contradict the 'looking forward' process, i.e. the compensatory lengthening is permitted to the extent that it does not violate SPC (3).

4.3. In this paper I have tried to determine the status of vowel-length in French. I have claimed that long vowels are derived by two different processes: by some late universal phonetic rules and by a major phonological phenomenon of compensatory lengthening, modified by an output condition requiring phonetic short vowels in open syllable.

NOTES

1. I have benefited greatly from discussing this paper with Dan Dinnsen. I also wish to acknowledge many helpful comments by Andreas Koutsoudas, Linda Norman, Gerald Sanders, and Albert Valdman. Needless to say, I alone am responsible for whatever errors may be found herein.

2. Some phonetic studies of French claim that [a] is submitted to the same lengthening as [o] and [ö]. The dialect I describe no longer makes the distinction between a front [a] and a back long [a] as exemplified in the classical distinction: <u>patte/pâte</u> ([pat]/[pa:t]). In the dialect concerned here, both words would have the same phoneme [a].

3. In some analyses of French set (c) is not recognized as having long vowels. Fouché says that although a vowel is long before a sequence of v+liquid (set (b)), it is not long before a sequence of r+ any consonant, as in set (c). In the dialect I describe there is no such distinction.

4. The hypothesis of compensatory lengthening has been suggested before. Martinet (1971:39) mentions a possible connection between length and deletion of /ə/: '. . . l'e caduc . . . se manifeste encore dans la prononciation par un allongement consécutif à sa syncope.' Delattre (1966:107), on the other hand, says that the extra-lengthening of a vowel may be historically attributed to the loss of a following segment. He also mentions that this lengthening occurs in closed syllable: 'Historiquement, on peut attribuer la durée vocalique . . . à la chute d'un son subséquent.' Schane (1968:55) also 'suspects that these long vowels are due to the deletion of a consonant.'

5. This rule cannot refer to the sequence /VN/ as syllable-final because of the following phonetic sentence-final forms:

[sɛ̃k] from /sink/ <u>cinq</u> 'we'
[gã̃g] from /gang/ <u>gang</u> 'gang'
[zɛ̃k] from /zink/ <u>zinc</u> 'zinc'
[tãk] from /tank/ <u>tank</u> 'tank'

6. Schane has pointed out that this conversion of /al/ to [o:] applies only to the nonlearned division of the lexicon (as appears in

learned forms like altitude, falsifier). Schane (1968:52, 143) has also discussed other O-Conversion rules, also restricted to non-learned lexical items, which apply roughly under the same conditions as the change /al/ to [o:] mentioned previously. These other O-Conversion cases are:

-/el/ becomes [o], e.g. belle [bɛ:l] beau [bo] 'beautiful (f. m.)'
-/ɔl/ becomes [u], e.g. collier [kɔlye] 'necklace' cou [ku] 'neck'
-/ɔs/ becomes [o], e.g. costal [kɔstal] 'coastal' (learned)
côte [ko:t] 'coast' (nonlearned)

However, these last cases do not seem to be very productive because of the multiplicity of learned words in which monophtongization does not occur. Therefore, I will not incorporate those cases in the O-Conversion rule formulated here. In many cases, no synchronic phonetic alternation occurs to support a two-segment underlying form: for example, saut [so] 'a jump', sauter [sote] 'to jump', saute [so:t] 'jumps (3 sg.)' is historically derived from Latin saltare, through an intermediate diphthongized stage: al > au > [o:]. I believe that the long [o:] in closed syllable is the reflex of a deletion. It might be assumed here that in Modern French a restructuring of the underlying form has taken place, establishing underlying long vowels specifically in those cases where the deletion-lengthening correlation historically existed, but vanished at a later stage. It is not essential for my purpose to decide on the best analysis to handle these cases.

7. Schane: French Phonology and Morphology, p. 54. 'A phonetic adjustment rule is required which shortens vowels in final position (for those vowels which have become long by the preceding rules and which eventually occur as final).'

Rule for final vowel shortening: 'In final position a vowel becomes short.'

8. Kisseberth (1973) discusses a case of compensatory lengthening in Klamath: the lengthening of a vowel is conditioned by the deletion of a glottal stop. He states this process in the following way: 'V → [+long] / if rule (i) deleted a glottal stop from a position immediately after this vowel.'

DOING THINGS OVER IN FRENCH

E. DEAN DETRICH

Michigan State University

The goal of this paper is to establish the appropriate phonological representation of the French prefix re- and demonstrate how it is mapped into its several phonetic representations. The phonological representations referred to in this paper are structured within the framework of Schane's analysis of French phonology (Schane 1968). It is assumed, therefore, that the French vowel system is made up of a set of underlying tense and lax vowels. The tense vowels (represented herein with the upper case symbols I, E, Ɛ́, A, Ɔ, O, U) undergo few changes by phonological rules, but the lax vowels (represented by the lower case symbols i, e, ɛ, a, ɔ, o, u) are radically modified. For example, the lax, front, nonhigh vowels e and ɛ diphthongize under stress; the lax, low vowels ɛ, a, and ɔ front under stress; unaccented, lax, low vowels are converted to schwa. These are not all the modifications of lax vowels, but they are some of those which are pertinent to the following discussion.

Another phonological characteristic of French phonology discussed by Schane and taken as a basic assumption in this paper is that there is a distinction to be made between learned and nonlearned pronunciation. This distinction is essential to the analysis which follows. Variations in the phonetic output of the phonological representations depend on the [±learned] specification.

I begin this discussion of the prefix re- by immediately considering its various pronunciations, putting off semantic considerations until later. Note the alternate pronunciations [r], [re], and [rə] in the examples in (1).

(1a)	(1b)	(1c)
renseigner	réunir	retailler
racheter	réimporter	redemander
rentrer	réformer	reformer
rassortir	réassortir	ressortir
rouvrir	réouverture	retravailler
rentoiler	rénover	renouveler
ranimer	réanimer	rechange
récrire	réécrire	repenser
rapporter	réduplicatif	redouble
rhabiller	réhabiliter	rechercher
ramollir	rémission	remettre
raffiner	rééditer	reconnaître

It is readily apparent that phonologically there is here, not a tripartite distinction among [r], [re], and [rə], but an opposition between [rə] and [re], the pronunciation [r] being the result of the application of the rule which deletes a lax vowel when it is contiguous to a tense vowel.[1] This means that the words in (1a) and (1c) all have a prefix whose underlying representation is r[V, -tense]. The lax vowel is deleted when followed by a tense vowel and is realized as schwa before a consonant.

If one chooses ɛ, which is both low and lax, as the vowel underlying re-, all the examples in (1a) and (1c) will be correctly generated. One can easily account for the pronunciation [re] in many of the words in (1b) by specifying them [+learned], in which case the underlying ɛ is tensed before the vowel deletion and schwa conversion rules apply, to generate the string rɛ. A late phonetic adjustment rule will rewrite the [+low] ɛ as [-low] [e] in open syllable.

There is ample evidence to support the contention that there is a distinction to be made between phonologically learned and nonlearned re- words. Examine the distinction as it is exemplified in the following pairs of words. The words in (2a) are learned; those in (2b) nonlearned.

(2a)	(2b)
réduplicatif	redoubler
répartir	repartir
récréer	recréer
réformer	reformer
rénover	renouveler
rétorquer	retordre
rébellion	rebelle
réviser	revoir
résurgence	resurgir

(2a)	(2b)
réprouver	reprouver
réversal	revers
répréhensif	reprendre
réhabiliter	rhabiller
récurrent	recourant
réfrigérer	refroidir
réception	recevoir
réfection	refaire
réflexion	reflet
réplétif	replet

I do not mean to imply by citing these examples that these pairs are necessarily doublets, that is, that they represent strings of morphemes containing identical underlying segments and whose differences of pronunciation are simply the result of different sets of phonological rules. This, however, may well be the case with the pairs *répartir/repartir*, *récréer/recréer*, *réformer/reformer*, *réprouver/reprouver*, and in the stems of the pairs *réception/recevoir*, *réflexion/reflet*, and *réplétif/replet*. My purpose in giving such a long list is simply to demonstrate a systematic opposition between learned [re] and nonlearned [rə/r].

Further evidence for the learned [re] / nonlearned [rə/r] distinction can be found by analyzing the phonetic makeup of the stems to which *re-* is affixed. Since all vowels in learned words are tensed before the application of other phonological rules, [2] it follows that words which exhibit pronunciations derived from underlying lax vowels should have a *re-* prefix pronounced either [rə] or [r]. Such is, in fact, the case in *revient*, *retient*, *relief*, and *rempiéter*, all of which contain the strings [jɛ] or [jɛ̃] derived from an underlying ɛ. The string [wa] in *reçoit*, *revoit*, *rassoit*, and *redoit* is similarly derived from the underlying lax vowel e. The [oe] of *repeupler*, *repleuvoir*, and *remeubler* is derived from an underlying ɔ. Consistently, [rə] and [r] appear as prefixes to roots with underlying lax vowels. Moreover, other characteristically nonlearned derivations can be correlated with the [rə/r] prefix. In French there is an alternation between learned [lj] and nonlearned [j] as in *foliation* versus *feuille*. There is a correlation between [rə/r] and [j] ← *li* (spelled *-ill-*): *refouiller*, *reconseiller*, *remouiller*, *réveiller*, *rempailler*. On the other hand, note the correlation between [re] and [lj] in *réconcilier* and *résilier*.

The [±learned] distinction does not, however, account for all the alternations between [re] and [rə/r]. In (1) one finds the alternations *réassortir/rassortir*, *réouverture/rouvrir*, *réanimer/ranimer*. To these can be added *réapprendre/rapprendre*, réapprovisionner/rapprovisionner, réassurer/rassurer, and réessayer/ressayer. These examples represent only those instances where the hesitation between [re] and [rə/r] has reached the dictionary. I have also heard subjects hesitate between réouvrir and rouvrir and between réoccuper and roccuper when asked which was 'correct'. It would be unsatisfactory to write off these examples simply by saying that they are alternately learned or nonlearned.

To explain this alternation one must begin by examining the semantics of re-. The Petit Robert gives the following definition:

> Re-, Ré, R-. Eléments qui expriment: le fait de ramener en arrière (ex. rabattre, recourber), le retour à un état antérieur (ex. refermer, rhabiller), la répétition (ex. redire, réaffirmer), le renforcement, l'achèvement (ex. réunir, ramasser) ou ce qui est explétif, équivalent de la forme simple vieillie (ex. raccourcir).

In explaining this alternation between [re] and [r] before vowels one must insist on the difference between those re's which have a clearly defined meaning of repetition and those which do not.

The last group of re- words specified in the Petit Robert definition is the largest single group which seems to convey no idea of repetition. These words are either synonyms of the forms without re- or have replaced a form without the prefix re-. There are raffiner, raffoler, ralentir, rapetisser, rallonger, ramollir, and raviver, to name just a few.[3] In these examples the re- prefix can be considered almost meaningless. In other instances re- can be analyzed as a prefix attached to a word with the result being, not a repetition of the meaning conveyed by the stem, but a different meaning for the word as a whole. Such is the case with reconnaître, which means 'to recognize', not 'to know again'; récréer means 'to enjoy one's self', not 'to create again'. For 'to create again' one uses recréer. A similar distinction can be made between réformer 'to convert' and reformer 'to reshape'. In many cases, however, a word in [rə] has two different interpretations: one implying repetition of the meaning of the stem word and another conveying an altogether different meaning. This is the case with remarquer which means both 'to mark again' and 'to take note of'. More words making similar distinctions are listed in (3).

(3a)	(3b)	(3c)
remonter	'to mount again'	'to rise (in value)'
rechercher	'to seek again'	'to do research'
recommander	'to order again'	'to recommend'
repartir	'to leave again'	'to retort'

(3a)	(3b)	(3c)
repasser	'to pass again'	'to iron'
représenter	'to present again'	'to represent'
reposer	'to place again'	'to rest'
reporter	'to carry again'	'to put back (a date)'
reprendre	'to take again'	'to criticize'

In English one can distinguish phonetically between [rɨ'muv] and ['rimuv], between ['rɛprɨˌzɛnt] and ['riprɨˌzɛnt], between [rɨ'pruv] and ['riˌpruv], etc. In some instances the distinction [re/rə] serves the same function in French as indicated in the preceding paragraph: *récréer*/*recréer*, *réviser*/*revoir*, *réformer*/*reformer*. But we have already maintained that the [re/rə] contrast in these pairs is the result of differences between learned and nonlearned pronunciation.

It is possible, though not obligatory, to disambiguate the homonyms of (3a) phonetically. In the *style familier*, and often in the *style soigné*, the word initial schwas of (3a) would be deleted under certain conditions, irrespective of the meaning of the words. However, a speaker can disambiguate meanings (3b) from (3c) by retaining the schwa and placing a secondary stress on it when he is being emphatic about the repetition of the meaning of the root, if he is insisting on the definitions (3b). Ex. [ˌrəprezɑ̃'te], [ˌrəpo'ze], [ˌrə'prɑ̃dr].

This raises questions concerning the derivation of stressed lax vowels in French. It is suggested above that the correct underlying vowel for the *re*- morpheme would be the lax, low, front vowel ɛ, as it is the one which can most easily generate learned [re] and nonlearned [rə]. It is also clear, however, that nonhigh lax vowels either front or diphthongize under stress. Since rɛ is stressed in the examples cited earlier, we must account for its not being realized as [rjɛ]. It is also interesting to note that there are other instances where [ə] ← [V, -tense] bears stress in French. The pronoun *le* is stressed when following the verb in an imperative, and the demonstrative *ce* is stressed in the expression: *Sur ce*! Note that in these cases the stress is primary. The easiest way to solve this problem is to specify that this secondary or emphatic stress is placed on schwa by a late rule applying after the schwa conversion rule.

This analysis casts further light on the doublets *réassortir*/*rassortir*, *réanimer*/*ranimer*, etc., but first consider the following list of words taken from the *Petit Robert*.

(4)			
	réabonner	réelire	réimporter
	réapparaître	réexporter	réimprimer
	réargenter	rééditer	réoccuper
	réagir	réévaluer	réorganizer
	réadapter	réhabituer	réunir

In all these [+learned] words the prefix [re] before a vowel clearly conveys repetition of the action of the root verb, as does the [r] in the [-learned] words rassortir, ranimer, rapprendre, remballer, rouvrir and ressayer. The [re] in the doublet forms réassortir, réanimer, etc. conveys the same kind of emphasis or insistence on repetition that is conveyed by the [ˌrə] before a root beginning with a consonant.

The question now is to account for the rewriting of an underlying rɛ, which conveys repetition and is followed by a vowel in a non-learned word, as [re] in the emphatic repetition realization of the same word. If it is the secondary stress discussed with reference to the distinction between [ˌrəpoˈze] and [rpoˈze] which constrains the tensing of ɛ before a vowel, then the secondary stress must be placed on rɛ early enough that the ɛ may be tensed before application of the rule which deletes lax low vowels when followed by another vowel. In fact, this would make the placement of secondary stress a fairly early rule and might again raise the problem of lax vowels fronting and diphthongizing under stress.

Allow me to suggest what I consider to be a better solution to this problem. When the repetition aspect of rɛ in formulations such as #rɛ#prEzANt+A+r#, #rɛ#AnIm+A+r# or #rɛ#Aʃɛt+A+r# is to be highlighted, an additional word boundary is inserted by a readjustment rule after the rɛ.[4] Since the lax vowel deletion rule does not apply if two word boundaries lie between the lax vowel and the following vowel, it is no longer necessary to use secondary stress as a constraint to tense ɛ in order to block vowel deletion. In other words I am saying that the prefix re- can function as a lexical item, at least phonologically. The formulation ##rɛ## not only blocks lax vowel deletion but dispenses with the need for a secondary stress placement rule. If we have the string ##rɛ##, the main stress rule will place primary stress on the vowel, and this stress will subsequently be reduced as are most other primary stresses in a phonological phrase.

In effect, I am saying that the emphasizing of repetition re- is the lexicalization of repetition re-.

Note that all the words in (4) are [+learned], therefore re- is consistently realized as [re]. The double word boundary is necessary, though, to generate the emphatic repetition forms: [ˌreadapˈte] and [ˌreeˈlir].

Note that all nonce words containing repetition re- will necessarily be emphatic, that is, they will have the form #rɛ##. A verb such as avertir, which does not normally have a re- derived form, will use the emphatic re- and will be pronounced [ˌreaverˈtir] if and when the re- prefix is used to convey avertir de nouveau.

One must now return again to the problem of not diphthongizing ɛ under stress. The only solution I can offer at present is an ad hoc rule tensing ε when it is followed by ##V. I am sure there will be other constraints on this rule and perhaps in its eventual form it will also account for the alternation between [ə] and [e] in the singular and plural of the masculine article (le+S# → [le(z)]). The same rule may also account for the alternation between the stressed diphthong [jε] in acquiert, which is derived from ε, and unstressed [e] in acquérir, which appears to be derived from ε.

This analysis of emphatic repetition re- having been given, let us consider again the semantic distinctions made between (3b) and (3c). For expository reasons I explored the method used by a French speaker to disambiguate phonetically the emphatic repetition definition of the words in (3a) from the other possible definition of the word. I indicated that it is possible to differentiate phonetically between the two meanings, but this does not mean that such a phonetic distinction is obligatory. The sentence Je vais le recommander pronounced without a secondary stress on re- is ambiguous. It can mean 'I am going to reorder it', or it can mean 'I am going to recommend it'. It is possible to disambiguate the two by stressing the re- in order to indicate the first meaning, but it is not imperative to do so. By the same token, the schwa of recommander 'to recommend' may never have secondary stress.

It is a difference in the makeup of the boundaries between rε and what follows which accounts for the differing meanings of the homonyms in (3a). When re- combined with a following stem yields a meaning other than repetition of the meaning of the root word, then we have an instance where the boundary between re- and what follows is + rather than #, even if the root which follows is phonologically identical to and semantically related to a string which is a lexical item bounded by #. Using this system to distinguish between [+repetition] and [-repetition] re's, one can easily account for the different phonetic outputs of the underlying representations in (5).

(5) #rε +pArtIr# → [repar'tir] 'to divide up'
[+learned]
#rε +pArtIr# → [rəpar'tir][5] 'to retort'
[-learned]
#rε #pArtIr# → [r(ə)par'tir] 'to leave again'
[-emp, -learned]
#rε ##pArtIr# → [ˌrəpar'tir] 'to leave again'
[+emp, -learned]
#rε #OvrIr# → [ru'vrir] 'to reopen'
[-emp, -learned]

#rɛ ##OvrIr# → [ru'vrir]   'to reopen'
[+emp, -learned]

The positing of the + rather than the # after re- also explains why there is no emphatic repetition form [re] for those vowel initial strings whose prefix [r] is purely 'explétif' in the words of the Petit Robert. We have ramollir, but not *réamollir; raffiner, but not *réaffiner; ralentir, but not *réalentir, etc. These words have the underlying form #rɛ+root# indicating that the rɛ does not convey repetition. If re- does not convey repetition, the repetition cannot be emphasized. The ɛ in ramollir, raffiner, and ralentir is naturally deleted before a vowel.

One can use the analysis developed so far to account for the differences among the words allonger, rallonger, and réallonger. In all the doublets discussed so far the phonetic variation has been between [r] and [re]. In this case allonger and rallonger are the doublets, and one must account for réallonger, which, according to what I have just stated, should probably be a starred form. Actually the explanation is quite simple. Allonger means, on the one hand, 'to lengthen', and the form rallonger ← #rɛ+allonger# is its synonym. On the other hand, allonger means 'to lay out' and its nonce form with repetition rɛ is réallonger ← #rɛ##allonger#.

For many rarely used words there is hesitation between #rɛ+...# and #rɛ#...#. While the Petit Robert and the Petit Larousse both give rempailler as the repetition form of empailler, indicating #rɛ#...#, two of my informants considered them synonymous, indicating #rɛ+...#.

An analysis of the verb écrire is also very interesting. On the basis of its alternation with description, inscrire, and transcrire one can posit an underlying root of the form skIr.... I will not try here to resolve the problem of the alternation p/b/v to account for scribe, description, and écrivain. The word initial vowel [e] of écrire is inserted by an epenthesis rule which is formulated in (6).

(6) $\emptyset \longrightarrow \begin{bmatrix} \text{V} \\ \text{-high} \\ \text{+front} \\ \text{-round} \end{bmatrix} \ / \ \# \ \_\_ \ \text{s} \ \begin{bmatrix} \text{C} \\ \text{-cont} \end{bmatrix}$ 6

After the application of rule (6) another nonlearned rule deletes [s] between [e] and a stop consonant.

The underlying representation of récrire being #rɛ#skrI...#, rule (6) will apply, followed by the lax vowel deletion rule and the [s] deletion rule, generating [re'krir]. The emphatic repetition form

[ˌreeˈkrir] will be generated regularly from #rɛ##skrI. . . #, a tense [ɛ] being inserted by rule (6), and the prefix vowel being tensed when followed by ##V. With this system of different boundaries one can account for the [+learned] word rescrit, meaning 'an ordinance or decree by a king or emperor in certain countries'. In this case the underlying representation is #rɛ+skrI. . . #. No [e] is inserted after a + boundary. Since rescrit is marked [+learned], the ɛ is tensed and [s] is not deleted before a consonant in learned words.

The nature of the boundary following the re- has other phonological repercussions as well. Consider the following list of examples.

(7a)	(7b)
ré[z]erver	con[s]erver
ré[z]orber	ab[s]orber
ré[z]oudre	dis[s]oudre
ré[z]ister	in[s]ister
ré[z]umer	con[s]umer
ré[z]ulter	con[s]ulter

Since the stems to which the prefixes in (7a) and (7b) are attached are not words, the boundary after the prefix is a derivational boundary =. The underlying phonological representation of all the stems in (7) begins with an /s/ as can be seen in the examples in (7b). Therefore we must have a rule voicing /s/ when it is between vowels. At the same time not all underlying /s/'s are voiced intervocalically. Such is not the case, for example, in re[s]entir, re[s]emeler, re[s]ortir, re[s]urgir, and re[s]embler. We must formulate the s voicing rule so that it applies to the words in (7), but not to the examples just given. Rule (8) is designed to allow for both eventualities.

(8) $s \rightarrow [+voice] / V = \_\_\_ V$

This brings up another problem of s voicing. While all the examples in (7) clearly are made up of a prefix and a stem which is not a word, there are other French words made up of re- followed by what looks like a complete word beginning in s, but which nevertheless undergo s voicing. What is more, they contrast with other words in which s is not voiced. We have ré[z]onner contrasting with re[s]onner, ré[z]urgence with re[s]urgir, and ré[z]igner with re[s]igner. Résonner, résurgence, and résigner are all the kind of [-repetition] re words to which has been assigned the underlying representation #rɛ+. . . #. Rather than extend rule (8) to include the environment V + ___ V, we can simply recognize that [-repetition] rɛ is a derivational affix always followed by the boundary = and a stem which in some cases looks like a word. The =connaître in reconnaître is no more a word than is the =sult of résulter.

This means that instead of three different boundaries #, =, and + after rɛ, there are only two, # and =. When # follows, rɛ is [+repetition]; when = follows, rɛ is [-repetition]. Now one sees that the homonyms of (3) are generated from rɛ attached to two identical phonological strings, one of which is a word, while the other is a stem. In (9) are a few example derivations to illustrate this.

(9)			
	#rɛ=mɔNt+A+r#	→ [r(ə)mɔ̃ˈte]	'to rise (in value)'
	#rɛ#mɔNt+A+r#		'to mount again'
	#rɛ=pAs+A+r#	→ [r(ə)paˈse]	'to iron'
	#rɛ#pAs+A+r#		'to pass again'
	#rɛ=pɔrt+A+r#	→ [r(ə)pɔrˈte]	'to put back'
	#rɛ#pɔrt+A+r#		'to carry again'

Before concluding this portion of the paper with a résumé of my analysis of the re- prefix, let me insist that much work needs to be done on this problem. While I believe that the analysis I have given accurately reflects the manner in which a speaker of French manipulates re-, what I have done is based primarily on examination of dictionary entries accompanied by informal interrogation of a small number of informants. The affixation of re- is productive in French and many occurrences of the re- emphasizing repetition are nonce forms. There is also considerable variation among speakers as to the 'normal' or 'correct' pronunciation of certain words. Most of these differences can be explained in terms of which boundary the particular individual inserts after the re-. A complete understanding of its manipulation will require a rigorous observation of unmonitored speech, together with some refined procedures for eliciting occurrences of re-. I feel confident, however, that such observation and elicitation will confirm my analysis.

I conclude with a brief résumé. There is a single underlying phonological representation for re- in French. This representation, rɛ, can be mapped into its pronunciations, [r], [rə], [ˌrə], [re], and [ˌre], by taking into account the phonological feature [±learned] and the type and number of boundaries which follow the prefix. The other crucial constraint is the feature specification of the following segment: is it followed by a vowel or by a consonant? The different possibilities are represented schematically in (10).

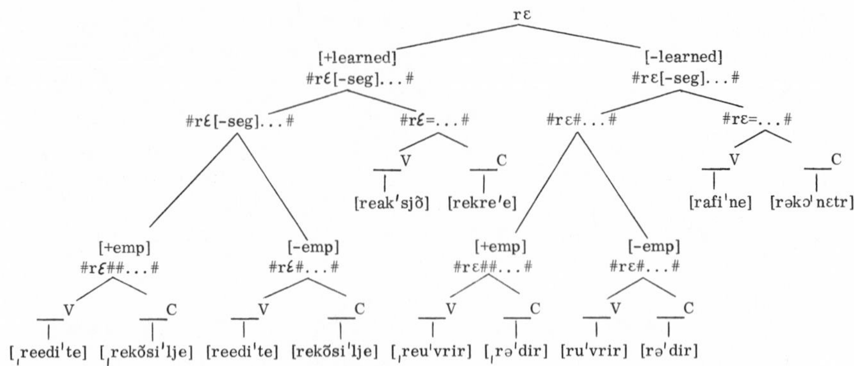

NOTES

1. The rule in question is the French truncation rule roughly as outlined by Schane in *French Phonology* and revised by Schane in 'There is no French truncation rule' (1974). The truncation rule used in this paper is specifically the vowel truncation rule. This rule is roughly stated: [V, -tense] $\rightarrow \emptyset$ / ___ {+, #} [-cons]. I have further refined this rule to the form [V, -tense] $\rightarrow \emptyset$ / ___ (#) [-cons]. Using this formulation, one can account for the [±learned] alternations between *Georges* [ʒɔrʒ] and *Géorgie* [ʒeɔrʒi], between *Jean* [ʒɑ̃] and *Johannique* [ʒɔanik]. In fact, this vowel truncation rule should be further refined as: [V, -tense, -high] $\rightarrow \emptyset$ / (#) [-cons, +voc] (a lax, nonhigh vowel is deleted when it precedes or follows the string (#) [-cons, +voc]). This last formulation will also account for the fact that schwa is never pronounced when it is preceded by a vowel. It can be argued that the *e* at the end of *amie* is purely orthographic and has no phonological reality. The verb ending *e* in *etudie*, *constitue*, etc. definitely has an underlying phonological representation. This final formulation of the vowel truncation rule deletes schwa preceded by a vowel and reinforces Schane's argument that instead of collapsing vowel truncation and consonant truncation as a single rule in French, we should use the vowel truncation rule outlined above and collapse the rules for consonant truncation and final consonant deletion. This consonant rule has the form C $\rightarrow \emptyset$ / ___ {+, #} {C, #}. For a more complete discussion of this last rule see my paper 'Constraints on final consonant deletion in French' (forthcoming).

2. There are a few rare instances where *re-* has the schwa pronunciation when affixed to a [+learned] stem as in *rechristianiser*, *retransmission* (*-mission* at least appears [+learned] in *rémission*) and *recalcification* (the verb *recalcifier* without the root final [k] and

the tense theme vowel is presumed to represent the [-learned] form). For the time being, I see no way to systematically identify [+learned] words or stems. Some general observations can be made, such as: Stems to which *-isme* is affixed are usually [+learned]. One could nevertheless question the learnedness of the stem of *je-m'en-fichisme.* It may be that the length or the morphemic complexity of *rechristianiser, retransmission* and *recalcification* may account for the *re-* having the schwa pronunciation characteristic of [-learned].

3. When pressed to convey repetition with reference to these verbs, an informant will usually say *de nouveau* or *encore*.

4. Note that this readjustment rule adding a word boundary after rɛ is a corollary to the readjustment rule suggested by Schane (1974) which deletes one of two word boundaries under certain circumstances in order to establish the appropriate environment for the application of the consonant deletion rule. Ex. #grɑ̃d##garsɔ̃# → #grɑ̃d#garsɔ̃# → [grɑ̃garsɔ̃].

5. Some French speakers hesitate about the learnedness of the noun *repartie/répartie.*

6. This is a nonlearned rule. It does not apply in the words *scribe, scriptural,* and *scripteur*. A similar [±learned] distinction can be made between *étude, étudier,* and *studieux*. In this case we also have a semilearned form *estudiantin*.

THEORETICAL IMPLICATIONS IN THE DEVELOPMENT OF *ACCUSATIUUS CUM INFINITIUO* CONSTRUCTIONS

MARIO SALTARELLI

University of Illinois

1. *Accusatiuus cum infinitiuo*. The following sentences exemplify three types of verb complements in Latin:

(1a) rogo *ut ueniat* 'I pray that he comes'
(1b) dicit *se latine scire* 'He_i says that he_i knows Latin'
(1c) *exire* uolo 'I want to go out'

Accusatiuus cum infinitiuo is the term which grammarians commonly reserve for the complement type (1b), where the logical subject of the subordinate clause is in the accusative case (normally the object case) and its verb is in the infinitive. Ernout and Thomas (1951:271-272) give the following account of this infinitival construction:

> La proposition infinitive a été tout d'abord un cas de double accusatif du type *doceo pueros grammaticam*. La phrase *sentio eum uenire* s'est analysée, d'une part, en *sentio eum* 'je l'aperçois', et, d'autre part, en *sentio uenire* 'j'aperçois venir'. Le nom à l'accusatif le considérèrent comme un véritable 'sujet'. La proposition infinitive est constituée dès les premiers texts. Son emploi très fréquent est en fait une des caractéristiques du latin, surtout littéraire. Il n'est pour ainsi dire pas de période cicéronienne qui n'en présente un ou plusieurs exemples. Cependant, la langue parlée s'en détournait. Elle préférait la complétive avec

quod: *gaudeo quod*, *dico quod*, qui, en maintenant le sujet au nominatif et le verbe à un mode personnel, évitait toute ambiguité.

The accusative-with-infinitive verb complement type (1b), seems to have had sociolinguistic relevance in the texts of the *aetas aurea* or *argentea*: the identification of the formal or 'literary' style as opposed to the informal or 'vulgar/popular' style. Examples of this construction are found in competition with the 'sentential' complement type (1a), in particular the subtype introduced by the complementizer *quod* (cf. Ernout and Thomas 1951), as well as in competition with the 'nominal' complement type (1c) (cf. Ronconi 1946:162; Sonnenschein 1914:213; Ernout and Thomas 1951:271). The three verb complement types--sentential (1a), accusative-with-infinitive (1b), and nominal (1c)--would then correlate with the two coexisting styles, literary and vulgar, as follows:

(2)

Latin verb complementation	
literary style	vulgar style
SENTENTIAL	SENTENTIAL
ACC-w-INF	Ø
NOMINAL	NOMINAL

There is one fundamental syntactic characteristic which distinguishes the two styles: the operations on equivalent subjects (better known as equivalent noun phrase deletion). This distinction, which I am going to define presently, is the conceptual identification of the socially more prestigious literary style which accounts for the more typical subtype of accusative-with-infinitive constructions and the well defined (as opposed to random) correlation between the two styles. Consider the literary and vulgar correspondences of (3a, b) in (4a, b):

(3a) he_i hopes that he_j comes (will come)
(3b) he_i hopes to come
(that he_i will come)

	'literary'		'vulgar'
(4a)	sperat eum uenturum esse	=	sperat quod ueniat
(4b)	sperat se uenturum esse	=	sperat uenire

Standard handbooks usually define both (4a) and (4b) as accusative-with-infinitive without any subclassification. If one focuses attention on the relation between the subject of the main verb and the subject of the dependent verb, two subtypes are noted: nonequivalent subjects, type (4a), and equivalent subjects, type (4b). This structural distinction accounts for the well defined correlation between the literary and the vulgar style. I claim, on the basis of present-day Romance complementation, that what characterized classical/literary Latin as opposed to vulgar Latin was the equivalent-subjects type, (4b), of the accusatiuus cum infinitiuo construction, and not (4a). The former type is entirely unknown in present-day Neo-Latin language, as far as I have been able to determine. The latter type is alive and well, as this paper intends to show. Further evidence for this claim might also be the fact that the data adduced by scholars to show the more general use of accusative-with-infinitive constructions in the texts of Cicero's time (106-43 B.C.), in comparison with the texts of Plautus' time (254-184 B.C.), usually involves the equivalent-subjects type of accusative-with-infinitive. For example, Ronconi (1946:162) compares the plautine ire dixi 'I said I would go' with the classical or ciceronian me ire or me iturum esse dixi, and the purely familiar/colloquial dare promitto 'I promise to give', the nominal type of complement still found in Caesar's Bellum Gallicum (ca. 50 B.C.) polliceor obsides dare 'I promise to give hostages'.

The foregoing discussion leads to the following preliminary hypotheses:

(5a) The syntactic characterization of the accusatiuus cum infinitiuo construction has a systematic definition in terms of subjects' equivalence. The equivalent-subjects subtype more narrowly defines the nature of the literary style in coexistence with the vulgar style.

(5b) The vulgar style remains dominant over the literary style.[1] This would offer an explanation for the fact that the equivalent-subjects subtype is not found in present-day Romance languages.

(5c) The acquisition of the literary/formal style in the aetas aurea involved the 'blocking' of the syntactic process of equivalent-subject deletion.

2. Case agreement. The blocking of the 'equivalent-subjects deletion', which is responsible for the subtype (4b), did not extend to all constructions which met the structural description. Some verbs like uolo, cupio, studeo, etc. allow either the complement type (1b) (accusative-with-infinitive) or (1c) (nominal), according to Ernout and Thomas (1951:271). What this means is that a characterization of the literary style must incorporate a variable constraint (defined on the above class of verbs) on equivalent-subjects processes.

The syntactician's problem is a formalization of the equivalence relation in pairs of sentences like (6b, c),

(6a) uolo Iuliam esse bonam 'I want Julia to be good'
(6b) uolo me esse bonum 'I want to be good'
(6c) uolo esse bonus 'I want to be good'

where the relevant distinctions are: the presence/absence of me co-occurring with the case alternation -um/-us.[2]

Robin Lakoff proposed (1968:75-85) to derive all accusative-with-infinitive constructions like (6a, b), as well as (6c), from underlying sentential complement structures by the following rules:

(7a) Accusative-Infinitive Complementizer Change[3]
(7b) Equi-NP-Deletion
(7c) Agreement Across Copula

I shall not argue here about the naturalness of a rule like (7a), which performs several seemingly unrelated operations in a deus ex machina fashion, nor shall I probe the empirical basis of (7b) defined on semantic coreference but used also to mop up the [+acc] marker introduced by (7a). As it stands, Lakoff's analysis leads to a theoretical paradox. Lakoff (1968:85) assumes that case is assigned at a level of derivation prior to the application of rules (7), and that Agreement Across Copula is ordered after Equi-NP-Deletion. Consider now the following derivations:

(8a)	uolo quod ego sim bon-	CASE ASSIGN
	uolo quod ego sim bonus	(7c)
	uolo ∅ me esse bonus	(7a)
	uolo ∅ me esse bonum	(7c)
(8b)	uolo quod ego sim bon-	CASE ASSIGN
	uolo ∅ me esse bon-	(7a)
	uolo ∅ ∅ esse bon-	(7b)
		(7c) fails to apply

It is evident that Agreement Across Copula (7c) cannot be extrinsically ordered after Equi-NP-Deletion (7b), or else unfinished derivations like (8b) are produced. It follows also that (7c) cannot be extrinsically ordered before (7b), because it would yield ungrammatical sentences like *uolo me esse bonus. As one can see in derivations (8a), Agreement Across Copula must apply before and after Equi-NP-Deletion.[4]

I propose that Agreement Across Copula is more precisely and generally characterized as a surface structure principle which I shall call 'functional dominance':

(9) An adjective is assigned the same case as the NP which 'immediately dominates' it.[5]

It is assumed, furthermore, that the NP's themselves are assigned primary case on the basis of the functional relations they enter into in the constituent structure of a given sentence (cf., however, Saltarelli 1973, for secondary or derived case assignment).

By way of exemplification, there is the surface structure analyses given in (10a, b, c):

(10a)

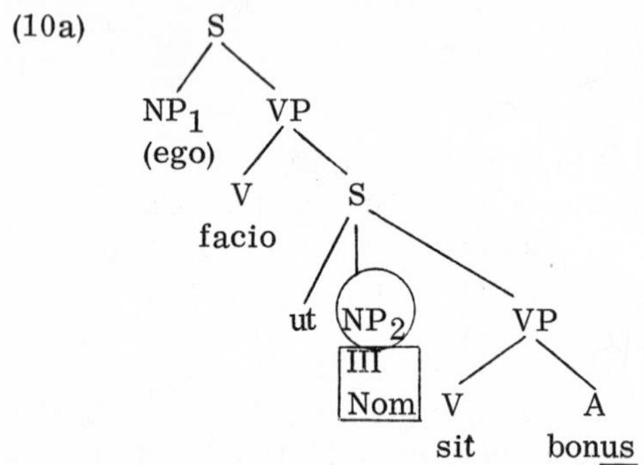

(10b)

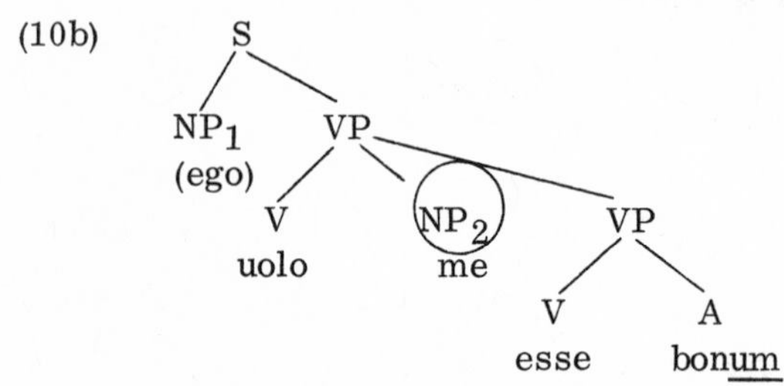

(10c)

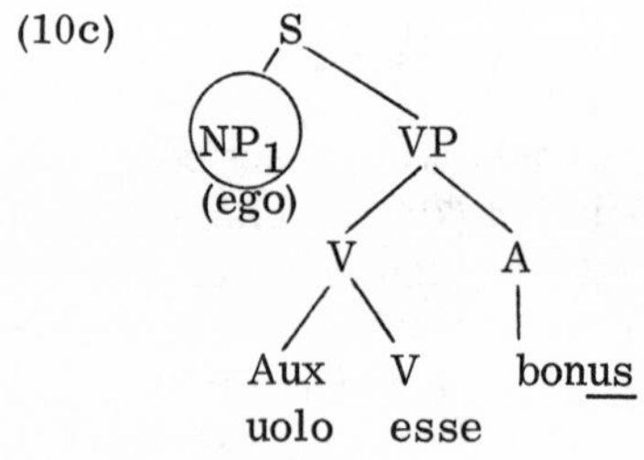

These exemplify, respectively, a sentential type of complement, an accusative-with-infinitive, and a nominal type. In (10a), NP_1 and NP_2 are assigned the nominative case by the functional relations principle. In (10b), NP_1 takes nominative and NP_2 takes accusative. In (10c), NP_1 is the only noun phrase left and it is assigned the appropriate case on the basis of the functional dominance principle (9). Bonus is nominative in (10a) in agreement with NP_2, the noun phrase which ‘immediately dominates’ it. Likewise, in (10b) bonum is accusative because it is ‘immediately dominated’ by NP_2, which is now in the accusative. Finally, in (10c) bonus is nominative because its ‘immediately dominating’ noun phrase is NP_1.

The surface structure of the sentences in (10a, b) needs little motivation. Example (10a) has a sentential complement in the sense that it has two finite verbs and two grammatical subjects. Example (10b) is an accusative-with-infinitive complement which has traditionally been considered a two-object structure: the infinitival predicate and its logical subject. Finally, in the nominal type, (10c), esse remains as the main verb, thus permitting Agreement Across Copula, while uolo functions as auxiliary verb. This analysis will be further supported in section 4.

3. Subject-Raising. Grammarians distinguish between ‘impersonal’ constructions like (11a) and ‘personal’ constructions like (11b) (cf. Ronconi 1946:217).

(11a) traditur Homerum caecum fuisse
‘It is said that Homer was blind’
(11b) (i) traditur Homerus caecus fuisse
‘Homer is said to have been blind’
(ii) Homerus traditur caecus fuisse
‘Homer is said to have been blind’

Examples (11a, b) are considered to be semantically equivalent, except for the ‘emphasis’ which Homerus is given in the personal construction. Examples (11b)(i, ii) are order variants. Whereas (11a) is considered an accusative-with-infinitive, (11b) is classified as nominative-with-infinitive. If the surface principle of functional dominance is assumed, a straightforward relation is found between personal and impersonal types in terms of the well-known syntactic process of Subject-Raising. In (12) are seen the principles of case assignment to NP and to Adjectives, discussed in connection with (10b, c), perfectly supported:

(12a)

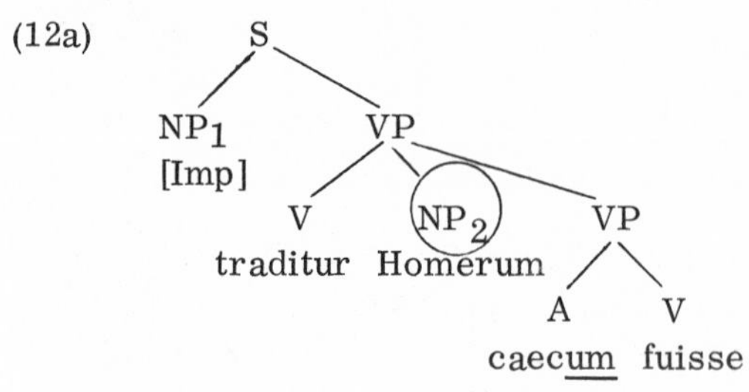

(12b)

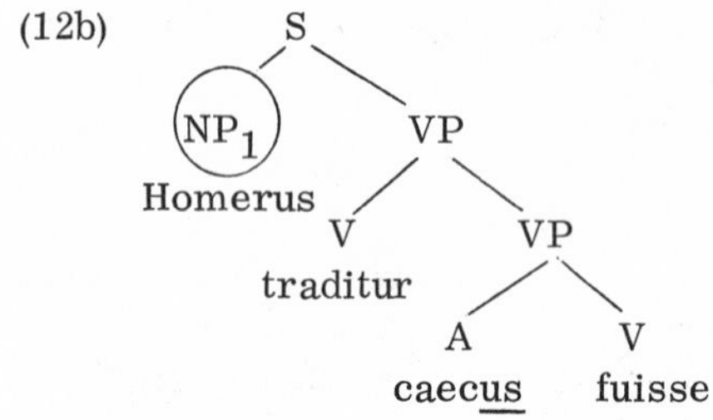

In (12a, b) 'Homer' is, respectively, in the accusative and nominative in accordance with its functional relations. Accordingly, 'blind' is in the accusative in (12a) because its immediately dominating NP_2 is accusative, but it is nominative in (12b) because NP_1 is nominative.

If the syntactician wishes to define the semantic equivalence between (12a) and (12b) by postulating the (logical) subject NP_2 raising to subject NP_1, he must assume that the impersonal and personal type are both derived from the same underlying structure which will end up being that of the sentential type of verb complement (10a), if the correlation between the accusative-with-infinitive in the literary style and the sentential and nominal in the vulgar style (presented in (2)) is considered. Under such analysis, (12a) (structurally equivalent to (10b)) is obtained by Subject-Raising-to-Object, and (12b) (structurally equivalent to (10c)) by Subject-Raising-to-Subject. The three types of verb complement thus related by formal syntactic processes represent degrees of reduction in complementation. Type (10a) is the most structured complement type, and (10c) the least structured.

4. Verb-Raising. So far I have argued for an analysis of Latin verb complementation on purely internal bases. Now, as a final point, I am going to discuss briefly a diachronic development in the verb complements of present-day Romance languages which supports the analysis proposed for Latin.

Although the three basic types discussed earlier (sentential, accusative-with-infinitive, and nominal) remain in general Romance, there is a new development whereby the sentential periphrastic causative <u>facere ut</u> + S has developed into a nominal periphrastic causative in the central regions of Romania. In the marginal regions, however, this construction has developed into an accusative-with-infinitive periphrastic causative. In particular, Italian and French have nominal periphrastic causatives, Portuguese and Rumanian have accusative-with-infinitive periphrastic causatives, and Spanish has only the nominal type with hacer but allows both the nominal and the accusative-with-infinitive with dejar.

The present-day Romance situation can be seen in (13) (for a full discussion of the phenomenon and its implications for functional syntax, cf. Saltarelli 1973, and in preparation).

(13)	Italian	Maria fa scrivere Gianni (DO)
		*Maria fa Gianni scrivere
	French	Marie fait écrire Jean (DO)
		*Marie fait Jean écrire
	Spanish	María hace escribir a Juan (DO)
		*María hace a Juan escribir
		María deja escribir a Juan (DO)
		María deja a Juan (DO) escribir
	Portuguese	*Maria deixou escrever João
		Maria deixou João (DO) escrever
	Rumanian	*Maria face scrie Ion
		Maria il face pe Ion (DO) să scrie

Note in (13) that Italian and French allow only the nominal type of complement fa scrivere Gianni, fait écrire Jean. These languages do not allow the accusative-with-infinitive *fa Gianni scrivere, *fait Jean écrire. Conversely, Portuguese and Rumanian allow only the accusative-with-infinitive type of complement deixou João escrever, îl face pe Ion să scrie. These languages do not allow the nominal *deixou escrever João, *face scrie Ion. Spanish appears to be in a diffusional period. It is moving toward the structurally more reduced nominal type but the acceptance of this type varies greatly from speaker to speaker.

As I mentioned briefly at the end of section 3, the three types of complements exemplified in (10a, b, c) represent a gradation in structure. The sentential type (10a) is the most structured type, the accusative-with-infinitive (10b) is less structured, and the nominal type (10c) is the least structured. The historical development, then, from sentential (Vulgar Latin) to accusative-with-infinitive (Portuguese, Rumanian) to nominal (French, Italian) can be described as the result of a complement structure reduction with consequent increase in functional opacity.

The question which remains to be answered now is the following:

what is the syntactic process involved in the development from sentential → accusative-with-infinitive → nominal?

The solution proposed in this paper is an extension of the principle of Raising and Pruning described as follows:

(14a) Sentential

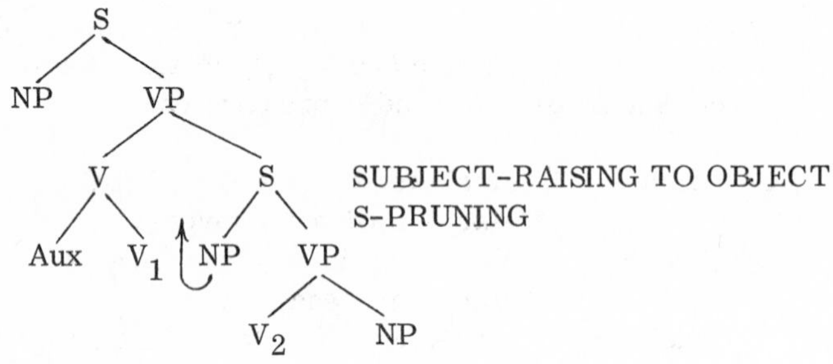

(14b) Accusative-with-Infinitive

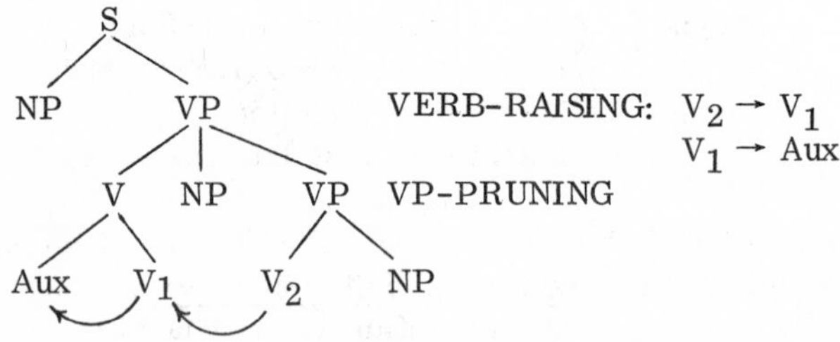

(14c) Nominal

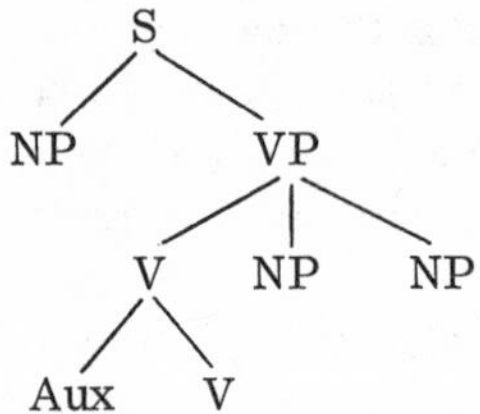

An historical account of the development of periphrastic causatives leads us to posit two stages, (14a) → (14b), and (14b) → (14c). This hypothesis is established on internal bases (they identify a gradation in structure reduction), as well as on comparative bases. The syntactic process assumed is that of Raising and Pruning. According to this analysis, causative verbs in nominal complements (14c) have the function of auxiliary verbs, whereas in accusative-with-infinitive complements they have the function of main verbs, in the same way as proposed in (10c) for the class of Latin verbs *uolo*, *cupio*, *studeo*, etc. (cf. section 2). I conclude that the process of Verb-Raising, assumed in deriving nominal complements in Vulgar Latin with a restricted class of verbs, has been extended in Romance to include periphrastic causative verbs. One might speculate that if the hypothesis is correct, Verb-Raising should eventually extend to Spanish in a general way, on the assumption that the diffusion of the process is not blocked.

NOTES

1. It seems reasonable to assume that literary/classical Latin was acquired by the young Roman at a later date during his formative period, in imitation of the more prestigious writers. In such sociolinguistic ambience it is easy to see how the spoken/vulgar style would remain the dominant one, the type of data on the basis of which Roman children would construct their grammar. That the literary style, the equivalent-subjects accusative-with-infinitive construction, was never incorporated in the spoken language is supported by the fact that there is no trace of it in Romance. One might also speculate that Equi-NP-Deletion is a relatively natural phenomenon, and that the literary style which 'blocked' this process would have little chance of survival in the spoken everyday language.

2. We are dealing here with the definition of the rule of Agreement, in particular Case-Agreement (as opposed to gender and number agreement, cf. paper by C. Quicoli in this volume). The time-honored rule in question is Agreement Across Copula. Given the surface structure (6a, b, c), the rule accounts for (6a, b) but not for (6c), where *bonus* appears to agree with the only possible nominative, i. e. *ego*, the subject of *uolo*. The standard solution to the agreement problem presented by (6c) within a generative-transformational grammar is to posit an underlying representation for that sentence like the following: $_{S}[\text{ego}_i$ uolo $_{S}[\text{ego}_i$ sum bon-]] which offers the proper structural description for the application of Agreement Across Copula. A later rule would yield the infinitival surface construction (6c). The theoretical questions which arise on closer inspection are the following: (1) do we need to appeal to hypothetical/underlying syntactic structures to define agreement? and (2) is the nature of case agreement the same as that of gender-and-number agreement?

3. Lakoff (1968:79) gives the following formulation:

(a) Accusative-Infinitive Complementizer Change
X_1 - quod - NP - VP - X_2 $\rightarrow$ 1 - ∅ - 3 - C+4 - 5
[+acc]
1 2 3 4 5
(C = -se + nonfinite)

which yields accusative-with-infinitive derivations with the following syntactic structure:

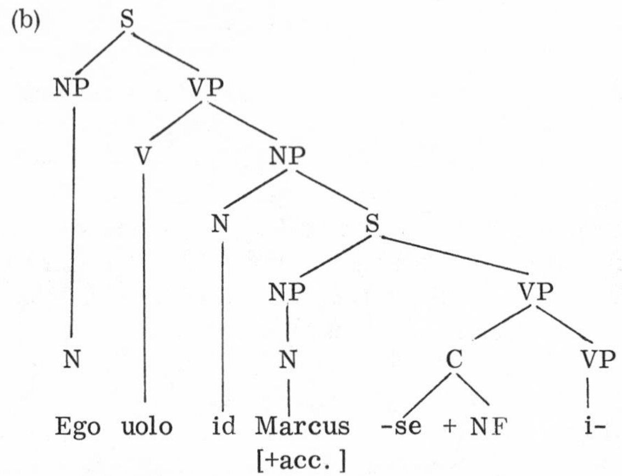

to yield uolo Marcum ire after other transformations (id-deletion among others) apply. Rule (a) is questionable on the following bases. First, it fails to meet a reasonable degree of 'operational unity'. If a rule brackets more than one phenomenon, they should be of the same general type. Rule (a) includes deletion (quod is ∅) as well as addition (3 is [+acc.], 4 is C+4). The addition process itself is not 'unitary' in that it inserts a feature as well as a constituent. Furthermore, within the very framework which the author assumes, the relation between quod-S and accusatiuus cum infinitiuo is not properly accounted for from a surface structure point of view. In fact, the latter is derived as a sentential type (b), whereas time-honored analyses would argue (to be sure, informally) its double-object function.

4. Another possible interpretation of Lakoff's statement (1968:85) is that there is a 'basic' case, the nominative, which is lexically assigned to adjectives (and nouns). Accordingly, we have the following derivation:

uolo quod ego sim bonus
uolo ∅ me esse bonus (7a)
uolo ∅ me esse bonum (7c)

in which (7c) is a highly limited phenomenon of case-change strictly required by the way that (7a) is formulated. In this view (7c) is not a formalization of the traditional Agreement Across Copula as a general case-assignment process (cf. (8)).

5. For the formalization of a transformational rule of case assignment, the principle of functional dominance can be defined on a domain of trees as follows: a noun phrase NP_i functionally dominates an adjective A_j if and only if there is a node X which dominates NP_i and A_j, and furthermore the distance (sequence of branches) between A_j and NP_i is shorter than that between A_j and any other noun phrase NP_k. Functional dominance would also have to have a straightforward definition in terms of an interpretive rule of coreference. The objection one might raise in this connection is that there is no reason for case agreement to be considered an interpretive rule, since case differences have no semantic import, as can be seen by observing the semantically equivalent (10b) and (10c).

MISSING SUBJECTS IN PORTUGUESE

A. CARLOS QUICOLI

Universidade Estadual de Campinas

1.0 Introduction. In the discussion that follows, I present evidence in favor of two syntactic rules which are operative in Portuguese.

The first rule, COMPLEMENT-SUBJECT DELETION (somewhat similar to the rule commonly referred to as EQUI-NP-DELETION), has the effect of deleting the subject of an embedded sentence under condition of identity with a noun phrase in the matrix sentence. This rule is responsible, for instance, for the derivation of the sentences in (2) from their simplified underlying structures in (1).

(1a) [Zeca queria--[Zeca jogar dominó]]
Zeca wanted--Zeca play dominoes

(1b) [Aldo persuadiu Lucia--[Lucia lavar os pratos]]
Aldo persuaded Lucia--Lucia wash the dishes

(2a) Zeca queria jogar dominó
'Zeca wanted to play dominoes'

(2b) Aldo persuadiu Lucia a lavar os pratos
'Aldo persuaded Lucia to wash the dishes'

In the derivation of (2a) from (1a) COMPLEMENT-SUBJECT DELETION deletes the subject of the embedded sentence--the underlined NP Zeca in (1a)--since it is identical to the subject of the matrix sentence. In the derivation of (2b) from (1b) COMPLEMENT-SUBJECT DELETION applies and deletes the subject of the embedded sentence--the underlined NP Lucia in (1b)--since it is identical to the object of the matrix sentence.[1]

The second rule, SUBJECT-PRONOUN DELETION, is a late rule which deletes 'nonemphatic' (i. e. 'noncontrastive') subject pronouns. This rule would account, for instance, for the existence of sentences such as those in (4), which are parallel to those in (3).

(3) Nós gostamos de limonada
'We like lemonade'
Eles foram ao cinema
'They went to the movie'

(4) Gostamos de limonada
Like (1st pl.) lemonade
'We like lemonade'
Foram ao cinema
Went (3rd pl.) to the movie
'They went to the movie'

Within the discussion, evidence based on facts from Portuguese will be presented in order to substantiate the following points: (1) The phenomenon involving 'missing' complement subjects which are understood to be identical to some NP in the sentence is to be accounted for by means of a syntactic rule of COMPLEMENT-SUBJECT DELETION and not by a semantic 'interpretive' rule as proposed in Jackendoff (1969). (2) COMPLEMENT-SUBJECT DELETION is a cyclic rule distinct from SUBJECT-PRONOUN DELETION which is a postcyclic rule. (3) COMPLEMENT-SUBJECT DELETION cannot be fragmented into two independent operations, one cyclic DOOM MARKING (which marks NP's fated for deletion), the other postcyclic DOOM ERASURE (which operates on pronominal structures and actually erases the 'doomed' NP's as proposed in Postal (1970a)).

2.0 On complement subject deletion. In his study of the English complement system, Rosenbaum (1967) pointed out the fact that in certain complement constructions the subject of an embedded sentence which is understood to be identical to a noun phrase in the matrix sentence is generally 'missing' in the superficial form of the sentence. In order to account for the phenomenon, he proposed an analysis in which the 'missing' element is actually represented in underlying structure and, to account for its absence in surface structure, he proposed a syntactic rule--IDENTITY-ERASURE TRANSFORMATION--which has the effect of deleting the subject of a complement sentence under condition of identity with a noun phrase in the matrix sentence. The IDENTITY-ERASURE TRANSFORMATION would thus account both for the absence of the complement subject in surface structure and for the fact that the missing subject is understood to be identical to another noun phrase in the sentence.

More recently, Rosenbaum's initial assumption that this process of 'deletion under identity' constitutes a syntactic phenomenon accountable for by a syntactic rule has been subject to critical discussion.

Thus in Jackendoff (1969) it is argued that there is no syntactic rule of the type proposed by Rosenbaum. The point at issue is that a syntactic rule such as the IDENTITY-ERASURE TRANSFORMATION (or EQUI-NP DELETION) would have to take into consideration the linguistic property of 'coreference' ('identity of reference') in its formulation. Jackendoff claims, however, that coreference is an 'exclusively semantic' property unavailable to the syntactic component; hence, no syntactic rule can refer to it in its structural description. Since a syntactic rule such as the IDENTITY-ERASURE TRANSFORMATION (or EQUI-NP DELETION) would have to mention coreference in its structural description, Jackendoff concludes that it cannot be a syntactic rule and he proposes an alternative analysis in which the alleged cases involving EQUI-NP DELETION are accounted for as part of the semantic component rather than in the syntax.

On the other hand, Postal (1970a) argues that the deletion of the complement subject under condition of identity is to be accounted for syntactically and, in another paper (Postal 1968), he argues that the syntactic principles must also include notions such as 'identity', 'nonidentity', which he refers to as 'syntactic coreferentiality'.

In this section I argue that, in Portuguese, the deletion of the complement subject under condition of identity constitutes a syntactic phenomenon to be accounted for by a syntactic rule of COMPLEMENT-SUBJECT DELETION. In particular, it will be shown that there are certain facts about Portuguese that can be adequately described if there is a syntactic rule of COMPLEMENT-SUBJECT DELETION and that the same facts are indescribable otherwise.

2.1 The deletion hypothesis. Let us begin the discussion by considering the following Portuguese sentence:

(5) As garotas queriam beijar o cantor
'The girls wanted to kiss the singer'

Following standard analyses within transformational grammar, one could propose for this sentence a deep structure roughly like (6).

(6)

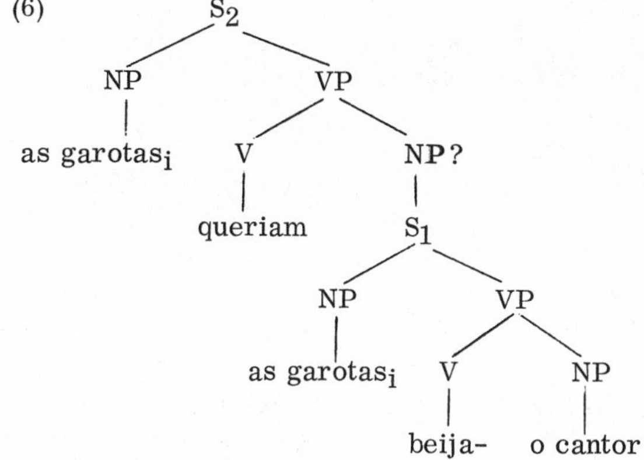

Now, since the subject of the complement sentence is identical to a noun phrase in the matrix sentence, COMPLEMENT-SUBJECT DELETION would apply to (6) and produce (7) as its output.

(7)

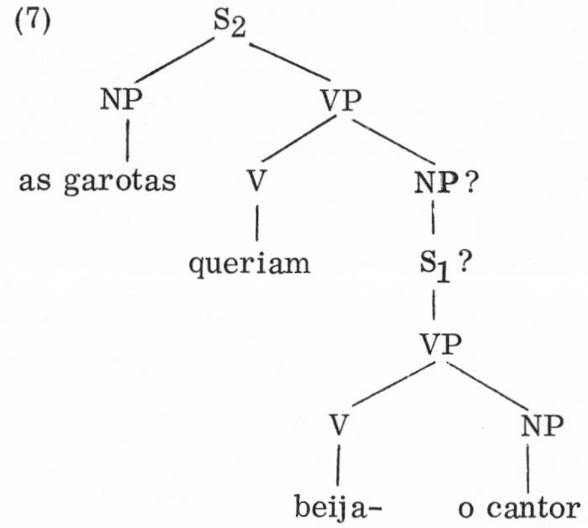

Subsequent transformation would then apply to this structure and (5) is derived.

Observe that if COMPLEMENT-SUBJECT DELETION is made obligatory, it is possible to block the derivation of ungrammatical sentences such as:

(8) *As garotas queriam as garotas beijar o cantor
'The girls wanted the girls to kiss the singer'

Notice also that sentence (8) is ungrammatical whether the two instances of <u>as garotas</u> are coreferential or not. That is, the Portuguese verb <u>querer</u> 'to want' does not appear in 'accusative plus infinitive' constructions.

Similarly, the obligatory character of the rule would also prevent the derivation of sentences such as (9), where the two instances of as garotas refer to the same group of individuals.

(9) *As garotas$_1$ queriam que as garotas$_1$ beijassem o cantor
The girls wanted that the girls kissed (subj.) the singer

I refer to the analysis just described as the 'deletion hypothesis'.

2.2 Inadequacies of the complex VP hypothesis. Consider now a first alternative analysis. Suppose one wished to extend the base component so as to allow the VP symbol to be expanded as in (10).[2]

(10) VP $\rightarrow$ V⁀VP

One could then argue that the structure underlying sentence (5) is something like (11) and not (6).

(11)

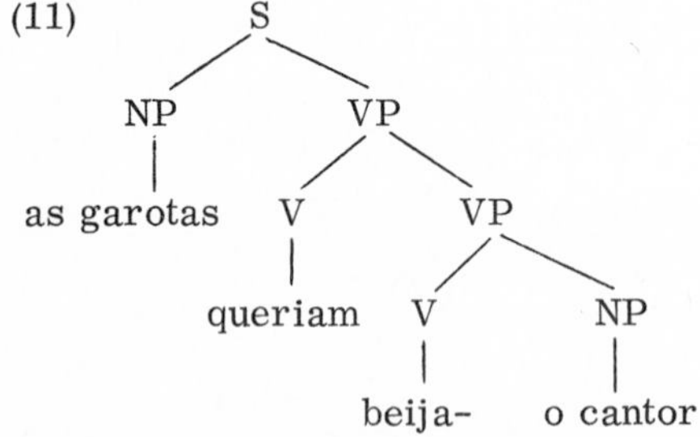

In this case, the deep structure would correspond closely to the surface structure and there would be no need for a 'deletion' rule in order to derive sentence (5). I refer to this analysis as the 'complex VP hypothesis'.

A priori, there is no reason why one should prefer one or the other analysis. However, closer examination of the two hypotheses shows that the complex VP hypothesis is deficient in ways in which the deletion hypothesis is not, and one is forced to choose the latter over the former.

Consider a first argument. In Portuguese, an embedded sentence may be introduced by the complementizer que in sentences like:

(12a) As garotas queriam que eu beijasse o cantor
The girls wanted that I kissed (subj.) the singer
'The girls wanted me to kiss the singer'

(12b) As garotas queriam que você beijasse o cantor
The girls wanted that you (sg.) kissed (subj.) the singer
'The girls wanted you to kiss the singer'

(12c) As garotas queriam que Tina beijasse o cantor
The girls wanted that Tina kissed (subj.) the singer
'The girls wanted Tina to kiss the singer'

Parallel to the sentences in (12), the infinitival complementizer appears in sentences like (6), repeated here:

(6) As garotas queriam beijar o cantor
'The girls wanted to kiss the singer'

The occurrence of both the que complementizer and the infinitival complementizer, however, is not without restriction. Thus, none of the sentences in (12) can appear with the infinitival complementizer as evidenced by the ungrammaticality of the sentences in (13).

(13a) *As garotas queriam eu beijar o cantor
The girls wanted I to kiss the singer

(13b) *As garotas queriam você beijar o cantor
The girls wanted you to kiss the singer

(13c) *As garotas queriam Tina beijar o cantor
The girls wanted Tina to kiss the singer

Similarly, the occurrence of the que complementizer is also restricted. Thus, there are no sentences like (14), where as garotas 'the girls' are understood to be the same girls.

(14) *As $garotas_1$ queriam que as $garotas_1$ beijassem o cantor
The girls wanted that the girls kissed (subj.) the singer

Nor are there sentences such as those in (15), where the subject of the embedded sentence and the subject of the matrix sentence can only be interpreted as being identical (see Postal 1968, 1969):

(15a) *Eu queria que eu beijasse o cantor
I wanted that I kissed (subj.) the singer

(15b) *Você queria que você beijasse o cantor
You (sg.) wanted that you (sg.) kissed (subj.) the singer

(15c) *Nós queriamos que nós beijassemos o cantor
We wanted that we kissed (subj.) the singer

(15d) *Vocês queriam que vocês beijassem o cantor
You (pl.) wanted that you (pl.) kissed (subj.) the singer

If one examines the facts presented, it is seen that the occurrence of the que complementizer and of the infinitival complementizer is entirely predictable: the que complementizer appears only in sentences where the subject of the embedded sentence is distinct from the subject of the matrix sentence, whereas the infinitival complementizer appears only in sentences where the subject of the embedded sentence is understood to be identical to the subject of the matrix sentence.

These generalizations can be captured in a very natural way within the deletion hypothesis. The COMPLEMENT-SUBJECT DELETION rule will apply obligatorily if the subjects of the matrix sentence and of the complement sentence are identical. Only in those cases where COMPLEMENT-SUBJECT DELETION has applied and deleted its subject will the embedded sentence be reduced to an infinitive (see Kiparsky and Kiparsky 1970; Perlmutter 1971 for a similar proposal).

In the complex VP analysis, however, there is no way in which these generalities can be expressed. The occurrence of the infinitival complementizer and of the que complementizer would be treated as two unrelated phenomena. The sentences with the infinitival complementizer and the sentences with the que complementizer would be assigned quite distinct underlying structures and, as a consequence, the generalization that the two cases are in complementary distribution would be lost.

Consider a second argument. In Portuguese there are sentences like the following:

(16) O doutor preferiu examinar Tina
'The doctor preferred to examine Tina'

(17) Tina preferiu ser examinada pelo doutor
'Tina preferred to be examined by the doctor'

These two sentences are clearly not synonymous. In (16) it is the doctor who 'prefers', whereas in (17) it is Tina who 'prefers'. The two sentences have quite distinct truth value and the meaning difference seems to reflect different deep structure configurations rather than the operation of rules of semantic interpretation on surface structure. In particular, it does not seem likely that (17) is the passive counterpart of (16), given the rather radical meaning difference between the two sentences.

Now I am going to examine how these facts would be accounted for within each hypothesis. Consider first the complex VP hypothesis. According to this hypothesis, the structure underlying sentence (16) would be roughly (18).

(16) O doutor preferiu examinar Tina
'The doctor preferred to examine Tina'

(18)

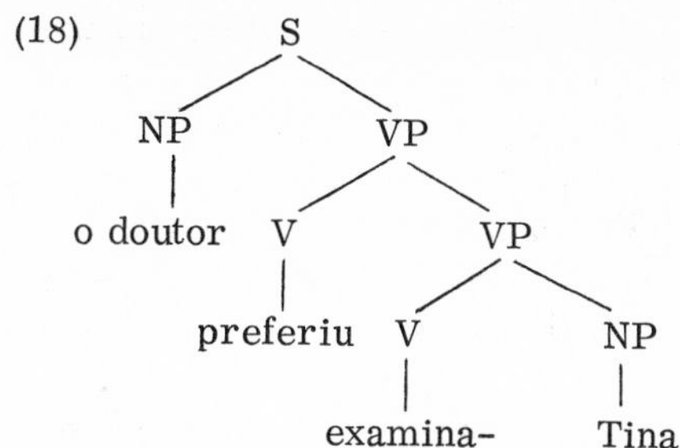

The derivation of (16) from this structure presents no problem. However, a serious problem for the analysis is posed by the existence of sentences like (17).

(17) Tina preferiu ser examinada pelo doutor
'Tina preferred to be examined by the doctor'

Notice, first of all, that if PASSIVE is formulated so as to apply solely to a string . . . NP-V-NP . . . as usual, there would be no way of explaining how the structural description of PASSIVE was met in the case of (17). In fact, the only way to account for (17) within the complex VP analysis is to reformulate the PASSIVE rule so as to allow it to apply also across VP's. One could then claim that both (16) and (17) are, in fact, transformationally related and that sentence (17) is derived from (18) by application of the revised PASSIVE rule. The lack of synonymy between (16) and (17) would be attributed to the operation of rules of semantic interpretation on surface structure.

However, it is not difficult to show that this account of the facts is incorrect. Observe first that in the normal cases where PASSIVE applies, there are no restrictions on what can be the superficial subject of the sentence:

(19a) O doutor preferiu esta hipótese
'The doctor preferred this hypothesis'

(19b) O doutor examinou esta hipótese
'The doctor examined this hypothesis'

(20a) Esta hipótese foi preferida pelo doutor
'This hypothesis was preferred by the doctor'

(20b) Esta hipótese foi examinada pelo doutor
'This hypothesis was examined by the doctor'

But observe now that nouns such as esta hipótese 'this hypothesis' can appear as the superficial subject of verbs such as preferir 'to prefer', examinar 'to examine', only in those cases where PASSIVE has applied. Thus the sentences in (20) are grammatical, but the sentences in (21) are impossible:

(21a) *Esta hipótese preferiu o doutor
'This hypothesis preferred the doctor'

(21b) *Esta hipótese examinou o doutor
'This hypothesis examined the doctor'

What these facts show is that the cooccurrence restrictions must be stated before the application of PASSIVE.

Consider now the following. In Portuguese there are sentences like:

(22) O doutor preferiu examinar esta hipótese
'The doctor preferred to examine this hypothesis'

According to the complex VP hypothesis, the deep structure for this sentence would be (23).

(23)

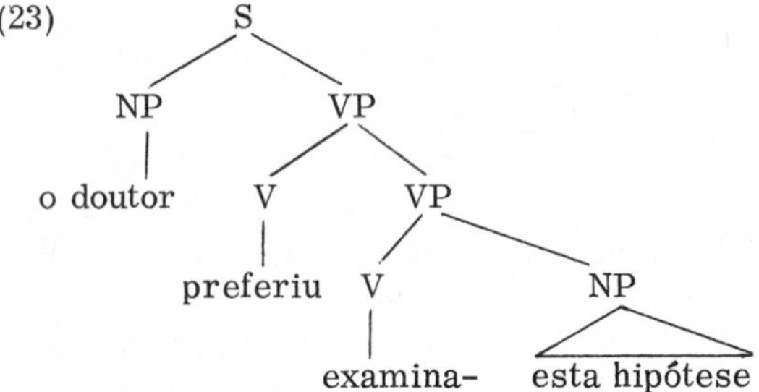

Notice that (23) is identical to (18) except for the noun phrase esta hipótese 'this hypothesis' instead of Tina. Now if it were true that PASSIVE applied across VP's in order to derive (17) from (18), one would also expect PASSIVE to be able to apply to (23) and produce a grammatical sentence, since (23) and (18) are structurally identical. However, sentence (24) is impossible:

(24) *Esta hipótese preferiu ser examinada pelo doutor
'This hypothesis preferred to be examined by the doctor'

As pointed out earlier, the cooccurrence restrictions have to be stated before PASSIVE in order to account for the facts in (19) through (21). Now, in order to exclude (24), it would be necessary to state the cooccurrence restrictions also after PASSIVE. The same cooccurrence restrictions would then have to be stated twice--before and after PASSIVE. The result is an inelegant and entirely unmotivated duplication of statements which is perfectly avoidable in a more articulated analysis.

Furthermore, since (20a) is grammatical but (24) is not, there is no explanation for the fact that esta hipótese 'this hypothesis' can appear as the superficial subject of preferir 'to prefer' due to the application of PASSIVE in (20a), but not in (24).

In short, if PASSIVE is allowed to apply across VP's the same cooccurrence restrictions would have to be stated twice: before PASSIVE because of the facts in (19) through (21), and after PASSIVE because of (24). But even so, there would be no natural way of blocking (24) while allowing (20a). It is clear, then, that if these problems are to be overcome, PASSIVE cannot be formulated so as to apply across VP's.

However, if PASSIVE cannot apply across VP's it will follow then that there is no way of accounting for sentence (17) within the complex VP analysis. This certainly constitutes strong empirical evidence for the rejection of the hypothesis.

On the other hand, it is not difficult to see that none of these difficulties arise in the case of the deletion hypothesis. According to the latter, sentences (16) and (17) would be assigned distinct deep structures--(25) and (26), respectively.

(16) O doutor preferiu examinar Tina
'The doctor preferred to examine Tina'

(17) Tina preferiu ser examinada pelo doutor
'Tina preferred to be examined by the doctor'

(25) [o doutor--preferiu--[o doutor--examinar--Tina]]
the doctor--preferred--the doctor--examine--Tina

(26) [Tina--preferiu--[o doutor--examinar--Tina]]
Tina--preferred--the doctor--examine--Tina

In the derivation of (16) from (25), it is necessary only that COMPLEMENT-SUBJECT DELETION apply, in the usual fashion. In the derivation of (17) from (26), the nonrevised PASSIVE rule would first apply, in the embedded sentence, since there is now a string NP-V-NP. Then, on the next cycle COMPLEMENT-SUBJECT DELETION would apply, and (17) is derived. Notice, furthermore, that there is also a natural explanation for the nonsynonymy of (16) and (17) within this analysis: the two sentences are not synonymous because they come from different deep structures.

Consider now the treatment of sentences (22) and (24):

(22) O doutor preferiu examinar esta hipôtese
'The doctor preferred to examine this hypothesis'

(24) *Esta hipôtese preferiu ser examinada pelo doutor
'This hypothesis preferred to be examined by the doctor'

According to the deletion hypothesis, sentence (22) would have a deep structure like (25):

(25) [o doutor--preferiu--[o doutor--examinar--esta hipôtese]]
the doctor--preferred--the doctor--examine--this hypothesis

The derivation of (22) is straightforward. It is necessary only that COMPLEMENT-SUBJECT DELETION apply to (25).

Observe now how ungrammatical sentences such as (24) are prevented. Under the deletion hypothesis, sentences such as (24) could only have come from a deep structure like (26), where esta hipôtese 'this hypothesis' is the deep structure subject of preferir 'to prefer'.

(26) [esta hipôtese--preferiu--[o doutor--examinar--esta hipôtese]]
this hypothesis--preferred--the doctor--examine--this hypothesis

However, this would never happen, for verbs such as preferir 'to prefer' would never select an NP like esta hipôtese 'this hypothesis' as its deep structure subject. For preferir is a verb which requires its subject to be 'animate'. In other words, sentence (24) is impossible for the same reason that (21a) is impossible:

(21a) *Esta hipôtese preferiu o doutor
'This hypothesis preferred the doctor'

The cooccurrence restrictions need only be stated once--before PASSIVE, as it must--and all these facts will follow automatically.

I conclude on the basis of the two foregoing arguments--namely, the one involving the complementary distribution holding between the que complementizer and the infinitival complementizer, and the one involving PASSIVE and cooccurrence restrictions--that the complex VP is empirically deficient in ways in which the deletion hypothesis is not, and that the latter must be chosen over the former if empirical adequacy is to be met.

2.3 Inadequacies of the interpretive hypothesis. A much more serious alternative to the deletion hypothesis can be construed following a recent proposal by Jackendoff (1969). In his dissertation, Jackendoff claims that 'coreferentiality' is an exclusively semantic property and hence no syntactic rule can be contingent on it.

Now a syntactic rule of complement subject deletion is incompatible with Jackendoff's claim since any such rule would require 'coreference' in its statement. In order to maintain the claim, Jackendoff examines the relevant facts used to justify the postulation of a syntactic rule of complement subject deletion, and he concludes that the phenomenon is to be accounted for by means of semantic 'interpretive' rules rather than by means of syntactic rules. He proceeds then to present an alternative analysis in which this is accomplished.

The essentials of this analysis are as follows. First, he assumes that lexical insertion is optional, so that deep structures can be generated containing unexpanded nonterminal nodes (represented by the symbol Δ) at the end of one or more branches. In earlier transformational work--as, for instance, in Chomsky (1965)--it was assumed that structures containing the symbol Δ would be blocked at the end of the transformations. However, Jackendoff proposes a modification to the effect that such structures containing Δ are to be blocked semantically rather than at the end of the transformations. That is, these structures would be taken to be semantically ill-formed by the semantic component if no semantic information were available for branches ending in Δ.

He introduces next a further modification in the theory so as to allow the rules of semantic interpretation to give readings also to the unexpanded nonterminal nodes Δ under certain conditions. The 'semantic blocking' of structures containing Δ can then be prevented just in those cases where Δ is interpreted. In this theory, then, the semantic rules which interpret the unexpanded nonterminal symbols would correspond to the transformations which delete items 'leaving no trace'.

Suppose a similar position is adopted here. In that case, sentences such as (5) would have a deep structure like (26).

(5) As garotas queriam beijar o cantor
'The girls wanted to kiss the singer'

(26) $[_{S_2}$ as garotas--queriam--$[_{S_1}$ Δ -beijar--o cantor$]]$
the girls--wanted-- Δ --kiss--the singer

The derivation of (5) from (26) would be as follows. On the first cycle, nothing important happens. On the second cycle, a semantic reference rule--COMPLEMENT-SUBJECT REFERENCE-- will apply, at the end of the cycle, marking as garotas 'the girls' as the antecedent of △ (cf. Jackendoff 1969:115ff.). Now, since the nonterminal symbol △ is interpreted, a well-formed surface structure, and a grammatical sentence, namely (6), will result. I refer to the analysis just described as the 'interpretive hypothesis'.

Consider now a more complex case represented by sentences such as (27) and (28).

(27) Pedro aconselhou Clara a vender a fazenda
'Pedro advised Clara to sell the farm'

(28) Clara foi aconselhada por Pedro a vender a fazenda
'Clara was advised by Pedro to sell the farm'

According to the interpretive hypothesis under consideration, the structure underlying both these sentences would be:

(29) $[_{S_2}$Pedro--aconselhou--Clara--$[_{S_1}$ △ --vender--a fazenda]]
Pedro--advised--Clara-- △ --sell--the farm

The derivation of (27) from (29) presents no problem. COMPLEMENT-SUBJECT REFERENCE would apply on the S_2 cycle, at the end of the cycle, and make Clara the antecedent of △. The derivation of (28), however, is not so obvious. Observe that COMPLEMENT-SUBJECT REFERENCE, which is a semantic rule, applies only at the end of the cycle after the syntactic transformations. Now, in the derivation of (28), PASSIVE, which is a cyclic transformation, would apply before the reference rule on the first cycle S_1 in (29), and produce (30) as a derived structure.

(30) $[_{S_2}$Clara foi aconselhada por Pedro $[_{S_1}$△vender a fazenda]]
Clara was advised by Pedro-- △ sell the farm

Now, as Jackendoff points out, if COMPLEMENT-SUBJECT REFERENCE were allowed to assign coreferentiality on the basis of the position of NP's in the structure, the rule would incorrectly mark Pedro instead of Clara as the antecedent of △. The problem is overcome in Jackendoff's analysis since he claims that the 'controller' of △ is determined not on the basis of the position of the NP's in the structure, but on the basis of 'thematic relations'.

Thematic relations, as Jackendoff (1969:116) points out, are not altered by transformations since they are properties of the semantic reading which correlate with the deep structure grammatical relations; hence, it does not matter for the selection of the 'controller' whether transformations have distorted the main clause, as in (30). What is relevant in the case of both (27) and (28) is that in terms of thematic relations Pedro is 'Agent', Clara is 'Theme', and vender a fazenda 'sell the farm' is 'Goal' (cf. Jackendoff 1969:143). For verbs such as aconselhar 'to advise', the 'controller' of the complement subject would always be associated with the Theme, regardless of its position in surface structure. The possibility of COMPLEMENT-SUBJECT REFERENCE assigning wrong coreferentiality in the case of (30) is thus eliminated and, as a result, sentence (28) would always be derived with the correct reading.

When one examines all the cases discussed, it is seen that the element which is understood to be 'missing' leaves no 'trace' behind, which makes the interpretive hypothesis even more attractive. However, the hypothesis becomes somehow less attractive in cases where it could be contended that the 'missing' subject leaves a 'trace' behind. This is the case, for instance, of reflexive sentences such as (31).

(31) Timoteo tentou barbear-se
'Timoteo tried to shave himself'

The way to account for this sentence within the interpretive hypothesis in question is to claim that reflexives are generated as lexical items in the base, and then to account for their presence in terms of semantic 'interpretive' rules (cf. Jackendoff 1969:41ff.). According to this view, sentence (31) would have a deep structure such as:

(32) $[_{S_2}$Timoteo--tentou--$[_{S_1}$ △ --barbear--se]]
Timoteo--tried-- --shave--himself

The derivation of (31) from (32) is as follows. The reflexive pronoun se 'himself' is generated by the base as a lexical item unmarked for reference like other noun phrases. On the first cycle S_1 an 'interpretive' rule of REFLEXIVIZATION would apply and mark se 'himself' as coreferential with △ . Then, on the second cycle S_2, COMPLEMENT-SUBJECT REFERENCE would apply as usual and mark Timoteo as the antecedent of △ . The chain of coreference is then correctly established and sentence (31), with the correct reading, would result.

Notice, however, that since reflexives are now being generated as lexical items, the question arises as to how ungrammatical sentences such as (33) are to be excluded.

(33) *Eu tentei barbear-se 'I tried to shave himself'

The way to prevent (33) within this hypothesis is as follows. The application of the 'interpretive' REFLEXIVIZATION rule (and of the COMPLEMENT-SUBJECT REFERENCE rule) would, in fact, make eu 'I' and se 'himself' coreferential, but the blocking would be accomplished by a general convention that coreferential NP's must be able to have the same reference and hence must agree in person, number, gender, as well as animacy, humanness, and other semantic properties (cf. Jackendoff 1969:45).[3]

I have so far limited myself to outlining some of the basic tenets of the interpretive hypothesis in order to provide a reasonable background for a critical appraisal. I am now going to argue against the interpretive hypothesis and in favor of the deletion hypothesis. It will become apparent from the discussion that there are certain facts in Portuguese that cannot be accounted for within the interpretive hypothesis, but which have a natural explanation within the deletion hypothesis.

Consider initially the following. In Portuguese, adjectives, nouns, and participles preceded by copula must agree in gender and number with the surface structure subject:

(34a) Esta moça é bonita
This girl (fem. sg.) is pretty (fem. sg.)
(34b) *Esta moça é bonito
This girl (fem. sg.) is pretty (masc. sg.)

(35a) Este homem é mecânico
This man (masc. sg.) is a mechanic (masc. sg.)
(35b) *Este homem é mecânica
This man (masc. sg.) is a mechanic (fem. sg.)

(36a) A bailarina foi seduzida por Miguel
The dancer (fem. sg.) was seduced (fem. sg.) by Miguel
(36b) *A bailarina foi seduzido por Miguel
The dancer (fem. sg.) was seduced (masc. sg.) by Miguel

The facts in (36) show also that the GENDER-NUMBER AGREEMENT rule must follow PASSIVE for it is only after PASSIVE that the NP a bailarina 'the dancer' becomes the subject of the sentence in (36a). The ungrammaticality of (36b), on the other hand, shows that the participle must agree across the copula in gender and number with the surface structure subject after PASSIVE only and not with the deep structure subject (or with the derived object).

Notice that the participle agrees with its subject only when it is preceded by a copula. If the participle is preceded by another auxiliary, agreement cannot occur:

(37a) A bailarina tinha seduzido Miguel
The dancer (fem.) had seduced (unmk.) Miguel
(37b) *A bailarina tinha seduzida Miguel
The dancer (fem.) had seduced (fem.) Miguel

I will show now that GENDER-NUMBER AGREEMENT is cyclic. The argument is based on the existence of sentences such as:

(38) Todos consideram Lucia bonita
Everybody considers Lucia (fem. sg.) pretty (fem. sg.)

Independent of the problem of what the correct structure of the complement of verbs such as considerar 'to consider' in (38) may be, it is clear that the adjective bonita 'pretty (fem. sg.)' must agree in gender and number with the NP Lucia which is the surface structure object of considerar 'to consider'. That the adjective cannot agree with the subject of considerar is evidenced by the ungrammaticality of (39).

(39) *Todos consideram Lucia bonitos
Everybody (masc. pl.) consider Lucia pretty (masc. pl.)

What these facts show is that in the case of verbs such as considerar 'to consider' in this construction, the rule of GENDER-NUMBER AGREEMENT has to be formulated so as to permit the agreement between the noun phrase which appears as the surface structure object of considerar 'to consider' and its modifier.

A very tentative rule of GENDER-NUMBER AGREEMENT to account only for the facts in (34) through (39) may be something like (40).

(40) GENDER-NUMBER AGREEMENT (Obligatory)

$$
\begin{array}{lllll}
\text{X--} & \underset{\left[\begin{array}{l}\alpha \text{ gender} \\ \beta \text{ number}\end{array}\right]}{\text{NP}} & \text{--(Copula)--} & \text{Predicate} & \text{--Y} \\
1 & 2 & 3 & 4 & 5 \Longrightarrow \\
1 & 2 & 3 & \underset{\left[\begin{array}{l}\alpha \text{ gender} \\ \beta \text{ number}\end{array}\right]}{4} & 5
\end{array}
$$

where the Predicate is expanded as follows:

$$
\text{Predicate} \longrightarrow \left\{\begin{array}{l}\text{Predicate Nominal} \\ \text{Adjective} \\ \text{Participle}\end{array}\right\}
$$

Now, parallel to (38) there are also grammatical sentences such as:

(41) Lucia é considerada bonita por todos
Lucia is considered (fem. sg.) pretty (fem. sg.) by everybody

The existence of sentences like (41) can only be explained if GENDER-NUMBER AGREEMENT applies twice: once before PASSIVE has had a chance to move the object of considerar, so as to permit the agreement relationship to be established between Lucia and bonita 'pretty (fem. sg.)'; and a second time, after PASSIVE, so as to permit the agreement between the NP Lucia, which becomes the derived subject via PASSIVE, with the participle considerada 'considered (fem. sg.)'. In other words, GENDER-NUMBER AGREEMENT has to apply both before and after PASSIVE, which is an ordering paradox.

The paradox is resolved, however, if one posits both GENDER-NUMBER AGREEMENT and PASSIVE as cyclic rules and orders the latter before the former. The derivation of (41) can now be explained. First, GENDER-NUMBER AGREEMENT will apply before PASSIVE on the 'cyclic node' containing Lucia and bonita 'pretty'. Then, on the next cycle, PASSIVE (which is ordered before GENDER-NUMBER AGREEMENT) will first apply placing the NP Lucia into subject position, followed by GENDER-NUMBER AGREEMENT which will establish the correct agreement between the derived subject and the participle. As a result, (41) can be derived with the correct agreement.[4]

A second fact which plays a role in this discussion is that, in Portuguese, infinitives must agree in person and number with their surface structure subject:

(42a) Rui pediu para os meninos lavarem o carro
Rui requested for the boys to wash (3 pl.) the car
'Rui requested that the boys washed his car'
(42b) *Rui pediu para os meninos lavar o carro
Rui requested for the boys to wash (unmk.) the car

I have argued elsewhere (Quicoli 1972; to appear) that the rule which is responsible for infinitival agreement (SUBJECT-VERB AGREEMENT) cannot be cyclic, but rather is a postcyclic rule. Evidence for this is as follows. First, SUBJECT-VERB AGREEMENT must apply after SUBJECT REPLACEMENT (or, 'raising into subject position') to produce the correct results in (43).

(43a) As coisas parecem estar quentes em Belfast
'Things seem (3rd pl.) to be (unmk.) hot (pl.) in Belfast'
(43b) *As coisas parecem estarem quentes em Belfast
Things seem (3rd pl.) to be (3rd pl.) hot (pl.) in Belfast

Second, SUBJECT-VERB AGREEMENT must apply after CLITIC RAISING so that (44a) but not (44b) is derived from deep structure (45) below.

(44a) Jonas nos viu sair
Jonas us saw leave (unmk.)
'Jonas saw us leave'
(44b) *Jonas nos viu sairmos
Jonas us saw leave (1st pl.)

(45) [Jonas viu [nós sair]]

SUBJECT REPLACEMENT and CLITIC RAISING are both rules which must wait until the matrix-S is reached in order to apply. Now, in order to account for the facts in (44) and (45), SUBJECT REPLACEMENT and CLITIC RAISING, respectively, must apply and move the subject of the embedded sentence before SUBJECT-VERB AGREEMENT has had a chance to apply; otherwise, the ungrammatical sentences with infinitival agreement would be produced. Since SUBJECT-VERB AGREEMENT must apply after SUBJECT REPLACEMENT and CLITIC RAISING to give the right results in these examples, and since the latter two rules can only take place once the matrix-S is reached, it follows that SUBJECT-VERB AGREEMENT cannot apply in the embedded clause before the matrix-S is reached. Hence, SUBJECT-VERB AGREEMENT cannot be cyclic but must be postcyclic.

I now pass to the arguments proper. In Portuguese, there are grammatical sentences like:

(46) Rosa queria ser examinada pelo especialista
Rosa wanted to be examined (fem. sg.) by the specialist

Within the 'interpretive' hypothesis under consideration, there are three plausible alternative analyses for this sentence.

Alternative A. Consider a first alternative. Suppose one assumes, following Jackendoff (1969), that agreement is a syntactic phenomenon to be dealt with in the syntactic component. In that case, Gender-Number Agreement would be formulated as a syntactic rule. Now, one might propose that the structure underlying a sentence like (46) is essentially:

(46) Rosa queria ser examinada pelo especialista
'Rosa wanted to be examined by the specialist'

(47) $[_{S_2}$Rosa--queria $[_{S_1}$o especialista--examinar-- △]]
Rosa--wanted the specialist--examine--△

According to this proposal, the derivation of sentence (46) from (47) could proceed as follows. On the first cycle S_1, PASSIVE would cyclically apply and produce (48) as its output:

(48) $[_{S_2}$Rosa--queria $[_{S_1}$△--ser--examinad--pelo especialista]]
Rosa--wanted △--be--examined--by the specialist

Notice that at the end of the first cycle in (48) the participle would still be uninflected for gender and number, since △ has no features to be copied. One might propose, however, a syntactic rule whose effect is to 'fill' △ with the features of, say, the closest NP to the left. This 'filling' rule could then be made to apply before GENDER-NUMBER AGREEMENT. Thus, if the 'filling' rule applied on the second cycle, in (48), it would copy the features of the NP <u>Rosa</u> into △, producing a derived structure approximately like:

(49) [Rosa--queria [$\underset{\begin{bmatrix}+\text{fem.}\\ +\text{pl.}\end{bmatrix}}{\triangle}$ --ser--examinad--pelo especialista]]

Now, in order to derive (46) it would be necessary only that GENDER-NUMBER AGREEMENT applied to (49) and copied the features of △ into the participle.

There is, however, evidence that this analysis is incorrect. First notice that under the analysis just outlined, the 'filling' rule must crucially apply before GENDER-NUMBER AGREEMENT, otherwise the structural description of the latter would not be met, since there would be no features to be copied. Notice now that the 'filling' rule must wait until the matrix-S in (48) is reached in order to apply. For only then will the NP Rosa be available to it. Now, since GENDER-NUMBER AGREEMENT must apply after the 'filling' rule, and since the latter can only take place once the matrix-S is reached, it follows that GENDER-NUMBER AGREEMENT cannot apply in the embedded-S until the matrix-S is reached. Hence, GENDER-NUMBER AGREEMENT cannot be cyclic but rather must be a postcyclic rule under this analysis. However, since it has already been shown that GENDER-NUMBER AGREEMENT must be cyclic, the suppositions underlying the analysis must be false and this alternative must be rejected.

Alternative B. Consider a second alternative. Suppose GENDER-NUMBER AGREEMENT is a syntactic cyclic rule. Suppose now that a modification is introduced in the 'interpretive' hypothesis so as to allow △ to be generated with lexical features for gender and number. In that case, the structure underlying sentence (46) would now be something like:

(50) $[_{S_2}$Rosa--queria $[_{S_1}$o especialista--examinar-- $\begin{bmatrix}\triangle \\ \text{+fem.} \\ \text{+sg.}\end{bmatrix}$]]

$[$Rosa--wanted [the specialist--examine-- $\begin{bmatrix}\triangle \\ \text{+fem.} \\ \text{+sg.}\end{bmatrix}$]]

The derivation of (46) from (50) could be accomplished as follows. On the first cycle PASSIVE would optionally apply and produce (51) as an output:

(51) $[_{S_2}$Rosa--queria $[_{S_1}$ $\begin{bmatrix}\triangle \\ \text{+fem.} \\ \text{+sg.}\end{bmatrix}$ --ser examinad--pelo especialista]]

Notice that after PASSIVE the participle is still uninflected for gender and number. But now, since △ has features for gender and number, GENDER-NUMBER AGREEMENT would apply cyclically on the first cycle in (51) and make the participle agree with △.

Then, on the second cycle, COMPLEMENT-SUBJECT REFERENCE would apply, at the end of the cycle, and make Rosa the antecedent of Δ, thus deriving (46).

There are, however, some crucial facts which show that this analysis is also empirically inadequate.

Thus, observe first that in Portuguese infinitives agree with their subjects:

(42a) Rui pediu para os meninos lavarem o carro
Rui requested for the boys to wash (3rd pl.) the car
'Rui requested that the boys washed his car'
(42b) *Rui pediu para os meninos lavar o carro
Rui requested for the boys to wash (unmk.) the car

However, in cases where the complement subject is obligatorily missing in surface structure, infinitives must not undergo agreement:

(52a) Os homens tentaram lavar o carro
The men tried (3rd pl.) to wash (unmk.) the car
(52b) *Os homens tentaram lavarem o carro
The men tried (3rd pl.) to wash (3rd pl.) the car

Observe now that in order to account for the facts involving gender-number agreement in sentence (46) within the present analysis, Δ must be generated with syntactic features for gender and number.

Suppose now that one substituted the NP as mulheres 'the women' for the NP Rosa in derived structure (51). In that case, before GENDER-NUMBER AGREEMENT is to take place, the derived structure would be something like:

(53) $[_{S_2}$ As mulheres--querer $[_{S_1}$ $\underset{\begin{bmatrix}+\text{fem.}\\+\text{pl.}\end{bmatrix}}{\Delta}$ --ser examinad--pelo especialista]]
$[$The women--wanted $[$ $\underset{\begin{bmatrix}+\text{fem.}\\+\text{pl.}\end{bmatrix}}{\Delta}$ to be examined by the specialist]]

Now, since Δ must contain syntactic features in order to account for GENDER-NUMBER AGREEMENT, and since infinitives agree, there is no natural way of permitting GENDER-NUMBER AGREEMENT to apply while, at the same time, blocking infinitival agreement.[5] As a result, not only would ungrammatical sentences like:

(54) *As mulheres queriam <u>serem</u> examinadas pelo especialista
The women wanted (3rd pl.) to be (3rd pl.) to be examined (fem. pl.) by the specialist

be produced, but also there would be no way to generate grammatical sentences where the participle undergoes agreement but the infinitive does not, as in (55):

(55) As mulheres queriam ser examinadas pelo especialista
'The women wanted (3rd pl.) to be (unmk.) examined (fem. pl.) by the specialist'

In view of these empirically inadequate results, this alternative must also be rejected.

Alternative C. There is still a third possibility to be considered. Thus one might claim that GENDER-NUMBER AGREEMENT is an 'interpretive' rule rather than a syntactic rule. One might then argue that adjectives and participles are randomly generated with features for gender and number, and propose to account for agreement in the semantic component, much in the same way as reflexivization is treated in Jackendoff (1969). According to this view, after PASSIVE applied on the first cycle of the structure underlying sentence (46), there would be a derived structure like:

(56) $[_{S_2}$ Rosa--queria $[_{S_1}$ Δ -ser $\underset{\begin{bmatrix}+\text{fem.}\\+\text{sg.}\end{bmatrix}}{\text{examinada}}$--pelo especialista]]

where the participle <u>examinada</u> is introduced in deep structure with features for gender and number. Also on the first cycle, after PASSIVE has produced (56), an 'interpretive' rule of gender and number agreement would apply to it, at the end of the cycle, and mark Δ with the appropriate features of the participle, yielding a derived structure like:

(57) $[_{S_2}$ Rosa--queria $[_{S_1}$ $\underset{\begin{bmatrix}+\text{fem.}\\+\text{sg.}\end{bmatrix}}{\Delta}$ --ser $\underset{\begin{bmatrix}+\text{fem.}\\+\text{sg.}\end{bmatrix}}{\text{examinada}}$ --pelo especialista]]

Later, on the second cycle in (57), interpretive COMPLEMENT-SUBJECT REFERENCE would then apply, at the end of the cycle, and make <u>Rosa</u> the antecedent of Δ. Now, since Δ would have an antecedent and since it would agree with it in gender and number, the result would be a grammatical sentence, namely:

(46) Rosa queria ser examinada pelo especialista
Rosa wanted to be examined (fem. sg.) by the specialist

Of course, since participles would now be generated randomly with features for gender and number, there is the problem of how to block ungrammatical sentences like:

(58a) *Rosa queria ser *examinado* pelo especialista
Rosa wanted to be examined (masc. sg.) by the specialist
(58b) *Rosa queria ser *examinadas* pelo especialista
Rosa wanted to be examined (fem. pl.) by the specialist
(58c) *Rosa queria ser *examinados* pelo especialista
Rosa wanted to be examined (masc. pl.) by the specialist

One might contend, however, that such sentences would be blocked 'semantically' much in the same way as ungrammatical sentences with reflexives like:

(33) *Eu tentei barbear-se
I tried to shave himself

would be blocked. That is, the interpretive rule of gender and number agreement would, in fact, mark △ with the corresponding features of the participle, and the COMPLEMENT-SUBJECT REFERENCE rule would make *Rosa* the antecedent of △. But the blocking would be accomplished by a general convention that coreferential NP's must agree in gender, number, person, animacy, etc. (see Jackendoff 1969).

It is not difficult to show, however, that this analysis is incorrect. For suppose one substituted the NP *as mulheres* 'the women' for the NP *Rosa*, and the participle *examinadas* 'examined (fem. pl.)' for the participle *examinada* 'examined (fem. sg.)' in derived structure (56). In that case, before application of interpretive gender-number agreement, there would be a derived structure like:

(59) $[_{S_2}$ As mulheres queriam $[_{S_1}$ △ ser examinadas pelo especialista]]
$\begin{bmatrix} +\text{fem.} \\ +\text{pl.} \end{bmatrix}$ (under *examinadas*)

If interpretive gender-number agreement applied on the first cycle, at the end of the cycle, in (59) it would mark △ with the appropriate features of the participle, thus yielding a structure like:

(60) [$_{S_2}$ As mulheres queriam [$_{S_1}$ $\underset{\begin{bmatrix}+\text{fem.}\\+\text{pl.}\end{bmatrix}}{\Delta}$ ser $\underset{\begin{bmatrix}+\text{fem.}\\+\text{pl.}\end{bmatrix}}{\text{examinadas}}$ pelo especialista]]

On the second cycle, COMPLEMENT-SUBJECT REFERENCE would then apply, at the end of the cycle as before, and make as mulheres the antecedent of Δ. However, since Δ would be marked with features during the cycle, due to the application of 'interpretive' gender-number agreement, there is no natural way of preventing postcyclic SUBJECT-VERB AGREEMENT from applying and causing wrong infinitival agreement. As a result one would always have the ungrammatical:

(54) *As mulheres queriam serem examinadas pelo especialista
The women wanted (3rd pl.) to be (3rd pl.) examined by the specialist

and not the grammatical:

(55) As mulheres queriam ser examinadas pelo especialista
The women wanted (3rd pl.) to be (unmk.) examined by the specialist

In view of the foregoing empirically inadequate results, I conclude that this third alternative analysis must also be rejected.

To recapitulate, in the course of this discussion I have examined three plausible alternative analyses for the treatment of certain facts involving gender-number and subject-verb agreement in Portuguese within the 'interpretive hypothesis'. It was shown that each one of these analyses is inconsistent with the facts about the language. I conclude, on the basis of the evidence presented, that the 'interpretive hypothesis' is incorrect and that a more general analysis must be found which is not subject to the same empirical deficiencies.

I will now show that the same facts which lead to the rejection of the interpretive hypothesis cannot be used as counterexamples to the deletion hypothesis. Thus, consider again sentence (46), repeated here:

(46) Rosa queria ser examinada pelo especialista
Rosa wanted to be examined (fem. sg.) by the specialist

According to the deletion hypothesis, the structure underlying (46) is essentially:

(61) [Rosa_i queria [o especialista--examinar--Rosa_i]]
S_2 S_1
Rosa_i wanted the specialist--examine--Rosa_i

The derivation of (46) is as follows. First, PASSIVE applies to (61) on the first cycle, producing a derived structure like:

(62) [Rosa_i queria [Rosa_i--ser examinad--pelo especialista]]
S_2 S_1
Rosa_i wanted Rosa_i--be examined--by the specialist

Notice that in (62) the participle is still uninflected for gender and number. Next, GENDER-NUMBER AGREEMENT, which is a cyclic rule and ordered after PASSIVE, will apply on the first cycle in derived structure (62) and establish the agreement between the subject of the embedded sentence and the participle, yielding a derived structure like:

(63) [Rosa_i queria [Rosa_i--ser examinada--pelo especialista]]
S_2 S_1
Rosa_i wanted Rosa_i--be examined (fem. sg.)--by the specialist

Finally, in order to derive (46) it is necessary only that COMPLEMENT-SUBJECT DELETION apply on the second cycle of (63) deleting the subject of the embedded clause.

Consider now how this analysis would prevent the derivation of ungrammatical sentences like:

(54) *As mulheres queriam serem examinadas pelo especialista
The women wanted (3rd pl.) to be (3rd pl.) examined (fem. pl.) by the specialist

According to the deletion hypothesis, the structure underlying this sentence is roughly:

(64) [As mulheres_i queriam [o especialista--examinar--as
S_2 S_1
mulheres_i]]
The women wanted the specialist--examine--the women

After cyclic application of PASSIVE and GENDER-NUMBER AGREEMENT on the first cycle in (64), the result will be a derived structure like:

(65) [As mulheres$_i$ queriam [as mulheres$_i$--ser examinadas--
S_2 S_1
pelo especialista]]
The women wanted the women--be (unmk.) examined (fem. pl.) by the specialist

Now, COMPLEMENT-SUBJECT DELETION is cyclic (as will be shown in section 3.0), whereas the rule which accounts for the agreement between the infinitive and its subject--SUBJECT-VERB AGREEMENT--is postcyclic. Given the cycle, COMPLEMENT-SUBJECT DELETION must always apply before SUBJECT-VERB AGREEMENT, since cyclic rules must necessarily apply before postcyclic rules. In that case, COMPLEMENT-SUBJECT DELETION would first apply to (65) and delete the subject of the embedded sentence before SUBJECT-VERB AGREEMENT had a chance to apply to it. Consequently, at the time SUBJECT-VERB AGREEMENT is to apply, there will be no subject in the embedded sentence and the structural description of the agreement rule will not be met. Hence, the rule cannot apply and the ungrammatical (54) will simply not be generated. The result would always be the grammatical:

(55) As mulheres queriam ser examinadas pelo especialista
The women wanted (3rd pl.) to be (unmk.) examined (fem. pl.) by the specialist

On the basis of the facts discussed so far in this section, I conclude that the deletion hypothesis is not subject to the empirical deficiencies which led to the disqualification of the interpretive hypothesis. Consequently, the former must be chosen over the latter. This conclusion has some important consequences.

First, it follows directly from the correctness of the deletion hypothesis that the process involving 'missing' subjects in complement sentences is to be accounted for syntactically, by means of a syntactic rule of COMPLEMENT-SUBJECT DELETION, and not semantically, by means of a purely semantic 'interpretive' rule as proposed in Jackendoff (1969).[6]

Second, since COMPLEMENT-SUBJECT DELETION is a syntactic rule which must make reference to notions of 'identity' vs. 'nonidentity' in its structural description, it follows that these notions must be available to the syntactic component of grammars. This supports the view advanced in earlier transformational studies (e.g. Chomsky 1965:145ff.), according to which 'deletion under identity' constitutes a syntactic phenomenon. At the same time, these findings show that Jackendoff's (1969) claim that coreferentiality is an exclusively semantic property unavailable to the syntactic component is incorrect.[7]

3.0 The cyclic nature of Complement Subject Deletion. In the preceding section, I have presented arguments justifying the status of COMPLEMENT-SUBJECT DELETION as a syntactic rule. I now argue that COMPLEMENT-SUBJECT DELETION is cyclic.

According to a general theoretical assumption within transformational grammar, rules can be of three types: precyclic; cyclic; and postcyclic. Under this assumption, in order to show that a rule R is cyclic, it is sufficient to show that:

(66a) R cannot apply before all cyclic rules; that is, that R is not precyclic.
(66b) R cannot apply after all cyclic rules; that is, that R is not postcyclic.

As a preliminary, consider the following. It was pointed out earlier in section 1.2 that PASSIVE and GENDER-NUMBER AGREEMENT must be cyclic rules because of the existence of:

(41) Lucia é considerada bonita por todos
Lucia is considered (fem. sg.) pretty (fem. sg.) by everybody

The argument given was that the existence of sentences such as these can only be explained if GENDER-NUMBER AGREEMENT applies twice: before and after PASSIVE. That is, GENDER-NUMBER AGREEMENT has to apply once, before PASSIVE, on the cyclic node containing Lucia and bonita so as to permit agreement between the noun and the adjective; and once again, this time after PASSIVE, in order to permit agreement between the NP Lucia (which becomes the derived subject via Passive) and the participle considerada 'considered (fem. sg.)'. The order of rule application in the derivation of (41) is as in (67).

(67) GENDER-NUMBER AGREEMENT
PASSIVE
GENDER-NUMBER AGREEMENT

As observed earlier, the way to overcome the ordering paradox illustrated in (67) is to formulate both PASSIVE and GENDER-NUMBER AGREEMENT as cyclic rules and order the former before the latter. The paradox is now overcome since the two applications of GENDER-NUMBER AGREEMENT will take place on different cycles, and on the cycle where both PASSIVE and GENDER-NUMBER AGREEMENT apply, PASSIVE precedes GENDER-NUMBER AGREEMENT. To illustrate, the order of rule application in the derivation of (41) will now be as in (68).

(68) First cycle: GENDER-NUMBER AGREEMENT
Second cycle: PASSIVE
GENDER-NUMBER AGREEMENT

The important point to remember here is that both PASSIVE and GENDER-NUMBER AGREEMENT are cyclic.

Now I am going to consider the COMPLEMENT-SUBJECT DELETION rule. In order to show that COMPLEMENT-SUBJECT DELETION is cyclic, one must first show that it cannot apply before all cyclic rules; that is, one must show that it cannot be precyclic. Evidence for this is as follows.

First, COMPLEMENT-SUBJECT DELETION must apply after GENDER-NUMBER AGREEMENT in the derivation of sentences like:

(69) Maria queria ser médica.
Maria wanted to be a doctor (fem. sg.)

Second, COMPLEMENT-SUBJECT DELETION must apply after PASSIVE and GENDER-NUMBER AGREEMENT in the derivation of (46).

(46) Rosa queria ser <u>examinada</u> pelo especialista
Rosa wanted to be examined (fem. sg.) by the specialist

Now, since GENDER-NUMBER AGREEMENT and PASSIVE are both cyclic, and since COMPLEMENT-SUBJECT DELETION has to apply after them in the derivation of sentences (69) and (46), it follows that COMPLEMENT-SUBJECT DELETION cannot apply before all cyclic rules. That is to say, COMPLEMENT-SUBJECT DELETION cannot be precyclic. Condition (65a) is therefore satisfied.

I am now going to show that COMPLEMENT-SUBJECT DELETION cannot apply after all cyclic rules. Evidence for this is as follows.

In Portuguese, there are sentences such as:

(70) Miro exortou a moça a ser boa
Miro exhorted the girl to be good (fem. sg.)

The intermediary structure for (70) before the application of COMPLEMENT-SUBJECT DELETION will be something like:

(71) [Miro--exortou--a moça--[a moça--ser--boa]]
S_2 S_1
Miro--exhorted--the girl--the girl--be--good (fem. sg.)

Observe now the following. In the derivation of (70) from the intermediary structure (71), COMPLEMENT-SUBJECT DELETION must be formulated so as to delete the subject of the complement sentence just in case it is identical to the object of exortar 'to exhort'. COMPLEMENT-SUBJECT DELETION cannot delete the complement subject under condition of identity with the subject of exortar 'to exhort' for there are no grammatical sentences like (72).[8]

(72) *Miro exortou a moça a ser bom
Miro exhorted the girl to be good (masc. sg.)

Now, let us examine structure (71) for a moment. Observe that on the matrix sentence cycle the structural description for PASSIVE is satisfied since there is a string NP - V - NP. It is already known that PASSIVE is cyclic. Suppose now that COMPLEMENT-SUBJECT DELETION is formulated so as to apply after all cyclic rules. That is, suppose that COMPLEMENT-SUBJECT DELETION is postcyclic.

In that case, PASSIVE, which is cyclic, would first apply to (71) (before COMPLEMENT-SUBJECT DELETION) and move the NP a moça 'the girl' into subject position. As a consequence, at the time COMPLEMENT-SUBJECT DELETION is to apply, the complement subject will no longer be identical to the object of exortar 'to exhort'. Hence, the structural description for COMPLEMENT-SUBJECT DELETION is not met and the rule cannot apply. The result would ultimately be the ungrammatical (73).

(73) *A moça foi exortada por Miro a moça ser boa
The girl was exhorted (fem. sg.) by Miro for the girl to be good (fem. sg.)

Suppose, alternatively, that one formulates COMPLEMENT-SUBJECT DELETION so as to apply before PASSIVE. In that case, COMPLEMENT-SUBJECT DELETION will first apply to (71) and correctly delete the complement subject under condition of identity with the object of exortar 'to exhort'. PASSIVE, which comes next, may optionally apply. If it does not apply, the result will be the grammatical sentence (70). If, on the other hand, PASSIVE does apply, the result will still be a grammatical sentence:

(74) A moça foi exortada por Miro a ser boa
The girl was exhorted (fem. sg.) by Miro to be good (fem. sg.)

It is clear then that in order to obtain the desired empirical results, COMPLEMENT-SUBJECT DELETION must be able to apply before PASSIVE. Now, PASSIVE is cyclic and it has just been seen that in the derivation of (74) COMPLEMENT-SUBJECT DELETION must apply before PASSIVE. Consequently, COMPLEMENT-SUBJECT DELETION cannot apply after all cyclic rules. Hence, COMPLEMENT-SUBJECT DELETION cannot be postcyclic, therefore, satisfying condition (65b).

COMPLEMENT-SUBJECT DELETION cannot be postcyclic, as has just been shown. On the other hand, I have already pointed out that COMPLEMENT-SUBJECT DELETION cannot be precyclic either. The logical conclusion, then, is that COMPLEMENT-SUBJECT DELETION must be cyclic.

A second argument comes from the existence of sentences such as (75) in the language.

(75) Maria foi persuadida por Ciro a ser operada pelo Dr. Óscar
Maria was persuaded (fem. sg.) by Ciro to be operated (fem. sg.) (on) by Dr. Óscar.

The order of rule application in the derivation of (75) can only be:

(76) PASSIVE
GENDER-NUMBER AGREEMENT
COMPLEMENT-SUBJECT DELETION
PASSIVE
GENDER-NUMBER AGREEMENT

The ordering paradox contained in (76) is transparent. COMPLEMENT-SUBJECT DELETION must both follow and precede PASSIVE and GENDER-NUMBER AGREEMENT. In a noncyclic theory of rule ordering there is no way to conciliate the facts. In a cyclic theory, however, the paradox is resolved if COMPLEMENT-SUBJECT DELETION is also made cyclic and ordered before PASSIVE and GENDER-NUMBER AGREEMENT. The order of rule application in the derivation of sentence (75) according to the latter view will be as in (77).

(77) First cycle: PASSIVE
GENDER-NUMBER AGREEMENT
Second cycle: COMPLEMENT-SUBJECT DELETION
PASSIVE
GENDER-NUMBER AGREEMENT

I conclude, on the basis of the two arguments presented, that COMPLEMENT-SUBJECT DELETION is cyclic.

4.0 Subject Pronoun Deletion. In this section I argue in favor of the existence of a rule of SUBJECT-PRONOUN DELETION as distinct from the rule of COMPLEMENT-SUBJECT DELETION discussed earlier. Arguments for distinguishing the two rules are as follows.

First, COMPLEMENT-SUBJECT DELETION must be restricted so as to delete the subject of a complement clause under condition of identity with a noun phrase in the matrix sentence. SUBJECT-PRONOUN DELETION, on the other hand, does not involve deletion under condition of identity. It deletes only 'nonemphatic', 'redundant' subject pronouns. The distinction between the two cases becomes apparent when one examines the contrast between cases like:

(78a) Zito queria sair
'Zito wanted to leave'
(78b) [Zito--queria--[Zito--sai-]]
Zito--wanted--Zito--leave

(79a) Zito queria que saíssem
Zito wanted that leave (3rd pl.) (subj.)
'Zito wanted them to leave'
(79b) [Zito--queria [eles--sai-]]
Zito--wanted--they--leave

The derivation of (78a) from deep structure (78b) can be explained by the application of COMPLEMENT-SUBJECT DELETION since the complement subject is identical to a noun phrase in the matrix sentence. But COMPLEMENT-SUBJECT DELETION cannot account for the absence of the complement subject in the derivation of (79a) from deep structure (79b), since the complement subject in (79b)--i.e. the NP Eles 'they'--is not identical to a noun phrase in the matrix S. The existence of sentences such as (79a) can be explained, however, if the complement subject is deleted by the independently motivated rule of SUBJECT-PRONOUN DELETION.

Second, COMPLEMENT-SUBJECT DELETION is restricted to perform deletion only on complement sentences; whereas there is no such restriction in the case of SUBJECT-PRONOUN DELETION. Thus consider the following:

(80a) Comemos o bolo
Ate (1st pl.) the cake
'We ate the cake'

(80b) Nós comemos o bolo
'We ate the cake'

There is a very natural explanation for these facts, if sentence (80a) is derived from the structure underlying (80b) by application of SUBJECT-PRONOUN DELETION. Observe, however, that there is simply no way to explain the absence of the subject in (80a) in terms of the rule of COMPLEMENT-SUBJECT DELETION: first, the derivation of (80a) does not involve deletion under identity; second, there is no complement sentence.

Third, COMPLEMENT-SUBJECT DELETION must precede SUBJECT-PRONOUN DELETION. This can be demonstrated quite easily. Consider the following:

(81a) Queremos jogar dominó
want (1st pl.) to play dominoes
'We want to play dominoes'

(81b) [Nós--querer [Nós--jogar--dominó]]
We--want we--play--dominoes

In order to derive (81a) from (82b), COMPLEMENT-SUBJECT DELETION must crucially apply before, and not after, SUBJECT-PRONOUN DELETION. For if the order of rule application were otherwise, it would be possible for SUBJECT-PRONOUN DELETION to apply first on the matrix sentence and delete the subject of querer 'to want', therefore eliminating the environment for COMPLEMENT-SUBJECT DELETION. As a consequence, ungrammatical sentences like (82) could be derived:

(82a) *Queremos nós jogar dominó
want (1st pl.) we to play (unmk.) dominoes

(82b) *Queremos nós jogarmos dominó
want (1st pl.) we to-play (1st pl.) dominoes

On the basis of the foregoing arguments, I conclude that SUBJECT-PRONOUN DELETION is an independent rule, distinct from COMPLEMENT-SUBJECT DELETION.

5.0 The non-cyclic nature of Subject Pronoun Deletion. In this section I present evidence showing that SUBJECT-PRONOUN DELETION is a postcyclic rule.

Notice first the following. In section 3.0, I have shown that SUBJECT-PRONOUN DELETION must apply after SUBJECT-VERB AGREEMENT in the derivation of sentences such as:

(83) Vimos Lucia em Ipanema
saw (1st pl.) Lucia in Ipanema
'We saw Lucia in Ipanema'

In fact, this order of rule application involving the two rules seems to be universally true (see Vago 1972).

Now, SUBJECT-VERB AGREEMENT is a postcyclic rule. Evidence for this is as follows. First, SUBJECT-VERB AGREEMENT must apply after SUBJECT REPLACEMENT (or, 'Raising' into subject position) to produce the right results in (84).

(84a) As coisas parecem estar quentes em Belfast (= 43a)
Things seem (3rd pl.) to be (unmk.) hot in Belfast
(84b) *As coisas parecem estarem quentes em Belfast (= 43b)
Things seem (3rd pl.) to be (3rd pl.) hot in Belfast

Second, SUBJECT-VERB AGREEMENT must apply after COMPLEMENT-SUBJECT DELETION to produce the right results in (85).

(85a) Os pivetes tentaram roubar o banco
The delinquents tried to rob (unmk.) the bank
(85b) *Os pivetes tentaram roubarem o banco.
The delinquents tried to rob (3rd pl.) the bank

SUBJECT REPLACEMENT and COMPLEMENT-SUBJECT DELETION are both rules which must wait until the second cycle to be applicable. Now, in order to account automatically for the facts in (84) and (85), SUBJECT REPLACEMENT and COMPLEMENT-SUBJECT DELETION, respectively, must apply, and affect the complement subject, before SUBJECT-VERB AGREEMENT has had a chance to apply. Now, since SUBJECT REPLACEMENT and COMPLEMENT-SUBJECT DELETION must wait until the second cycle to be applicable, and since they have to be made to apply before SUBJECT-VERB AGREEMENT, it follows that SUBJECT-VERB AGREEMENT cannot apply on the first cycle before the second cycle is reached. Hence, SUBJECT-VERB AGREEMENT cannot be cyclic but rather is postcyclic.

SUBJECT-VERB AGREEMENT is postcyclic. Now, since SUBJECT-PRONOUN DELETION has to apply after SUBJECT-VERB AGREEMENT, which is postcyclic, I conclude that SUBJECT-PRONOUN DELETION is also a postcyclic rule.

6.0 The 'Doom' hypothesis. Postal (1970a) gives several arguments purporting to show that application of COMPLEMENT-SUBJECT DELETION is subordinated to prior application of PRONOMINALIZATION

However, since in Postal's theory PRONOMINALIZATION is a lastcyclic or postcyclic rule and the complement-subject rule must be cyclic, it is necessary for him to fragment COMPLEMENT-SUBJECT DELETION into two separate rules:[9]

(86) (i) DOOM MARKING, which applies cyclically (before PRONOMINALIZATION) and marks the NP's fated for deletion with a special feature [+Doom];
(ii) DOOM ERASURE, which applies last--or post-cyclically (after PRONOMINALIZATION), and actually erases those 'doomed' complement subject NP's that are deleted.

Postal claims that the dependence of the deletion rule (DOOM ERASURE) on prior application of PRONOMINALIZATION is not an accidental property of English but rather follows from a general principle of grammar common to all languages, which requires all rules deleting NP's under condition of identity to delete only pronominal NP's (cf. 1970a:489). The principle is stated as follows:

(87) Universal Deletion Constraint:
If a transformation T deletes an NPa subject to the existence of a coreferent NP, NPb, in the same structure, then at the point where T applies, NPa must be pronominal.

There are, however, several objections to this analysis. The first one has to do with the obvious ad hoc character of the analysis: an arbitrary feature [+Doom], which plays no role anywhere else in the grammar, is introduced as a device to circumvent a problem of rule ordering.

There is, I believe, a metatheoretical paradox in this proposal. On the one hand, an arbitrary feature is proposed in order to overcome an ordering problem. This is done under the assumption that rule ordering is the important empirical notion to be preserved. For it would be senseless to make a proposal to resolve an ordering problem if one assumes that rules are not ordered. On the other hand, if arbitrary features are used in this fashion to overcome ordering problems, the empirical claim that rules are ordered is considerably weakened. Thus, at the same time that the proposal seeks to resolve an ordering problem in order to maintain the claim involving rule ordering, it trivializes the empirical content of the claim (see also Jackendoff 1969).

Apart from these objections based on metatheoretical considerations, there are also objections based on the negative consequences of the analysis.

Consider a first case. In the preceding sections, I have argued, at some length, in favor of a cyclic rule of COMPLEMENT-SUBJECT DELETION as distinct from the postcyclic rule of SUBJECT-PRONOUN DELETION.

As pointed out earlier, SUBJECT-PRONOUN DELETION is postcyclic and must be restricted so as to delete only pronominal NP's. Now, in Postal's analysis, DOOM ERASURE is also construed as a lastcyclic or postcyclic rule whose application is also restricted so as to delete only pronominal NP's.

One might then very well argue that SUBJECT-PRONOUN DELETION and Postal's DOOM ERASURE can be collapsed together as a single rule. Notice that if this could be done, Postal's hypothesis would have the interesting consequence of relating the rule which deletes complement subjects under condition of identity with the rule which deletes 'nonemphatic' subject pronouns, which in my earlier analysis were regarded as unrelated. One could then claim that the introduction of the Doom marker permits the expression of a generalization, otherwise inexpressible, that the two deletion rules are related. This would lend some plausibility to the Doom marker.

I now present evidence showing that DOOM ERASURE cannot be collapsed with SUBJECT-PRONOUN DELETION.

Consider initially the following. It was pointed out earlier in section 3.0 that SUBJECT-PRONOUN DELETION must apply after SUBJECT-VERB AGREEMENT in the derivation of sentences such as:

(83) Vimos Lucia em Ipanema
Saw (1st pl.) Lucia in Ipanema
'We saw Lucia in Ipanema'

The order of rule application is:

(88) SUBJECT-VERB AGREEMENT
SUBJECT-PRONOUN DELETION

I show now that the same is true in the case of infinitives. Compare, for instance, the sentences in (89).

(89a) Convém <u>comprarmos</u> uma ratoeira
Be-convenient to buy (1st pl.) a mousetrap
'It is convenient (for us) to buy a mousetrap'

(89b) Convém nós comprarmos uma ratoeira
Be-convenient we to buy (1st pl.) a mousetrap
'It is convenient for us to buy a mousetrap'

The only visible difference between these two sentences is that in (89a) the subject of the 'infinitival' complement is 'missing', although its presence is easily traceable due to the presence of the morpheme -mos (1st person plural) attached to the infinitive comprar 'to buy'; whereas in the case of (89b), the subject of the infinitive--the 'nominative' subject pronoun nós [nɔ́s] 'we' appears in the surface form of the sentence.

Notice first that the absence of the complement subject in (89a) cannot be explained in terms of 'deletion under identity'. Thus, (89a) cannot be explained in terms of deletion under identity with the subject of convém 'be-convenient' for there are no sentences like (90) in the language.

(90a) *Nós convém comprarmos uma ratoeira
We be-convenient to buy (1st pl.) a mousetrap
(90b) *Nós convém comprar uma ratoeira
We be-convenient to buy (unmk.) a mousetrap

Nor can (89a) be explained in terms of deletion of the complement subject under condition of identity with the object of convém 'be-convenient', for in (89a) convém 'be-convenient' does not appear with an object. Furthermore, in cases where convém 'be-convenient' appears with the 'objective' pronoun nos [nus] as its object, the infinitive cannot be inflected:

(91a) Convém-nos comprar uma ratoeira
Be-convenient-for-us to buy (unmk.) a mousetrap
'It is convenient for us to buy a mousetrap'
(91b) *Convém-nos comprarmos uma ratoeira
Be-convenient-for-us to buy (1st pl.) a mousetrap

Notice, however, that the facts in (89) will follow automatically if (89a) is derived from the structure underlying (89b) by application of SUBJECT-PRONOUN DELETION and if the order of rule application in (88) is observed. This analysis would automatically account both for the absence of the complement subject in (89a), and also for the fact that the infinitive agrees since, as shown in (88), SUBJECT-PRONOUN DELETION would apply only after the SUBJECT-VERB AGREEMENT rule had established the agreement relationship between the infinitive and its subject.

The analysis is corroborated by the existence of sentences such as:

(92a) Zito crê termos feito uma boa escolha
Zito believes to have (1st pl.) made a good choice
'Zito believes that we have made a good choice'
(92b) Zito crê termos nós feito uma boa escolha
Zito believes to have (1st pl.) we made a good choice
'Zito believes that we have made a good choice'

Notice that in the derivation of (92a) there is no possibility of deletion under identity for the subject of the complement--nós 'we', as indicated by the presence of the morpheme -mos (1st person plural) attached to the infinitive ter 'to have'--is not identical to any NP in the structure. These facts, however, follow automatically if (92a) is derived from the structure underlying (92b) by application of SUBJECT-PRONOUN DELETION and if the order of rule application in (88) is observed.

It is clear then from the foregoing facts that SUBJECT-PRONOUN DELETION must be formulated so as to apply after SUBJECT-VERB AGREEMENT, and that this order of rule application is equally valid for finite verb forms as well as infinitives.

I show now that SUBJECT-PRONOUN DELETION cannot be collapsed with DOOM ERASURE. Thus consider the following:

(93a) Nós tentamos comprar uma ratoeira
We tried to buy (unmk.) a mousetrap
(93b) *Nós tentamos comprarmos uma ratoeira
We tried to buy (1st pl.) a mousetrap

(94) [Nós--tentamos--[Nós--comprar--uma ratoeira]]
We--tried We--buy--a mousetrap

Sentence (93a) is derived from deep structure (94) via deletion of the complement subject under condition of identity. Thus, according to Postal's analysis, it must involve application of DOOM ERASURE.

Suppose now that DOOM ERASURE and SUBJECT-PRONOUN DELETION were the same rule.

In the discussion immediately preceding, it was shown that SUBJECT-PRONOUN DELETION must apply after SUBJECT-VERB AGREEMENT, as in (88). Now, if SUBJECT-PRONOUN DELETION and DOOM ERASURE were the same rule, then DOOM ERASURE would also have to apply after SUBJECT-VERB AGREEMENT. Suppose this were so. In that case, since DOOM ERASURE applies after SUBJECT-VERB AGREEMENT, SUBJECT-VERB AGREEMENT would first apply to deep structure (94) and trigger infinitival agreement. DOOM ERASURE, which comes next, would then apply and the result would always be the ungrammatical (93b) with the inflected infinitive.

The only way to account correctly for the facts in (93) would be to formulate DOOM ERASURE so as to apply to (94) before SUBJECT-VERB AGREEMENT. Thus, the facts in (93) require the order to be:

(95) DOOM ERASURE
SUBJECT-VERB AGREEMENT

This is to be compared with the earlier order in

(88) SUBJECT-VERB AGREEMENT
SUBJECT-PRONOUN DELETION

The ordering in (95) shows that DOOM ERASURE must apply before SUBJECT-VERB AGREEMENT; whereas the order in (88) requires that SUBJECT-PRONOUN DELETION apply after SUBJECT-VERB AGREEMENT. I conclude that DOOM ERASURE and SUBJECT-PRONOUN DELETION cannot be the same rule for there is a different rule--SUBJECT-VERB AGREEMENT--intervening between them.

This conclusion has some important consequences. First, the fact that DOOM ERASURE cannot be collapsed with SUBJECT-PRONOUN DELETION shows that the arbitrary [Doom] marker proposed by Postal does not have any far-reaching consequences. In fact, it cannot be extended in any way beyond the facts for which it was originally postulated; and, furthermore, there is no clear way in which it can be shown to be independently motivated.

Second, it is now clear that DOOM ERASURE will have to be an extra rule, thereby adding extra complexity to the grammar.

Third, since DOOM ERASURE would have to be distinct from SUBJECT-PRONOUN DELETION, in order to maintain Postal's analysis it would be necessary to make the rather suspicious claim that there are two rules, both of them postcyclic (or lastcyclic), for the deletion of pronouns, namely, SUBJECT-PRONOUN DELETION, which deletes 'nonemphatic' pronouns, and must be in the grammar independently; and in addition, DOOM ERASURE, which will delete pronouns just in case they bear the arbitrary feature [Doom].

Consider now a second case. It was argued in section 2.0 that COMPLEMENT-SUBJECT DELETION, viewed there as a single rule, is cyclic.

Now, Postal (1970a:482ff.) claims that the complement-subject rule cannot be a cyclic deletion rule. The crucial basis for this claim is Postal's argument that this deletion rule must follow

WH-MOVEMENT, which in his theory is a last- or postcyclic rule. The essentials of Postal's arguments are as follows.

Postal observes that there is a principle which blocks derivations in which a transformational rule has the effect of crossing one coreferential NP over another. This principle would explain, for instance, the difference in grammaticalness between the sentences in (96).

(96a) Who$_i$ claimed Mary kissed him$_i$?
(96b) *Who$_i$ did he$_i$ claim Mary kissed?

These facts, Postal observes, follow from the 'crossover' principle since in the case of (96a), where the wh-word has not crossed over its coreferent, the sentence is grammatical; whereas in (96a), where the wh-word does cross over its coreferent, the sentence is ungrammatical.

He points out next that the same principle is responsible for ungrammaticality of sentences like (97).

(97) *Who$_i$ did you think discovering that Bill was dead annoyed the most?

The same principle would also exclude:

(98a) *Who$_i$ did you think his$_i$ discovery that Bill was dead annoyed the most?
(98b) *Who$_i$ did you think the Doom$_i$ discovery that Bill was dead annoyed the most?

According to Postal's analysis, sentences like (97) would have an underlying structure like (99).

(99) [$_{S_3}$You think [$_{S_2}$his$_i$ discovering [$_{S_1}$that Bill was dead]$_{S_1}$ annoyed who$_i$ the most]$_{S_2}$]$_{S_3}$

The ungrammaticality of (97) would follow from the crossover principle since in the derivation of (97) from (99) under the application of WH-MOVEMENT the wh-word who would cross over its coreferent, namely, the subject of discovering.

However, as Postal points out, in order to block (97) by means of the 'crossover' principle, it is necessary that WH-MOVEMENT apply to deep structure (99) before the subject of discovering is deleted by COMPLEMENT-SUBJECT DELETION. Otherwise, if WH-MOVEMENT applied after the deletion of the subject of discovering at the time WH-MOVEMENT were to apply, there would be no coreferent NP in the structure for the wh-word who to cross over. Consequently, there would be no way of stating the restrictions on (97) as 'crossing restrictions'. Postal concludes, then, that in order to block (97) WH-MOVEMENT must apply to (99) before COMPLEMENT-SUBJECT DELETION.

Now, since WH-MOVEMENT is applicable only on the last cycle S_3 in (99), and since it must apply before the complement-subject rule deletes the subject of discovering on the earlier cycle S_2, Postal concludes that the complement-subject rule cannot be a 'cyclic deletion rule'. In order to account for the facts, he proposes a fragment of grammar with essentially the properties of (100).

(100) DOOM MARKING (cyclic)
WH-MOVEMENT (last- or postcyclic)
DOOM ERASURE (last- or postcyclic)

Notice, first of all, that the English facts discussed by Postal are parallel to similar Portuguese facts. Thus, parallel to the English facts in (96) we have:

(101a) Quem$_i$ disse que Maria o$_i$ havia beijado
'Who$_i$ said that Mary had kissed him$_i$?'
(101b) *Quem$_i$ ele$_i$ disse que Maria havia beijado?
'Who$_i$ did he$_i$ say that Mary had kissed?'

And parallel to the facts in (98) we have:

(102a) *Quem$_i$ você acha que sua$_i$ descoberta que Bill estava morto perturbou mais?
*'Who$_i$ do you think his$_i$ discovery that Bill was dead disturbed the most?'
(102b) *Quem$_i$ você acha que a Doom$_i$ descoberta que Bill estava morto perturbou mais?
*'Who$_i$ do you think the Doom$_i$ discovery that Bill was dead disturbed the most?'

In view of the similarity between the two languages with respect to these facts, one would expect the fragment of grammar (100) to be equally valid for Portuguese.

I show now that this is not the case, and that Postal's analysis represented in (100) is incompatible with the facts of Portuguese.

Consider first the following. It was pointed out earlier in this section that if there is a rule of DOOM ERASURE this rule would have to apply before SUBJECT-VERB AGREEMENT because of cases like (93), repeated here:

(93a) Nós tentamos comprar uma ratoeira
We tried to buy (unmk.) a mousetrap
(93b) *Nós tentamos comprarmos uma ratoeira
We tried to buy (1st pl.) a mousetrap

The facts just listed would require the order to be:

(95) DOOM ERASURE
SUBJECT-VERB AGREEMENT

Consider now the following. In Portuguese it is possible to question or relativize the subject of a 'tensed' complement sentence. Thus, there are grammatical sentences like:

(103a) Que homens você disse que haviam saído?
Which men you said that had (3rd pl.) left
'Which men did you say had left?'
(103b) Os homens que você disse que haviam saído estão aqui
The men who(m) you said that had (3rd pl.) left are here
'The men whom you said had left are here'

In the derivation of these sentences, SUBJECT-VERB AGREEMENT must clearly apply before WH-MOVEMENT. Otherwise, if WH-MOVEMENT applied first, it could move the subject of haver saído 'to have left' indefinitely far and there would be no possibility for the agreement rule to apply. The order of rule application must then be:

(104) SUBJECT-VERB AGREEMENT
WH-MOVEMENT

If one simply places together the correct ordering statements in (95) and (104), respectively, one would have a fragment of grammar with the characteristics of (105).

(105) DOOM ERASURE
SUBJECT-VERB AGREEMENT
WH-MOVEMENT

This is to be compared with Postal's analysis in (100).

(100) DOOM MARKING
WH-MOVEMENT
DOOM ERASURE

If one examines the facts just listed, it is seen that the order of rule application in (105) and the order of rule application in Postal's analysis in (100) are clearly incompatible. In particular, as (105) shows, DOOM ERASURE would have to apply before WH-MOVEMENT, and not after WH-MOVEMENT as predicted by Postal's analysis. Postal's analysis cannot, therefore, be maintained.

This conclusion has some important consequences. First, it shows that Postal's claim that the English sentences in (97) and (98)--and (if one assumes close correspondence with the facts of Portuguese) the parallel Portuguese sentences in (102)--are blocked by the 'crossover' principle is incorrect since it leads to incorrect ordering in (100). This raises serious doubts as to the validity of the 'crossover' principle as a general principle of grammar.[10]

Second, and more importantly, since the analysis in (100) cannot be maintained, Postal's claim that COMPLEMENT SUBJECT DELETION cannot be a cyclic deletion rule but must be divided into two subrules--one cyclic, and the other last- or postcyclic--is unsupported by the facts.

I conclude, on the basis of the arguments presented above, that COMPLEMENT-SUBJECT DELETION is a SINGLE RULE, and that COMPLEMENT-SUBJECT DELETION is CYCLIC.

NOTES

The research on which this paper is based was done at Massachusetts Institute of Technology. I am greatly indebted to David Perlmutter and Noam Chomsky, who commented on an earlier version of the paper and made numerous suggestions for its improvement. Responsibility for eventual mistakes is solely mine. The paper is a revised fragment of my dissertation Aspects of Portuguese Complementation, State University of New York at Buffalo, 1972.

1. Alternatively, it may be the case that the subject of the embedded sentence is a pronominal element (PRO) which deletes. In this case, instead of (1a-b), the structure underlying (2a-b) would be:

[Zeca queria [PRO jogar dominó]]
[Aldo persuadiu Lucia [PRO lavar os pratos]]

2. Arguments for a phrase structure like (10) are found in Bresnan (1971). Since the facts used by Bresnan to motivate such a rule are quite distinct from the ones discussed here, one might

claim that Bresnan's analysis provides independent motivation for this expansion of the VP node.

3. For a different account of reflexivization within an interpretive theory which does not raise such problems, see Helke (1971).

4. One further argument for the cyclicity of Gender-Number Agreement is provided by the existence of sentences like:

Estes livros parecem ser difíceis de ser encontrados
These books seem (3rd pl.) to be (unmk.) difficult (pl.) to be (unmk.) found (pl.)
'These books seem to be difficult to find'

The order of rule application to derive this sentence is as follows: Passive (estes livros which is the underlying subject of encontrar 'to find' shifts to the position of subject of encontrar); Gender-Number Agreement (causes agreement between estes livros and the participle encontrados 'found-pl.'); Tough-Movement (moves estes livros to the position of subject of ser difícil 'be difficult'); Gender-Number Agreement (causes agreement between estes livros and difíceis 'difficult (pl.)'); Raising into Subject Position (estes livros becomes the derived subject of parecer 'seem') and, finally, post-cyclic application of Subject-Verb Agreement (causing agreement between parecer 'seem' and estes livros). As is seen in the derivation of this sentence, Gender-Number Agreement must apply both before and after Tough-Movement, which can only be done if the rule is cyclic. Furthermore, agreement in this sentence must take place before Raising into Subject Position which is a rule known to be cyclic. Since Gender-Number Agreement cannot be precyclic (it must apply after Passive in the derivation of this sentence) and since it must apply before Raising into Subject Position which is cyclic, it must be cyclic.

5. It would make no difference if one were to argue that what triggers infinitival agreement is the presence of a feature for person. Since Δ would be generated with syntactic features for gender and number, there would be no nonarbitrary way to present Δ to be generated also with a feature for person. Anyway, it seems rather doubtful that one would make such claim in the case of nouns. More likely, nouns are unmarked for 'person' which seems to be rather a feature of pronouns.

6. But see Wasow (1972) for a more recent discussion.

7. It should be emphasized, however, that this conclusion in no way argues against 'interpretive' theories in general. The arguments given constitute negative evidence against the 'interpretive' treatment of Equi proposed in Jackendoff (1969).

8. The inexistence of sentences like these can be explained in terms of the existence of 'deep structure' constraints as proposed in Perlmutter (1971). According to this theory, verbs like exortar 'to exhort' would require that the subject of the embedded sentence be identical to the object of the matrix sentence. (For an alternative proposal see Jackendoff 1969).

9. In a more recent study, Postal (1972b) has abandoned this proposal.

10. Postal (1972b) himself has admitted that it is untenable. In the paper, he argues for a less general, language specific 'global derivational constraint' to account for the so-called 'wh-constraint'. For an alternative proposal not involving 'derivational constraints' see Wasow (1972).

COMPLEMENT SUBJECT DELETION AND THE ANALYSIS OF MENACER

GILLES FAUCONNIER

University of California at San Diego

Until recently, generative linguistics has kept in line with the rigorous structuralist tradition of accounting for distributions and word patterns without reaching into the quicksand of meaning. Typically, surface sequences have been accounted for by means of rules which are sensitive to syntactic categories, formal configurations, and various types of features--subcategorization, exception, morphologically related features, etc. Take, for example, Rosenbaum's[1] treatment of complement subject deletion, written ten years ago; the rule that erases complement subjects in order to eventually produce strings like (1):

(1) Dick persuaded Henry to perjure himself.

depends on the following: (a) a structural configuration including a verb with a sentential subject or complement; (b) a feature on the verb indicating that it belongs to the appropriate type; (c) a principle for determining which noun phrase, Dick or Henry in (1), controls the deletion (this principle is purely formal: it refers to the 'distance' in terms of number of nodes between the possible deletors and the deletee in the syntactic configuration which triggers the rule); (d) the structural identity of the deletor and the deletee.

In such a treatment, nothing about the meaning of the governing verb or of the complement clause is relevant to whether and how the rule applies. For example, English could have a verb sorfe meaning 'force' except that its object would be the agent of the forcing.

A sentence like (2) would then be grammatical, according to Rosenbaum's distance principle:

(2) Jane sorfed Dick to kiss her.

The deleted subject would be Dick and the corresponding interpretation something like Dick forced Jane to be kissed by him. Or swear might be an EQUI-verb, [2] like jurer in French, and sentence (3) would have the same source as (4).

(3) Mary swore to Joseph to regret what he had done.
(4) Mary swore to Joseph that he would regret what he had done.

Obviously, nonsentences like (2) and (3) do not in any way count against Rosenbaum's analysis: they are only intended to illustrate what his syntax allows. As we know, the analysis fails on its own grounds because of the existence of verbs and expressions like promise, make an offer, receive instructions, etc. [3]

In recent generative work, the stringent structuralist attitude mentioned earlier has been dropped and the extensive interaction between some syntactic phenomena and the logical or pragmatic properties of the sentences in which they are observed has come to be realized. Some outstanding instances are Ann Borkin's study of TO-BE Deletion, [4] George Lakoff's 'The Role of Deduction in a Grammar', [5] work by the Kiparskys[6] and by Karttunen[7] on complementation, etc.

The major aim of this paper is to present a case in French for which 'independently' motivated logical characteristics determine the manner of application of a rule of grammar; I will suggest that this approach is inherently more powerful than even a formally equivalent purely syntactic one because it handles directly cases of 'fuzzy acceptability' constituting a fully productive phenomenon which in principle falls outside the scope of traditional syntactic research. I have chosen the verb menacer to illustrate this last point in some detail, because it has interesting superficial distributional properties which have already received attention from eminent transformationalists.

Specifically, the question I wish to ask is the same as Rosenbaum's, mentioned earlier: given an EQUI-verb with three arguments, one sentential and the other two ordinary noun phrases, most often 'animate', and referential, which of the two referential arguments controls the deletion of the complement subject? The following examples and contrasts show that sometimes only the subject, sometimes only a direct or indirect object, and sometimes either one of two referential arguments may serve as controllers:

(5a) J'ai juré à ma mère de me réformer.
'I swore to my mother that I would reform.'
(5b) *J'ai juré à ma mère de se réformer.

(6a) Mon fils m'admire de m'être adapté à cette vie.
'My son admires me for having adapted myself to this life.'
(6b) *Mon fils m'admire de s'être adapté à cette vie.

(7a) J'ai conseillé à Julien de s'enfuir.
'I advised Julien to run away.'
(7b) *J'ai conseillé à Julien de m'enfuir.

(8a) J'ai supplié Ernestine de venir avec moi.
'I begged Ernestine to come with me.'
(8b) J'ai supplié Ernestine d'aller avec elle.

(9a) J'ai promis à Gustave de me faire nommer à Collioure.
'I promised Gustave that I would be appointed at Collioure.'
(9b) J'ai promis à Gustave d'être nommé à Collioure.
'I promised Gustave that he would be appointed at Collioure.'

Notice in particular that no straightforward semantic or derivational principle rules out the ill-formed examples cited: parallel to the ungrammatical (5b) and the grammatical (9b) are the full forms (10) and (11), which are both fine:

(10) J'ai juré à ma mère qu'elle se réformerait.
'I swore to my mother that she would reform.'

(11) J'ai promis à Gustave qu'il serait nommé à Collioure.
'I promised Gustave that he would be appointed at Collioure.'

Parallel to (6b) and (8b) are (12) and (13):

(12) Mon fils m'admire de lui permettre de s'adapter.
'My son admires me for allowing him to adapt.'
(13) J'ai supplié Ernestine de me permettre d'aller avec elle.
'I begged Ernestine to let me go with her.'

Because formal accounts such as Rosenbaum's distance principle also fail to make correct predictions, the phenomenon is treated in an ad hoc way in transformational grammars by marking verbs individually for their control properties. In looking for logical properties to replace these ad hoc features, one must be careful not to beg the question. For example, take (14) and (15):

(14) Othello méprise Iago d'être aussi lâche.
'Othello despises Iago for being so cowardly.'

(15) *Othello méprise Iago que son fils soit aussi lâche.

One has the intuition here that the complement sentence must be 'about' the object (one despises somebody because of some characteristic or action of that somebody). However, this cannot be tested independently of EQUI, since the rule here is obligatory in the strong sense that its SD must be met. Consequently, the most revealing cases will be those in which the verb can surface with three arguments, and no EQUI has taken place. Here are some examples:

(16) J'ai ordonné à Walter que son fils quitte le pays.
'I ordered Walter to [have] his son leave the country.'

(17) Nous avons décidé le ministre à ce qu'on construise le barrage.
'We convinced the minister to [have] the dam built.'

(18) Ils ont obligé le directeur à ce que le bar reste ouvert la nuit.
'They made the director [let] the bar remain open at night.'

(19) Les locataires ont demandé au propriétaire que la maison soit repeinte.
'The tenants asked the landlord to [have] the house repainted.'

(20) Nous avons proposé au patron que la nourriture soit gratuite.
'We suggested to the owner that the food be free.'

(21) Le patron a promis aux clients que la nourriture serait gratuite.
'The owner promised the customers that the food would be free.'

(22) L'agent immobilier nous a assurés que la maison serait belle.
'The real estate agent assured us that the house would be beautiful.'

In all the foregoing examples I have underlined the noun phrases which might be controllers if EQUI could apply. The complement clause describes an event or a state of affairs; a native speaker of the language, because he knows the 'meaning' of ordonner, décider, obliger, demander, etc., can infer an active relationship between the potential controller in these sentences and the event or state affairs described in the complement.[8] That is, in (16) it is known that 'I' want Walter to make his son leave the country, in (17) that 'we' want the minister to bring about the construction of the dam, in (18) that 'they' want the director to let the bar stay open, and so on. Examples (16)-(20) have the structure:

(23) x V y P

and in every case one can extract a component of the meaning:

(24) x want [y bring about P]

Examples (20)-(22) have the form

(25) y V x <u>P</u>

and again (24) is part of their meaning. A difficult point here, however, is the distinction between meaning and derivable consequence. Under current proposals, (24) might be related to the logic of the verb <u>ordonner</u> by means of lexical decomposition, as in (26) (given for illustrative purposes only):

(26) :L: x express to y [x want [y bring about P]]
+ appropriateness condition for <u>ordonner</u>:
x think 'x superior to y'
+ semantics of superiority:
x superior to y → (L → y bring about P)

or (24) might be related to (23) by means of meaning postulates like (27):

(27) xVyP → x want [y bring about P]

But from forms like (23) one can also conclude indirectly that 'x try [x bring about P]'. And such consequences can indeed be derived from representations like (26) or (27) (with other meaning postulates). For our present purpose it is sufficient to note that

(28) [y bring about P]

will be a necessary component of any logical characterization of verbs like <u>ordonner</u>, whereas propositions like [x bring about P] need only appear in derived consequences.

For sentences like (19) and (21) a relationship holds between the other argument (x) and the complement proposition, roughly characterized by (29):

(29) P is $\left\{\begin{matrix}\text{good}\\ \text{bad}\end{matrix}\right\}$ for x

Thus in (19), having the house painted will benefit the tenants; in (21), free food will be to the good of the customers. The distinction here between (19) and (16) is not straightforward because (29) will appear in many contexts as a derived consequence with verbs like <u>ordonner</u>: one normally gives orders that are compatible with one's desires. However, again, this is a frequent but not necessary consequence of (24): if x wants [y bring about P], there is a likelihood but not a certainty that x desires <u>P</u>: P may be good for x only insofar as it is y who brings it about, as in (30):

(30) L'adjudant a ordonné au caporal que la cour soit balayée.
'The adjutant ordered the corporal to [have] the yard swept.'

If the corporal fails to execute the order and the commanding general decides to do the sweeping himself, P will have been brought about with no benefit to the 'adjudant'. Verbs like <u>conseiller</u>, <u>permettre</u>, <u>recommander</u> are more clearly free of a condition like (29).

(31) Jules a conseillé à Jim de vendre sa voiture.
'Jules advised Jim to sell his car.'

Relationships between a referential argument and the complement proposition of a verb, such as (28) and (29), appear as subparts of primary consequences of the meaning of that verb; that is, the notion that (28) or (29) is related to structure (23) must be viewed as part of the native speaker's linguistic competence; the fact that he can use and understand <u>ordonner</u>, <u>demander</u>, <u>obliger</u>, etc. and give judgments as to the consequences they allow or demand, and their appropriateness, must be reflected in an adequate theory. Sentences (16) through (22) show that such logical relations operate for EQUI-verbs regardless of whether EQUI applies or not, so that the characterization cannot be viewed as an automatic consequence of the application of EQUI as it might have been for example (14).

Given these observations, I would like to propose the following Controlling Principle for EQUI-verbs with two referential arguments in French:

(C) If x, y and P are arguments of an EQUI-verb V and if the characterization of the meaning of V crucially involves one of the following:
1. [x bring about P]
2. [P is {good / bad} for x]
3. P describes a property of x
then x can serve as a controller for EQUI.

Form 1 appears in the meaning of all the verbs in Appendix samples (1a), (1b), (2), (3), and (5), with x the underlying object, and in sample (6) with x the underlying subject, and accordingly, the respective objects and subjects of these verbs are possible controllers:

(32) Le général autorise Camembert à partir en permission.
'The general authorizes Camembert to go on leave.'

(33) Joséphine supplie l'empereur de lui rendre sa liberté.
'Josephine begs the emperor to give her back her freedom.'

(34) J'admire Néron d'avoir brûlé Rome.
'I admire Nero for having burnt Rome.'

(35) Nous approuvons Richardson d'avoir démissioné.
'We approved of Richardson's having resigned.'

(36) Sa mère envoie Jean chercher du lait.
'John's mother sends him to get some milk.'

(37) Mme de Sévigné a promis à sa fille d'aller aux Tuileries.
'Mme. de Sévigné promised her daughter to [let her] go to the Tuileries.'

Form 2 appears in the meaning of the verbs in Appendix sample (1) and also pardonner and proposer with x as the subject:

(38) Nous avons pardonné au gardien que les meubles aient été volés.[9]
'We forgave the guard for letting the furniture be stolen.'

It also appears in the meaning of assurer, promettre, and menacer with x as the object:

(39) Ils ont menacé Daniel que sa femme lui soit enlevée.
'They threatened Daniel that his wife would be kidnapped.'

The complement clause here must represent something bad for the object, at least in the subject's mind.[10]

(40) Le FBI a promis à Getty que son fils serait retrouvé.
'The FBI promised Getty that his son would be found.'

In all these cases, as predicted by the principle, x is a possible controller:

(41) Platon m'a {demandé / supplié / imploré} de m'accompagner.
'Plato asked me if he could come with me.'

(42) J'ai pardonné à ce traitre d'avoir passé toute ma vie en prison.
'I forgave this traitor for [having caused] me to spend my life in prison.'

(43) César a menacé Pompée d'être envoyé en Egypte.
'Caesar threatened Pompey with being sent to Egypt.'

(44) Le FBI a promis à Getty d'être tenu au courant.
'The FBI promised Getty that he would be kept posted.'

Form 3 is part of the meaning of the verbs in Appendix samples (3a) and (4), and the complement P is a presupposition of the sentences constructed with the former.[11]

(45) Elle envie sa soeur d'être aussi aimable.
'She envies her sister for being so gracious.'

(46) Nous destinons notre enfant à être éveque.
'We destine our child to be a bishop.'

Principle (C) makes a number of predictions which are testable.[12] For example, it predicts that if a verb can be used with a derived meaning, there will be changes in the possible controllers corresponding to the status of 1, 2, and 3 in the derived meaning. This claim can be tested on demander which can be used with the imperative force of 'order', thereby losing Form 2 as an essential component of its meaning.

(47) Le capitaine vous demande que la cour soit balayée avant midi.
'The captain asks you to [have] the yard swept before noon.'

Now the captain may order that you place him next to you at dinner; but the following sentence cannot convey this:

(48) Le capitaine vous demande d'être placé à coté de vous à table.
'The captain asks you to let him sit next to you at the table.'

Example (48) is perfectly appropriate as a request (for example, if vous is a general). Therefore, one sees that if demander is used with the meaning of 'order', its subject can no longer serve as a controller and this bears out the prediction made by (C). A syntactic account of control here would force one to posit two different verbs demander. However, even this ad hoc lexical treatment would not be sufficient in cases where the meaning of the verb is modified by some other part of the sentence. Yet this can happen, as in (49):

(49) La servante me demande de la part de sa maîtresse que j'apporte des fleurs au palais.
'The servant asks me on behalf of her mistress to bring flowers to the palace.'

Adding de la part de z to x demande à y P shifts the benefit of P from x to z and thus Form 2 is no longer valid: P is now assumed to be good not for x but for z. Correspondingly, one finds that x can no longer be a controller in this case: suppose the mistress' request is that her servant accompany me, and that the servant transmits this request; (50) is inappropriate to convey this:

(50) *La servante me demande de la part de sa maîtresse de m'accompagner.

Especially interesting in this perspective is the case of a verb like proposer; again, its logic can be studied independently of EQUI on the basis of sentences like:

(51) J'ai proposé à Marianne que nous allions au bois de Chaville.
'I suggested to Marianne that we go to the Bois de Chaville.'

(52) Haddock a proposé à Milou que le bateau s'appelle 'Fleur de Lotus'.
'Haddock suggested to Milou that the boat be called 'Fleur de Lotus'.'

In general the form

x propose (à) y P

has a meaning which involves one of the following: (a) x want [x + y agree [x bring about P]]; (b) x want [x + y agree [y bring about P]]; (c) x want [x + y agree [x + y bring about P]]. (51) and (52) are examples of component (c). Components (a) and (b) can be found in (53) and (54):

(53) L'entrepreneur a proposé à son client que la maison soit construite en moellon.
'The contractor suggested to his client that the house be built of stone.'

(54) Le client a proposé à l'entrepreneur que la maison soit construite en moellon.
'The customer suggested to the contractor that the house be built of stone.'

That is, in (52) Haddock and Milou will jointly give the boat a name. In (53) and (54), it is the contractor who will build the house, but he must be in agreement with his customer.

The consequence of this is that condition 1 of the controlling principle (C) is met for x, for y, and also for x + y; and we find that x, y, and x + y are all possible controllers:[13]

(55) L'entrepreneur a proposé à son client de construire la maison en moellon.
'The contractor proposed to his customer to build the house of stone.'

(56) Le client a proposé à l'entrepreneur de construire la maison en moellon.
'The customer suggested to the contractor that he build the house of stone.'

(57) J'ai proposé à Gertrude de nous marier dimanche prochain.[14]
'I suggested to Gertrude that we get married next Sunday.'

Equipped with controlling principle (C), I now turn to the analysis of menacer. Gross (1969) characterizes the control properties of menacer in the following way: if the matrix is passivized, the complement clause must also be passivized and the subjects are coreferential before passivization:

(58) Pierre a été menacé par Paul d'être battu.
'Pierre was threatened by Paul with a beating.'

(59) *Pierre a été menacé par Paul de le battre.

However, Ruwet (1972) notes the following well-formed sentences:

(60) Justine a été menacée par le marquis
'Justine was threatened by the marquis
{de subir les pires tortures.
with the worst tortures.'
de recevoir des coups de bâton.
with being beaten with a stick.'
de se faire fouetter.
with being whipped.'}

Accordingly, he proposes the following principle:

'(I) le sujet (effacé par Equi) de la subordonnée est obligatoirement coréférentiel du sujet <u>superficiel</u> de la principale.
(II) si la principale est au passif le sujet subordonné ne peut pas être sémantiquement un agent.'

'(I) The subject (deleted under EQUI) of the subordinate is obligatorily coreferential with the surface subject of the matrix.
(II) If the matrix is in the passive, the subordinate subject cannot semantically be an agent.'

For most speakers, however, part (I) of this principle does not hold; the following sentences are fine:

(61) Le marquis a menacé Justine de recevoir des coups de bâton.
'The marquis threatened Justine with being beaten with a stick.'

(62) Le Directoire m'a menacé d'être nommé à Tombouctou.
'The director threatened to send me to Timbuktu.'

(63) L'arbitre a menacé Bobby Orr {d'être suspendu. / de se voir infliger une amende.}
'The referee threatened Bobby Orr {with being suspended.' / with the infliction of a fine.'}

In all these cases the surface object of <u>menacer</u> controls the deletion of the complement subject.

I am going to attempt to sketch a partial logical analysis of menacer, as it appears in:

(64) x menacer y (de) P (si ~ Q)

The action expressed by a threat such as (64) consists in the proclamation by x that he will bring about P unless Q occurs, i. e.

Assertion: x express to y[(x bring about P) if ~ Q]

For menacer to be appropriate here a number of conditions must be met. x must believe that it is in y's power to bring about Q:

Appropriateness condition 1:
x believe ◊ [y bring about Q]
x must believe that y does not wish to bring about Q: otherwise a threat is unnecessary.
Appropriateness condition 2:
x believe [y want ~ Q]
x must believe that y is scared of P, so that he may prefer $Q \wedge \sim P$ to $\sim Q \wedge P$:
Appropriateness condition 3:
x believe [y believe [P is bad for y]]

The apparent complexity of this last condition is justified by sentences like:

(65) Brer Fox threatens to throw Brer Rabbit into the brier patch.

Example (65) is appropriate even though the brier patch is harmless to Brer Rabbit. Moreover, even if Brer Fox knows this, (65) will be appropriate as long as he thinks that Brer Rabbit believes otherwise.[15]

The minimal analysis presented in the foregoing is adequate for examples such as (61)-(63), also (39) in which EQUI does not apply, and examples cited by Ruwet, in which the argument y does not appear explicitly in the complement P:

(66) Ney a menacé Napoléon de refuser la Légion d'honneur.
'Ney threatened Napoleon that he would refuse the Legion of Honor.'

Now the Controlling Principle (C) applies straightforwardly: one finds Form 1 (x bring about P) in the Assertion, and Form 2 (P is bad for y) in Appropriateness condition 3. Thus either x or y can serve as controllers and this is borne out by facts in (61), (62), (63), and (66).

Moreover, if x controls the deletion, x must be subject of P, and may therefore very often be an agent in P because of Form 1, in the Assertion; but this is by no means necessary: sentence (61) can easily be understood with the interpretation that it is le marquis who will receive the blows, provided that the context allows le marquis to be able to bring this about (cf. condition (ii) in note 15). The active and intentional nature of P when x is a controller can be tested distributionally:

(67) *Pierre a menacé Paul de le frapper involontairement.

(68) *Pierre a menacé Paul de savoir le Latin.

Compare this with:

(69) Pierre a menacé Paul de savoir le Latin d'ici trois semaines.
'Pierre threatened Paul that he (Paul) would know Latin within three weeks.'

Form 1 in the Assertion shows that the argument x is the primary agent of P. Therefore, y will normally not be an agent in P. In particular then, if y controls the deletion in accordance with principle (C), the coreferential subject of the complement clause P will not be an agent and this accounts for Ruwet's principle (II). This is not entirely correct, however, since y could be an agent in P provided that P was exclusively under the control of x--that is, y's performing P or not would depend on x's decision. Here again the prediction made by the logical analysis contrary to Ruwet's principle is borne out by the facts. One finds the following sentences:

(70) Mon père m'a menacé d'aller à l'école du dimanche.
'My father threatened to [make] me go to Sunday school.'

(71) Jean a été menacé de partir faire la guerre au Tchad.
'Jean was threatened with being made to go fight in Chad.'

(72) On a menacé ma soeur d'accoucher sans docteur.
'They threatened my sister with having to give birth without a doctor.'

In all of these sentences, the underlying object of menacer controls the deletion of a subject which is a semantic agent. This happens because the context makes it possible to assume that the subject of menacer has control over whether or how the agent will perform the action mentioned in P. An extreme case of this phenomenon is when the lexical meaning of the embedded verb strongly implies that only one agent is involved. Se suicider, for instance, has this property and correspondingly the following sentence would initially be rejected by anyone:

(73) J'ai menacé Paul de se suicider.
'I threatened Paul that I would make him commit suicide.'

But if je is a hypnotist, (73) sounds much better.

This brings one to the question of fuzzy acceptability. It is clear that if a verb is logically specified in the way that we have suggested for menacer, then the form of the context and the internal form of the embedded proposition P may be more or less compatible with the logical specification. For example, in the case of menacer, the a priori most compatible proposition P will be one with an agent subject identical to x, because of the logical Assertion, and an object or prepositional complement identical to y, because of Appropriateness condition 3:

(74) Catilina a menacé Cicéron de le dénoncer.
'Catiline threatened Cicero that he would denounce him.'

(75) Jeanne a menacé Charles de se retourner contre lui.
'Jeanne threatened Charles that he would turn against him.'

If it is agreed that given the logic, this is in some sense the most probable construction, it is seen that passivization of the matrix, which rules out x as a controller,[16] will allow y to control deletion only if it is a subject in the lower clause; and this in turn can happen if the lower clause is passivized. This state of affairs corresponds directly to the observation originally made by Gross, and one sees that it does not represent an accidental syntactic property of menacer, as a treatment in terms of features might suggest, but follows instead from independently attested logical properties.

Cases like (61), (62), (63) are not quite as good semantically as (74), (75), because they leave unspecified the manner in which x can bring P about, and therefore they require more context. Cases (70)-(73) are worse because the embedded clause P has the form:

y do Q

which is in conflict with subparts of the assertion:

x bring about P

and of Appropriateness condition 3:

y believe [P is bad for y]

Thus even more context is required to counteract the apparently conflicting consequences of (70)-(73).

The influence of context on acceptability judgments has been often noted in recent work, for instance, Boons (1973) and Householder (1973). The present study shows that an explanatory account of deletion control and corresponding degrees of acceptability must take into consideration the interaction of syntax, logic, and pragmatics. Moreover, the fact that too little is yet known about semantics to produce really rigorous arguments is no reason for claiming that one must therefore do without it: it is only if the existence of such phenomena is accepted that appropriate techniques can be developed to deal with them. To let the available techniques define exclusively the relevant phenomena is to engage in a vicious and circular enterprise.

APPENDIX

Equi-verbs with two arguments

Sample

(1a)
décider
ordonner
conseiller
recommander
permettre
astreindre
autoriser
contraindre
engager
exhorter
forcer
habituer
inviter
obliger
charger
persuader
dire, écrire, hurler, crier, téléphoner } + Subj
. . .
enseigner
apprendre

(1b)
défendre
empêcher
déconseiller
dégouter
dispenser
dissuader

(2)
demander
prier
implorer
supplier

(3a)
admirer

féliciter
applaudir
critiquer
envier
mépriser

(3b)
approuver
désapprouver
comprendre
gronder
haïr
rabrouer
récompenser
réprouver
respecter

(3c)
pardonner
accuser
soupçonner

(4)
destiner
prédestiner
preparer

(5)
écouter
entendre
regarder
sentir
voir
laisser
expédier
envoyer
emmener

(6)
proposer
suggérer
assurer
menacer
jurer
promettre
comploter

(7)
dire, écrire, hurler } + IND
. . .

NOTES

1. Cf. Rosenbaum (1965).

2. EQUI (from 'Equi noun phrase deletion') is the name given to the transformation that deletes complement subjects. EQUI-verbs are those for which the deletion is possible.

3. Cf. Langendoen (1973), who cites these expressions, and Gross (1967) for numerous counterexamples in French such as jurer, garantir, menacer, and the class of dire, raconter, confesser.

4. Cf. Borkin (1973).

5. Cf. G. Lakoff (1971b).

6. Cf. Kiparsky and Kiparsky, and R. Lakoff's (1973) review of their article.

7. Cf., e.g., Karttunen (1971a).

8. Only one of the two possible controllers has this property in examples 19-22.

9. For some speakers EQUI is obligatory (its SD must be met) with pardonner.

10. This is inaccurate; see what follows for a more precise statement.

11. As noted earlier, the test for this cannot be direct because EQUI is obligatory with the verbs in question. Indirect evidence could be adduced from sentences like:

(i) Je méprise Iago parce que son fils est lâche.
'I despise Iago because his son is a coward.'

(ii) Susanne admire Claude parce que son père est ministre.
'Susan admires Claude because her father is a minister.'

Thus for verbs in Appendix sample (3a) there is the equivalence:

x V y P $\leftrightarrow$ [x V y] because [P]

and in the second part of the equivalence P must be a property of y.

12. The verbs of class 7 are not handled by principle (C), since their logic does not establish any special relationship between x and P:

(i) J'ai raconté à Jean que les Allemands étaient entrés en Pologne.
'I told Jean that the Germans had entered Poland.'

(ii) J'ai raconté à Jean m'être promené en Pologne.
'I told Jean that I had travelled in Poland.'

It is possible that a distinct deletion rule is operating here.

The verb habituer in Appendix sample (1a) is also exceptional in that

x habituer y à P

does not necessarily involve

y bring about P

Elle habitue son mari à ce que son amant leur rende visite tous les soirs.

and yet y is the possible controller:

Elle habitue son mari à recevoir son amant tous les soirs.

Perhaps Form 2 of the principle is at work here, since the meaning of habituer implies that its object y was not ready to accept P spontaneously.

13. Suggérer has similar properties; but both suggérer and proposer can be used with a derived meaning close to that of

conseiller; this derived meaning precludes the use of x + y as a controller, as predicted by (C).

14. Sentences like (57) are examples of the split controller phenomena; strictly speaking, principle (C) will work here if x is interpreted either as one of the referential arguments or a Boolean combination of them.

15. Other conditions might be:

(i) x believes [y prefer $Q \wedge \sim P$ to $\sim Q \wedge P$]
(ii) x believe [y believe $\Diamond$ [x bring about P]]

16. Quite generally, if

x V y P

is passivized to:

y être V par x P

x can no longer serve as a controller:

(i) *Jean a été prié par moi de l'accompagner.
'I was asked by me to accompany him.'
(ii) *Le patron a été supplié par Marie d'être reprise.
'The boss was begged by Mary to be taken back.'
(iii) *Le traître a été pardonné par moi d'avoir passé ma vie en prison.
'The traitor was pardoned by me for having passed my life in prison.'
(iv) *Pierre a été menacé par Paul de le battre.
'Peter$_i$ was threatened by Paul with hitting him$_i$.'

SUBJECT-RAISING AND EXTRAPOSITION

NICOLAS RUWET

Université de Paris VIII (Vincennes)

'Let my subjects rise,
wherever they come from.'
Nobunaga, Instructions to the daimyo
n 10-27-32; Month of the Bear, 1570

1. I would like to deal here with the question of how the rule of 'Subject raising into subject position' (henceforward SRS) should be stated; this is the rule which derives sentences such as (1a), (2a), from underlying structures which are similar, maybe identical, to those which underlie (1b), (2b):

(1a) Hideyoshi seems to have succeeded in making the cuckoo sing
(1b) it seems that Hideyoshi succeeded in making the cuckoo sing
(2a) Hideyoshi semble avoir réussi à faire chanter le coucou
(2b) il semble que Hideyoshi a réussi à faire chanter le coucou

I will limit myself to the discussion of French examples, though most of what I will have to say is probably relevant to English syntax as well.

The existence of an SRS rule seems to be uncontroversial.[1] However, disagreement comes in as soon as one tries to state it in a precise way. Leaving aside a number of details which, for my present purpose, may be considered irrelevant,[2] one can basically discern three main proposals which have been made in the literature of transformational grammar:

(i) The 'standard' solution, which is that of Rosenbaum (1967). A verb like seem (or sembler) has a sentential subject in the underlying structure; this complement sentence is subjected to the rule of extraposition (henceforward EXTRAP) which gives sentences like (1b), (2b); then SRS applies to the output of EXTRAP and, by means of a right-to-left movement, substitutes the subject NP of the complement sentence for the main subject, which is either an 'impersonal' pronoun (it) or a dummy element (delta), which has been left behind by the application of EXTRAP.

(ii) The solution which is probably the most commonly accepted and which has been adopted by the proponents of generative semantics; it goes back to relatively early researches by Ross and Lakoff and has recently been expounded in detail in Postal (1974). These linguists agree with the standard analysis in attributing to seem a deep structure sentential subject. However, they diverge from it in that they consider EXTRAP and SRS as two unrelated processes, the second of which is in no way dependent on the first. SRS applies directly to the deep structure configuration and can be conceived of as being composed of two parts: the first substitutes the complement subject for the main subject, and the second attaches the remainder of the complement sentence to the right of the main VP. Thus, assuming that the proposed deep structure of (1) is:

(3) $[_{NP}[_{S}$Hideyoshi succeed in making the cuckoo sing]] seems

according to (i), (1a) will be generated by successively applying EXTRAP (which gives (1b)) and SRS; according to (ii), (1a) and (1b) will be generated independently, (1a) by directly applying SRS to (3), and (1b) by applying EXTRAP to (3).

(iii) The third solution basically differs from the first two in that it gives a different deep structure to sentences in which verbs like seem occur; for the linguists who adopt it (Kajita 1966; Gross 1968; Emonds 1969a, 1972; Ruwet 1972; Bresnan 1972) a deep structure such as (3) has no justification, and the deep structure in which verbs such as seem (or sembler in French) enter is basically the same as the surface structure of (1b), (2b). The question of how EXTRAP and SRS should be related does not arise, the complement sentence of seem (sembler) being from the start in 'extraposed' position. SRS can then be defined (as in (i)) as a rule which moves a complement subject from right to left and substitutes it for an empty main subject; in order to get (1a), the rule, which has essentially the form (5), starts from (4):

(4) $[_{NP}\triangle]$--seems--$[_{S}$Hideyoshi succeed in making the cuckoo sing]

(5) $[_{NP}\ \Delta\ ] - V - [_S\ NP - \underline{X] - Y} \Rightarrow 3 - 2 - \emptyset - 4$

Though the choice between these three alternatives might seem at first sight to be of very limited interest, it soon becomes obvious that this choice entails important consequences from the point of view of general linguistic theory.

First, depending on the solution one chooses, one will be led to adopt different views as to the relation between syntax and semantics, especially as to whether an autonomous level of syntactic deep structure plays a significant role in such a relation. It is clear that compared to (i) and (ii), solution (iii) leads to a view of the deep structure which is at the same time less abstract (that is, less far removed from the surface) and more varied (insofar as it allows frames such as Δ V S X--see (4)--besides $[_{NP}$ S]V X). Accordingly, if one adopts (iii), one's view of the interrelation between the syntactic structure and the logico-semantic representation is likely to be less straightforward than if one chooses solutions (i) or (ii). In another sense, solution (iii) can be considered more abstract than the other two, insofar as it allows the presence at the deep structure level of empty terminal symbols (delta elements) which lack any natural semantic or referential counterparts.

Second, according to one's chosen solution, one will be led to raise different questions as to the nature of the rules permitted by the theory and the character of the constraints to which these rules are subject. Solutions (i) and (iii) are still compatible with the standard definition of transformations as rules which analyze a terminal string in terms of a sequence of categories and variables. It is much less clear whether solution (ii) is. In fact, it is not so in the informal presentation of SRS I have given in terms of solution (ii); substituting a subordinate NP to the main NP of which it is a part cannot be represented as an operation that analyzes a string into a sequence of categories and variables. As a matter of fact, Postal and Perlmutter have recently proposed[3] a new class of rules (the so-called 'promotion rules'), of which this version of SRS would be a typical example and which, making crucial use of the notion of grammatical function, cannot any longer be considered transformations in the standard sense of the word. What is more interesting is that according to Postal and Perlmutter the promotion rules would be subject to a general principle (the 'Functional Succession Principle', henceforward FSP) which puts severe constraints on their form and application.[4] If this principle should reveal itself to be well-founded, it would represent an important step toward establishing a general theory of language which would constrain the form of grammars. For this principle to be valid, it is apparently essential that SRS be stated in a way close to that sketched in (ii). Should one succeed in showing that one of the other solutions--in particular solution (iii)--is to be preferred for empirical reasons, one would have produced a crucial counterexample to Postal's and Perlmutter's theory, leading to its rejection or radical modification.

Finally, any solution to the problem raised must bring one to a close examination of the relations between SRS and EXTRAP and of the status of the latter rule. Several theories of EXTRAP have been proposed. In particular, Emonds (1972) has presented a theory according to which EXTRAP in the standard form given by Rosenbaum (1967) does not exist. According to Emonds, complement sentences are never NPs; they never occur in NP positions in deep structure; they are only generated at the right side of various phrases, for instance, at the right side of verb phrases, as in (4). Deep structures such as (3) are excluded in principle, and the occurrence of complement sentences or verb phrases in subject position in surface structure (as in que Bashō ait pu faire cela me déplaît) are due to the application of a rule of 'Intraposition' which in some respects is a sort of inverse of EXTRAP. Within Emonds' theoretical framework (see Emonds 1969a), this rule is a 'root transformation' and its application is subject to very strict limitations. It goes without saying that for Emonds the only way of stating SRS is as in (iii).

I will try to show here that in French and for at least some of the verbs which allow SRS, the only possible solution is solution (iii). In other words, if one considers the two possible deep structure frames:

(6) $[_{NP}S]$ V X

(7) $[_{NP}\triangle]$ V S X

one can construct a number of empirical arguments which justify positing the deep structure (7) alongside of (6).[5] Concretely, this will amount to showing that the various predicates which can occur at the surface level in the frame il . . . que S[6] fall into two groups whose syntactic behaviors strikingly differ in several respects. These differences can be explained most naturally if one posits that the first group (8) enters into deep structures of type (6), while the second group (9) enters into deep structures of type (7) (the predicates in list (9a) optionally allow SRS, while those of (9b) do not allow SRS at all):[7]

(8) advenir (à NP), convenir (à NP), plaire à NP, déplaire à NP, répugner (à) NP, être probable, être évident, être intéressant, être difficile (à NP), être possible (à NP), être convenable, etc.

(9a) sembler (à NP), paraître (à NP), s'avérer, se révéler, se trouver, etc.
(9b) falloir (à NP), s'agir de NP, souvenir de NP à NP,[8] être question, être temps, se faire, etc.

If one can show that nothing justifies positing deep structure (6) for the verbs of (9a), it follows that solution (iii) for SRS is the only possible one. This, in turn, casts doubts on Postal's and Perlmutter's claim as to the validity of FSP. If, on the other hand, deep structure (6) turns out to be justified for the predicates in list (8), it also follows that Emonds' theory of 'intraposition' is to be abandoned. A question I will leave aside is whether there exist, besides the verbs in (9a), predicates which allow SRS while also occurring in deep structures of type (6). While there exist such predicates in English (likely, certain), the facts are much less clear in French. Granting their existence, and given that solution (iii) is the only possible one for the predicates of (9a), the most natural way to account for their behavior would be to have recourse to solution (i), with SRS, stated as in (5), applying on the output of EXTRAP.[9]

2. Let us now review the arguments in favor of solution (iii). Some of them have been known for quite a while, and it is interesting that they have not been taken seriously by the majority of transformational grammarians. I briefly return to this point in section 4.

2.1 As everybody has noticed (see, for English, Kajita 1966, Rosenbaum 1967; for French, Gross 1968), the verbs in (9) as opposed to those in (8) never allow a sentential subject in surface structure. Compare (10)-(11) to (12)-(13):

(10a) que Murasaki porte ce kimono me plairait beaucoup
(10b) il me plairait beaucoup que Murasaki porte ce kimono

(11a) que Saigō ait pu commettre une telle erreur est bizarre
(11b) il est bizarre que Saigō ait pu commettre une telle erreur

(12a) *que Sakamoto soit très intelligent (me) semble[10]
(12b) il (me) semble que Sakamoto est très intelligent

(13a) *que Nobunaga ait brûlé le temple s'avère
(13b) il s'avère que Nobunaga a brûlé le temple.

If this were an isolated fact, one would not be in a position to choose between the various solutions. One could either: (a) enter all the predicates of (8)-(9) in a deep structure of type (6) and mark sembler, etc., by means of a rule feature, as obligatorily undergoing

EXTRAP--then solutions (i) or (ii) are still possible; (b) along Emonds' lines, enter all the predicates of (8)-(9) in the deep structure (7) and mark *sembler*, etc., also by means of a rule feature, as obligatorily blocking 'Intraposition'; or (c) differentiate the predicates of (8) and (9) at the deep structure level by attributing to them, respectively, the strict subcategorization features [+S___] and [+Δ___S]. Up to now, these various solutions are strictly equivalent and equally ad hoc.[11]

2.2 In French, though I think this is not so in English, there exists another type of facts, concerning at least *sembler* and *paraître*, from which it is possible to draw a more interesting argument. It is a general fact that, whenever an 'extraposed' sentence has been reduced by EQUI or the deletion of an indefinite subject, the resulting infinitival VP is obligatorily preceded by the complementizer *de*.[12] To my knowledge, there are no exceptions to that rule in the case of the predicates of list (8); see for instance:

(14a) que Bernard apprenne à jouer du shô me plaît
(14b) il me plaît que Bernard apprenne à jouer du shô
(14c) apprendre à jouer du hichiriki me plairait
(14d) il me plairait $\left\{\begin{matrix}*\emptyset \\ \text{d'}\end{matrix}\right\}$ apprendre à jouer du hichiriki

(15a) que Kiyomori ait trahi les Heike est impossible
(15b) il est impossible que Kiyomori ait trahi les Heike
(15c) trahir les Heike est impossible
(15d) il est impossible $\left\{\begin{matrix}*\emptyset \\ \text{de}\end{matrix}\right\}$ trahir les Heike

(16a) lire Saikaku dans le texte (m') est difficile
(16b) il (m') est difficile $\left\{\begin{matrix}*\emptyset \\ \text{de}\end{matrix}\right\}$ lire Saikaku dans le texte

On the other hand, in the clear cases when the complement sentence has been generated to the right of the verb in deep structure (in 'direct object' position), the facts are more complex. If the complement subject has been deleted, the complementizer is sometimes *de*, obligatorily, as in the 'extraposed' case, sometimes, obligatorily, Ø, and sometimes there is a choice between *de* and Ø; see for instance:[13]

(17a) Onatsu craint que Seijuro l'abandonne
(17b) Onatsu craint $\left\{\begin{matrix}\text{d'} \\ *\emptyset\end{matrix}\right\}$ être abandonnée par Seijuro

(18a) Oharu regrette que ses parents l'aient vendue comme concubine à un grand seigneur
(18b) Oharu regrette {d' / *∅} avoir été vendue comme concubine à un grand seigneur

(19a) les filles de Yoshiwara adorent que Yonosuke leur caresse les seins
(19b) les filles de Yoshiwara adorent {de / ∅} se faire caresser les seins par Yonosuke

(20a) Junichiro veut que Katsuko aille en pélerinage à Ise
(20b) Junichiro veut {*d' / ∅} aller en pélerinage à Ise

(21a) Katsu croit que Sakamoto a compris ses intentions
(21b) Sakamoto croit {*d' / ∅} avoir compris les intentions de Katsu

(22a) Hideyoshi estime que Konishi mérite une récompense
(22b) Konishi estime {*de / ∅} mériter une récompense

The point is that, in French, verbs such as *sembler* and *paraître* allow EQUI to apply, under certain conditions, the controller being the main indirect object.[14] Thus we have, besides (23) (in which, in (23b), we have a case of SRS), cases like (24) where, in the (24b) case, it is clear that EQUI has applied:

(23a) il me semble qu'Oshichi s'est évanouie
(23b) Oshichi me semble s'être évanouie

(24a) il me semble que je me suis évanoui
(24b) il me semble {*de / ∅} m'être évanoui

Thus, from the point of view of the choice of the complementizer, *sembler* (and *paraître*) do not behave like the predicates of list (8), but rather like *vouloir*, *croire*, *estimer*, etc. This is an argument against theories (i) and (ii) which would derive the sentences in which *sembler* occurs by means of EXTRAP, insofar as these theories would have to treat *sembler* as exceptional not only with respect to EXTRAP but also with respect to the insertion (or deletion) of the complementizer *de*--these two facts being unrelated.

If, on the contrary, the complement sentence of sembler is generated directly to the right of the verb in deep structure, the absence of the complementizer de ceases to be exceptional.[15]

2.3 (Kajita 1966, Ruwet 1972). Generally, predicates which allow complement sentences in subject position also allow ordinary NPs in the same position. However, such NPs are totally excluded as subjects of sembler, etc. Compare (25)-(26) to (27)-(28):

(25) { que Shoshichi joue de la flûte / le visage de Mikasa / sa jeune servante } plaisait beaucoup à Yonosuke

(26a) il est évident que Sōseki était génial
(26b) le génie de Sōseki est évident

(27a) il (me) semble que Sōseki est génial
(27b) *le génie de Sōseki me semble

(28a) il s'est avéré que Hiroshima avait été totalement détruite par la bombe
(28b) *la destruction totale de Hiroshima par la bombe s'est avérée

Notice that only an analysis which distinguishes plaire, etc., on the one hand, from sembler etc., on the other hand, at the level of deep structure, by attributing to them different strict subcategorization features, (6) and (7) respectively, allows one to treat the properties (2.1)-(2.3) in a unified and non-ad hoc way. Rosenbaum's analysis, as well as Postal's and Perlmutter's or Emonds', are forced to deal with these facts as if they were unrelated. The proponents of solutions (i) and (ii) would have to impose a special constraint (independent of the constraint on the obligatory character of EXTRAP) on the subject of sembler etc., providing that 'ordinary' NPs are excluded. As for Emonds, he would have to say that plaire, probable, etc., can occur in two distinct frames, that of (7), on the one hand, and NP ___, on the other hand; while it is possible to treat this by means of a redundancy rule, sembler, etc. would then have to be treated as exceptions to this redundancy rule, just as they are to be treated as exceptions to 'Intraposition'.

We now turn to a series of arguments which all have the same structure: (2.4)-(2.10). In each case, the complement sentence has been replaced by a pronoun, whether personal, demonstrative, relative, or interrogative; in each case, the predicates of (8) and those of (9) pattern in a different way: in the case of (8), the pronouns substituted for the complement sentence are subject pronouns;

on the contrary, in the case of (9), the pronouns are object pronouns, while the dummy subject il is still present. This suggests that, while keeping (6) as an appropriate deep structure frame for the predicates of (8), we should modify (7) as in (29):[16]

(29) $[_{NP}\Delta]$ V $[_{NP}$ S] X

An important point to notice is that the dummy subject il (impersonal pronoun) never has a referential property; whenever a referential subject pronoun (which is coreferential with a sentence) is needed, ce (c'), cela or ça shows up instead of il--which differs in this respect from the homonymous regular masculine third person pronoun.[17] Compare (30) with (31):

(30) où est Shigeyuki ?
  (a) il est à San Diego
  (b) *c'est à San Diego

(31) est-il étrange que Mishima ait fait harakiri ?
  (a) *non, il n'est pas étrange
  (b) non, ce n'est pas étrange
  (c) non, cela n'est pas étrange
  (d) oui, c'est étrange

2.4 Consider first the so-called 'cataphoric' pronouns.[18] We have the following paradigm:

(32a) ceci est probable: la flotte US coulera le Yamato
(32b) *il est probable ceci: la flotte US coulera le Yamato

(33a) *ceci me semble: le général Tojo est paranoïaque
(33b) il me semble ceci: le général Tojo est paranoïaque[19]

Given proposal (i) or (ii) and granting the necessary constraints on EXTRAP (see (2.1)) and ordinary subject NPs (see (2.3)), one would expect (32a) to be grammatical and (33a) to be ungrammatical. Given also the standard treatment of EXTRAP, which optionally moves a bare S, one would also expect (32b) to be ungrammatical. The problem, however, is how to generate (33b). This sentence would have no source, unless one is ready to introduce two different extraposition rules, the standard one to deal with probable, plaire, etc., and a new one, which would obligatorily extrapose the whole NP, to deal with sembler, etc.; I will come back later to this proposal.

2.5 We have similar facts with anaphoric pronouns (facts (2.4) and (2.5) have been noted in Gross 1968); thus:[20]

(34) est-ce qu'il est possible de visiter le Palais Impérial?
(a) oui, c'est possible
(b) *oui, il (l') est possible
(c) *oui, il en est possible

(35) est-ce qu'il te semble qu'Okubo est intelligent?
(a) *oui, cela (ça) me semble
(b) Oui, il me le semble

With respect to facts (2.4) and (2.5), sembler and paraître[21] behave exactly like the verbs which take regular object sentential complements, such as croire (see (36)-(37)):

(36) je crois ceci: Mishima est devenu subitement fou
(37) est-ce que tu crois que Genji vaincra Heike?
oui, je le crois

Under certain conditions (see Cornulier 1973) the clitic object le of sembler can be missing; but, here again, sembler patterns like croire:

(38) est-ce que Gengobei est amoureux?
(a) oui, il me semble
(b) oui, je crois

2.6 The situation is similar when the predicates of (8) or (9) occur within parentheticals. Thus (39) contrasts with both (40) and (41):

(39a) la conquête de la Corée, c'est évident, sera longue et difficile
(39b) *la conquête de la Corée, il est évident, sera longue et difficile

(40a) *la conquête de la Corée, ça me semble,[22] sera longue et difficile
(40b) la conquête de la Corée, il me semble, sera longue et difficile

(41) la conquête de la Corée, je crois, sera longue et difficile

Here, as in (38), the clitic object of sembler or croire has been deleted; it can, however, be present, as in:

(42) la guerre, du moins il me le semble, va durer longtemps
(43) la guerre, du moins je le crois, va durer longtemps

Notice, by the way, that these facts raise a serious problem for any analysis (such as the one which has been proposed for English by Ross 1973) which derives sentences such as (39)-(43) from sentences such as (44)-(46) by means of a sentence-raising rule (passing through an intermediary stage in which the parenthetical is to the extreme right of the 'raised' sentence):

(44) il est évident que la conquête de la Corée sera longue et difficile
(45) il me semble que la conquête de la Corée sera longue et difficile
(46) je crois que la conquête de la Corée sera longue et difficile

First, this analysis would predict that (39b), rather than (39a), is grammatical. Second, it could not account for the presence of le in sentences like (42)-(43). Third, it would not account for the difference in meaning between, for instance, (43) and (47):

(47) du moins je crois que la guerre va durer longtemps

[(47) is natural only as the continuation of a discourse, du moins 'at least' introducing a restriction with respect to the preceding part of the discourse; by contrast, (43) can stand in isolation.]

On the other hand, these facts are predicted by an analysis (such as the one suggested for English by Emonds 1974) which simply derives (39)-(43) from 'two successive independent clause S's concatenated without a coordinating conjunction, the second of which contains a proform referring back to the first' (Emonds 1974:200); under this hypothesis, the deep structures of (39), (42), (43), would be (48), (49), (50), respectively:

(48) la conquête de la Corée sera longue et difficile; PRO est évident
(49) la guerre va durer longtemps; du moins il me semble PRO
(50) la guerre va durer longtemps; du moins je crois PRO

There is no longer any problem from the semantic point of view, (49) and (50) being synonymous with (42) and (43), respectively. The fact that we get (39a) instead of (39b) follows from the nonreferential nature of the 'impersonal pronoun' il (see (31)). The presence of le in (42)-(43) will be due to the cliticization of the object pronoun in (49)-(50); its absence in (40)-(41) will be dealt with by the same proform-deletion rule which applies in (38) (as for the reduction of cela to ce or c', see Kayne 1973).

Another interesting difference between the predicates of (8) and sembler or paraître when they appear within parentheticals is the following. Sembler or paraître, like croire or dire, allows subject-clitic inversion (see again Kayne 1973) within parentheticals, while subject-clitic inversion is prohibited in the case of the predicates of (8). So (51) contrasts with (52):[23]

(51) la guerre, {me semblait-il / croyait-il / disait-il}, allait durer longtemps

(52) *la guerre, {(a) est-ce évident / (b) est-ce possible}, va durer longtemps

2.7 As far as English is concerned, it has been known for some time (see, for instance, Bresnan 1972, Emonds 1972) that the sentential complements of sentences with seem cannot be questioned or pseudoclefted, as the contrast between (53) and (54), (55) and (56) demonstrates:

(53) *what seems to you?
(54) what is obvious to you?
(55) *what seems to me is that Akechi has gone crazy
(56) what is obvious to me is that Akechi has gone crazy

In French, the facts are more interesting and more complicated. Let us first consider the case of questions.

As is well known, French has various ways of forming questions. In the simplest case, there is a still unexplained constraint which prohibits questioning an inanimate subject. So, while (57b) is a possible question, (58b) is ungrammatical:

(57a) Yonosuke a vécu dans la débauche
(57b) qui a vécu dans la débauche?

(58a) le sort du Yamato concerne Jimmu
(58b) *que concerne Jimmu?

It is thus impossible to form simple questions using predicates of the list (8) (see (59)-(60)) and one has to use questions such as (61)-(62):

(59) *que te plairait?
(60) *qu'est étrange?
(61) qu'est-ce qui te plairait?
(62) qu'est-ce qui est étrange?

There is no such constraint when the direct object is questioned, and we get sentences such as:

(63) que crois-tu?
(64) que te donnera-t-il?

The interesting fact is that we get sentences such as (65)-(66) which parallel in a striking way (63)-(64), while sentences such as (67)-(68) are completely excluded:

(65) que te semble-t-il?[24]
(66) que s'est-il avéré?
(67) *que te plairait-il? (compare with (59)-(61))
(68) *qu'est-il étrange? (compare with (60)-(62))

This is once more a case where the complement sentence of <u>sembler</u> etc. patterns like a direct object,[25] while that of <u>plaire</u>, <u>étrange</u> etc. patterns like a subject.

When we come to the 'complex' kind of question, exemplified by (61)-(62), the facts are somewhat blurred for a phonetic reason: <u>qui</u> and <u>qu'il</u> (before consonant) are both pronounced [ki] in standard spoken French. So while there is a clear contrast between (62), repeated here as (69), and (70), which confirms the subject nature of the sentential complement of <u>être étrange</u>,

(69) qu'est-ce qui est étrange?
(70) *qu'est-ce qu'il est étrange?

native speakers accept sentences such as:

(71) qu'est-ce [ki] te semble?

where it is not immediately clear whether (72) or (73) is involved:

(72) qu'est-ce qui te semble?
(73) qu'est-ce qu'il te semble?

If we build sentences such as (74)-(75), however:

(74) qu'est-ce qu'il avait semblé à Go-Daigo?
(75) ?*qu'est-ce qui avait semblé à Go-Daigo?

it is clear that (74) is far better than (75).[26] Moreover, the [l] can be optionally pronounced in (73). I take this to indicate that the interrogative pronoun corresponding to the complement sentence of sembler, here as in (65), is a direct object and not a subject. The fact that for some speakers (75) does not sound as bad as one would expect is probably due to some performance factor, owing to the confusing nature of the phonetic facts.

2.8 The facts are similar in pseudocleft sentences.[27] While there is a clear difference between (76a) and (76b):

(76a) ce qui est probable, c'est que les Minamoto battront les Taira
(76b) *ce qu'il est probable, c'est que les Minamoto battront les Taira,

both (77a) and (77b) would normally be pronounced as in (77c):

(77a) ce qui me semble, c'est que les Minamoto battront les Taira
(77b) ce qu'il me semble, c'est que les Minamoto battront les Taira
(77c) ce [ki] me semble, c'est que les Minamoto battront les Taira

But, once again, an [l] can be optionally pronounced, which indicates that we have a case of (77b) rather than (77a). Moreover, there is a clear difference in acceptability between (78a) and (78b):[28]

(78a) ?*ce qui avait semblé à Go-Daigo, c'est que Takauji le trahissait
(78b) ce qu'il avait semblé à Go-Daigo, c'est que Takauji le trahissait

2.9 There exists in French a type of 'concessive' construction which is exemplified by:

(79) { qui que tu sois / où que tu ailles / quoi que tu fasses }, la vengeance des dieux te poursuivra toujours

This type of sentence is probably derived, by means of WH-MOVEMENT, from underlying structures such as:

(80) { que tu sois qui / que tu ailles où / que fasses quoi } , la vengeance des dieux te poursuivra toujours

Cf. sentences such as:[29]

(81) { que tu sois l'empereur ou le shōgun / que tu ailles à Ise ou à Shimonoseki / que tu fasses des offrandes ou des pénitences }, la vengeance . . .

This construction is subject to a number of constraints, one of which is the following: if the WH-word is a subject, it cannot be extracted,[30] cf.:

(82a) que Heike ou Genji gagne la bataille, l'empereur sera perdu
(82b) *qui { qui / que } gagne la bataille, l'empereur sera perdu

(83a) que tes prières ou tes offrandes plaisent aux dieux, tu n'en seras pas moins damné
(83b) *quoi { qui / que } plaise aux dieux, tu n'en seras pas moins damné

(84a) que la victoire des Heike ou celle des Gengi soit imminente, l'empereur sera perdu
(84b) *quoi { qui / que } soit imminent, l'empereur sera perdu

This constraint manifests itself strikingly in the case of constructions which have been subjected to the rule of 'Indefinite NP-Extraposition' (see Ruwet 1972:21; also Kayne 1975). Given that there are sentences such as:

(85a) des choses étranges sont arrivées pendant la fête à Gion
(85b) il est arrivé des choses étranges pendant la fête à Gion

we have the contrast:

(86a) *quoi qui arrive pendant la fête à Gion, Yonosuke respectera toujours les geisha
(86b) quoi qu'il arrive pendant la fête à Gion, Yonosuke respectera toujours les geisha

Now, sentences like (87) are acceptable:

(87) quoi [ki] te semble, le shōgun respecte profondément l'empereur

which, given the unacceptability of (83b)-(84b), seems to indicate that (87) really corresponds to (88a) rather than (88b):

(88a) quoi qu'il te semble, le shōgun respecte profondément l'empereur
(88b) *quoi qui te semble, le shōgun respecte profondément l'empereur

Once again, as contrasted with the complement sentences of plaire, probable, etc., those of sembler behave like direct objects (or predicate complements) (see (79)).

2.10 The so-called 'presentative' element voilà (also voici) occurs in a variety of constructions, some of which it has in common with the verb voir, from which it derives diachronically.[31] These are mainly the following: (a) voilà + NP (see (89)); (b) voilà + que S (see (90)); (c) voilà + NP + 'pseudo-relative clause' (see (91)); (c) voilà + indirect question (see (92)):

(89a) voilà Bōtchan
(89b) me voilà
(89c) voilà quelque chose à quoi tu ne t'attendais pas

(90a) voilà que subitement la Honda tombe en panne
(90b) voilà que les cerisiers fleurissent à Katsura

(91a) voilà la Honda qui tombe en panne
(91b) voilà Nobunaga qui incendie les temples
(91c) le voilà qui arrive

(92a) voilà quelles sont le décisions de Shōtoku Taishi
(92b) voilà comment (tu peux) séduire les femmes de Yoshiwara
(92c) voilà pourquoi nous ne boirons plus jamais l'eau de Kiyomizudera

Voilà also occurs in a special construction, which it is important not to confuse with those of (89)-(92). This construction is composed of voilà plus a headless relative clause, it is restricted to the 'style élevé', and it normally occurs in special discourse conditions. For instance, to sentence (93), uttered by speaker A,

(93) la guerre va se prolonger,

speaker B can add the comment:

(94) voilà qui {me déçoit terriblement / est insupportable / ne plaira à personne}

(This can be roughly paraphrased by: 'Haha! This is terribly disappointing,' etc.)

This construction is subject to the following constraint (which is almost the reverse of the one considered in (2.9): if the WH-word corresponds to a direct object, the construction is ungrammatical; see, for instance:

(95a) *voilà que je ne peux pas croire
(95b) *voilà que je n'aurais pas prévu

If the complement sentence of <u>sembler</u> were a subject, one would expect <u>sembler</u> to occur in that type of construction; on the other hand, if the complement sentence is a direct object (or a predicate), one would not expect <u>sembler</u> to occur in such a construction. As a matter of fact, there is no way to get sentences involving <u>sembler</u> here; neither (96a) nor (96b) is a possible comment on (93):

(96a) *voilà qui me semble
(96b) *voilà qu'il me semble

This follows from our analysis: (96a) is excluded because <u>sembler</u> does not take a sentential subject, and (96b) is excluded by the constraint, peculiar to the construction involving <u>voilà</u>, which we have just mentioned.

Until now, I have concentrated on the differences in the behavior of the predicates of (9a) and (8). To illustrate these differences, I have mainly used <u>sembler</u>, for which the facts are the clearest. I will now give a few examples to show that the same differences can be found in the case of the predicates of (9b)--which differ from those of (9a) in that they do not allow SRS. Take <u>falloir</u>, for instance; we have the following facts:

(97a) il faut que tu partes
(97b) *que tu partes faut (cf. (2.1))
(97c) il faut (*de) partir (cf. 2.2))
(97d) *notre départ faut (cf. (2.3))
(97e) il me faut {ceci, de l'argent, cette femme} (cf. (2.4))[32]

(97f) il le faut, que tu partes (cf. (2.5))
(97g) que (te) faut-il? (cf. (2.7))
(97h) ce qu'il aurait fallu à Go-Daigo, c'est un général fidèle (cf. (2.8))

Another example is souvenir;[33] we get, for instance:

(98a) il me souvient des cerisiers en fleur de Kyoto
(98b) *les cerisiers en fleur de Kyoto me souviennent (cf. (2.3))
(98c) il m'en souvient (cf. (2.5))
(98d) un soir, t'en souvient-il, nous voguions en silence (cf. (2.7))
(98e) ce dont je me souviens, c'est des cerisiers en fleur de Kyoto (cf. (2.8))

Consider also il est temps . . .:

(99a) il est temps {que tu partes / de partir}
(99b) * {que tu partes / partir} est temps (cf. (2.1))
(99c) il en est temps, de partir[34] (cf. (2.5))

2.11 I will now present a different type of argument. It is based on the existence in French of a construction which is exemplified by (100b), (101b):

(100a) je trouve que le Nō est merveilleux
(100b) je trouve le Nō (*être) merveilleux

(101a) je croyais que Nobunaga était plus magnanime
(101b) je croyais Nobunaga (*être) plus magnanime

Sentences such as (100b), (101b) have generally been derived from deep structures similar to those of (100a), (101a) by means of a rule of 'Subject raising into object position' (henceforward SRO; in French 'Formation d'Objet'; see Gross 1968, Ruwet 1972, Fauconnier 1974; also, for a different view, Kayne 1973).[35] It is well known that SRO can only apply if the main verb of the complement sentence is être, this être being subsequently deleted (which is different from the case of SRS, see Ruwet 1972:222).

Now consider the following sentences:

(102a) je crois qu'il est nécessaire de partir
(102b) je crois nécessaire de partir

(103a) Mizoguchi trouve qu'il est étrange que Tanaka se maquille si outrageusement
(103b) Mizoguchi trouve étrange que Tanaka se maquille si outrageusement

(104a) Michiko estime qu'il est convenable de procéder à la cérémonie du thé
(104b) Michiko estime convenable de procéder à la cérémonie du thé

(105a) je crois qu'il est temps de partir
(105b) *je crois temps de partir

(106a) je crois que Takauji est foutu de trahir Go-Daigo
(106b) je crois Takauji foutu de trahir Go-Daigo

(107a) je crois qu'il est foutu de pleuvoir sur le mont Fuji
(107b) *je crois foutu de pleuvoir sur le mont Fuji

(108a) je crois que Perry est sur le point de bombarder Edo
(108b) je crois Perry sur le point de bombarder Edo

(109a) je crois qu'il est sur le point de neiger sur Nara
(109b) *je crois sur le point de neiger sur Nara

(110a) Nakaoka jugeait que Sakamoto était trop subtil pour tomber dans ce guet-apens
(110b) Nakaoka jugeait Sakamoto trop subtil pour tomber dans ce guet-apens

(111a) Takamitsu a jugé qu'il était trop tard pour visiter le Todaiji
(111b) *Takamitsu a jugé trop tard pour visiter le Todaiji[36]

The distribution of the facts follows from two assumptions: (a) the hypothesis we have made that the predicates of (8) (see nécessaire, étrange, convenable in (102)-(104)) enter into the deep structure (6), while those of (9) (see être temps in (105), être (trop) tard in (111)) enter into the deep structure (7) or (29); (b) the assumption that there is a constraint on 'Subject-raising into object position' which prohibits raising an empty or nonreferential NP into object position.[37] Let us call this the Empty Subject Constraint (ESC). Given that

EXTRAP is optional,[38] sentences such as (102)-(104) may still have a complement sentence in subject position (within the object sentence) by the time SRO applies; thus for (102) the structure at that stage may still be (112) and for (103), (113):

(112) je crois [$_{S}$[$_{NP}$[$_{S}$partir]] être nécessaire]

(113) Mizoguchi trouve [$_{S}$[$_{NP}$[$_{S}$Tanaka se maquille si outrageusement]] être étrange]

The complement subject being nonempty, ESC will not block SRO, which will be free to apply, giving:

(114) je crois [$_{NP}$[$_{S}$partir]][$_{S}$être nécessaire]

(115) Mizoguchi trouve [$_{NP}$[$_{S}$Tanaka se maquille outrageusement]] [$_{S}$être étrange]

Être-deletion and (in the case of (115)) *que*-insertion will convert (114) and (115), respectively, into (116) and (117):[39]

(116) ?je crois partir nécessaire
(117) *Mizoguchi trouve que Tanaka se maquille outrageusement étrange

Now EXTRAP can still apply[40] and convert (116), (117) into (102), (103) (with *de*-insertion applying in the case of (116)-(102)).

On the other hand, sentences such as (105), (111) will have the following deep structures:

(118) je crois [$_{S}$[$_{NP}$ Δ]être temps de partir] (for (105))

(119) Takamitsu a jugé [$_{S}$[$_{NP}$$\Delta$] être trop tard pour visiter le Todaiji] (for (111))

Since the complement subject is empty, ESC will block the derivation of (105b), (111b).

Sentences (106)-(109) require a word of explanation. *Foutu* (see Gouet 1971) and *sur le point* are among the few adjectival or adverbial predicates which allow (and even require) SRS to apply, as the behavior of the clitic *en* shows (see Ruwet 1972:ch. 2):

(120a) la construction du temple est {foutue / sur le point} d'être interrompue

(120b) la construction est {foutue / sur le point} d'en être interrompue

SRS must obligatorily apply, as (121) shows; on the other hand, there is no reason to believe that the complement sentence has ever been in subject position, cf. (122)-(123):

(121) *il est {foutu / sur le point} que la construction du temple soit interrompue

(122) *que la construction du temple soit interrompue est {foutu / sur le point}

(123) *l'abdication de l'empereur est {foutue[41] / sur le point}

Now sentences such as (106), (107) will have the following deep structures, respectively:

(124) je crois $[_S[_{NP}\Delta]$ être foutu $[_S$Takauji trahir Go-Daigo]]

(125) je crois $[_S[_{NP}\Delta]$ être foutu $[_S[_{NP}\Delta]$ pleuvoir sur le mont Fuji]]

SRS (which is not subject to ESC), will apply on the second cycle, replacing the dummy subject, in (124) by Takauji, and in (125) by the embedded dummy subject of pleuvoir, giving, respectively:

(126) je crois $[_S[_{NP}$Takauji] être foutu $[_S$trahir Go-Daigo]]

(127) je crois $[_S[_{NP}\Delta]$ être foutu $[_S$pleuvoir sur le mont Fuji]]

Now the situation is similar to that we had before in the case of (102)-(104) (or (100)-(101)) vs. (105)-(111). Either SRO does not apply, and que-insertion (plus il-insertion in the case of (127)) will give (106a), (107a), or SRO will apply normally in the case of (126), while being blocked by ESC in the case of (127).

Let us now try to see how these facts could be dealt with if one had chosen either Rosenbaum's solution (solution (i)), Postal's and Perlmutter's (solution (ii)) or Emonds'. For Rosenbaum, given that in his framework EXTRAP must be cyclical, the only problem would reside in the ad hoc nature of the deep structures he might postulate (such as (99b) or (122))[42] and in the equally ad hoc rule feature on être temps, être foutu, etc., which would mark them as obligatorily undergoing EXTRAP; but by the time SRO would apply, the required difference between (102)-(104) and (105)-(111) would be at hand. For Postal and Perlmutter, given that they claim (see Postal 1974) that EXTRAP is postcyclical, the facts would be more damaging unless they choose to derive sentences such as (99a) by other means than EXTRAP. I will leave it to them to provide a convincing alternative, noting simply that, if (99a) is derived by means of obligatory EXTRAP from something like (99b) and if EXTRAP is postcyclical, then, by the time SRO applies, there will be no way to distinguish (105) from, say, (102), and consequently, no way to use ESC in order to block (105b).

Let us consider now what Emonds could say about these facts. There are two possibilities. (i) All 'extraposed' constructions are generated as such in deep structure, with a dummy subject: in that case, there is no difference between (102)-(104) and (105)-(111) by the time SRO applies; given ESC, one would expect (102b)-(104b) to be as ungrammatical as (105b)-(111b). (ii) One reverts to Emonds' original proposal (see note 11 of this paper), according to which predicates like plaire, probable, on the one hand, sembler, etc., on the other, are differentiated at the level of deep structure. The former take 'referential' pronominal subjects while the latter take dummy subjects. This would account for the difference between (102)-(104) and (105)-(111) with respect to ESC (see note 37). However, it also raises serious problems. We have seen that the normal form of the 'referential' pronominal subject is either cela, ça, or ce (c'); so a natural source for sentences such as (128a) would be (128b), 'Intraposition' substituting the complement S for the coreferential cela:

(128a) que Tanaka se maquille si outrageusement est étrange
(128b) cela_i est étrange $\text{que Tanaka se maquille si outrageusement}_i$

Though sentences such as (129)-(130) exist:

(129) c'est étrange, que Tanaka se maquille si outrageusement
(130) {cela / ça} me plairait, que tu fasses un pélerinage au mont Hiei

they are cases of 'dislocated', not 'extraposed', sentences. So, since 'Intraposition' is optional, the question arises as to what is the source for il in sentences such as (102a)-(104a). Remember that this il differs in no way from that which appears as a surface subject of sembler, etc. Moreover, since 'Intraposition' is a 'root' transformation, it would play no role in the generation of (102)-(104). But, whenever a 'referential' pronoun is generated, if it has become an object by SRO, it normally shows up in the surface structure; see, for instance:

(131a) je trouve cela intéressant
(131b) Sakamoto, je le trouve intelligent
(131c) cette idée, je la trouve sublime

So one would expect to get, instead of (102b)-(104b), (132) or (133) for instance:

(132a) *je le crois nécessaire de partir
(132b) *je crois cela nécessaire de partir

(133a) *Mizoguchi le trouve étrange que Tanaka se maquille si outrageusement
(133b) *Mizoguchi trouve cela étrange que Tanaka se maquille si outrageusement

(Sentence (133b) must be pronounced without any intonational break between <u>étrange</u> and <u>que</u>; if there is an intonational break, we have a case of 'dislocation'; see examples (129)-(130).)

So these 'referential' pronouns, whose only use was to save sentences such as (102)-(104) from being subject to ESC, would have to be deleted by means of an ad hoc rule, while another unrelated ad hoc rule would presumably be necessary to replace them by the dummy pronoun <u>il</u> in order to account for (102a)-(104a).[43]

3. Given the arguments in section 2, it seems clear to me that we must abandon the claim that <u>sembler</u> etc. take sentential subjects in deep structure. Consequently, solution (iii) for the statement of SRS seems to be unavoidable (see section 1). This, however, raises two problems, which must be clearly distinguished from each other.

(A) We are forced to introduce dummy terminal symbols in the deep structure; accordingly, there is a discrepancy between the semantic representation of <u>sembler</u> (which is, presumably, a two-place predicate) and the syntactic frame in which it occurs in deep structure (a 'three-position' frame).
(B) Postal's and Perlmutter's FSP seems to be falsified, given that SRS now raises an NP from within an object (or predicate) complement into a subject position.

One might try to avoid these (to some people) unpleasant consequences by trying to invent a new solution which, while taking the fundamental difference between the predicates of (8) and those of (9) into account, would get rid of dummy subjects and save FSP. In this section, I will briefly discuss three such conceivable solutions, and I will try to show that all of them are inadequate, given the present state of our knowledge of French syntax.

3.1 A first alternative can be easily dismissed.[44] It is well known that verbs like sembler, s'avérer, etc., can occur in sentences such as the following:

(134a) Sei Shōnagon (me) semblait songeuse
(134b) Katsu s'est révélé fidèle et astucieux
(134c) à l'aube, quand ils s'habillent l'un l'autre, les amants paraissent tristes

Sentences such as these have generally been derived from SRS sentences (such as Sei Shōnagon (me) semblait être songeuse) by means of an optional être-deletion rule. However, to my knowledge, they could just as well be directly generated in the base, sembler, etc. being taken as simple copulative verbs with the feature +___AP (PP). Now, sentences such as (135a-b) seem to be synonymous:

(135a) il (me) semble que Katsu a vu juste
(135b) il (me) semble vrai que Katsu a vu juste

This might give one the idea of generating sentences such as (135a) in the following fashion. Sembler would be entered into the lexicon with only the feature +___AP (PP), without any special restrictions on its subject besides those imposed by the choice of the AP; so we would have deep structures such as (136):[45]

(136) $[_{NP}[_{S}$que Katsu a vu juste]]semble vrai (à moi)

Then (135b) would be derived by means of EXTRAP (which is anyway necessary), and an optional rule of VRAI-deletion would apply in the context sembler ___ S.[46] This would save one feature (+△ ___ S (PP)) in the lexical entry of sembler, and at the same time get rid of the dummy subject problem and explain why sembler never occurs intransitively with a sentential subject (see fact (2.1)) or a 'full' subject NP (see fact (2.3)).

However, this proposed solution immediately gets us into lots of trouble. First, notice that it is not clear that it would allow us to save FSP. To do this, we would have to state SRS in terms of the following structure:

(137) $[_{NP}[_{S}$ NP X]] sembler VRAI (à NP)

Given that (138a) is ungrammatical:

(138a) *Katsu semble vrai avoir vu juste
(138b) Katsu semble avoir vu juste

we would have, either to order SRS after EXTRAP and VRAI-deletion (thus reverting to statement (iii) of SRS and violating FSP) or to complicate VRAI-deletion and make it obligatory in the context /___ VP or something of the sort.

Notice anyway that, in both of its forms, VRAI-deletion is quite ad hoc. Granting that sentences like (135a-b) are synonymous,[47] one would expect such a rule to be based on some general principle of a semantic nature (stating something like the following: 'Whenever an element is semantically redundant, it can be optionally deleted'); so one would expect VRAI-deletion to apply in the context /sembler ___ without any additional condition. The fact that it is subject to special conditions of a purely syntactic nature makes the existence of such a rule very dubious and reduces its explanatory power (with respect to facts (2. 1) and (2. 3), to zero.

The important point, however, is that this analysis still fails to account for all the other facts discussed in section 2 (especially facts (2. 2) and (2. 4) through (2. 11)). Given that the complement sentence is placed by means of EXTRAP, the source of the various object pronouns (such as in il me le semble, etc.) remains to be explained. Moreover, this solution fails to apply to the predicates of (9b), such as falloir. Indeed, at least one of the verbs of list (9a), se trouver, normally never occurs in the frame ___ AP (see Gross 1968); être must be present, cf.:

(139a) il se trouve que Sei Shōnagon est songeuse
(139b) Sei Shōnagon se trouve être songeuse
(139c) *Sei Shōnagon se trouve songeuse[48]

(140a) il se trouve être vrai que Katsu est fidèle et astucieux
(140b) *il se trouve vrai que Katsu est fidèle et astucieux

This means that, at least in the case of se trouver (as well as falloir etc.), we cannot dispense with the feature $+\Delta$ ___ S. There are still other problems with this proposal (for instance, cf. fact (2. 2), the ungrammaticality of *m'être évanoui me semble vrai, *il me semble *vrai (de) m'être évanoui*), so we can safely reject it as a reasonable alternative to the solution I suggest.

3.2 A second alternative might seem more attractive at first sight. I have mentioned it briefly in Ruwet (1972:ch. 5; 197-198). It is related to Postal's (1971) proposal that verbs like *seem* (*sembler*) etc. be treated as PSYCH-MVT predicates. According to this view, a sentence like (141a) would have the deep structure (141b):

(141a) il me semble que Narihira est bien mélancolique
(141b) [$_{NP}$moi] semble [$_{NP}$[$_{S}$Narihira est bien mélancolique]]

The difference with Postal's treatment would be that, instead of permuting the subject and object NPs by means of PSYCH-MVT, one would only apply a part of PSYCH-MVT, that is, the rule which postposes the subject NP into the indirect object position; nothing would happen to the object complement. This rule of 'indirect object formation' would convert (141b) into (142) (which CLITIC-PLACEMENT and IL-insertion would finally convert into (141a):

(142) $\triangle$ semble [$_{NP}$[$_{S}$Narihira est bien mélancolique]] à moi

As can easily be seen, this proposal accounts for all the properties of the complement sentence of *sembler* which have been discussed in section 2. The question is whether it is preferable to my own solution. Notice that it is a case of the classical choice between a phrase structure and a transformational solution to a problem; there is no a priori reason to choose one over the other. There is a technical problem concerning the insertion of the preposition *à* in (142), but one may consider this a minor matter.

Inasmuch as I have dealt at length elsewhere with the difficulties involved in the PSYCH-MVT analysis in general (see Ruwet 1972: ch. 5), I will be brief. One of the main problems with the 'indirect object formation' rule is that, apart from *sembler*, *paraître*, *se souvenir*, and *falloir*, many of the verbs in list (9) lack an indirect object; sentences such as the following are ungrammatical:[49]

(143) *il s'est avéré à Katsu que l'empereur devait être restauré
(144) *il se trouve à Sei Shōnagon que l'aube est délicieuse au printemps
(145) *il est temps à Hideyori de se préparer au seppuku
(146) *il m'est question d'être adopté par le clan des Minamoto

This would force a would-be proponent of the 'indirect object formation' rule to postulate for these verbs 'abstract' underlying subjects, whose semantic status is unclear and which would be obligatorily deleted. This, to my mind, deprives this proposal of much of its plausibility.

On the other hand, if, coming to the raising cases, one wants to maintain the validity of FSP, one is once again faced with serious difficulties. If one wants to derive (147) from (141b):

(147) Narihira me semble être bien mélancolique

either (a) one applies SRS, in the way I have stated it (see (5), after 'Indirect object formation' has applied--thus violating once again FSP, or (b) one reverts to Postal's original claim (see Postal 1970b, 1971), according to which sentences such as (147) are not directly generated by means of SRS, but rather by applying SRO followed by PSYCH-MVT (or here rather by a rule of 'Object preposing'). However, I have shown (Ruwet 1972:221-222) that the raising rule involved in the <u>sembler</u> case cannot possibly be collapsed with SRO, so this solution seems to be out of the question too.

I might add that, given the general framework of Postal's and Perlmutter's theory of functional rules, if I understand them, a rule such as 'Indirect object formation' would be excluded on principle; they claim indeed that there is a hierarchy subject/direct object/indirect object and that, within this hierarchy, a NP can only be promoted (as is the case of the object becoming a subject in passive sentences) and that it can never be 'demoted' while keeping its functional status, which it seems to do in the <u>sembler</u> case.[50]

3.3 We are left with a last proposal, to which I have alluded (see section (2.4)), namely, that <u>sembler</u>, etc. have a deep structure sentential subject after all. This allows SRS to apply according to FSP and, when it does not, the whole subject NP is extraposed by an NP-extraposition rule distinct from EXTRAP (which moves a bare S).

Actually, there exists a rule in French which at first sight seems similar to the one postulated here. This is the so-called 'Indefinite NP Extraposition' (abbreviated IND-EX) which I have already mentioned (see section (2.9)). This is the rule which derives (85b) from (85a) (repeated here as (148a-b) and (149b) from (149a):[51]

(148a) des choses étranges sont arrivées pendant la fête à Gion
(148b) il est arrivé des choses étranges pendant la fête à Gion

(149a) quarante-sept rōnin sont venus à Harima
(149b) il est venu quarante-sept rōnin à Harima

It is hard to tell whether it would be possible to use IND-EX to deal with the sembler case, given that the rule is still poorly understood.[52] Keep in mind that its name is somewhat misleading; in spite of some very strict constraints, it sometimes applies to definite NPs, as for instance, when they are of the nature of a list or an enumeration (see (150)) or when they are 'cataphoric' expressions (see (151)):

(150) il est venu d'abord Tsuruko, et puis Sachiko, et puis Yukiko, et enfin Taeko

(151a) il arrivera ceci: un grand tremblement de terre ravagera la province d'Echizen
(151b) il arrivera la chose suivante: les vents divins disperseront la flotte mongole
(151c) il m'est venu l'idée suivante: Nobunaga devrait se méfier d'Iyeyasu

The facts of (151), of course, remind us of those discussed in section (2.4) (see especially note 19). In other respects too, the extraposed NP behaves like a direct object (see especially Gaatone 1970). For instance, it can be questioned (see (152) and compare with the facts in section (2.7)).[53] It can also occur in concessive constructions (see section (2.9), (86), repeated here as (153)):

(152a) qu'est-il arrivé pendant la fête à Gion?
(152b) que se passera-t-il après l'abdication de l'empereur?

(153a) *quoi qui arrive pendant la fête à Gion, Yonosuke respectera toujours les geisha
(153b) quoi qu'il arrive pendant la fête à Gion, Yonosuke respectera toujours les geisha

Moreover, some of the verbs which allow IND-EX can have a sentential complement in extraposed position, see (154)-(155):

(154) il arrive trop souvent que Yonosuke boive immodérément du saké
(155) il se passe parfois qu'un grand tremblement de terre dévaste la province de Musashi

Notice that, just as in the case of sembler, sentences like (154), (155) can be understood as answers to questions like (156), (157), respectively:

(156) qu'arrive-t-il trop souvent?
(157) que se passe-t-il parfois?

In spite of these similarities, in other respects verbs like *arriver*, etc., on the one hand, and *sembler*, etc., on the other, behave in very different ways. First, as already shown by examples (148)-(149), IND-EX is an optional rule, even when it applies to complement sentences;[54] see (158)-(159):

(158) que Yonosuke boive immodérément du saké arrive trop souvent
(159) ?qu'un grand tremblement de terre dévaste la province de Musashi pourrait bien se passer

So we cannot use this rule to explain fact (2.1). The same is true as regards fact (2.2) (the presence vs. absence of the complementizer *de* in a reduced extraposed sentence). Compare (24) with (160):

(160) il arrive à Oharu {de / *Ø} s'évanouir de plaisir

Thirdly, IND-EX never applies to a pronoun (or in general to a definite NP) if it is used anaphorically (see Gaatone 1970); so there is a sharp contrast between (35) and (161):

(161) est-ce qu'il arrive souvent que Yonosuke boive immodérément du saké?
(a) *oui, il (l') arrive souvent
(b) oui, {cela / ça} arrive souvent

Similarly, only the (b) cases are possible within dislocated sentences (see (162)) and sentences which involve parentheticals (see (163)):

(162a) *il l'arrive souvent, que Yonusuke boive immodérément du saké
(162b) ça arrive souvent, que Yonosuke boive immodérément du saké

(163a) *les femmes de Yoshiwara, il (l') arrive, se suicident parfois par amour pour un beau seigneur
(163b) les femmes de Yoshiwara, ça arrive, se suicident parfois par amour pour un beau seigneur

The case of pseudo-cleft sentences (see section (2.8)) is less clear and differs in this respect from that of questions. To me, (164b) is better than (164a):

(164a) ??ce qu'il arrive souvent, c'est que les femmes de Yoshiwara se suicident par amour pour un beau seigneur
(164b) ce qui arrive souvent, c'est que les femmes de Yoshiwara se suicident par amour pour un beau seigneur

For these various reasons, it seems to me unrealistic to use IND-EX in order to save the sentential subject analysis of sembler etc., and we are left with the solution I suggested in the first place.[55]

4. As I mentioned earlier (see beginning of section 2), it would be an interesting point to inquire why most linguists did not take solution (iii) seriously, in spite of the fact that some of the arguments in its favor had been at hand for quite a while. I see two main reasons for this. First, the earlier proponents of solution (iii) (Kajita 1966, Gross 1968) were working in a semitaxonomical semitransformational framework; they justified their analyses by referring to heuristic tests. Now, I take it that no generative linguist will ever be completely convinced by such an approach, which eschews building and comparing alternative grammars (remember the discussion in (2.1)).

Second, and more important, in spite of Chomsky's repeated warnings (in Syntactic Structures, for instance), there has been an implicit assumption at the high tide of the standard theory that there is a simple correspondence between syntactic structures and semantic representations; this is very clear in the early works of Katz, Fodor, and Postal, as well as in Rosenbaum (1967). Potential discrepancies between syntax and semantics tended to be brushed aside rather than carefully studied--thanks to the rich means provided by the formalism, such as rule features, etc.

I think I have shown that no such simple solution is available. This does not mean that the result reached is satisfactory and that there is no problem with the discrepancy between syntax and semantics which the behavior of sembler etc. exhibits--the more so as the resemblances in this respect between French and English, as well as, apparently, German, Italian, etc., can hardly be due to mere chance. The main merit of this study, as I see it, is that it has put the problem in full light: why is there such a structural difference between the predicates of (8) and those of (9)? The problem now becomes one of interpreting structures.

I will not try to solve it here. I will only make a few speculative remarks, indicating a possible line of research.

Suppose we take seriously, in spite of its present vagueness, the theory of 'thematic relations' as it is sketched in Jackendoff (1972) (see also Ruwet 1972:ch. 5). If we concentrate on the distinction between the 'theme' and the 'experiencer',[56] we note that there is no one-to-one relation between thematic functions and grammatical functions. So, given simple (direct or indirect) transitive sentences, there are at least the following possibilities:

(165a) subject = 'experiencer'; direct object = 'theme' (croire, aimer, vouloir, etc.)
(165b) subject = 'theme'; direct object = 'experiencer' (amuser, dégoûter, étonner, etc.)
(165c) subject = 'experiencer'; indirect object = 'theme' (penser, songer, rêver, etc.)
(165d) subject = 'theme'; indirect object = 'experiencer' (plaire, déplaire, être facile, etc.; many of the predicates of (8) belong here)

I have only considered two-place predicates. When one takes three-place predicates into consideration, there are at least some cases in which, while the subject has some 'causative' function, the direct object is 'theme' while the indirect object corresponds to the 'experiencer'. This is the case with verbs like inspirer, suggérer, or révéler in sentences such as:

(166) ses amours ont inspiré de beaux poèmes à Ono no Komachi
(167) personnellement, dit Yonosuke, la vue de cette jolie courtisane m'inspire des sentiments folâtres[57]
(168) la rencontre de Katsu suggère à Sakamoto qu'il a fait fausse route jusqu'à présent
(169) la lecture du Manyoshū m'a révélé tout un monde inconnu

Given that complex interplay between thematic and grammatical functions, the facts about sembler etc. become a little less puzzling. They are a case of the same type of relations as in (166)-(169): the direct object is 'theme' and the indirect object is 'experiencer'. The difference is that with sembler etc. the subject has no thematic function at all. Notice the syntactic and semantic parallelism between (170) and (171):

(170) personnellement, ceci me suggère que tu as tort
(171) personnellement, il me semble que tu as tort

Now let us imagine that we have a theory of the relations between grammatical and thematic functions. In spite of the variety involved, we know that there are some regularities (for instance, only a (deep) subject can be an 'agent'; see Ruwet 1972). We might try to relate the semantic differences which have been noticed (see Postal 1970b: 114ff.) between predicates like sembler on the one hand and croire etc. on the other (for instance, the more 'subjective' character of sembler vs. croire) to the differences they present in the relations between thematic and grammatical functions. Notice, for instance, that croire behaves in certain respects like an agentive verb while sembler is purely stative (see 172)):

(172a) Katsu a forcé Sakamoto à croire qu'il avait tort

(172b) Takauji a osé croire que l'empereur abdiquerait

(172c) {je croirais / *il me semblerait} volontiers que tu n'as rien compris

The relative freedom in the relations between grammatical and thematic relations might be conceived of as a means of conveying certain subtle semantic differences, and this might ultimately explain why predicates like sembler exist with their special syntactic properties.

Another question stays open. I have shown that Postal's and Perlmutter's FSP cannot be maintained in view of the syntactic properties of sembler, etc. This is unfortunate in a way because, had it worked, FSP would have imposed very strict constraints on the form of grammars. I would like to suggest that an alternative to FSP can be conceived along the following lines. First, Emonds' structure-preserving principle accounts for at least a part of the constraints on raising transformations. Second, we might constrain raising transformations in terms of thematic functions. Notice that it seems always to be the case that the raised element is a part of a complement sentence whose thematic function within the higher sentence is that of 'theme'. This is true for SRS as well as SRO or TOUGH-MVT.[58] We might impose the further condition that the raised element (whatever its thematic function within its own simple sentence is) can only be raised to the least thematically marked position within the higher sentence. Here again, this does not seem to raise any special problem in the SRO and TOUGH-MVT cases. In the sembler case, one can either: (a) consider a dummy element by definition as the least marked element in terms of thematic relations, or (b) if sentences of the form NP sembler AP are basic (see section 3.1), this would indicate that the subject position is that of the theme, which seems to be generally true in the case of copulative sentences. Notice that, if this worked, it would allow us to get rid of an ad hoc condition which Jackendoff must adopt in order to make his 'Thematic Hierarchy Condition' work (see Jackendoff 1972:154). In order to explain the facts about reflexivization within SRS sentences, he has to assume that a raised element ceases to participate in thematic relations and that 'lack of thematic relation counts as the lowest position on the Thematic Hierarchy' (Jackendoff 1972:154). Though intuitively reasonable, this proposal is formally ad hoc, in that it would be as easy to assume that lack of thematic relation counts as the highest position on the Thematic Hierarchy.[59]

NOTES

1. Though this has recently been questioned, e.g. by Shopen (1972) and Brame (to appear); their discussion leaves me unconvinced. For a purely syntactic argument in favor of SRS in French, see Ruwet (1972: ch. 2).

2. For instance, the question of the precise status of the complementizer in sentences such as (1) and (2), as well as the question of how the presence vs. absence of tense is to be treated. As far as solution (ii) is concerned, its basic assumption leaves open various ways of stating SRS. I will not consider them; the most common one relies on the assumption that English (or, for that matter, French) has underlying VSO order--which, to my mind, has been conclusively disproved by Berman (1974a).

3. In still unpublished work. My acquaintance with this proposal is, in the main, due to a lecture given by Postal at Vincennes in the spring of 1973 and to conversations with Perlmutter in the fall of the same year; for a 'preview' of this proposal, see now Postal (1974: Part VIII, D).

4. According to Postal (1974:Part VIII, D), this principle 'holds not just for RAISING [that is, subject raising to subject and object position; for the latter, see section (2.11)] but for a whole class of partly similar cyclical rules . . . which have the effect of extracting one NP from a larger containing NP. The principle in question . . . says in effect that when a promotion rule extracts one NP, NP_a, from a containing NP, NP_c, in the output NP_a takes on the grammatical function manifested by NP_c in the input. Such a principle makes it automatic that when RAISING extracts an NP from a sentential subject . . . it becomes a subject, and that when RAISING extracts an NP from a sentential object . . . it becomes an object. _The principle in question claims that no promotion rule can extract an NP from a subject and make it an object, or conversely_' (emphasis mine, N.R.).

5. Given that verbs such as _sembler_ and _paraître_ optionally take indirect objects (see, for instance: _il semblait à Murasaki que Sei Shônagon était trop prétentieuse_), the question arises whether one should allow a PP position between the V and S in (7). I will not discuss this point here, for it is not crucial for my main purpose.

However, I think there are reasons to prefer generating the complement S directly to the right of the verb (see note 16).

6. Where il is the so-called 'il impersonnel'.

7. For more details on these predicates, see the lists in Gross (1975).

8. Souvenir appears in two different frames; cf. je me souviens des cerisiers en fleurs vs. il me souvient des cerisiers en fleurs; the second one, which concerns us here (see example (98)) has an archaic flavor. See Ruwet (1972:193, 197).

9. For the adjectives which allow STS to apply (susceptible, foutu), there are no reasons to postulate a deep structure sentential subject (see examples (106)-(107) and the discussion which follows). The only case I am aware of which might lead one to have recourse to solution (i) is that of sentences which involve both the application of PASSIVE and SRS, such as Katsu a longtemps été supposé (par tout le monde) avoir trahi l'empereur, which presumably has a deep structure similar to that of on (or tout le monde) a longtemps supposé que Katsu avait trahi l'empereur. The question whether EXTRAP is involved in the generation of such sentences depends on a number of assumptions; an answer to it must await a more detailed analysis of the so-called 'impersonal passives' such as il a été supposé que Katsu avait trahi l'empereur, il a été réfléchi à cette question.

10. I have put these ungrammatical sentences in the subjunctive mood (soit vs. est) because there is a general constraint in French according to which, whatever main predicate has been chosen, a sentence-initial sentential complement must have its verb in the subjunctive mood.

11. Unless there were more general, theoretical reasons for preferring the strict subcategorization solution to the other one (or vice versa); see Kayne (1969) and Bresnan (1972) for discussion.

As a matter of fact, Emonds (1972:55ff.) deals with these facts in a different way from the one I have suggested; he claims that predicates like irritate, be necessary, etc., on the one hand, and seem, appear, on the other hand, are differentiated at the level of deep structure in that the first group are cases of what he calls 'antecedent complementation' (the 'extraposed' sentence being coreferential with the subject pronoun it), while the second group are cases of 'oblique complementation', their subject being empty in deep structure. As he states 'intraposition' as a rule which substitutes the 'extraposed' sentence for a coreferential subject pronoun, this would account for the facts without any need for rule features. However, I argue that, in French at least, the 'impersonal' pronoun il has the same properties in both cases (see section (2.4), ff.) and that it would be extremely arbitrary to derive it from two different sources in deep structure. I will return to this later (see section (2.11)).

12. On the nonprepositional nature of de in these instances, see Gross (1968) and Long (in this volume). For some speakers, the same de occasionally also shows up in front of the VP in sentence-initial position; so, instead of (14c) these speakers sometimes get d'apprendre à jouer du hichiriki me plairait. I will not deal here with the precise way in which the presence of the complementizer is to be treated; one could as well consider a deletion or an insertion analysis. Long's treatment is not quite convincing to me.

13. Sometimes, the complementizer is à; see, for instance, in some dialects, j'aime à lire Gengi Monogatari (vs. j'aime lire Gengi Monogatari and j'aime que tu lises Gengi Monogatari); also j'apprends à jouer du hichiriki (vs. j'apprends le japonais). See Gross (1968) and Long (this volume).

14. See Sandfeld (1965:39) for examples. Only paraître and sembler (and falloir, see ex. (97c) in this paper) are relevant here; s'avérer, se trouver, se révéler do not take an indirect object. Sandfeld (id., ibid.) quotes two literary examples where the extraposed complement sentence of plaire appears without de, but to me these are simply mistakes; all the informants I have asked about such sentences reject them.

15. Notice that many of the verbs which do not allow de in front of the reduced object sentence also allow 'Raising into object position' (see section (2.11)); this is the case for croire, estimer, juger, maybe vouloir. So there is a similarity between these verbs and sembler or paraître; maybe there is some generalization lurking here.

16. Two remarks are in order here. First, the facts which we are going to review can be accounted for by an analysis which treats the sentential complement of sembler not as a direct object stricto sensu but rather as a predicate nominal; it is well known, for instance, that predicative NPs or APs can be replaced by the clitic le (see section (2.5)); cf. Sakamoto l'est, le meilleur ami de Nakaoka, or très intelligent, Katsu l'est incontestablement. Maybe this analysis is to be preferred, in view of the facts: (i) that sentences whose main verb is sembler do not passivize; and (ii) that sembler, paraître, can appear in the frame NP ___ Predicate (cf., for instance, Yonosuke semble amoureux); see section (3.1) of this paper.

Second, if pronouns are generated in the base, it may not be necessary to have an NP dominate the complement sentence of sembler, etc. Sembler could be marked in the lexicon with the features + ___ NP (allowing only for a restricted class of 'semantically void' NPs (see note 19)), and + ___ S, and the interpretative rules which account for coreference would allow a pronoun to be 'coreferential' with a sentence.

As I am mainly interested in showing that the complement sentence of sembler, etc. is not a subject and must be generated to the right of the verb, I will not discuss these points further and will keep to the analysis proposed in (29). Notice that if the complement sentence of sembler is to be treated either as a direct object or a predicate nominal, it seems that it must be generated directly to the right of the verb and to the left of the indirect object (see note 5).

17. This impersonal il must probably be inserted by a late rule; see Ruwet (1972:67, note 3). These properties of il render even more dubious, at least for French, Emonds' proposal to treat the 'extraposed' S as coreferential with the subject pronoun. For other criticisms of Emonds' proposal, see Higgins (1973a).

18. I have borrowed this term from Higgins (1973b).

19. Some informants even accept sentences such as:

(i) il me semble quelque chose: . . .

(ii) il me semble une chose étrange: . . .

(iii) il me semble la chose suivante: . . .

20. See also:

(i) est-ce qu'il te répugnerait de manger du sashimi?

(a) non, cela ne me répugnerait pas du tout

(b) *non, il ne me (le) répugnerait pas du tout

I have added example (34c) in order to show that de + VP here is not a prepositional phrase; contrast this with:

(ii)(a) Go-Toba parle d'abdiquer le trône

(b) Go-Toba en parle

21. For s'avérer, se trouver, se révéler, the facts are somewhat different; while they behave like sembler with respect to (2.4) (see (i)-(ii)), they do not allow the clitic le (see (iii)):

(i) il s'est avéré ceci: Michinaga est le vrai maître du Japon

(ii) il se révèle ceci: Kōmei a sans doute été empoisonné

(iii) *il se le {révèle / avère}, que Michinaga a fait des dépenses extravagantes

This might be related to the 'accusative' character of the intrinsic reflexive clitic se (see Ruwet 1972:ch. 3 and Kayne 1975), which would make its presence incompatible with that of the accusative clitic le. Notice that, when these verbs occur parenthetically, se trouver, etc., pattern like sembler (see section (2.6)) if the object pronoun has been deleted, cf.:

(iv) Michinaga, il (*ça) se trouve, est l'homme le plus puissant du Yamato

22. As a parenthetical, ce me semble, however, is possible (though not *ce me paraît, etc.), but is felt as archaic. See note 24. On the alternation ce/ça, see Kayne (1973:134). Ce, as a clitic, has a limited distribution; it mainly occurs with être. For instance, we do not get *ce me plairait but only cela (or ça) me plairait.

23. Example (52b) is acceptable with a different intonational

pattern and a different (interrogative or exclamatory) meaning. This would be derived from:

(i) la guerre va durer longtemps; {est-ce possible? / est-ce possible!}

Notice also that sentences like (ii) but not (iii) are acceptable:

(ii) la guerre, à ce {qu'il paraît / qu'il me semble / que je crois / qu'on dit}, va durer longtemps

(iii) *la guerre, à ce qui est {probable / évident}, va durer longtemps

24. We also get que t'en semble? (without il and with an en whose source is unclear), though not *que t'en paraît, etc. But first this is archaic, and second, the unacceptability of (58)-(60) may indicate that que here is not a subject but an object, the subject pronoun (il) having been deleted. The possibility of having ce me semble (see note 22), which is also archaic, might be related to this. See Foulet (1967:177-178).

25. Or (see note 16) as a predicate nominal. Cf. questions like:

(i) qu'as-tu été pendant toutes ces années?
--j'ai été (la) concubine de Michitaka
--j'ai été moine au mont Hiei
--j'ai été amoureuse de Yonosuke

26. Sentences such as (74) are somewhat clumsy; in general, sentences with sembler, when the indirect object is present, are better if it is a clitic (il lui semble . . .) than if it is an ordinary PP. This is not an isolated case (see Gross 1968 and Kayne 1975 for other cases of constructions where cliticization of an indirect object makes the sentence better).

27. For a detailed study of pseudocleft constructions in French, see Moreau (to appear).

28. By the way, C. L. Baker (personal communication) has told me that sentences such as (i) can sometimes be heard in spoken American English:

(i) ?What it seems to me is that Akechi has gone crazy (contrast with (55))

though apparently the corresponding questions are quite bad:

(ii) *what does it seem to you? (compare with (53) and (65))

29. Notice that, just as in questions, the modifier d'autre (que NP) (which normally modifies only quelqu'un/quelque chose or qui/quoi (que), can be left behind by WH-MVT, see:

(i) j'ai rencontré quelqu'un d'autre (que Kūkai)
(ii) qui as-tu rencontré d'autre (que Kūkai)?
(iii) qui que tu puisses avoir rencontré d'autre (que Kūkai), . . .

This seems to indicate that these concessive constructions are closely related to questions. Notice also that the WH-word quel, which can occur as a predicate in questions but not in relatives, can also occur in concessive constructions; see:

(iv) le fidèle disciple de Kūkai {que / *quel} je suis est prêt à se sacrifier
quel est le plus fidèle disciple de Kūkai?
quel que soit le plus fidèle disciple de Kūkai, . . .

However, certain WH-words, which occur quite normally in questions though not in relatives, are prohibited from occurring in concessive constructions; see:

(v) Kiyomori combat d'une manière terrifiante
comment combat Kiyomori?
*la manière comment combat Kiyomori est terrifiante
*comment que combatte Kiyomori, ses ennemis sont terrifiés

(vi) Kiyomori combat pour la gloire
pourquoi combat Kiyomori?
?la raison pourquoi Kiyomori combat m'échappe totalement
*pourquoi que combatte Kiyomori, ce n'est pas pour l'argent

(vii) Kiyomori est mort le troisième jour du mois du Tigre
quand est mort Kiyomori?
*le jour quand est mort Kiyomori, tout le Yamato a pleuré
*quand que soit mort Kiyomori, tout le Yamato l'a pleuré

The reason for these irregularities still escapes me, as does the reason why quelque shows up instead of quel within the paraphrastic concessive constructions which replace the ungrammatical examples in (v) through (vii); see:

(viii) de quelle manière combat Kiyomori?
de {*quelle / quelque} manière que combatte Kiyomori, il terrifie tous ses ennemis

30. It is interesting to remark that, though both variants (with qui or que) of the (b) sentences are unacceptable, those with que are definitely worse. At an earlier time in the history of French, the said constraint on the extraction of subjects was not operative. At that time, apparently, only the version with qui was acceptable. This is an indirect corroboration of Gross' (1968) and Moreau's conjecture (1971) that the so-called subject 'relative pronoun' qui should be treated as a morphological variant of the complementizer que in the context /___ V. This proposal is not without its problems, however (see Kayne, in this volume).

31. As can be seen, for instance, from the placement of clitics in (89b), (91c) voilà still behaves like a verb in certain respects.

32. This example shows that falloir can take any kind of direct object NP. Notice the following interesting fact: falloir can occur, as a parenthetical, within sentences, such as:

(i) Go-Daigo, il le faut, doit abdiquer

The comparison with:

(ii) *il faut que Go-Daigo doive abdiquer

(iii) Go-Daigo doit abdiquer; il le faut

gives one more argument in favor of the analysis of parentheticals suggested in section (2.6). (The pronoun le in il le faut refers to the sentence Go-Daigo . . . abdiquer and not to Go-Daigo doit abdiquer).

33. See note 8.

34. This example shows that here de + VP is a prepositional phrase. Notice that not all the predicates of (9b) have the same properties; for instance, contrast (99) with (i):

(i) il s'agit que tu partes
il s'agit de partir
*(de) partir s'agit
*il s'en agit
*il se l'agit

This can be dealt with by means of strict subcategorization features: falloir will be subcategorized + ___ NP (à NP), être temps + ___ PP, and s'agir + ___ S.

35. Kayne suggests that croire, etc. be entered into two different frames, + ___ S (which would give (100a), (101a), and + ___ NP S (which would give (100b), (101b) by means of EQUI). This would explain the constraint I am going to talk about. Apparently, we have the choice between imposing an ad hoc constraint on SRO and introducing an arbitrary subcategorization bifurcation in the lexicon. Some facts seem to favor a raising analysis (see, for instance: je crois justice rendue, je crois la solution susceptible d'en être publiée). I have chosen the SRO solution for expository purposes; nothing crucial for my argument depends on this choice.

36. This example is grammatical on a different reading, in which trop tard . . . is a time adverbial modifying the main verb constructed intransitively; compare with: Takamitsu s'est décidé trop tard pour visiter le Todaiji.

37. See note 35 and Kayne (1975). ESC does not apply to the subject pronoun cela or ça which occurs as a subject of plaire, amuser, probable, etc.; see:

(i) je crois {cela / ça} probable, que Go-Toba abdique le trône
je crois {cela / ça} foutu de te déplaire, que Yonosuke fréquente les filles de Yoshiwara

On the other hand, it does apply to the ça which is the only possible subject of idiomatic expressions such as ça barde, ça marche, ça va; see:

(ii) ça barde entre les Taira et les Minamoto
ça semble barder entre les Taira et les Minamoto

c'est foutu de barder entre les Taira et les Minamoto
*je crois ça foutu de barder entre les Taira et les Minamoto

38. If EXTRAP is post- (or last-) cyclic, the question does not arise; but even if it were proven that EXTRAP is cyclical, its being optional would still permit the complement sentence to be in subject position by the time that SRO applies on the higher cycle. I will not deal here with this question; as far as I can see, nothing crucial for my purpose depends on it.

39. On the status of sentences such as (116)-(117), see note 43.

40. Or EXTRAP could have applied before _être_-deletion and _que_-insertion; this is immaterial.

41. _L'abdication de l'empereur est foutue_ is grammatical, but with a different meaning; see Gouet (1971).

42. Instead of (99b), one could imagine having a deep structure such as *_maintenant est temps de partir_ (with _de partir_ being a PP complement on _temps_); I see no syntactic justification for this. The ad hoc rule feature (in terms of EXTRAP) would have to be replaced by an equally ad hoc deletion rule (or, in view of sentences such as _il est maintenant temps de partir_, _il sera temps de partir dans 20 minutes_, by an obligatory time-adverbial formation rule).

43. In a conversation in March, 1974, Emonds told me that he has now abandoned his 'Intraposition' theory. He still wants to generate complement sentences to the right of the verb phrase, both for sentences such as _it seems to me that Murasaki is sublime_ or _it irritates Yonosuke that the young geisha is so frigid_; sentences such as _that the young geisha is so frigid irritates Yonosuke_ would be generated by means of a sort of 'generalized transformation' operating on two sentences: _The young geisha is so frigid_; _that irritates Yonosuke_; this rule would substitute the first sentence for the pronoun _that_ and would still be a root transformation. Though this might solve some of the problems raised by the 'Intraposition' analysis (see Higgins 1973a), I still do not see how it could solve the problem mentioned in the text; moreover, there are some semantic difficulties involved; a sentence such as (i) is not synonymous with the discourse (ii):

(i) que Yonosuke fasse jouir la jeune geisha est impossible
(ii) Yonosuke {fera / fait} jouir la jeune geisha; c'est impossible

Emonds' main reason for rejecting the standard treatment of EXTRAP was that, given the restrictions on the occurrence of sentence-initial complement sentences, Rosenbaum (1967) had to impose several ad hoc constraints on EXTRAP. However, in French at least, those restrictions seem to be less strict than Emonds claims. First (as 116) shows), infinitives are often allowed within embedded structures; see, for instance, (iii):

(iii) Sei Shōnagon trouve que se promener à l'aube est délicieux il me semble que rendre hommage aux ancêtres de cette manière n'amuse pas Yonusuke

(see also Ronat 1974). Second, even tensed sentences are sometimes allowed in subject position within embedded structures; a sentence like (iv), though stylistically awkward, seems to me to be acceptable:

(iv) le fait que, plus que vraisemblablement, que Yonusuke séduise la jolie servante déplaise à la jeune veuve, ne semble pas le tracasser beaucoup

So, with Higgins (1973a), I think that sentences such as (117) are excluded due to performance factors rather than grammatical constraints; it is quite possible that perceptual strategies are involved. This does not mean that there are no problems left with the EXTRAP theory and the idea that complement sentences are dominated by NP in deep structure; for some of these, see Ronat (1974).

44. This solution was suggested to me, though not quite in earnest, by Gilles Fauconnier.

45. Sentences such as <u>que Katsu ait vu juste me semble vrai</u> are grammatical anyway.

46. The rule should, of course, not mention <u>sembler</u> but rather the class of verbs which appear in list (9a).

47. Even this is dubious; the following (a) sentences convey a feeling of a direct personal experience which is lacking in their (b) counterparts:

(ia) il me semble avoir aperçu un fantôme monstrueux

(ib) il me semble vrai que j'ai aperçu un fantôme monstrueux

(iia) il me semble, s'exclama Oharu, que je vais défaillir de plaisir

(iib) il me semble vrai, s'exclama Oharu, que je vais défaillir de plaisir

48. On another reading, which corresponds to:

(i) Sei Shōnagon trouve qu'elle est songeuse,

this sentence is grammatical; it would derive from (i) by SRO.

49. In view of the fact that sentences such as (i) (compare with (145)) are possible:

(i) il est temps pour Hideyori de se préparer au seppuku

one might try to maintain that 'Indirect object formation' applies in these cases too, <u>pour</u> being inserted instead of <u>à</u>. However, this raises problems too; see Ruwet (1972:195-196). In fact, sentences such as (ii) and (iii) (which compare with (143)-(144)) are far from perfect:

(ii) ??il s'est avéré pour Katsu que l'empereur devait être restauré

(iii) ??il se trouve pour Sei Shōnagon que l'aube est délicieuse au printemps

50. In all respects (for instance, with respect to CLITIC-Placement), the à NP complement of sembler behaves like an indirect object. In fact, in his lecture at Vincennes in 1973, Postal acknowledged that PSYCH-MVT is a counterexample to his new functional theory and that 'it was a very dubious rule anyway'.

51. We also get sentences with indirect objects, such as:

(i) il m'est arrivé une expérience très étrange
    il m'est venu une idée bizarre

52. Though some recent studies (see Gaatone 1970, Martin 1970) contain interesting material on IND-EX, in particular on the semantic constraints to which it seems to be subject.

53. If the extraposed NP is animate, it cannot be questioned; compare (i) with (149):

(i) qui est venu à Harima?
    *qui est-il venu à Harima?

We find similar facts within relative clauses:

(ii) *les rōnin qu'il est venu à Harima étaient résolus à mourir
     les rōnin qui sont venus à Harima étaient résolus à mourir

(iii) ?les choses qu'il est arrivé pendant la fête à Gion sont étranges
      les choses qui sont arrivées pendant la fête à Gion sont étranges

54. This formulation is confusing. If pronouns are generated in the base, que in (156)-(157) as well as ceci in (151a) would be placed in object position by IND-EX, while the complement S in (154)-(155) could simply be positioned by the usual, equally optional, rule of EXTRAP.

55. Notice, by the way, that IND-EX, which converts a subject into something which behaves in many respects like a direct object, is a 'demotion' rule and would thus raise a problem within Postal's and Perlmutter's framework. It is also probably cyclical, because, if SRS is cyclical, IND-EX must be able to apply on an earlier cycle than the one on which SRS applies, as is shown by the behavior of clitics (en) in the following sentences:

(i) il semble en être arrivé plusieurs, des samurai sans maître
    ??il en semble être arrivé plusieurs, des samurai sans maître

(ii) il commence à en arriver beaucoup, des rōnin
     *il en commence à arriver beaucoup, des rōnin

56. I use the notion of 'experiencer' (see Postal 1970b), though it does not appear in Jackendoff's work, because it is not clear whether this function must be identified with that of 'goal' (Jackendoff's choice) or that of 'location' (my choice, Ruwet 1972). This is immaterial here.

57. The occurrence of personnellement here indicates that the indirect object is to be interpreted as 'experiencer'. See Ruwet (1972:212ff.).

58. This is the rule which relates sentences such as *il sera difficile de convaincre Sakamoto* and *Sakamoto sera difficile à convaincre*. See Postal (1971) and Fauconnier (1974).

59. I would like to thank the following people for their help, advice, encouragement, and criticism: C. L. Baker, Arlene Berman, Gilles Fauconnier, Mike Helke, Paul Hirschbühler, Richie Kayne, E. S. Klima, S.-Y. Kuroda, Hans Georg Obenauer, and Mike Szamosi. Special thanks are due to Mike Helke, who took the trouble to read the final version of this paper and who helped me to improve its style and content. All errors left are due to the influence of the evil spirits of the night.

FRENCH INFINITIVAL COMPLEMENTIZERS AND THEIR PLACE IN A GENERATIVE GRAMMAR

MARK E. LONG

Indiana University

1.1 A considerable number of French infinitives are preceded by de and à, which normally function as prepositions meaning 'of' and 'to' respectively. However, not all sequences of à or de + Infinitive seem to have a distribution corresponding to that of PP. Compare the following sentences:

(1a) Il a oublié de nettoyer la chambre. 'He forgot to clean the room.'
(1b) Il a oublié cette tâche. 'He forgot (about) that job.'
(2a) Elle rêve d'aller en Suisse. 'She dreams of going to Switzerland.'
(2b) Elle rêve de ce voyage. 'She dreams about that trip.'

In Long (1974), the de or à encountered in structures such as (1a) were termed 'infinitival particles',[1] and certain constraints on their appearance were discussed. I would now like to propose that the particle de is the basic complementizer for French infinitives and that its absence, or replacement by à, is possible only in a restricted number of syntactic environments. Having presented evidence for this claim, I will go on to discuss formal means of inserting and/or deleting infinitival complementizers in three current versions of generative grammar.

1.2 In this paper, it will be suggested that morphemes previously referred to as particles are in fact complementizers. Such an identification is by no means novel (see, for example, Langacker 1966:80-85), but it calls for some comment, regarding both its justification and the exact use of the term 'complementizer'.

Reference to complementizers dates back to Rosenbaum (1967: 24-32), who applied the term to English that, for-to, and Poss-ing. It has appeared in most of the subsequent literature on predicate complementation and has continued to designate a rather wide variety of morphemes, both those which introduce complement clauses (that, for) and those which may be considered verbal particles or inflections (to and -ing). In most studies, moreover, these elements 'have been viewed as markers of syntactic subordination having neither semantic nor significant syntactic function' (Bresnan 1970: 297).

It was pointed out in Long (1974) that presence or absence of particles can reflect major semantic distinctions, as between differing uses of the verb dire 'say, tell':

(3a) Elle nous dit ne pas avoir peur. 'She tells us she isn't afraid.'

(3b) Elle nous dit de ne pas avoir peur. 'She tells us not to be afraid.'

Bresnan (1970:302-303) also gives examples of semantic contrasts involving English for and that. In any case, my reference to French de and à as complementizers should not be taken to mean that they are without any semantic value. Even if they are only 'markers' in some sense, they nevertheless serve to mark something, that is, semantically distinct constructions after matrix verbs.

A more troublesome question is that of syntactic function. As indicated above, the term complementizer can be used in various ways. Bresnan would seemingly restrict it to introductory elements like for and that, partly on the assumption that occurrences of to and Poss-ing are entirely predictable (1970:300, note 3; 313-314, note 16), partly because 'true' complementizers are for her associated with a specific, clause-initial COMP node (1970:300). In the French cases, however, these two criteria turn out to be incompatible, since de is not a predictable element, [2] certainly not in the purely syntactic sense intended by Bresnan, but cannot, on the other hand, be shown to occur in absolute clause-initial position, as does English for. Assuming that the first criterion carries more weight and that evidence regarding the second is indecisive, [3] I will consider the term complementizer to be applicable, at least in principle, to the French infinitival particles de and à. [4]

Whether this use of the term is in fact justified is less clear. It must be shown that particles are morphemes which may serve to introduce a wide variety of infinitives and that they cannot be considered mere transitional elements between verbs and following complements. Evidence is provided by the wide range of environments in which the particle de may occur:

(4a) After some matrix verbs:
J'ai refusé de partir 'I refused to leave'

(4b) After verbs and adjectives with impersonal surface subjects:[5]
C'est/Il est difficile de chanter comme elle 'It's hard to sing like her'

(4c) In dislocated constructions:
De chanter comme elle, c'est difficile 'Singing like her, it's hard'

(4d) In subject position:[6]
De chanter comme elle est difficile 'Singing like her is hard'

(4e) In comparative constructions:
J'aimerais mieux aboyer comme un chien que de chanter comme elle 'I'd rather bark like a dog than (to) sing like her'

(4f) In 'historical' or 'independent' infinitives:
Et les enfants de rire 'And so the kids started laughing'

(4g) After a few prepositions and conjunctions:
Avant de partir . . . 'Before leaving . . .'

Occurrences of à as an infinitival particle are far less frequent. A may follow certain matrix verbs:

(5a) Elle commence à chanter. 'She's starting to sing.'

(though even in many of these cases de would be an acceptable alternative for some speakers). This particle likewise appears after adjectives of the so-called 'tough' class, where these have subjects which are logical objects of the following infinitive:

(5b) Ce morceau est difficile à chanter. 'This piece is hard to sing.'

Compare:

(6) C'est/Il est difficile de chanter ce morceau. 'It's hard to sing this piece.'

More numerous are the instances in which there is no particle at all in surface structure. Again, however, such cases are relatively restricted, when we consider the distribution of de (4). Infinitives must appear without particles only in two types of environments:

(7a) After some matrix verbs:
Je ne veux pas chanter comme elle 'I don't want to sing like her'

(7b) After most prepositions and conjunctions:
Il songe à partir en vacances 'He's thinking about going off on vacation.'

Particles may also be optionally omitted in two other instances:

(7c) In dislocated constructions:
Chanter comme elle, c'est difficile [Same reading as (4c)]

(7d) In subject position:
Chanter comme elle est difficile [Same reading as (4d)]

De, however, is also possible in such cases.

Occurrence of de in (4c) and (4e) above constitutes especially strong evidence for considering this particle the basic complementizer for French infinitives. Take, for example, the sentence:

(8a) D'aller à pied, il ne fallait pas y songer.[7]
'Going on foot was out of the question/one couldn't think about it.'

Songer 'think, reflect' takes infinitival complements preceded by the preposition à, which normally excludes particles (7g):

(8b) Il ne fallait pas songer à aller à pied.

(8c) *Il ne fallait pas songer à d'aller à pied.

Thus, the exclusion of particles with prepositions seems to be a kind of local constraint, applying only where the complement immediately follows the preposition in question. The same may well be true of constraints imposed by certain matrix verbs, (7a), as can be seen in comparative constructions:

(4e) J'aimerais mieux aboyer comme un chien que de chanter comme elle.

Here, the second infinitive is preceded by de even though it is understood to be a complement of aimer mieux 'prefer', which disallows particles. Thus, the two conditions for obligatory absence of de turn out to be quite limited in their scope.

2. We will assume, then, that infinitival particles are to be considered complementizers (hereafter abbreviated COMP) and that de

is in some sense the most basic. We must next ask what formal account can be given for the presence or absence of infinitival COMP in surface structure. Given the current diversity of models in generative grammar, it may be desirable to consider not only standard theory (ST) accounts (for example, Rosenbaum 1967, Langacker 1966, R. Lakoff 1968, P. and C. Kiparsky 1970, UESP 1968, Gross 1968) but also solutions which suppose an interpretive-lexicalist (IL) framework (as in Long 1974) or which allow for lexicalization in derived structures (Sanders 1970, Hochster 1973a, 1973b).

The ST approaches will be examined first. If we assume that de is the primary COMP for French infinitives, then we must account for the absence of this morpheme in certain surface environments (as well as for its occasional replacement by à). In so doing, we need to answer the even more basic question of how infinitival COMP (or any COMP) comes to be inserted in embedded constructions.

Let us begin with this second question. There are at least two logically possible sources for COMP:

(I) Transformational insertion, governed by rule features on matrix verbs and prepositions;[8]

(II) Insertion in the base, governed by lexical features--strict-subcategorization features.

Since (I) is adopted in most ST accounts (except Langacker 1966 and Bresnan 1970), we will consider it first. If we provisionally assume the validity of (I), then a further choice arises between two possible means of constraining the occurrences of de. These alternative approaches are:

(A) Restricted insertion, such that de is introduced in environments of (4), but not of (5) or (7);

(B) General insertion, with subsequent Deletion in (7).[9]

The choice of (A) or (B) is far from clear. (B), if judged preferable, would provide a formal correlate for our suggestion that de is basic with respect to ∅. However, formal justification for such a choice is also necessary. It might be argued that (B) would allow the most general application of the COMP-Insert rule and that rules should always be formulated so as to apply in the most general manner. It could be objected, on the other hand, that (B) permits such generality only at the expense of additional (deletion) rules.

A more decisive argument might be found by examining the relative complexities of (A) and (B). The insertion 'rule' of (A) would in fact consist of at least seven distinct operations (really, seven separate rules) for the various environments (4) in which de may occur. These are repeated here, for the sake of convenience:

(4a) After some matrix verbs
(4b) After verbs and adjectives with impersonal subjects
(4c) In dislocated constructions
(4d) In subject position
(4e) In comparative constructions
(4f) In 'historical' infinitives
(4g) After prepositions and conjunctions (no more than a few)

Cases (4a) and (4g) would require a rule feature [+/- COMP-Insert], since presence or absence of COMP, as well as the choice between à and de, will vary according to the specific lexical item; other occurrences of COMP would not be restricted in this way. Cases (4c) and (4d) would involve optional insertion, whereas in other instances COMP, where possible, is inserted obligatorily. There seems to be no natural way of collapsing these rules, with the possible exception of (4a) and (4b).[10]

Solution (B), on the other hand, would be less complex. If COMP were inserted before all infinitives by a general rule, then only four subsequent deletion rules would be necessary to account for the absence of COMP in (7). Presence of de in (4b), (4e), and (4f) would not require special rules, but would result naturally from the general rule of COMP-Insert, since no deletion transformation would refer to these environments. Thus solution (B) would apparently involve fewer rules than (A).[11]

There would be still more problems with (A) if it were to be incorporated into certain specific ST accounts of predicate complementation. In the formulations adopted by Rosenbaum (1967) and R. Lakoff (1968), for example, choice of COMP, and thus of complement type, is of decisive importance for the application of subsequent rules, such as Equi-NP-Deletion. A description of this sort, if applied to French, would require the presence of an infinitival COMP (distinct from that of tensed clauses) in order to derive:

(9a) Tu crois travailler dur. 'You think you're working hard.'

from:

(9b) Tu crois que tu travailles dur.

This is true even though no COMP appears on the surface before infinitival complements of croire 'believe'. It might be proposed, in an (A) solution, that verbs like croire require the phonological value ∅ for infinitival COMP. It would, however, be necessary to change this value at later points in some derivations, e.g. where there are reduced comparative structures of the type:

(4e) J'aimerais mieux aboyer comme un chien que de chanter comme elle.

In such a sentence, the infinitive de chanter comme elle 'to sing like her', would have undergone two rules specifying COMP, on two different cycles. These awkward consequences would be avoided in a (B) version of Rosenbaum's description: a general COMP-Insert rule[12] could apply early in the cycle involving matrix verbs of (9a) or (4e), with deletion rules applying later (perhaps postcyclically).

Other ST analyses of predicate complementation (P. and C. Kiparsky 1970, UESP 1968) make selection of infinitival structure--and of the appropriate COMP--dependent upon prior operation of Equi-NP-Deletion and various raising rules. Given this approach, a COMP-Insert rule could apply to any VP not preceded by a subject NP under the same S-node. Note, however, that the absence of a subject NP would have to be specified in the structural description of every rule for inserting COMP.[13] Under this analysis, then, a solution involving a single insertion rule, such as (B), would be more highly valued than one requiring up to seven such rules. For these and other reasons,[14] then, we will provisionally adopt (B) as the preferred means of transformationally introducing COMP.

The principal rules for solution (B) would be of the following form:

(10) T_{obl}: Inf-COMP-Insert[15]

$$\begin{array}{lll} X - [_S VP - Y & \Rightarrow 1 - \begin{bmatrix}+COMP\\+INF\\+DE\end{bmatrix} + 2 - 3 \\ 1 \quad\ 2 \quad\ 3 & \end{array}$$

(11) T_{obl}: Inf-COMP-Del (Post-verbal)

$$\begin{array}{cccccc} X - & \begin{bmatrix}+V\\+COMP\text{-}Del\end{bmatrix} & - \left(\begin{Bmatrix}NP\\PP\end{Bmatrix}\right) & \begin{bmatrix}+COMP\\+INF\end{bmatrix} & - Y \\ 1 & 2 & 3 & 4 & 5 \\ \Rightarrow 1 - & 2 & - \ 3 \ - & \emptyset & - 5 \end{array}$$

(12) T_{obl}: Inf-COMP-Del (Post-prepositional)

$$\begin{array}{ccccc} X - & \begin{bmatrix}+Prep\\+COMP\text{-}Del\end{bmatrix} & - & \begin{bmatrix}+COMP\\+INF\end{bmatrix} & - Y \\ 1 & 2 & & 3 & 4 \Rightarrow 1 - 2 - \emptyset - 4 \end{array}$$

(13) T_{opt}: Inf-COMP-Del (Pre-verbal or subject position)

$$\begin{array}{ccccc} X - & \begin{bmatrix}+\text{COMP}\\ +\text{INF}\end{bmatrix} & - \text{VP} - & [_{vp} & Y \\ 1 & 2 & 3 & & 4 \Rightarrow 1 - \emptyset - 3 - 4 \end{array}$$

In addition to the above rules, one or more transformations will be necessary for deleting *de* in dislocated infinitives. This optional rule, or set of rules, will no doubt be similar in some respects to (13). Its exact form will be determined partly by details of the Dislocation rule(s) which cannot be discussed here.

Transformations (11) and (12) require a rule feature [+/-COMP-Del] which characterizes some matrix verbs (*pouvoir* 'can, may', *vouloir* 'wish, want', *croire* 'believe, think') and some prepositions (*de, à*), but not others (*oublier* 'forget', *décider* 'decide', *commencer* 'begin', *avant* 'before'). A feature of this sort would seemingly be part of the necessary cost of any transformational solution of type (I). This cost is somewhat less than might be expected, since the value of [+/- COMP-Del] is predictable for many verbs. Thus, all verbs of stating, believing, and knowing (the 'propositional' verbs of Long 1974) are [+COMP-Del]:[16]

(9) Tu crois travailler dur. 'You think you're working hard.'
(14) Il affirme avoir rencontré l'accusé. 'He states that he met the defendant.'

[+COMP-Del] is also predictable for verbs which occur only before infinitives (that is, not before NP, PP, or tensed clauses)[17] and which might be termed 'modals' in a loose sense:

(15) *avoir beau* [*faire*] '[do] in vain'; *oser* 'dare'; *daigner* 'deign, condescend'; *pouvoir* 'can, may';[18] *devoir* 'must, should, be supposed to';[19] *faillir* [*faire*] 'nearly [do]';[20] *savoir* 'know [how], be able'.[21]

Other verbs which would always require deletion of infinitival COMP, (11), are those whose verbs are directly followed (at least optionally) by infinitival complements and may be preceded by clitics of the subordinate VP:

(16a) Ils ont fait réparer la voiture. 'They had the car repaired.'
(16b) Ils l'ont fait réparer. 'They had it repaired.'

Also:

(17a) On fera chanter la soprano. 'They/we will have the soprano sing.'
(17b) On la fera chanter. 'They/we will have her sing.'

Such behavior is shared (with differences of detail) by:

(18) *faire* 'make, cause, have'; *laisser* 'let'; *voir* 'see'; *entendre* 'hear'; *regarder* 'watch'; *écouter* 'listen'; *sentir* 'feel';

and perhaps one or two others.

There remain a large number of verbs, however, for which the value of [+/-COMP-Del] could be predicted in no principled way. This is true especially of the emotive class, which includes some verbs subject to rule (11):

(19) *vouloir* 'wish, want'; *aimer autant* 'would just as soon'; *aimer mieux* 'prefer';

some verbs which require the COMP *de*:

(20) *craindre* 'fear'; *regretter* 'regret, be sorry'; *déplorer* 'lament';

and some which may have either value for [+/- COMP-Del]:

(21) *préférer (de)* 'prefer'; *aimer (à)* 'like'; *désirer (de)* 'wish, desire'.

The fact that presence or absence of COMP is in some instances idiosyncratic might be taken as an argument for determining the form of complements at the point of lexical insertion. It is to this formal alternative that I now turn.

3. So far I have been attempting to characterize a generative framework in which infinitival COMP is inserted by transformation (I). It has been assumed, moreover, that such insertion would be a step in the derivation of infinitive VP's from underlying subordinate S's, where the latter also underlie tensed clauses introduced by *que*. Now, there is reason to believe that infinitives and *que*-clauses should already be distinct (probably in terms of their complementizers) at the point where lexical insertion takes place. Evidence for this claim has been presented by Bresnan (1970) and Long (1974) and may

be further supplemented by the idiosyncratic behavior of emotive verbs (19-21), for which choice of à, de, or ∅ must be specified for each individual item. It would thus be desirable to consider solution (II), whereby COMP would be introduced by rules of lexical insertion, allowing us to express the constraints on postverbal COMP as strict-subcategorization features of verbs.

One form of (II) has already been worked out in a standard theory (ST) description of French. Langacker (1966:43-44, 82-85) proposes that matrix verbs be strictly subcategorized for the types of COMP they will accept: que, de, à, or ∅. Such complementizing morphemes then determine the application of rules for forming infinitives, as in Rosenbaum (1967). In addition, Langacker suggests that infinitives be assigned a special 'infinitival' tense (TN$) in deep structure (1966: 85-89). I will not go into the details of Langacker's argumentation here. One important consequence of his claim is that it requires filtering out various deviant structures, produced by the insertion of infinitival COMP (or of TN$) in inappropriate environments (1966:89). This would seemingly be necessary in any form of (II)--including that described by Bresnan (1970)--where infinitives are derived from full S complements.[22]

Use of a filter might be avoided, on the other hand, in an interpretive-lexicalist (IL) framework, in which infinitives could be directly generated in the base as VP's (as in Long 1974). There would be provision for two sorts of infinitives in the phrase-structure rules rewriting VP:[23]

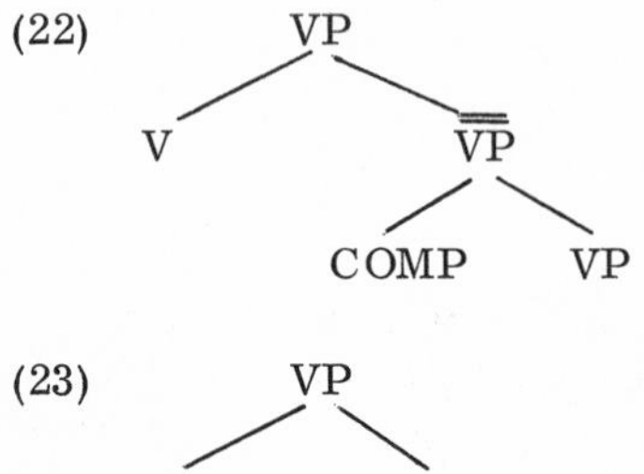

Matrix verbs could then be marked for strict-subcategorization features of roughly the following form:[24]

(24) [+/- ___ $\overline{\overline{\overline{VP}}}$]

(25) [+/- ___ VP]

Values for these features would be partly predictable (cf. the case of [+/- COMP-Del], § 2).

The forms of approach (II) described here involve restricted, rather than general, insertion of infinitival COMP. In this way, they more nearly resemble solution (A) than solution (B). This fact seems to follow naturally from the use of lexical insertion, and not syntactic transformations, as the formal mechanism for introducing COMP. Notice, however, that I have so far discussed only the occurrences of COMP after matrix verbs (4a, 5a, 7a). It is not clear whether all other constraints on the appearance of *de* can be adequately stated in strict-subcategorization features. Problems arise in particular for infinitives in dislocated position (4c). It is necessary, above all, to determine whether such constructions are derived transformationally or whether they represent further alternatives in the base. If they are considered derived structures, then the presence or absence of infinitival COMP cannot be adequately constrained at the point of lexical insertion: infinitives optionally containing *de* will have been transformationally dislocated from positions where this morpheme is excluded in surface structure:

(8a) D'aller à pied, il ne fallait pas y songer.
(8c) *Il ne fallait pas songer à d'aller à pied.

In this instance, it would be necessary either to give up (II) or else to modify it, so that some surface occurrences of COMP are determined transformationally.

There may, however, be motivation--in an IL approach--for giving dislocated constructions a distinctive representation in deep structure. The arguments for this would be especially strong if it could be shown that pronouns (even redundant ones) ought to be directly generated in clitic position. In such a case, choice of *a* structure like (22) would always be a possibility, provided that $\overline{\overline{VP}}$ cooccurs with a coreferential clitic (e.g. *y* of (8a)).[25] Sentences like (8a) would then constitute no problem for solutions of type (II).

4. The principal advantage of solutions which insert COMP in the base is the possibility of stating constraints on infinitival *de* (and on the form of predicate complements generally) in terms of lexical restrictions. On the other hand, adoption of (II) leaves no means of stating the wider distribution of *de* with respect to other infinitival complementizers. It is also necessary, in the IL version, to accept deep structures which many will find insufficiently abstract.[26]

In view of these facts, it might seem desirable to find some middle ground between hypotheses (I) and (II). A possible compromise solution would be one in which lexical insertion itself takes place late, after at least some syntactic transformations have applied, so that strict-subcategorization features will, in fact, refer to derived structures.

A proposal of just this sort has been made by Hochster (1973b), utilizing a form of lexicalization described by Sanders (1970:53-59). In such an approach, it might be possible to allow transformations (10-13) to apply freely, with no reference to rule features. Incorrect outputs could be avoided by restrictions on the (subsequent) insertion of lexical items (verbs, adjectives, prepositions, etc.). These restrictions could take the form of strict-subcategorization features like (24) and (25).

Though this lexicalization solution seems, on the whole, to be an appealing one, it offers certain difficulties of its own. First, it is incompatible with certain views of Hochster, who places lexical insertion in shallow structure (1973b) but would insert COMP only by very late postcyclic rules (1973a:29, note 14). If these positions cannot be modified, then a lexicalization approach would differ in no interesting ways from ST solutions (at least as far as infinitival COMP is concerned). It should be further noted that late lexicalization must function as a syntactic filter. This is because lexicalization does not allow free insertion of lexical items as in ST. Rather, only those forms which correspond to predetermined feature matrices may be inserted. Thus, if a given verb (say, oublier) fails to be inserted--as it must--in a string where Inf-COMP-Del (11) has applied, there is no way of substituting another, more appropriate item (e.g. vouloir). Instead, the derivation would simply block. The most that can be said is that such a filtering mechanism is more highly constrained and (in some intuitive sense) more natural than others which have been proposed.

5. To summarize, I have suggested that infinitival particles are complementizers and that de is the basic infinitival complementizer of French. This priority of de would be expressed directly in a generative description where COMP is transformationally inserted before all infinitives--the (B) version of approach (I)--with subsequent deletion (or substitution of à for de) in some environments. Evidence was given for preferring this account over a context-restricted insertion of COMP by transformation (A). There turned out to be certain arguments, however, for letting COMP be chosen in terms of restrictions on lexical insertion (II). If COMP is to be inserted in the base, then de will be on the same footing as à and Ø. Such a solution would also require deep structure representations which differ only slightly from those found on the surface. For this and other reasons, a compromise solution was examined, whereby COMP would be inserted and/or deleted transformationally, with

subsequent introduction of lexical items. This account, however, would involve the acceptance of a filtering device.

NOTES

This paper has been rather extensively revised since its presentation at the Texas Symposium on Romance Linguistics (1974). Many of the ideas presented in this final version have been shaped by discussions with Gilles Fauconnier, Fred Householder, Richard Kayne, Michael Mazzola, Nicolas Ruwet, and Albert Valdman, all of whom I would like to thank for their comments and (especially) their criticisms. Needless to say, none of them is necessarily in agreement with the conclusions at which I have arrived.

1. The use of this term does not exclude the possibility that such morphemes are likewise prepositions (compare the use of English to, German zu, Italian di). That there is only a very subtle distinction between object complements introduced by particles and oblique complements dominated by PP is suggested by examples like: Il demande à Marie à ce qu'elle vienne 'He's asking Marie to come', where ce que is the complementizer (or Pronoun and COMP) generally used for introducing tensed clauses after prepositions. Such cases might suggest that particles are not completely limited to infinitival complements and may have more characteristics of prepositions than is suggested elsewhere in this paper or in Long (1974). It has been pointed out to me, however, (by Gilles Fauconnier and Nicolas Ruwet) that such behavior is to be observed only for à, never de. This would support my contention that the latter is more closely bound up with infinitival structure than the former.

2. That is, choice of à, de, or Ø cannot be predicted in any straightforward way for postverbal infinitives. This is especially clear in the case of emotive verbs (see § 2 below).

3. The problem of determining whether de occurs in absolute clause-initial position is complicated by the absence, in modern Standard French, of infinitives with surface subjects. That is, it is virtually impossible to say whether French particles correspond more closely to English for or English to. There is, of course, the argument that French infinitives already have a distinctive ending, so that the quasi-inflectional role of English to does not fall to de. In Old French, moreover, where infinitives could have surface subjects, the latter were sometimes preceded by de: dist . . . que ce astoit grief chose de riche home entrer ou regne dou ciel 'He said that it was a difficult matter for a rich man to enter the kingdom of heaven'; Pour quel raison fu establi/De deus homes combattre ainsi/Encontre un seul 'For which reason it was decided/For

two men so to fight/Against a single one'. (Both examples are cited by Tobler 1886:89-90). Finally, in modern French dialects where infinitives may have surface subjects after prepositions, there is no separate de preceding the VP: Je ne suis pas très partisan de les vieux changer leur arrangement de tête 'I'm not much in favor of old people changing their ways of thinking' (cited by D'Amourette and Pichon 1933:491).

4. The exact syntactic function of complementizers, here or elsewhere, remains an open question. Probably no more can be said in the present instance than that complementizers mark subordinate clauses as such and sometimes serve (as in (3a)/(3b)) to distinguish between semantically divergent complement types.

5. It is not crucial at this point to determine whether such complements have been shifted into predicate position by a rule of Extraposition (as in Rosenbaum 1967:71-80).

6. Although the use of infinitival de in subject position is frowned upon in normative grammars, its existence in some dialects is not subject to doubt (cf. Sandfeld 1965:34).

7. Cited by Gamillscheg (1957:455).

8. For Rosenbaum (1967:29-30), at least some features of this type are copied onto the pronoun it, which is posited as the head N of sentential NP's.

9. Both (A) and (B) leave open the question of à. Presumably this morpheme will be inserted later, either by a substitution rule (in solution B) or by a separate addition rule (solution A). The substitution approach--and thus (B)--might seem to derive some support from the hesitation between de and à after many of the verbs which must be specially marked for the latter (commencer 'begin', forcer 'force', etc.).

10, It might be claimed that (4a) and (4b) involve a single rule (i) if adjectives are considered verbs and (ii) if the feature [+COMP-Insert] is predictable for [+V, +Adj] or [+V, +[IMPERSONAL]___]. Any statement about (ii) will depend upon acceptance or rejection of the Extraposition rule.

11. There would, of course, be a further substitution rule for introducing à (see note 9). This represents no increase in complexity with respect to (A).

12. Some problems would remain even for this form of Inf-COMP-Insert, since Rosenbaum chooses to generate the infinitives of (4b) in subject position, with subsequent Extraposition (see note 5). If, on the other hand, one were to accept the arguments of Emonds (1969a), who would generate such structures in postverbal position, it would be far simpler to insert COMP on the basis of verb features.

13. Actually, there is some reason to wonder whether the Kiparsky/UESP approach could be made to account for all the possible

infinitival constructions of French. In particular, historical infinitives (4f) appear to have surface subjects: Et les enfants de rire. Perhaps these could be explained in terms of an abstract matrix verb (like 'COMMENCER') which is transformationally deleted.

14. Further motivation for (B) would appear in accounts like those of R. Lakoff (1968:29-39) or Ruwet (1968:288-293), where all complement types are derived from S and contain the COMP 'that' or que at some point in the derivation. It would seem more reasonable to alter the features of an already existing COMP (i. e. replace French que with de before infinitives) and then delete in some specific cases, rather than to first erase COMP before S's which are to undergo infinitive formation and then recreate the node by means of a new insertion rule. The validity of this argument, however, depends upon acceptance of the analyses in question.

15. Rule (10) assumes an account of infinitive formation along the lines of Kiparsky (1970) and UESP (1968). If it can be shown that the S dominating VP has been pruned before this point, then a more involved statement will be required.

16. Even here, [+COMP-Del] cannot be redundantly assigned to propositional verbs, but to verbs which are used propositionally, since a number of verbs of speaking can be followed either by statements (3a) or by commands (3b). If, as argued in Long (1974), such verbs are to be assigned single lexical entries, then they will have to be marked [+/- COMP-Del], with later specification of a positive or negative value in terms of the following complement type.

17. These verbs are similar, in some respects, to certain of the English items which Rosenbaum (1967) considers to take VP complements.

18. Pouvoir does appear to take NP objects in sentences like Je le peux 'I can [do] it', J'y peux quelque chose 'I can [do] something about it/ along those lines', Je n'en peux plus 'I can [do] no more'. In fact, these pronominal expressions seem to exhaust the possible NP objects of this verb, and all of them apparently stand for unspecified infinitival complements.

19. Devoir takes direct and indirect objects where it means 'owe': Je lui dois 5. 000 francs 'I owe him 5000 francs'. In such instances, infinitival complements of devoir are preceded by COMP: Je devais à mon oncle d'avoir trouvé une situation 'I owed finding a position to my uncle'.

20. With the meaning 'fail', faillir can be followed by PP. It also sometimes follows the pattern of synonymous manquer 'miss, fail' and takes the COMP de (Sandfeld 1965:81).

21. Used propositionally, in the sense of 'know (for a fact)', this verb takes NP objects, clauses with que, and infinitives as well (these last also without COMP).

22. One major problem with Langacker's solution--and also Bresnan's--is that choice of a specific COMP in deep structure often implies coreference constraints between NP's in the subordinate and superordinate clauses. These in turn must be stated in terms of derived structures, since application (or not) of rules like T-Passive can alter the grammaticality of either major complement type, after some verbs: Il veut être aimé de tout le monde 'He wants to be loved by everyone', *Il veut tout le monde l'aimer 'He wants everyone to love him'; Il veut que tout le monde l'aime 'He wants everyone to love him', *Il veut qu'il soit aimé de tout le monde 'He wants himself to be loved by everyone'. This problem can be gotten around, though not without some formal difficulties, where Passive is an obligatory transformation, triggered by a deep structure formative of some kind. Otherwise, some sort of filter will have to be adopted (or else the Passive rule given up).

23. The Chomsky adjunction is adapted from Bresnan (1970). It should also be noted that I am disregarding the possible presence under VP of other elements, such as NP or PP.

24. Further features, or refinements in those given, might permit a choice between à and de.

25. The actual process of dislocation, and assignment of surface position to the dislocated constituent, can be carried out by transformations.

26. Generation of VP complements in deep structure would imply the abandonment of all rules which alter grammatical relations among NP's: e.g. Il veut être aimé de tout le monde or He wants there to be room for his golf clubs. As can be seen, constraints on infinitival subjects apply to derived subjects of the subordinate clause (see note 22), and proper coreference could be assured only where infinitives are at some point full S's.

ASSERTION AND PRESUPPOSITION IN SPANISH COMPLEMENTS

TRACY D. TERRELL

University of California at Irvine

1. Introduction. Much of the recent work in theoretical linguistics has been directed to developing an understanding of the relationship between semantics and syntactic processes. The work of the Kiparskys (1970) established the importance of the semantic notion of PRESUPPOSITION for explaining certain syntactic phenomena in English. Hooper and Terrell (1974) postulated a correlation between the semantic notion of ASSERTION and the use of mood in Spanish sentences containing sentential complements.[1] In particular, we tried to show that in sentences with sentential complements, the relation of both the mood of the verb in the complement and the matrix into which the complement is embedded is dependent upon this factor of assertion, and that the choice of mood is meaningful and not transformationally derived.

In this paper we analyze the Spanish system of complementation in order to examine in semantic terms the relationship between ASSERTION and PRESUPPOSITION and their correlation with certain syntactic processes and their associated classes of matrix predicates. We make no attempt to formalize our theories; we consider such formalizations inappropriate because (a) there is no global theory which would further elucidate the data to be presented here, and (b) we doubt that a syntactic-semantic theory can be developed until the relationships between syntax and semantics have been better defined.

2.0 Definitions. The term PRESUPPOSITION has been widely used by both philosophers and linguists. In this paper we are concerned with the notion of presupposition as defined by Keenan (1971), which we take to be essentially the same as the notion used by the Kiparskys.[2] Keenan gives two criteria for the recognition of presupposition in complements. First, the truth of the complement is presupposed by the entire sentence.

(1) Le sorprendió que María se enojara.
'It surprised him that Mary got mad.'

If the proposition, que María se enojara is, in fact, untrue, then the entire sentence (1) is neither true nor false; it simply has no truth value. In addition, the truth value of a presupposed proposition will remain constant under the normal processes of sentence negation or questioning.

(2) No le sorprendió que María se enojara.
'It didn't surprise him that Mary got angry.'

(3) ¿Le sorprendió que María se enojara?
'Did it surprise him that Mary got angry?'

The Kiparskys showed that presupposition in English is associated regularly with a variety of syntactic processes.[3] Presupposition was said to occur in English with matrices which group themselves into two semantic types: matrices which describe some subjective or emotional reaction to a proposition (to be significant, odd, tragic, exciting, relevant, to regret, deplore, etc.),[4] or those which describe cognitive or other mental acts with regard to a proposition (be aware of, grasp, comprehend, take into account, forget, ignore, etc.).

In the case of sentences with matrices from the former class, Spanish normally requires the subjunctive:[5] see (1), (2), and (3). With matrices of mental acts the verb forms are normally indicative:

(4) Se dió cuenta de que no iban a poder llegar antes de las seis.
'He realized that they weren't going to be able to arrive before six.'

Consequently, it was thought that presupposition, although semantically operative in Spanish as well as in English, had very few syntactic consequences and certainly played no role in the use of moods. In Hooper and Terrell (1974), the matrices of mental acts were considered to be exceptions to the rule that the indicative forms are used in assertive propositions and subjunctive forms in all others, including presupposed ones, since we knew of no independent evidence to show that these propositions were also assertive. We showed that the presupposition in these propositions differs from that found in the sentence of subjective comment and that these sentences are indeed assertive in many fundamental ways.

Kartunnen (1971b) first suggested that there may be two kinds of presupposition with differing semantic and syntactic correlates for English. These differences were further investigated in Hooper (1974), where strong presupposition was distinguished from weak presupposition. In sentences with strong presupposition, the complement is accepted as true under any conditions. With complements only weakly presupposed, it is possible to construct sentences in which the truth of the complement cannot be inferred. Consider the following sentences.

(5) No me sorprende el hecho de que hayan podido hacer el viaje sino que hayan podido quedarse allî por tanto tiempo.
'It doesn't surprise me that they were able to take the trip, but rather that they were able to stay so long.'

Even in a contrastive situation the complement in (5) remains presupposed.

(6) No supe que se había cancelado el vuelo sino que todavía no había llegado.
'I didn't find out that the flight had been canceled, only that it hadn't arrived.'

In (6), however, the proposition may or may not be presupposed.

Kartunnen points out questions in English which are ambiguous between a presupposed and a nonpresupposed reading. Let us examine such questions in Spanish.

(7) ¿Sentiste que no dijeras la verdad?
'Were you sorry that you didn't tell the truth?'

(8) ¿Supiste que no habías dicho la verdad?
'Did you learn that you hadn't told the truth?'

In (7) the speaker assumes that the addressee had not told the truth. In (8), however, there are two possibilities of interpretation: one in which the matrix is questioned (¿Lo supiste?) and the complement presupposed, and the other in which the speaker actually wishes to question the complement, i.e. 'Did or did you not tell the truth?'

We assume that it has been demonstrated that in strictly following our definition there are two types of presupposition which we label strong and weak. What remains to be shown is that the notion of weak presupposition is compatible with the notion of assertion.

2.1 In this paper we use the term ASSERTION loosely to mean a proposition expressed in a declarative sentence. More specifically, the speaker claims the proposition which he has announced to be true to the best of his knowledge.[6] An assertion is a claim to truth which, on at least one reading, may be taken as the semantically dominant proposition in the discourse context. Suppose the speaker wishes to assert that he believes a certain proposition to be a true statement. This may be done syntactically in a number of different ways, depending on whether or not he wishes to qualify the assertion. If there is no qualification, he states the proposition directly.

(9) María irá a la playa con nosotros.
'Mary will go to the beach with us.'

He may, of course, qualify in various degrees his belief in the validity of the proposition, with the use of an appropriate matrix.

(10) Me parece (creo, es seguro, etc.) que María irá a la playa con nosotros.
'It seems to me (I believe, it's sure, etc.) that Mary will go to the beach with us.'

Assertions may also be indirect; that is, we may report the assertions of others and describe the way in which the assertion was reported to us.

(11) Juan me dijo (confesó, comunicó, explicó, etc.) que María iría a la playa con nosotros.
'John said to me (confessed, communicated, explained, etc.) that Mary would go to the beach with us.'

This in no way commits the speaker to the truth of the reported assertion.

We shall also try to show that an assertion may be embedded in a matrix which describes the way in which knowledge was obtained or perceived.

(12) Sabía (me enteré, reconocí, vi, noté, etc.) que María iba a la playa con nosotros.
'I knew (learned, recognized, saw, noted, etc.) that Mary was going to the beach with us.'

In all the foregoing cases, the verbs are indicative in form. In fact, all simple declarative sentences (both positive and negative) are assertions and are expressed with indicative verb forms. Questions simply request an affirmation as a reply. There are only two types of nonembedded sentences in which indicative verb forms are not used: imperatives and sentences of doubt.

Imperatives are clearly not assertions and subjunctive verb forms are used in all cases except one. [7]

(13) ¡No hables con ella!
'Don't talk to her!'

(14) ¡Vuelva mañana, señor!
'Come back tomorrow, sir!'

The assertion in (14), if there is one, is something close to 'I want something', not 'You come back tomorrow.' Commands may also be reported or qualified just as in the case of assertions. Matrices of the latter type are referred to variously as matrices of volition, persuasion, or influence.

Reported commands:

(15) Carlos nos dijo (escribió, insistió en, gritó) que pasáramos las vacaciones con él en el campo.
'Carlos told (wrote, insisted, shouted) (for) us to spend our vacation with him in the country.'

Volition:

(16) Marta quería (prefería, propuso, permitió) que nos fuéramos immediatamente.
'Marta wanted (preferred, proposed, permitted) us to leave immediately.'

The verb forms of the matrices are indicative since the matrix predicate is always asserted. Commands, direct or qualified, embedded or nonembedded, are never assertions; the verb forms of the command are subjunctive.

Since both assertions and commands may be reported, there is a minimal formal contrast between the indicative and subjunctive verb forms. [8]

(17) Le dijo que regresara.
'She told him to return.'

(18) Le dijo que regresaba.
'She told him that he was returning.'

There are simple nonembedded sentences which express degrees of doubt in the mind of the speaker as to the validity of the proposition.

(19) Acaso (tal vez, quizás) {viene / venga} mañana.
'Perhaps (maybe, possibly) he's coming tomorrow.'

If the proposition is felt to be essentially an assertion with qualification, then the indicative forms are used. If, in the speaker's mind, there is sufficient doubt so that he wishes to avoid making a clear assertion, then the subjunctive forms are used.

Usually, doubted propositions are embedded so that the matrices express varying degrees of doubt.

(20) Es dudoso (no es seguro, es posible, es probable, etc.) que llegue temprano.
'It's doubtful (it's not certain, it's possible, it's probable, etc.) that I'll arrive early.'

Negation of matrices of belief often results in matrices of doubt. In this case the subjunctive forms will be used in the complement.

(21) No creo (no es cierto, no es evidente, no parece, etc.) que hayan podido terminar.
'I don't believe (it isn't certain, it isn't evident, it doesn't seem, etc.) that they have been able to finish.'

In summary, the correlation of mood with assertion and presupposition appears to be clear. The indicative is used in cases of assertion and weak presupposition, the subjunctive in cases of nonassertion, including strong presupposition. We will now examine other syntactic correlates of assertion and presupposition other than mood with two purposes in mind: we wish to show that (1) weak presupposition is treated syntactically and semantically as a type of assertion and that (2) the syntactic processes involved may be explained by the semantic properties of the class of matrices to which they are restricted.

2.2 The following classification is given for ease of reference in the discussion. Many matrices are semantically ambivalent and may be used in more than one sense. We will return to this problem. For the present we have listed those which, with rare exceptions, are used only as members of a single class. The subclassifications are according to syntactic structure: (1) contains matrices which take object complements; (2) contains matrices consisting of the copula plus an adjective or noun which take subject complements; (3) contains other matrices which take subject complements, mostly intransitive verbs.

(a) Factives (strong presupposition)

(1) deplorar, sentir, resentir, lamentar, alegrarse de, entristecerse de, estar contento (alegre, triste, avergonzado, furioso, enojado) de.
(2) ser ridículo, triste, significativo, raro, trágico, emocionante, divertido, natural, extraordinario, una tragedia, una cosa de risa.
(3) dar náusea, dar asco, dar vergüenza, sorprender, alegrar, molestar, tener sentido, gustar, divertir, emocionar, extrañar, encantar, indignar, facinar, enojar.

(b) Semifactives (weak presupposition)

(1) poner en claro, revelar, clarificar, descubrir, ver, darse cuenta de, fijarse en, olvidar(se de), aprender, tomar en consideración, precibir, ver, reconocer, reflexionar sobre, acordarse de, contar con.

(c) Opinion (announcing assertion)

(1) saber, sostener, opinar, asegurar, jurar, concluir, mantener, juzgar, creer, pensar, suponir, imaginarse, no dudar, tomar por dado, estar seguro, cierto.
(2) ser verdad, cierto, seguro, claro, indiscutible, obvio.
(3) parecer, pasar, ser, resultar.

(d) Reporting (indirect assertion)

(1) contar, explicar, relatar, predecir, confesar, repostar, afirmar, intimar, declarar, prometer, proclamar.

(e) Doubt (lack of assertion)

(1) dudar, no creer, no estar seguro de.
(2) ser inseguro, probable, dudoso, no ser seguro, verdad, obvio, evidente, ser una mentira.

(f) Volition (command)

(1) anhelar, querer, preferir, desear, oponerse a, exigir, pedir, sugerir, proponer, rogar, mandar, dejar, permitir, aconsejar, impedir, ordenar, suplicar, recomendar, evitar, implorar.
(2) ser necesario, recomendable, inevitable, preferible, deseable.

3.0 Let us now turn to supporting our claim that weakly presupposed matrices are also cases of assertion. To see this, we will examine the effects of negation and questioning on sentences with a matrix from each of the six classes.

3.1 Simple sentence negation does not, of course, affect the strong presupposition of sentences with factive matrices (subjective comment).

(22) Estoy contento (de) que hayan podido hacer el viaje.
'I'm glad that they were able to take the trip.'

(23) No estoy contento (de) que hayan podido hacer el viaje.
'I'm not happy that they were able to take the trip.'

In either case, the presupposed proposition remains constant; only the comment is varied.

The negation of matrices of volition only changes the assertion, that is, the matrix itself; the complement remains a nonassertion.

(24) Quiero que vayan con nosotros.
'I want them to go with us.'

(25) No quiero que vayan con nosotros.
'I don't want them to go with us.'

In sentences with matrices of doubt, if the effect of negation does not change the semantic class of the matrix, the proposition remains a nonassertion.

(26) Es probable que lo compren.
'It's probable that they'll buy it.'

(27) No es probable que lo compren.
'It isn't probable that they'll buy it.'

If, however, the negated matrix turns out to be equivalent to a positive opinion matrix, it will naturally be treated as assertive.

(28) Dudo que lo leyeran.
'I doubt that they were reading it.'

(29) No dudo que lo leían.
'I don't doubt that they were reading it.'

Thus, in general, negation of a nonassertive matrix does not affect its complement.

The negation of sentences with assertive matrices, on the other hand, is quite complex. The negation of an opinion matrix may cause the meaning to be equivalent to that of a doubt matrix. In this case, the proposition is not affirmed and the subjunctive must be used.[9]

(30) Es seguro que irán.
'It's sure that they'll go.'

(31) No es seguro que vayan.
'It's not sure that they'll go.'

This is the case when the opinion is personal, that is, the speaker's own. However, if the opinion is someone else's and is being reported by the speaker, there may be complications. The speaker may choose simply to report the opinion as given.

(32) Juan cree que irán.
'John thinks they'll go.'

(33) Juan no cree que vayan.
'John doesn't think they'll go.'

However, if the speaker wishes to affirm as true a proposition another speaker has doubted, he may do so by using the indicative.[10]

(34) Juan no cree que Uds. fueron al cine.
'John doesn't believe that you went to the movies.'

The negation of matrices of reporting is also quite complex.

(35) Juan no dijo que Uds. querían ir.
'John didn't say that you wanted to go.'

(36) No predijeron que el temblor ocurriría tan pronto.
'They didn't predict that the earthquake would occur so soon.'

(37) Tu no dijiste que mis padres estaban en casa.
'You didn't say that my parents were at home.'

Out of context and without any indication of emphasis, it is difficult to interpret the negation. In (35), without any special emphasis, the interpretation seems to be that 'You wanted to go' is a possible assertion (neither presupposed nor rejected), but that in this case it just simply is not the assertion which Juan uttered. That is, it is not the complement which is negated, but its relation to the matrix.

If emphasis is added, one can negate various parts of the sentence.

(38) Juan no <u>dijo</u> que Uds. querían irse sino que lo <u>gritó.</u>
'John didn't <u>say</u> you wanted to go, he <u>yelled</u> it.'

(39) Juan no dijo que <u>Uds</u>. querían irse sino que <u>ellos</u> querían irse.
'John didn't say that <u>you</u> wanted to go, but that <u>they</u> wanted to go.'

(40) Juan no dijo que Uds. <u>querían</u> irse sino que <u>tenían</u> que irse.
'John didn't say that you <u>wanted</u> to go, but that you <u>had</u> to go.'

(41) Juan no dijo que Uds. querían <u>irse</u> sino que querían <u>quedarse</u>.
'John didn't say that you wanted <u>to go</u>, but that you wanted <u>to stay</u>.'

In (38), the complement is not affected. However, in (39) to (41), although the proposition is still a possible affirmation, various parts are negated. The mere fact that with negation of the matrix different parts of the complement may be negated shows that these complements contain an assertion. Now let us examine sentences with semifactive matrices of perception or knowledge.

(42) No vio que Uds. habían salido.
'He didn't see that you had left.'

(43) No supieron que se había cancelado el vuelo.
'They didn't find out that the flight had been cancelled.'

(44) No tomó en consideración que hacía calor.
'He didn't take into consideration that it was hot.'

The preferred reading for most speakers is that the complement is presupposed to be true. However, if contrastive stress is added, these sentences behave similarly to sentences of reporting.

(45) No vio que Uds. habían salido, solamente que ya no estaban allí.
'He didn't see that you had left, only that you were no longer there.'

(46) No supieron que se había cancelado el vuelo, sino que no había llegado todavía.
'They didn't learn that the flight had been cancelled, only that it hadn't yet arrived.'

(47) No tomó en consideración que hacía calor, solamente que no llovía.
'He didn't take into consideration that it was hot, only that it wasn't raining.'

If used personally, the semifactives may be similar to matrices of opinion; if so, the negated form may be used to express doubt and the subjunctive is used.

(48) No era obvio que fuera tan importante.
'It wasn't obvious that it was so important.'

(49) No vi que hiciera tanto trabajo.
'I didn't see that she did so much work.'

(50) Yo no me acordé de que fuera tan lejos.
'I didn't remember that it was so far.'

If the speaker, however, wishes to assert the proposition but negate its relationship to the matrix, the indicative is used.

(51) No era obvio que era tan importante.
'It was important, but it wasn't obvious that it was.'

(52) No vi que hacía tanto.
'She did a lot; I just didn't see it.'

(53) Yo no me acordé de que era tan lejos.
'It was far, but I didn't remember it.'

The negation of a semifactive used in the present tense first person singular is anomalous if the combination of the meaning of the matrix and assertion is contradictory.

(54) *No me doy cuenta de que ella está adelantada.
*'I don't realize she's ahead.'

Sometimes contrastive stress can make the sentence acceptable.

(55) No véo que empieza a llover.
'I don't see that it's starting to rain.'

In general, then, it is seen that the semifactives are similar to both matrices of reporting and opinion with regard to sentence negation and have little in common with nonassertions.

3.2 Effects of interrogation. Just as with sentence negation, question formation has no effect on the complements of nonassertive sentences unless the effect of interrogation is to change the semantic class of the matrix.

(56) ¿Estás contento que tomaran tanta cerveza?
'Are you glad that they were drinking so much beer?'

(57) ¿Le aconsejaste que fuera al médico?
'Did you advise him to go to the doctor?'

(58) ¿Era dudoso que no la pudieran alcanzar?[11]
'Was it doubtful that they couldn't reach her?'

In assertive sentences the effects of interrogation are more complicated, as might be expected. In sentences of reporting, i.e. indirect assertion, there are two possibilities of interpretation: parenthetical and nonparenthetical.[12]

(59) ¿Dijo Juan que iba a salir temprano?
'Did John say he was leaving early?'

(60) ¿Anunciaron que el partido terminó ya?
'Did they announce that the game is already over?'

On the nonparenthetical reading we are interested in whether John actually said something or whether something was announced. On the parenthetical reading the speaker is really interested in questioning the proposition.

(61) ¿Iba a salir temprano Juan?
'Was John going to leave early?'

(62) ¿Terminó el partido ya?
'Did the game already end?'

With matrices of belief the parenthetical reading is most common:

(63) ¿Crees que ganará mañana?
'Do you think she'll win tomorrow?'

(64) ¿Es verdad que irán los dos?
'Is it true that both of them will go?'

(65) ¿Te parece que quieren quedarse?
'Does it seem to you that they want to stay?'

If, however, the matrix is used nonparenthetically to cast doubt on the proposition of the complement, then the subjunctive forms appear.[13]

(66) ¿Crees que gane mañana?
'Do you really think she'll win tomorrow?'

Questions with matrices of knowledge also seem to have a parenthetical and a nonparenthetical reading in most cases.

(67) ¿Te diste cuenta que no lo hiciste?
'Did you realize you didn't do it?'

(68) ¿Viste que no lo terminaron?
'Did you see that it wasn't finished?'

Although by far the most common interpretation is that the question applies to the matrix, it is easy to imagine contexts in which the complement itself is being questioned.

(69) Viste que no lo terminaron, o ¿es que lo terminaron?
'Did you see that they didn't finish it, or did they finish it?'

Let us now turn to syntactic evidence to support our claims concerning assertion and nonassertion.

4.0 In a recent paper (1973), Hooper and Thompson investigated certain syntactic processes first studied by Emonds (1969a) and found a correlation between their application and the semantic notion of assertion as used in this paper. It is important to examine these notions in detail since, even though examples from Spanish seem to refute the Hooper-Thompson hypothesis, they actually support it.

Most of the syntactic processes defined by Emonds as Root Transformations are movement transformations which result, in English, in a shift of emphasis in the sentence.[14] Directional Adverb Preposing is a typical example.

(70) 'Over the trees flew the birds.'
(71) 'The birds flew over the trees.'

Hooper and Thompson demonstrate that these 'emphatic' transformations such as Directional Adverb Preposing, Negative Constituent Preposing, VP Preposing, and so forth, may occur only in assertive sentences.

(72) 'He said that over the trees flew the birds.'
(73) *'I'm happy that over the trees flew the birds.'
(74) *'It's doubtful that over the trees flew the birds.'

Their point was that emphatic RT's apply in assertions, but not presupposed clauses or other nonassertions because it is inappropriate, in general, to emphasize backgrounded material.

Although there are differences of opinion among English speakers on the acceptability of many of these types of sentences, the main thrust of the argument seems to be valid.

Let us now turn to Spanish and examine the possibilities. If the hypothesis of Hooper and Thompson is correct, it must be also valid for Spanish. In that case, emphatic transformations should be restricted to assertive sentences, i.e. those with indicative verb forms.[15] However, consider the following sentences, all perfectly acceptable in Spanish.

(75) Dijo que sobre los árboles volaban miles de aves.
'He said that above the trees were flying thousands of birds.'

(76) ¡Qué maravilloso que sobre los árboles volaran tantas aves!
*'How wonderful that above the trees flew so many birds.'

(77) Dudo que por las calles se viera tanto de interés.
*'I doubt that in the streets could one see so many interesting things.'

These results lead us to conclude that either the Hooper-Thompson hypothesis is incorrect, our indicative mood-assertion hypothesis is incorrect, or that something is wrong with our definition of emphasis.

Consider the following pairs of sentences.

(78) Miles de aves volaban sobre los árboles.
(79) Sobre los árboles volaban miles de aves.
(80) 'Thousands of birds flew above the trees.'
(81) 'Above the trees flew thousands of birds.'

It is immediately apparent to anyone who knows Spanish and English well that the correspondences are not at all exact. Sentence (81) is definitely less common that (80) and is used only for special emphasis. In Spanish, on the other hand, (79) is as common as (78) and certainly draws no special attention to itself as does the English transformed sentence (81). In (78) the focus[16] (but not the emphasis) is on the place where the birds flew and in (79) the focus is on the fact that it was birds that were flying over the trees, instead of something else, perhaps insects. One is simply not more emphatic than the other. Therefore, since Directional Adverb Preposing is quite common in Spanish and not at all emphatic, it may freely occur in nonassertions; in English, it does not.[17]

The task now, then, is to ascertain which of these movement transformations actually result in emphasis and to test their correlation with the assertion-nonassertion distinction.

4.1 Bolinger (1968) very perceptively described in detail perhaps the most important case of an emphatic transformation, which he labeled Postposed Main Phrases and which we term Complement Preposing. Complement Preposing is an operation which fronts all or part of the complement clause. Thus, the structure underlying (82) may yield (83) or (84) when Complement Preposing is applied.

(82) Creo que la situación se ha vuelto muy complicada.
'I believe that the situation has become quite complex.'

(83) La situación, creo, se ha vuelto muy complicada.
'The situation, I believe, has become quite complex.'

(84) La situación se ha vuelto muy complicada, creo.
'The situation has become quite complex, I believe.'

Bolinger showed that this process in English and Spanish is correlated almost exactly with the use of the subjunctive in Spanish; he did not at that time try to relate the process to notions of assertion or presupposition. Emonds (1969a) assumed that Complement Preposing was restricted to nonpresupposed complements. Hooper (1974) showed that for English, at least, the distinction between matrices which allow Complement Preposing and those that do not is the assertion-nonassertion distinction; this is equally true for Spanish complements. All classes of assertive matrices allow Complement Preposing:

Reporting

(85) No ha hecho su trabajo, me confesó (dijo, explicó, etc.).
'He hasn't done his work yet, he confessed (said, explained, etc.) to me.'

Knowledge

(86) No lo iban a completar, (como) pronto se dieron cuenta.
'They weren't going to finish it, as they soon realized.'

Belief

(87) Irán todos, creo (me parece, estoy seguro, etc.).
'Everyone will go, I think (it seems to me, I'm sure, etc.).'

Nonassertive matrices do not allow Complement Preposing.

Doubt

(88) *Lo buscó en el diccionario, dudo.
*'He looked for it in the dictionary, I doubt.'

Volition

(89) *No lo encontrarás, quiero.
*'You won't find it, I want.'

Comment

(90) *Guillermo quería estudiar para abogado, me alegro.
*'Bill wanted to be a lawyer, I'm happy.'

In other words, nonassertive matrices may not be used parenthetically in their predicate forms.[18]

The effect of Complement Preposing is to make the complement proposition the main assertion of the sentence. The original main element, the matrix, is reduced to secondary, almost parenthetical, status. The explication for the restriction of this process to assertions is simple. All simple, declarative sentences are taken to be assertions (or commands: see further). If we utter a sentence like 'John doesn't eat much', this is equivalent to saying 'I say (believe, affirm, etc.) that John doesn't eat much.' Thus any preposed complement will be taken to be an assertion, and Complement Preposing cannot therefore be applied to nonassertions.[19]

There are two classes of sentences which are apparent exceptions to the rule of Complement Preposing. First, certain nonassertions may be preposed.

(91) Me dijo que fuera a comprarme uno.
'He told me to go buy one.'

(92) Vaya a comprarse uno, me dijo.
'Go buy one, he said.'

Matrices of volition may not be used in this manner, however.

(93) *Vaya a comprarse uno, quiere.
*'Go buy yourself one, he wants.'

In fact, the only matrices which can be so used are those which can report either an assertion or a direct imperative.

(94) Venga a visitarnos, me escribió.
'Come to see us, he wrote.'

(95) No saltes, gritó.
'Don't jump, he shouted.'

Since independent sentences are either assertions or commands,

(96) Juan va al cine.
'John is going to the movies.'

(97) Juan, no vayas al cine.
'John, don't go to the movies.'

therein lies the explanation as to why, in these cases only, the complement may be preposed.[20]

The other class of exceptions consists of what appear to be assertions which cannot be preposed.

(98) Juan no me dijo que Uds. habían estudiado tanto.
'John didn't tell me that you all had studied so much.'

(99) *Uds. habían estudiado tanto, Juan no dijo.
*'You all had studied a lot, John didn't say.'

In the section on negation we saw that, without emphasis, the effect of negation on matrices of reporting was to negate the relationship between the matrix and its complement. In (98) the proposition that you all had studied so much is a possible assertion, hence the indicative mood, but in this case it was not the assertion which John uttered. If we were to front the complement, it would be interpreted as a direct assertion followed by a contradiction. The sentence would make sense only if we used <u>but</u>.

(100) Uds. habían estudiado mucho, pero Juan no lo dijo.
'You all had studied a lot, but John didn't say it.'

4.2 Another transformation which in Spanish results in emphasis is what Emonds termed Verb Phrase Preposing. Although highly restricted in Spanish, the transformation does apply in certain cases of auxiliary plus main verb.

(101) Juan quiere que Lola se case con él, pero ella no puéde casarse con él.
'John wants Lola to marry him, but she can't marry him.'

(102) Juan quiere que Lola se case con él; pero, casarse con él, no <u>puede</u>.
'John wants Lola to marry him; but, marry him, she <u>can't</u>.'

Now let us compare the effects of a matrix, one assertive and one nonassertive.

(103) Juan quiere que Lola se case con él; pero, parece que casarse con él no puede.
'John wants Lola to marry him; but it seems that marry him she can't.'

(104) *Juan quiere que Lola se case con él; pero, ella duda que casarse con él, pueda.
*'John wants Lola to marry him; but she doubts that marry him she can.'

The other movement transformations discussed by Emonds (1969a) and Hooper and Thompson (1973) do not produce emphasis in Spanish and are not restricted to sentences of assertion.

Negative Constituent Preposing

(105) Es verdad que jamás he visto yo tanta gente.
'It's true that never have I seen so many people.'

(106) Estoy contento de que jamás tenga yo que regresar aquí.
*'I am pleased that never will I have to return here.'

Preposing around be

(107) Es obvio que más significativo sería el desarrollo de una teoría semántica.
'It's obvious that more significant would be the development of a semantic theory.'

(108) Dudo que más significativo sea el desarrollo de una teoría semántica.
*'I doubt that more significant would be the development of a semantic theory.'

(109) Me di cuenta de que este libro lo habían encontrado hace años.
*'I realized that this book they had found years ago.'

(110) Quisiera que este libro lo leyeran antes de clase mañana.
*'I want this book for you to read before class tomorrow.'

5.0 We have tried to show that the syntactic properties discussed here, the use of mood in Spanish, and the application of the various movement transformations, are directly related to the semantic notions of assertion and presupposition. We showed that by distinguishing two types of presupposition, weak and strong, we can at least partially account for the seemingly aberrant nature of the knowledge matrices. We believe that this is more evidence against the claims of some transformationalists that the use of mood is syntactically based, and it supports the traditional view that its use is meaningful. However, we do not mean to imply that vague statements about factualness, truth, or reality so often found in grammars and in texts used to teach the subjunctive are anything other than incorrect and misleading.

NOTES

1. This paper is the result of long hours of conversation and correspondence with Professor Joan B. Hooper, without whose help it would never have been completed.

2. In the only other article of which I am aware dealing with presupposition and mood in a Romance language, María-Luisa Rivero (1971) discusses what she considers to be presupposition in complements with matrices such as creer, parecer, and certain others. Her notion of presupposition is never precisely defined in the paper, but is certainly different from Keenan's and from that which is adopted in this paper. In fact, as will be seen, her use of presupposition correlates closely in some respects with my notion of assertion.

3. Most of these processes which are relevant for English do not operate in Spanish. (a) Only presupposed complements may be used with the full range of gerundive constructions. The professor's not knowing the answer was surprising. (b) Presupposed complements do not allow subject raising. *He is tragic to finish his paper. (c) Vacuous extraposition from object is optional with presupposed complements. I hate it that we have to get up so early. (d) Presupposed complements do not allow the accusative and infinitive construction. *He supposes the president to be responsible. (e) Only presupposed complements allow the phrase the fact that + S. I am pleased about the fact that she will remain on this campus. Only the last item (e) may be applied to Spanish since the other syntactic processes, (a)-(d), do not exist.

4. This is the same definition used by the Kiparskys for their class of emotive matrices. The emotive category for the Kiparskys cut across the lines of presupposition. However, their emotive factive (presupposition) matrices correspond roughly to our true factive matrices, and most of their emotive nonfactive matrices fall into our category of volition.

5. Actually, there are many Spanish speakers who do not use subjunctive forms in these sentences. I will return to this matter shortly.

6. That does not imply, of course, that the speaker cannot lie or deliberately mislead his listeners.

7. Only the singular familiar positive commands are not subjunctive in form. Most traditional grammarians have posited an imperative mood for Spanish but this analysis is purely semantic, since there are no forms which differ from indicative or subjunctive forms. The second person singular positive command is identical in form to the third person singular indicative form (except in a few cases which are verbal stems: sal, ven, ten, haz, etc.).

8. As is well known, this formal contrast exists also in English for many, although certainly not all, speakers.

(i) I insist that he is there now.
I insist that he be there tomorrow.

9. It must be pointed out, however, that there exists much variation in the Spanish-speaking world with regard to the use of mood with matrices of opinion or doubt. Theoretically, there could be four basic possibilities combining mood and negation:

(i) Creo que irá. Most certainty.
(ii) Creo que vaya. Some doubt.
(iii) Creo que va. Some doubt.
(iv) No creo que vaya. Most doubt.

However, many factors weigh against the full use of such a system. Most matrices of opinion or doubt are not as flexible as are perhaps creer, parecer, and others; most are fairly clear-cut cases: dudo, no dudo. In addition, there is a tendency on the part of most speakers to regard any opinion, however qualified, as an assertion and sentences like (ii) are unacceptable. Also important is the fact that except for subtle differences in intensity of the doubt, the use of the subjunctive or indicative is quite redundant because the main thrust is carried by the matrix. Many speakers, therefore, use the subjunctive only when the doubt (nonassertion) is clear and indicative if they do not wish to deny completely the possibility that the assertion may be true. We also would not wish to deny that for some speakers the assertion-nonassertion contrast for mood does not operate and that any use of the subjunctive in sentences of doubt may be formulaic.

10. Such cases are discussed in detail by María-Luisa Rivero (1971), where she describes such complements as presupposed. This is clearly not the case using our definition of presupposition since (a) the truth of the proposition is not implied by the sentence as a whole, and (b) the truth of the proposition is affected by the processes of negation and questioning. It seems clear that such cases are examples of assertion; the fact that the proposition is known to the listener does not prevent the speaker from (re)affirming it. Many speakers, of course, do not make the semantic distinction and simply use subjunctive in all cases.

11. In certain cases, if the speaker wishes to affirm the complement, he may use the indicative (although many speakers do not accept the combination of affirmation and doubt and hence always use the subjunctive).

(i) ¿Dudaste que lo hice yo?
'Did you doubt that I did it?'

12. The terms 'parenthetical' and 'nonparenthetical' in this sense are taken from Hooper (1974) and Urmson (1963). I quote from Hooper (1974): 'The reading in which the main (assertive) verb itself makes the main assertion of the sentence is called the nonparenthetical reading. On the reading in which the complement proposition is the main proposition, the assertive verb is used in its parenthetical sense.'

13. I do not mean to imply that all speakers use the subjunctive forms in these sentences.

14. Two are not: Tag-Question Formation, which does not exist as such in Spanish, and Subject-Auxiliary Inversion, which also is quite different in Spanish. I will not discuss these two transformations in this paper.

15. Joan Hooper has pointed out (personal communication) that Spanish may be a VSO language, and if this is the case, then one would not expect correspondences of items such as Root Transformations. See note 16 for another hypothesis.

16. Helas Contreras (in this volume) has suggested that these data be explained in terms of theme (old material) and rheme (new material). In this framework neither word order is basic; rather, both derive from the native speaker's selection of different elements as the rheme of the sentence.

17. I suspect that this will also explain why some English speakers also accept certain of these transformations in nonassertive sentences.

18. There are, however, sentence adverbials which may be used in this manner.

(i) Estarán allí a las nueve, a lo mejor.
'They will be there at nine o'clock, in all likelihood.'

(ii) El tren llegará dentro de poco, probablemente.
'The train will arrive soon, probably.'

One might argue that the hypothesis that the mood is directly correlated with assertion-nonassertion is falsified by these examples since one can find minimal pairs in which the difference is only syntactic.

(iii) Es posible que vengan.
'It's possible that they'll come.'

(iv) Posiblemente vendrán.
'Possibly they'll come.'

(v) Vendrán, posiblemente.
'They'll come, possibly.'

However, I would argue that there are semantic differences between these sentences, slight though they may be. In (iii) no assertion is made; a proposition is stated as a possibility. In (v) it is asserted that they will come and then the assertion is qualified; (iv) is intermediate between (iii) and (v), and one also finds the sentence (vi):

(vi) Posiblemente vengan.
'Possibly they'll come.'

according to how doubtful the speaker feels about the proposition. We could find no sentence adverbs of volition.

Sentence adverbials of comment are completely different, both syntactically and semantically, from their corresponding matrices.

(vii) Es interesante que fueran a Acapulco en vez de Puerto Vallarta.
'It's interesting that they went to Acapulco instead of Puerto Vallarta.'

(viii) Interesante que sea, fueron a Acapulco en vez de Puerto Vallarta.
'Interesting that it may be, they went to Acapulco instead of Puerto Vallarta.'

In (vii) it is presupposed that they went to Acapulco; in (viii) this same proposition is asserted.

19. For an even more detailed discussion of the details of Complement Preposing see Bolinger (1968). A syntactic process which appears to be quite similar to Complement Preposing is Extraposition. The Kiparskys (1970) give credit to Jespersen for the introduction of this term. Ross's (1967) study of extraposition in English is perhaps the cause of recent interest in the phenomenon. The Kiparskys correlated extraposition in English to lack of presupposition: non-presupposed complements must be extraposed.

Extraposition is the process which describes the relationship between sentences such as (i) and (ii).

(i) Que no querían ir con Uds. es evidente.
'That they didn't want to go with you all is evident.'

(ii) Es evidente que no querían ir con Uds.
'It's evident that they didn't want to go with you all.'

Since sentence (ii) is far more common than (i), it appears at first glance that this is just another case of Complement Preposing. There are, however, certain syntactic and intonational differences.

(iii) Querrán ir, es seguro.
'They will want to go, it's sure.'

(iv) Que querrán ir es seguro.
'That they will want to go is sure.'

(v) Es seguro que querrán ir.
'It's sure that they will want to go.'

In (iii) the matrix is parenthetical; in (iv) the sentence follows the normal subject-predicate order. In (v), with extraposition the subject (complement) has been moved to the end of the sentence. (Emonds presents considerable evidence that sentential subjects such as these are actually generated in the 'extraposed' position and moved by a transformation he calls Subject Replacement to this position.)

The complements in sentence initial position will not be taken necessarily as assertions, since they must be preceded by que, and they are usually followed by the copula or another intransitive verb. Therefore, subject complements may appear in sentence initial position with all classes of matrices. This is not necessarily the most common or preferred position.

(vi) Que no compraron el carro es evidente.
'That they didn't buy the car is evident.'

(vii) Que Juan no había sacado buenas notas no me fue explicado muy bien.
'That John hadn't gotten good grades wasn't explained to me very well.'

(viii) Que Alfredo es un buen nadador es reconocido en todas partes.
'That Alfred is a good swimmer is recognized everywhere.'

(ix) Que se queden conmigo es dudoso.
'That they stay with me is doubtful.'

(x) Que se vayan inmediatamente es preferible.
'That they leave immediately is preferable.'

(xi) Que te lo hayan regalado es magnífico.
'That they gave it to you is magnificent.'

In sentences in which the matrix is not the copula, if the complement is asserted, then it must be preposed.

(xii) Resulta que se irán mañana.
'It turns out that they'll leave tomorrow.'

(xiii) Que se irán mañana resulta.
*'That they'll leave tomorrow turns out.'

However, nonassertions are not so restricted.

(xiv) Que nos devuelva el dinero basta (importa, cuenta, emociona).
'That he return the money to us is enough (is important, counts, is exciting).'

It is not entirely clear why the extraposed sentences are preferred. Perhaps it is to avoid misinterpretation of all subject-complements as (preposed) assertions.

20. Although it is clear that this is the explanation for the possibility of either assertions or commands in first position in the

sentence with the predicate for reporting in parenthetical position, it is not at all clear that these commands are completely parallel to the sentences we have taken to be the result of Complement Preposing. However, this does not affect my claims and I will not pursue the matter further. Note also that it is obvious that reported commands differ syntactically from sentences with regular matrices of volition. In most work done within the transformational framework, sentences of volition were 'derived' from underlying commands. Consider the following sentences.

(i) Me dijo que viniera a las nueve.
'He told me to come at nine.'

(ii) Me dijo 'Venga a las nueve.'
'He said to me "Come at nine".'

(iii) Venga a las nueve, me dijo.
'Come at nine, he said to me.'

Although (i) may be 'derived' from (ii) or even (iii), such is not the case for the following set of sentences in which (v) and (vi) do not even exist.

(iv) Quería que viniera a las nueve.
'He wanted me to come at nine.'

(v) *Quería, 'Venga a las nueve.'
*'He wanted "Come at nine".'

(vi) *Venga a las nueve, quería.
*'Come at nine, he wanted.'

However one may wish to formalize this difference, it is clear that the syntactic difference is a direct result of the semantic difference between matrices of reporting and volition.

SABER: TOWARD A GRAMMAR OF KNOWLEDGE IN SPANISH

MARÍA-LUISA RIVERO

University of Ottawa

In this paper I consider certain aspects of the grammar of the epistemological term saber 'to know' in Spanish, and, in a secondary way, its relationship with conocer 'to be acquainted with'.

In Spanish, the verb saber can enter into various syntactic constructions with different semantic consequences:

(1a) Juan sabe que la canción está pasada de moda
'John knows that the song is old-fashioned'
(the SABER QUE construction)
(1b) Juan sabe si la canción está pasada de moda
'John knows whether the song is old-fashioned'
(the SABER SI construction)
(1c) Juan sabe qué canción está pasada de moda
'John knows which song is old-fashioned'
(the SABER QUESTION-WORD construction)
(1d) Juan sabe la canción que está pasada de moda
'John knows the song which is old-fashioned'
(the SABER NP construction)
(1e) Juan sabe cantar la canción que está pasada de moda
'John knows how to sing the song which is old-fashioned'
(the SABER INFINITIVE construction).

Among the various semantic aspects which differentiate the foregoing examples, I mention only one at this point: the label 'factive' (Kiparsky and Kiparsky 1970) applies to saber in (1a) but is inapplicable elsewhere.

When we observe the foregoing paradigm, a number of interesting questions come to mind: (a) Are we dealing with one verb saber, or with several? (b) Are we dealing with only one verb and several complementizers having semantic import? (c) Are we dealing with a combination of several verbs saber and several complementizers? These questions will be treated in what follows.

To complete the list of constructions indicating basic knowledge in Spanish, another set of examples must be added to the paradigm in (1), those including conocer 'to be acquainted with':

(2) Juan conoce la canción que está pasada de moda
'John is acquainted with the song which is old-fashioned'

Is conocer an independent verb, or is it the surface realization of a Phrase-Marker which also includes saber (or one of the several kinds of saber) within a separate syntactic configuration? These problems are not dealt with here, but they must be answered before a complete grammar of saber can be formulated.

The questions I have raised within a purely syntactic context are important from other points of view as well. They constitute a translation into current linguistic terminology of some of the problems encountered by philosophers when speaking of different kinds of knowledge and different types of objects of knowledge and perception. [1]

I propose to demonstrate that there is one particular construction involving saber, the SABER INFINITIVE in (1e), which differs from all the others both syntactically and semantically. My conclusion is that example (1e) exhibits a different type of verb from those in the other sentences. By distinguishing this different kind of saber, the hypothesis that there is only one epistemological verb underlying all the syntactic constructions presented in (1) and (2), is refuted. I present the claim that the saber which precedes the infinitival complement is a verb belonging to the category of personal or root modals in Spanish (together with poder 'to be able to' and deber 'to have the obligation to'). [2] This kind of saber is not a verb of propositional attitude such as creer 'to believe' or saber que 'to know that'. It must therefore be separated from other epistemological verbs.

It should be pointed out first of all that saber in connection with an infinitive has the meaning of skill, similar in its range to poder 'to be able to' (Sé hablar inglés is sometimes rendered into English by 'I can speak English'). This modal meaning is the only one exhibited by the infinitive construction in Spanish, unlike the know how construction in English, which is ambiguous. Hintikka (1972) has pointed out that the sentence Do you know how to play the piano? can be understood as a question about skill and capacity, or in the sense of 'Do you know the answer to the question . . . ?' (the 'knowing-the-way' sense). In the second case, a possible answer is *Surely, everyone knows how a piano is played; but nevertheless not everyone can play the piano, myself included.* I do not find this type of ambiguity in the SABER INFINITIVE construction in Spanish. *¿Sabes tocar el piano?* is a question about skill, while the 'knowing-the-way' sense is realized by a different syntactic form in *¿Sabes cómo se toca el piano?* with *cómo* and no Infinitive in the complement sentence, or in *¿Sabes cómo tocar el piano?* with *cómo* and an Infinitive in the complement sentence. A question such as *¿Sabes abrir la puerta?* 'Do you know how to open the door?' is a request for directions. Analogously, somebody watching a swimming lesson could conclude *Ahora sé cómo se nada* 'Now I know how one swims', or *Ahora sé cómo nadar* 'Now I know the way to swim', but not *Ahora sé nadar* 'Now, I can swim'. *Ahora sé cómo se nada* and *Ahora sé cómo nadar* are examples of SABER QUESTION WORD constructions; they are related to the indirect questions discussed by Baker (1970). *Ahora sé nadar* is related to sentences with modal verbs. I am going to return briefly to this point at the end in order to distinguish these sentences on syntactic grounds as well.

As I have already pointed out, the SABER QUE sequence is factive, while the SABER INFINITIVE is not. The modals *poder* and *deber* are also nonfactive.

In addition to the above semantic properties, there are a number of syntactic characteristics that relate the SABER INFINITIVE sequence to modal verbs in Spanish and which separate it from other *saber* constructions. I now proceed to examine some of these.

Even though *saber* is a transitive verb, the SABER INFINITIVE sequence has no passive counterpart and behaves in this respect like the modals *deber* and *poder*. All other constructions with *saber* and those with *conocer* can be passivized.

(3a) Que la canción está pasada de moda es bien sabido
'That the song is old-fashioned is well known'
(SABER QUE)

(3b) Si la canción está pasada de moda será ya bien sabido
'Whether the song is old-fashioned is probably well known already' (SABER SI)

(3c) Qué canción está pasada de moda es bien sabido
'What song is old-fashioned is well known'
(SABER QUESTION WORD)

(3d) La canción que está pasada de moda es bien sabida
'The song which is old-fashioned is well known'
(SABER NP)

(4) La canción que está pasada de moda es bien conocida
'The song which is old-fashioned is well known'

(5a) *Cantar la canción que está pasada de moda es bien sabido
*'To sing the song which is old-fashioned is well known'
(SABER INFINITIVE)
(5b) *Cantar la canción que está pasada de moda es debido
(5c) *Cantar la canción que está pasada de moda es podido

Infinitive complements can also enter into passive sentences: Fue decidido cantar la canción que estaba pasada de moda '(It) was decided to sing the song which was old-fashioned'. Therefore, the constraint must be intrinsically connected with saber, poder, and deber, and not with the complement sentence or the form of the complementizer.

The SABER INFINITIVE sequence shares its pattern of pronominalization with the modals poder and deber, and not with the rest of the constructions with saber or conocer:

(6a) Juan sabe que la canción está pasada de moda y María lo sabe también
'John knows that the song is old-fashioned and Mary knows it too'
(6b) Juan sabe si la canción está pasada de moda y María lo sabe también
'John knows whether the song is old-fashioned and Mary knows it too'
(6c) Juan sabe qué canción está pasada de moda y María lo sabe también
'John knows which song is old-fashioned and Mary knows it too'
(6d) Juan sabe la canción que está pasada de moda y María la sabe también
'John knows the song which is old-fashioned and Mary knows it too'.

(7) Juan conoce la canción que está pasada de moda y María la conoce también
'John knows the song which is old-fashioned and Mary knows it too'

(8a) Juan sabe cantar la canción que está pasada de moda y María {*lo sabe / sabe hacerlo} también
'John knows how to sing the song which is old-fashioned and Mary knows {*it / how to do it} too'

(8b) Juan debe cantar la canción que está pasada de moda y María {*lo debe / debe hacerlo} también
'John must sing the song which is old-fashioned and Mary must {*it / do so} too'

(8c) Juan puede cantar la canción que está pasada de moda y María {*lo puede / puede hacerlo} también
'John can sing the song which is old-fashioned and Mary can {*it / do so} too'

A string of the form Juan sabe cantar la canción y María lo sabe 'John knows how to sing the song and Mary knows it' is grammatical when the pronoun lo 'it' has as its reference the full string Juan sabe cantar la canción 'John knows how to sing the song'. This, of course, is the pronominalization of a SABER QUE construction.

Certain Spanish modals are ambiguous in that they exhibit personal or root senses versus impersonal senses. A string such as Juan puede venir mañana can be understood in the sense of Puede que Juan venga mañana 'It is possible that John will come tomorrow' in which the modal assigns a degree of probability to John's coming, or it can be interpreted as 'John is able to come tomorrow', in which case there is a direct relationship between John and the modality. When there is a sequence of two modals in Spanish, the first must be interpreted in an impersonal sense while the second one receives a personal interpretation. El debe poder venir is understood as 'It must be that he is able to come', and not as 'He has the obligation to be able to come', nor as 'He has the obligation that it is possible that he comes'. In the same manner, El puede saber nadar is equivalent to 'It is possible that he knows how to swim', in which poder is impersonal. This syntactic peculiarity of modal verbs is shared by saber in an interesting way. Saber in its modal sense is always personal and can never be said to modify a proposition in the way impersonal poder and deber do. As a consequence, saber can never be the first verb in a sequence of two modals, only the second one:

(9a) *El sabe poder nadar.
(9b) *El sabe deber nadar.

(10a) El puede saber nadar
'It is possible that he knows how to swim'

(10b) El debe saber nadar
'It must be that he knows how to swim'

Other constructions with saber, nonmodal in nature, are not constrained in their order of occurrence with modals:

(11a) El sabe que puede nadar 'He knows that he can swim'
(11b) El sabe si puede nadar 'He knows if he can swim'
(11c) El sabe cómo puede nadar 'He knows how he can swim'
(11d) El sabe cómo poder nadar 'He knows the way to be able to swim'

(11c) and (11d) are examples of the SABER QUESTION WORD construction.

This syntactic fact must be correlated with the personal character saber has as a modal. It could never be correlated with the infinitive complement nor with verbs of propositional attitude, given that many of these verbs can be followed by modals within infinitival constructions:

(12a) El cree poder nadar
'He believes that he is able to swim'
(12b) El quiere poder nadar
'He wants to be able to swim'

It is my contention that the best way to treat the facts associated with the SABER INFINITIVE construction is to analyze this saber as a personal modal verb which is unrelated, both syntactically and semantically, to the other saber and conocer constructions. However, another possible solution exists which I am going to consider before concluding my paper, and which is to be rejected on syntactic grounds.

The differences between the various constructions with saber could be explained by positing different complementizers in underlying structure. The Infinitive Complementizer would then account for the semantic and syntactic peculiarities of the SABER INFINITIVE construction and its similarities with the modals poder and deber, given that they, too, can be followed by Infinitive Complementizers.

It must be pointed out, however, that propositional attitudes do not acquire modal meaning when followed by Infinitive Complementizers. The verb saber is uniquely different in this respect. For instance, creer 'to believe' and recordar 'to remember', when followed by infinitives, have the same meaning as when followed by que complementizers. The complement sentence likewise remains constant in meaning:

(13a) Creo ser discreto
(13b) Creo que soy discreto 'I believe that I am discreet'

(14a) Recuerdo haber corrido toda la noche.
(14b) Recuerdo que corrí toda la noche 'I remember that I ran all night'

The meaning attributed to the Infinitive Complementizer with saber would separate this verb from other verbs of propositional attitude.

There is, however, a purely syntactic argument which indicates that the distinctions which I have discussed should be connected with saber itself and not with the complementizers. In an article dealing with the hypothesis that complementizers are present in deep structure, J. Bresnan (1970) points out that 'how' constructions followed by an infinitive ('how to swim') could constitute a counterexample to her proposal. Such sequences, she argues, could be viewed as manifesting two separate complementizers, namely, wh- and 'for-to'. But she then concludes that wh- is the only complementizer since the infinitive is the result of Subject Deletion and not of complementation. Consider the following examples in Spanish and suppose that we adopt the proposal that the differences between (15a) and (15b) below are due to the complementizers they exhibit:

(15a) Juan no sabía entretenerse
'John did not know how to amuse himself'
(15b) Juan no sabía cómo entretenerse
'John did not know the way to amuse himself'

(15a) would have an Infinitive Complementizer present at the level of deep structure, and (15b) would have a wh Complementizer in deep structure, an infinitive appearing in the course of the derivation following deletion of the embedded subject. The differences between the two examples would be due to the presence of the Infinitive Complementizer in the first case, and to the wh Complementizer in the second.

This solution is not valid in Spanish because the infinitives in (15a) and (15b) must be considered complementizers in both cases. The deletion of the embedded subject is not the factor determining the appearance of the infinitive in (15b). Sentences in which the subject has not been deleted can also have an infinitive, as (16a) and (16b) indicate:

(16a) Juan no sabía entretenerse él
'John did not know how to amuse himself (he)'

(16b) Juan no sabía cómo entretenerse él
'John did not know the way to amuse himself (he)'

(16a) and (16b) have retained the subject of the embedded clause, él, in a pronominal form with all the original case markings. If one tried to explain the differences between (15a) and (15b) and (16a) and (16b), in terms of their complementizers, one would have to conclude that there are two complementizers in (15b), and two complementizers in (16b).

In summary, the syntactic and semantic behavior of saber followed by an infinitive separates it from other constructions with saber and conocer, and connects it with the modals poder and deber. The differences between the modal saber and the other epistemological constructions cannot be explained through the complementizers, but follow from the hypothesis that there is a separate verb saber which is a personal or root modal, unrelated to verbs of propositional attitude.

NOTES

The research for this paper was completed under Grant S73-0482 from the Canada Council. I wish to thank Merle Horne for her help.

1. The philosophical literature dealing with this question is, naturally, very extensive. I will simply refer the reader to Hintikka (1972) for an interesting survey and bibliography.

2. The relationship between the meaning of savoir and pouvoir in French seems to be closer than that found in Spanish between poder and saber, with a number of semantic and syntactic consequences. For instance, French allows nonhuman subjects with savoir and pouvoir, Spanish only with poder. Compare the following paradigm, which shows the closer link between savoir and pouvoir in French:

(i) a. Un tel crime ne saurait rester impuni.
(i) b. *Tal crimen no sabría quedar sin castigo.
(i) c. Tal crimen no podría quedar sin castigo.

(ii) a. Son innocence ne saurait être niée.
(ii) b. *Su inocencia no sabría ser negada.
(ii) c. Su inocencia no podría ser negada.

(iii) a. Ce bois ne saurait brûler.
(iii) b. *Esta madera no sabría quemarse.
(iii) c. Esta madera no se podría quemar.

(iv) a. Il ne saurait rien arriver de plus fâcheux.
(iv) b. *No sabría ocurrir nada más fastidioso.
(iv) c. No podría ocurrir nada más fastidioso.

FRENCH RELATIVE QUE

RICHARD S. KAYNE

Université de Paris VIII (Vincennes)

1. Identification of relative que with complementizer que

1.1 The following claim serves as the point of departure for this article: all embedded tensed sentences in French begin with que. Included in the scope of such a claim are sentences embedded as verbal complements, whether prepositional:

(1) Elle tient à ce que Jean s'en aille.
Cela provient de ce que Marie n'aime pas le vin rouge.

or nonprepositional:

(2) Elle a dit que tout irait bien.
Jean croyait qu'elle était malade.
On voudrait que tu sois là à 5h.

and those embedded as adjectival complements:

(3) Elle est heureuse que tu sois là.
Je suis sûr qu'ils sont venus.
Cela est imputable à ce que Marie n'aime pas le vin rouge.

or as noun complements:

(4) L'idée que Jean aurait pu faire ça est absurde.
Le fait que Jean soit parti tôt n'a aucune importance.

Sentences embedded as subjects also begin with que:

(5) Que tu ais dit cela ne m'a pas surpris du tout.

as do extraposed sentences:

(6) Il me plaît qu'ils disent cela.
Il est important que tu reviennes bientôt.

Que also introduces tensed sentences associated with comparatives and related structures:

(7) Jean est aussi bête que je le croyais.
Elle a moins d'argent qu'on ne le pense.
Tant de personnes sont venues qu'il a manqué de bonnes places.
Elle a plus d'argent qu'ils n'en ont, eux.

In none of (1)-(7) is it possible to delete the que:

(8) *Cela provient de ce Marie n'aime pas le vin rouge.
*Jean croyait elle était malade.
*Elle est heureuse tu sois là.
*L'idée Jean aurait pu faire ça est absurde.
*Tu ais dit cela ne m'a pas surpris du tout.
*Il est important tu reviennes bientôt.
*Tant de personnes sont venues il a manqué de bonnes places, etc.

Similar facts obtain with almost all subordinating conjunctions, e.g.[1]

(9) Avant qu'elle ne soit entrée, Paul est parti.
Je suis tout prêt à le croire, à moins que tu me dises le contraire.
Pendant que Jean chantait, Marie dansait.
Bien qu'elle soit là, elle n'a pas répondu.

(10) *Avant elle ne soit entrée, Paul est parti.
*Je suis tout prêt à le croire, à moins tu me dises le contraire.
*Pendant Jean chantait, Marie dansait.
*Bien elle soit là, elle n'a pas répondu.

The validity of the claim that all embedded tensed sentences begin with que cannot, of course, be demonstrated by a list, however long, of cases compatible with that claim. One may therefore ask what kinds of counterexamples can be found, and what modifications they entail.

There are, for instance, a small number of subordinating conjunctions which take tensed sentential complements not introduced by que:

(11) Quand elle joue aux cartes, elle s'amuse follement.
Si tu restais là, tu verrais quelque chose de formidable.
Comme il n'a pas de fric, il ne peut pas se payer à boire.

However, even these cooccur with que under coordination:[2]

(12) Quand elle joue aux cartes et qu'elle réfléchit à l'avenir, . . .
Si tu vas au cinéma et que tu y restes longtemps, . . .
Comme il n'a pas de fric et qu'il en a drôlement besoin, . . .

which suggests that the absence of que in (11) (and the first half of (12)) be attributed to some marginal rule specific to the lexical items in question.[3]

The only systematic case of que being absent in embedded tensed sentences is that of WH-constructions, i.e., embedded interrogative and relative structures:

(13) On ne sait pas où elle habite.
Dis-moi avec qui je dois parler.
Je me demande quand elle a pu partir.

(14) La fille avec qui tu parlais s'appelle Marie.
La table sur laquelle tu es assis appartient à Jules.
Le problème dont il est question est important.

In summary, then, I have claimed that French embedded tensed sentences are introduced by que, with the significant exception of interrogatives and relatives.[4]

Interestingly, interrogatives and relatives taken together display a gap in the WH-word paradigm which I would claim interacts strongly with the que data just presented. Consider the WH-words, lequel, laquelle, lesquel(le)s. In interrogatives, these can appear both as prepositional and as nonprepositional objects:

(15) Dites-moi lesquelles Jean photographiera.
Je ne sais pas lequel Marie préfère.

(16) Elle se demande à laquelle elle devrait se fier.
Tu devrais savoir avec lesquels il est sorti.

In restrictive relatives, however, only the prepositional object use is grammatical:

(17) *Le garçon lequel Marie préfère s'appelle Georges.
*La table laquelle Paul a cassée est celle-lá.
*Les villes lesquelles mon ami a visitées ont l'air bien.

(18) Le garçon auquel Marie pense s'appelle Georges.
La table sur laquelle Paul s'est assis est celle-là.
Les villes pour lesquelles mon ami a la plus grande admiration sont Paris et New York.

whether *lequel* has an animate or inanimate antecedent. (The facts of (15)-(16) are likewise independent of animacy/inanimacy).

The gap represented in (17) is filled by:

(19) Le garçon que Marie préfère s'appelle Georges.
La table que Paul a cassée est celle-là.
Les villes que mon ami a visitées ont l'air bien.

where *lequel* is replaced, informally speaking, by *que*. Such 'replacement' is impossible in (15), (16), (18):

(20) *Dites-moi que Jean photographiera.
*Elle se demande à que elle devrait se fier.
*La table sur que Paul s'était assis est celle-là, etc.

The situation can be summed up in the following way: The WH-word *lequel* oddly fails to occur as a nonprepositional object in restrictive relatives, (17). Relatives are a significant exception to the general occurrence of *que* in embedded tensed sentences, (14). In precisely that case where object *lequel* is impossible, there appears a *que*, (19), i.e. precisely the morpheme which might have been expected in relatives in the first place, if relatives were regular with respect to the above generalization.

As a first step toward the disentanglement and illumination of the preceding sets of observations, one could propose that the general absence of *que* in embedded tensed sentences which are relatives or interrogatives is related to the presence of the WH-word which generally introduces such relatives and interrogatives. Put another way, one could say that *que* and WH-words are mutually incompatible in Standard French:

(21) * La fille avec qui que tu parlais s'appelle Marie.
*La fille qu'avec qui tu parlais s'appelle Marie.

*Elle se demande lesquels que Jean préfère.
*Elle se demande que lesquels Jean préfère.

*La table sur laquelle que Jean s'est assis est celle-là.
*La table que sur laquelle Jean s'est assis est celle-là.

That is, the presence of the WH-word is what prevents the appearance of que, which otherwise would be expected, given the tensed character of the embedded sentence.

Turning now to the gap observed in the distribution of lequel ((17) vs. (15), (16), (18)), I interpret that gap as evidence of a rule which deletes lequel in restrictive relatives when lequel is not preceded by a preposition.

In this framework, the appearance of que in the relatives of (19) is immediately comprehensible. When lequel is deleted (by the rule just mentioned), there is no longer any WH-word present. Consequently, the tensed and embedded character of the relative S will provoke the appearance of que.[5] The que of (19) is thus the same morpheme, conditioned by the same syntactic environment, as the que of (1)-(9).

If, borrowing a term from Rosenbaum (1967), we call the que of (1)-(9) a 'complementizer', then this analysis claims that the que found in relative clauses is a complementizer. Conversely, one could call 'relative pronoun' any (complex) element which represents the spelling out in surface structure of a relativized NP, i.e. of the NP moved leftward by the transformation WH-movement. In this sense, lequel (as well as qui, quoi, see the following) will be a relative pronoun, but que will not be a relative pronoun. In relatives with que, the NP moved by WH-movement, which would have been spelled out as a relative pronoun, has been deleted, so that the relative is introduced in surface structure by a complementizer, que, rather than by a relative pronoun.

1.2 In this section, I extend my analysis of relatives to the relative pronouns qui and quoi, and examine an alternative analysis which I shall argue to be less desirable than that proposed in the foregoing.

The rule deleting prepositionless object lequel in restrictive relatives should be considered to apply under the same conditions to the relative pronoun qui. The gap with lequel, illustrated in (15)-(18), is duplicated in the case of qui:

(22) Dites-moi qui Jean photographiera.
Je ne sais pas qui Marie préfère.

(23) Elle se demande à qui elle devrait se fier.
Tu devrais savoir avec qui il est sorti.

(24) *Le garçon qui Marie préfère s'appelle Georges.
*La fille qui Jean photographiera est là.

(25) Le garçon à qui Marie pense s'appelle Georges.
La fille avec qui il est sorti est là.

In interrogatives, qui can correspond either to a prepositional object (23) or to a nonprepositional object (22). In relatives, however, qui can only correspond to a prepositional object (25), and not at all to a nonprepositional one (24). The ungrammaticality of (24) can be accounted for in the same way as that of (17), i.e. via an obligatory deletion rule.

The output of that deletion rule will be a relative clause lacking a relative pronoun; as noted earlier, such a relative clause will be introduced by the complementizer que:[6]

(26) Le garçon que Marie préfère s'appelle Georges.
La fille que Jean photographiera est là.

The fact that the deletion rule in question can apply both to lequel and to qui means that (26) can be viewed as the nonprepositional counterpart to both (25) and (18); while there are two possibilities with (human) prepositional objects--la fille avec laquelle/avec qui tu parlais--there is only one with nonprepositional objects. In other words, (26) arises through the deletion of a relativized NP which might otherwise have been spelled out either as lequel or as qui.[7]

The patterning together here of lequel and qui suggests that the deletion rule be formulated in such a way as to apply to any relativized nonprepositional object NP, i.e. that it might not be necessary to mention the specific elements qui and lequel in the rule itself. Such a more general formulation is compatible with the behavior of the third French relative pronoun, quoi:

(27) *Ce quoi Marie préfère, c'est le cinéma.
*Je cherche quelque chose quoi je pourrais mettre là.

(28) Ce à quoi Marie pense, c'est au cinéma.
Je cherche quelque chose sur quoi je pourrais m'asseoir.

Although possible as the object of a preposition, quoi does not work as a nonprepositional relativized object, a fact which would follow from the applicability to (27) of the same obligatory deletion rule as that operative in the case of qui and lequel. Again, the output is a relative introduced by que, just as in (26) (and (19)):[8]

(29) Ce que Marie préfère, c'est le cinéma.
Je cherche quelque chose que je pourrais mettre là.

Furthermore, such a generalized obligatory deletion rule permits an account of comparable asymmetries existing in the case of NP's which are subject to WH-movement as a result of what Ross (1967) called 'Pied-Piping':

(30) L'homme avec la femme de qui tu t'es disputé s'appelle Georges.
L'homme avec la femme duquel tu t'es disputé s'appelle Georges.

(31) *L'homme la femme de qui tu as insultée s'appelle Georges.
*L'homme la femme duquel tu as insultée s'appelle Georges.

In (30) and (31), the relative pronoun qui, lequel, in being moved leftward by WH-movement, has 'dragged along' the more inclusive phrase (avec) la femme de qui / duquel. The result is grammatical in the case where the preposition is present, but not in the other. This will follow from the interpretation of the deletion rule as one deleting any nonprepositional object NP moved to sentence-initial position by WH-movement. In (30), the rule is inapplicable because of avec. In (31), the rule will be applicable, and will obligatorily delete la femme de qui / duquel, thereby accounting for the ungrammaticality of (31).[9]

The deletion of la femme de qui / duquel in (31) will yield, given the automatic appearance of que: L'homme que tu as insulté(e) s'appelle Georges, which is clearly impossible in the sense of (31). This impossibility is accounted for by the principle of recoverability of deletion (cf. Chomsky 1964a; 1965), which will mark as ungrammatical the derivation in which such a deletion takes place. It should be noted that the fact that the deletion applied to (31) violates a general condition on transformations does not allow one to relax the obligatory character of that deletion; if it did, then (31) itself would be grammatical.[10]

1.3 At this point, one could pause to ask whether an alternative analysis to the one I am developing is feasible. In particular, would it be possible to deny the twin claims that que in relatives is a complementizer rather than a relative pronoun and that there exists in relatives a rule deleting nonprepositional object NP's moved by WH-movement?

The most plausible alternative would seem to be the following, especially if one focuses one's attention on qui and quoi, for which one might claim that rather than being deleted when nonprepositional objects, they assume an 'accusative' form, namely, que. In other words, que in la fille que je vois, ce que tu fais would be a simple morphological variant of qui in la fille à qui je parle and of quoi in ce à quoi je pense. In this framework, it would be fortuitous that the que in relatives has the same shape as the normal complementizer for tensed S's (a priori not inconceivable), and the supposed que/qui and que/quoi alternations would derive some plausibility from their phonological similarity, as well as from the fact that all are monomorphemic. In addition, a special form for 'accusative' would appear plausible, since other instances of 'accusative' forms exist in French.[11]

Unfortunately, such an analysis is far less plausible in the case of lequel. To account for la table sur laquelle elle est assise vs. *la table laquelle elle a repeinte, la table qu'elle a repeinte without a deletion rule, and parallel to the comparable qui facts, one would have to say that just as que is the accusative of qui, que is also the accusative of lequel. But lequel is not monomorphemic, and is in fact composed of the definite article le plus the WH-word quel, as shown by: the series lequel, laquelle, lesquelles parallel to le, la, les; the appearance of the fused forms with de and à, i.e. duquel, auquel, desquelles, auxquelles parallel to du pain, au garçon, etc.; the alternation between interrogative lequel and quel, i.e. Quel livre vous plaît?, *Lequel livre vous plaît? vs. Lequel vous plaît?, *Quel vous plaît?;[12] the similarity between quel and lequel with respect to ce, i.e. *ce auquel je pense, *Quel est-ce? In addition, the very fact that the definite article appears (obligatorily) with quel in relatives should probably be related to the definitization in relatives discussed by Kuroda (1969) and Browne (1970a, 1970b).

To call que the accusative form of lequel would thus raise the embarrassing question of the disappearance of the definite article.

Moreover, an analysis based on accusative alternations cannot relate the facts concerning la femme de qui / duquel to those concerning qui, lequel, and quoi. In the deletion rule/complementizer que analysis I am proposing, the ungrammaticality of *l'homme la femme de qui tu as insultée, *l'homme qui tu vois, *la table laquelle tu vois, and *ce quoi tu fais, i.e. of (31), (24), (17), and (27) can be attributed to a unique (deletion) process.[13] If, however, the last three are attributed to the supposed accusative spelling of qui, lequel, and quoi as que, then what of (31)? It seems evident that it would make little sense to speak of la femme de qui/duquel as having an accusative spelling que, but if it does not, then the ungrammaticality of (31) remains obscure, in particular given the grammaticality of (30).

The superiority of the deletion rule/complementizer que analysis of relatives, as compared with the accusative alternation analysis, is further suggested by the syntax of infinitival relatives. With respect to object qui, lequel, quoi, these pattern like their tensed counterparts.

(32) Elle cherche quelqu'un avec qui parler.
Elle cherche une chaise sur laquelle s'asseoir.
Elle a trouvé quelque chose avec quoi réparer sa voiture.

(33) *Elle cherche quelqu'un qui photographier.
*Elle cherche une chaise laquelle repeindre.
*Elle a trouvé quelque chose quoi offrir à son mari.

The crucial observation is that, unlike their tensed counterparts, infinitival relatives do not allow que, even in the case of nonprepositional objects:

(34) *Elle cherche quelqu'un que photographier.
*Elle cherche une chaise que repeindre.
*Elle a trouvé quelque chose qu'offrir à son mari.

(Cf. Elle cherche quelqu'un qu'elle pourrait photographier, Elle cherche une chaise qu'elle pourrait repeindre, Elle a trouvé quelque chose qu'elle pourrait offrir à son mari, where que is perfect.) The accusative alternation analysis would in no way lead one to expect that 'accusative' que would not be compatible with infinitival relatives.

The deletion rule/complementizer que analysis, however, provides an immediate explanation for the ungrammaticality of (34), in terms of a much more general incompatibility between complementizer que and infinitives. Consider the following paradigm:

(35) Jean voudrait qu'elle parte.
Ils ont avoué qu'ils étaient coupables.
Elle tient à ce que tu restes.
Il faut que tu restes là.
Je lui ai dit qu'il devait se taire.

(36) Jean voudrait partir.
Ils ont avoué être coupables.
Elle tient à rester.
Il faut rester là.
Je lui ai dit de se taire.

A tensed sentential complement is introduced by que, as noted earlier. Corresponding infinitival complements occur without que, as in (36). The appearance of que there is impossible:[14]

(37) *Jean voudrait que partir.
*Ils ont avoué qu'être coupables.
*Elle tient à (ce) que rester.
*Il faut que rester là.
*Je lui ai dit que de se taire.

The complementizer status of relative *que* allows the ungrammaticality of (34) to be assimilated to that of (37). It is a general fact about French that sentences whose main verb is an infinitive do not take *que* as their complementizer. Consider, for example, the derivation of the first sentence of (33), (34), and that of its tensed counterpart. The latter will contain an NP of the form: 'quelqu'un $_S$[elle pourrait photographier NP$_{+WH}$]'; WH-movement will yield 'quelqu'un $_S$[NP$_{+WH}$ elle pourrait photographier]'; the deletion rule will delete NP$_{+WH}$ (which otherwise would have been spelled out *qui*), yielding 'quelqu'un $_S$[elle pourrait photographier]'; *que* will appear as a function of the tensed main verb, yielding *quelqu'un qu'elle pourrait photographier*.[15]

The infinitival relative will have a structure of the form: 'quelqu'un $_S$[PRO photographier NP$_{+WH}$], (where PRO is the subject deleted by EQUI); WH-movement will yield 'quelqu'un $_S$[NP$_{+WH}$ PRO photographier]'; the deletion rule will obligatorily delete NP$_{+WH}$ (whence the impossibility of (33)), yielding: 'quelqu'un $_S$[PRO photographier]'. The ungrammaticality of (34) follows at this point from the fact that the infinitive prevents the appearance in its S of complementizer *que*, just as in (37).[16]

The identification of relative *que* with complementizer *que* thus allows an account of a gap in the distribution of infinitival relatives, and thereby supports the deletion rule/complementizer *que* analysis of relatives.

1.4 One might wonder what happens to the structure 'quelqu'un $_S$[PRO photographier]', which has been seen not to accept *que*. The mere application of EQUI is not sufficient to produce a grammatical sentence:

(38) *Elle cherche quelqu'un photographier.
*Elle cherche une chaise repeindre.
*Elle a trouvé quelque chose offrir à son mari.

What is possible is:

(39) Elle cherche quelqu'un à photographier.
Elle cherche une chaise à repeindre.
Elle a trouvé quelque chose à offrir à son mari.

I shall return in section 3.4 to these infinitival relatives in à, and to the mechanisms which might account for the appearance of that à.

2. Relativized subjects and nonrestrictives

2.1 Relativized subjects. The deletion rule that I have postulated will account for the impossibility of sentences like: *La fille laquelle tu as vue hier s'appelle Anne, if stated as obligatorily deleting in restrictive relatives any prepositionless object NP preposed by WH-movement. A transformation incorporating the notion 'object NP' is, however, not statable in the standard transformational formalism (e.g. that of Chomsky 1961). Interestingly, there exists a straightforward simplification of the deletion rule which would (desirably) eliminate it as a possible argument for an increase in the power of transformations. Let us in particular remove the specification 'object' used until now. This (simpler, and formally less problematic) revised rule will now read: obligatorily delete in restrictive relatives any prepositionless NP that has been preposed by WH-movement.

Such a revised deletion rule clearly has a wider scope than its predecessor, specifically in the case of subject NP's preposed by WH-movement in restrictive relatives. The revised rule, henceforth to be called Rel-NP-Del (relative noun-phrase deletion), will not distinguish WH-moved subject NP's from the WH-moved object NP's, and so will obligatorily delete the former just as it does the latter.

The facts concerning lequel support this revised interpretation of the deletion rule:

(40) La table sur laquelle tu étais assis nous appartient.
(41) *La table laquelle tu as cassée hier nous appartient.
(42) *La table laquelle te plaît nous appartient.

In (40), laquelle is the object of a preposition, and the restrictive relative is well formed, just as seen earlier in (18). In (41), laquelle is a nonprepositional object, and the sentence is ungrammatical, as in (17). The crucial point is now that (42), in which laquelle corresponds to a subject NP, patterns like (41).

The ungrammaticality of (42) is a consequence of the obligatoriness of Rel-NP-Del.

Relative quoi exhibits the same behavior here as lequel:

(43) Ce à quoi je pensais, c'est à ceci. (Like (28))
(44) *Ce quoi j'ai fait, c'est ceci. (Like (27))
(45) *Ce quoi serait arrivé, c'est ceci.

The ungrammaticality of (45), like that of (41), (42), (44), will follow from the obligatoriness of Rel-NP-Del.

Furthermore, complex WH-moved relative NP's of the form la femme de qui (or la femme duquel) display behavior like that of lequel and quoi:

(46) L'homme avec la femme de qui tu t'es disputé s'appelle Georges.
(47) *L'homme la femme de qui tu as insultée s'appelle Georges.
(48) *L'homme la femme de qui t'a insulté s'appelle Georges.

The contrast between (47) and (46) was noted earlier (see the discussion of (30), (31)) to be explicable in the same terms as the comparable facts concerning lequel and quoi. The ungrammaticality of (48) will likewise follow from the obligatoriness of Rel-NP-Del, if that rule applies to 'prepositionless NP' rather than to 'prepositionless object NP'.

Both (47) and (48) (along with (41), (42), (44), (45)) will be marked as instances of an obligatory rule having failed to apply. The actual application of Rel-NP-Del in (47) and (48) (although not in the others) will violate the recoverability of deletion condition, as noted previously.

The application of Rel-NP-Del in structures corresponding to (41), (42), (44), (45) will lead to relatives with que:

(49) La table que tu as cassée hier nous appartient.
(50) *La table que te plaît nous appartient.

(51) Ce que j'ai fait, c'est ceci.
(52) *Ce que serait arrivé, c'est ceci.

which is the desired result in the case of (49), (51). The ungrammaticality of (50), (52) indicates that the application of Rel-NP-Del in the subject case, if combined merely with the appearance of que, is not sufficient to generate the correct output, which is rather:

(53) La table qui te plaît nous appartient.
Ce qui serait arrivé, c'est ceci.

The qui of (53) is strictly limited to the subject cases:

(54) *La table qui tu as cassée hier nous appartient.
*Ce qui j'ai fait, c'est ceci.

(55) *La table sur qui tu étais assis nous appartient.
*Ce à qui je pensais, c'est à ceci.

The facts of (49)-(55) will fall into place if a rule is postulated which introduces qui as a replacement for que in structures resembling (50) or (52) (thereby yielding (53)). The qui-introduction rule will not be applicable in (40) or (43) (whence the impossibility of (55)), nor will it be applicable in (49) or (51) (whence the impossibility of (54)). More precisely, let us say that que is replaced by qui when que is immediately followed by a verb.

The derivation of the second sentence in (53) will contain as a subpart: 'Ce $_S$[quoi serait arrivé]' ---> Rel-NP-Del ---> 'Ce $_S$[serait arrivé]' ---> appearance of que ---> 'Ce $_S$[qui serait arrivé]' ---> replacement by qui ---> 'Ce $_S$[qui serait arrivé]'. The derivation of la table qui te plaît will proceed in similar fashion, with the introduction of qui triggered by the following V = te plaît.[17]

The analysis just sketched implies that the qui of (53), which originates as a replacement for que, is distinct from the qui of la fille à qui tu parlais, which originates as the spelling out of a WH-moved element. The postulation of two distinct qui is given additional motivation by the observation that the qui of (53) is unrestricted as to the animacy of its antecedent: la fille/la table/ce qui est là, while that occurring with prepositions must have an animate (perhaps human) antecedent, as shown by (55).

It should be noted that in this analysis, the qui of la fille qui est là is identified with that of (53), rather than with that of la fille à qui tu parlais. This is so, since in the derivation of la fille qui est là, the WH-element, being nonprepositional, is obligatorily deleted; the que which would otherwise be expected to appear in surface structure instead gives way to qui, just as in (53).

The postulation of a rule replacing que by qui in certain contexts, which will complement the 'complementizer que/Rel-NP-Del' analysis proposed earlier, is supported by two constructions containing instances of qui which would, independently of one's analysis of (53), be extremely difficult to analyze as relative pronouns, but which lend themselves to an analysis in terms of a rule replacing que by qui. The first construction has specifically been argued by Moreau (1971) to justify just such a rule. It involves the extraction via WH-movement of an element contained in a sentence embedded under a verb like croire:

(56) Qui crois-tu que Jean a photographié?
(57) *Qui crois-tu que viendra le premier?

In both examples, the sentence-initial qui is an interrogative pronoun extracted from the embedded S. In (56), this interrogative qui corresponds to the object of the embedded verb, and the derivation is straightforward (cf. Tu crois que Jean a photographié qui?). In (57), which is comparable to (56) except that the interrogative qui originates as the subject of the embedded verb, the derivation is less straightforward (despite the existence of Tu crois que qui viendra le premier?). For the result to be well formed, an additional change must take place: the complementizer que introducing the S-complement of croire must give way to qui:

(58) Qui crois-tu qui viendra le premier?

This change takes place only when que would be immediately followed by the verb (cf. (53) vs. (54)):[18]

(59) *Qui crois-tu qui Jean a photographié?

Since, as argued by Moreau, sentences such as (58) do not lend themselves to analysis in terms of an embedded relative,[19] they support the idea of a que/qui alternation valid for complementizer que. Now I have argued that the que of relative clauses is to be identified with complementizer que; consequently, the que/qui alternation will automatically extend to relatives, as in (53).

The second construction is one for which the intervention of a que ---→ qui rule was proposed by Gross (1968:124). It involves sentences such as:

(60) Je l'ai vu qui sortait du cinéma.
Je l'ai rencontré qui sortait du cinéma.

The S introduced by qui does not lend itself to analysis as a relative clause, for many reasons (cf. Kayne 1975:section 2.10), one of which is that no true relative pronoun can occur there:

(61) *Je l'ai vu lequel sortait du cinéma.
*Je l'ai rencontré à qui Marie parlait.
*Je l'ai vu sur quoi Marie s'asseyait.

The qui of (60) can, however, be plausibly attributed to the application of a que ---→ qui rule applying to a S introduced by complementizer que whose subject has been deleted.[20]

Taking together, then, (60), (58), and (53), we conclude that a single que/qui rule is at work. The rule allows us to integrate the case of relativized subjects, (53), into the Rel-NP-Del/complementizer que framework developed in earlier sections.[21]

2.2 Nonrestrictives. Before considering the formulation of the rules so far discussed, we briefly note the extent to which nonrestrictive relatives behave like restrictive relatives with respect to those rules. In the case of quoi, Rel-NP-Del is applicable and obligatory in nonrestrictives too (cf. (43)-(45)):

(62) Tout cela, sur quoi elle médite depuis longtemps, . . .
(63) *Tout cela, quoi tu étudies depuis longtemps, . . .
(64) *Tout cela, quoi la fascine depuis longtemps, . . .

The same can be said of Rel-NP-Del and qui in nonrestrictives:

(65) Cette fille, à qui Jean pense souvent, . . .
(66) *Cette fille, qui Jean connaît très bien, . . .

As expected, the deletion of the relative pronoun in (63) and (66) leads to relatives introduced in surface structure by the complementizer que:

(67) Tout cela, que tu étudies depuis longtemps, . . .
Cette fille, que Jean connaît très bien, . . .

and in (64), with the change from que to qui, a relative introduced by qui:

(68) Tout cela, qui la fascine depuis longtemps, . . .

In the subject case corresponding to (66), the deletion of the WH-moved element which would have been spelled out as qui is followed by the application of the que/qui rule, with a result to be aligned with (68):

(69) Cette fille, qui me fascine depuis longtemps, . . .

The transformation Rel-NP-Del is also applicable in nonrestrictives in the case of lequel:

(70) Cette table, sur laquelle j'étais assis, . . .
(71) Cette table, que tu as cassée, . . .
(72) Cette table, qui nous appartient maintenant, . . .

The derivation of (71) involves the deletion of the WH-moved element, which otherwise would have been spelled laquelle, and the appearance of complementizer que. The derivation of (72) is comparable to that of (71), with the additional application of the que/qui rule, just as in restrictives. However, alongside (71) and (72) we have:

(73) ??Cette table, laquelle tu as cassée, . . .
(74) ?Cette table, laquelle nous appartient maintenant, . . .

In a literary style, (74) is acceptable ((73) less so); consequently, in such a style, Rel-NP-Del cannot be obligatory with lequel in nonrestrictives.[22]

3. Formulation of rules

3.1 Que/Qui. Sentences (68), (69), and (72) of the preceding section are instances of the que/qui rule applying in nonrestrictives. As in the other cases in which that rule was seen to be operative, the relevant environment can be taken as 'immediately before a verb' (with the proviso of note 18 concerning parentheticals). Let us therefore entertain the formulation: X que V Y --> 1 qui 3 4.
1 2 3 4

The above formulation appears to be inadequate in the following cases:

(75) Elle ne fait que chanter.
Elle a plus que chanté.
Elle a autant chanté que dansé.
(76) Bien qu'étant très jeune, . . .
(77) Ce que voyant, elle est partie. (archaic)
(78) ?Le seul garçon que chanter amuse beaucoup s'appelle Jean

since in none is que replaceable by qui:

(79) *Elle ne fait qui chanter.
*Elle n'a qui chanté.
*Elle a autant chanté qui dansé.
*Bien qui étant très jeune, . . .
*Ce qui voyant, elle est partie.
*Le seul garçon qui chanter amuse beaucoup s'appelle Jean.

despite the fact that in all que immediately precedes a V.

There are in principle at least two ways of accounting for (75)-(79). First, one could take advantage of the difference between the verbs following que in (75)-(78), all of which are nontensed, and those which trigger the *que*/*qui* rule. In particular, all the instances of a *qui* derived through that rule involve tensed verbs. By 'tensed' here, we mean either indicative or subjunctive. Thus, one could add to the rule the specification that V be indicative or subjunctive, in which case the rule would become inapplicable to any of (75)-(78).[23]

A second possibility would be to claim that, despite appearances, *que* is not really immediately followed by V in (75)-(78). For example, in (76), the underlying NP subject of *étant* has been deleted by a kind of EQUI-NP-deletion. If that deletion were ordered after the *que*/*qui* rule, then the latter would be blocked in (76) by the presence of that NP. The same reasoning concerning EQUI holds for (77) and (78). In (75), the same approach could be taken with respect to comparative deletions; i. e. if the sentence with *autant* has a deep structure more closely resembling: *Elle a autant chanté qu'elle a dansé*, so that the derivation includes deletion of the embedded subject (among other things), and if that deletion is ordered after *que*/*qui*, then the latter will be blocked by the presence of that NP subject.[24]

An appraisal of the two preceding approaches (which are not necessarily mutually exclusive) might be made on grounds of 'independent motivation', if the specification 'tensed' required by the former turned out to be needed in any case, or if the orderings required by the latter were found to be otherwise justified by principles having the effect that certain types of deletion are derivation-final (cf. Postal 1970a:489; Wasow 1972). In Wasow's framework, for example, one would say that (60) involves a true deletion rule, occurring before *que*/*qui*, whereas EQUI and subject-deletion in (75) are interpretive rules on dummy elements.

3.2 Relative-NP-Deletion. Before attempting to make precise the rule(s) responsible for *que*, let me state the transformation Rel-NP-Del which, as seen, plays an important role in the syntax of *que*. Let me furthermore adopt the framework developed by Bresnan (1970, 1972), Chomsky (1973; MIT lectures), and Vergnaud (1974). The grammar will contain the PS-rule: S --> COMP S', where S' is then expandable via the familiar: S' --> NP VP. The symbol COMP will be rewritten: COMP --> Δ $\underline{+}$WH, where $\underline{+}$WH is a nonterminal feature, with +WH occurring in interrogatives (embedded or not) and -WH in relatives and in sentences not exhibiting any form of WH-movement. The transformation WH-movement will, in both interrogatives and relatives, move some element into the position of Δ, e. g. 'Je ne sais pas $_{S}$[$_{COMP}$[Δ +WH] $_{S'}$[tu as vu $_{NP}$[qui]]]' --> 'Je ne sais pas $_{S}$[$_{COMP}$[$_{NP}$[qui] +WH] $_{S'}$[tu as vu]] or, in the case of relatives: 'Cette table $_{S}$[$_{COMP}$[Δ -WH] $_{S'}$[tu étais assis $_{PP}$[sur laquelle]]]' --> 'cette table $_{S}$[$_{COMP}$[$_{PP}$[sur laquelle] -WH] $_{S'}$[tu étais assis]]'.[25]

Rel-NP-Del can now be stated as: $_{NP}$[NP $_{COMP}$[NP -WH] X] -->
1 2 3 4

1 ∅ 3 4.[26]

It will apply as follows: 'cette table $_{S}$[$_{COMP}$[$_{NP}$[laquelle] -WH] $_{S'}$[tu as cassée]] --> Rel-NP-Del --> 'cette table $_{S}$[$_{COMP}$[∅ -WH] $_{S'}$[tu as cassée]]'.

In accordance with the principle of recoverability of deletion (Chomsky 1965), term 2, which is erased by term 1, must be nondistinct from term 1, if a violation is not to occur. If laquelle (and similarly for quoi, qui) has at the point of application of Rel-NP-Del the representation 'wh-Det-table', then that condition will be satisfied as long as the Det's are nondistinct (Chomsky 1965:234-235 and Vergnaud 1974), since 'wh-', as a 'noninherent feature', will not count in determining nondistinctness.[27]

The NP status of term 2 of Rel-NP-Del will render that transformation inapplicable in cases such as: 'cette table $_{S}$[$_{COMP}$[$_{PP}$[sur laquelle] -WH] $_{S'}$[j'étais assis]]', where the element moved by WH-movement is a PP. Thus the following will not be derived:

(80) *Cette table, que j'étais assis, est très belle.

The correct output is: Cette table, sur laquelle j'étais assis, est très belle, the grammaticality of which, it should be noted, supports the claim that Rel-NP-Del is simply inapplicable to PP's. (If Rel-NP-Del were applicable, in which case (80) might be excluded via recoverability,[28] we would expect the sur laquelle sentence to be ungrammatical as a violation of the obligatoriness of Rel-NP-Del.)

The inapplicability of Rel-NP-Del to PP's leads to the conclusion that NP and PP are (at least partially) distinct categories (cf. Kayne 1975:section 2.11).

Given a structure 'cette table $_{COMP}$[$_{PP}$[sur $_{NP}$[laquelle]] -WH] . . .', Rel-NP-Del will thus not be applicable to the PP. Nor will it be applicable to the NP laquelle in such a structure, since the structural description of Rel-NP-Del does not allow for a preposition immediately preceding the NP corresponding to term 2. Consequently, the following is excluded:

(81) *Cette table, sur j'étais assis, est très belle.

The insertion of a que would not have any effect, and the same is true for all other prepositions, e.g. *Ce candidat, pour j'ai voté, . . . etc.

The ungrammaticality of (81) in French can be attributed to the formulation of Rel-NP-Del. Notice, however, that it would be straightforward to formulate a deletion rule which would allow (81); since recoverability is not involved, it would suffice to have

'. . . $_{\text{COMP}}$[(P) NP -WH] . . .', i.e. to add the term (P), while leaving the structural change as NP --> Ø. The question now is whether some dialect of French, or some related language, could possibly have (81) as a grammatical sentence. If the answer is negative, as I suspect, then (81) (in addition to being excluded by that formulation, in French) must be excludable in at least one way not dependent on the formulation of Rel-NP-Del. It is of interest, then, that the interpretation rules for COMP proposed by Chomsky (1973; MIT lectures, fall 1972) will, in the case of relatives, fail to assign a well formed interpretation to a -WH COMP containing, as in (81), a bare preposition.[29]

Rel-NP-Del does not apply in:

(82) La fille dont je vous disais du mal s'appelle Marie.

although dont, since it is a single morpheme, might be (mistaken for) a NP. The inapplicability of Rel-NP-Del to dont is not surprising, in fact, since dont is best analyzed as a PP: it corresponds in all cases to 'de+NP' (e.g. Je vous disais du mal de cette fille), and is subject to the same constraints on movement transformations as PP's having the surface form 'de+NP' (see Kayne 1975:section 2.7):

(83) *De quoi est-il appuyé contre le pied?
*De qui penses-tu au père?

(84) *La table dont il est appuyé contre le pied est belle.
*La fille dont il pensait au père s'appelle Marie.

(vs. De quoi a-t-elle cassé le pied?, La table dont elle a cassé le pied).

Dont could be regarded as a possible spelling out in COMP position of $_{\text{PP}}$[de PRO], where 'de PRO' is the string which is, via the transformation CLitic-PLacement, the source for the clitic en.[30] More precisely, one could write: $_{\text{COMP}}$[$_{\text{PP}}$[de PRO] -WH] --> dont 2.
1 2

This rule (DONT-FORMation) expresses succinctly a number of notable facts about dont. First, the specification -WH excludes dont from interrogatives:[31]

(85) *Dont parlais-tu?
*Je sais très bien dont il a cassé le pied.

Second, the absence from the rule of an initial variable within COMP correctly excludes:

(86) *la fille au père dont je me suis adressé

(vs. *la fille au père de qui je me suis adressé*). Third, the specification COMP will insure that *dont* is not generated in sentences such as:

(87) *Dont que tu parles, cela m'est égal.

(vs. *?De quoi que tu parles, cela m'est égal*), if the WH-word in this construction is not in COMP, as I am going to suggest. Fourth, if no conjunction transformation can apply to COMP subsequent to DONT-FORM, and if relatives like *la fille de qui et avec qui j'ai parlé* have: $_{COMP}$[PP et PP -WH], rather than $_{COMP}$[$_{COMP}$[PP -WH] et $_{COMP}$[PP - WH]], then DONT-FORM as stated will exclude:[32]

(88) *la fille dont et avec qui j'ai parlé
*la fille avec qui et dont j'ai parlé

(Cf. *la fille dont j'ai parlé et avec qui j'ai parlé*.)

The ungrammaticality of *dont* in the somewhat archaic construction represented by: *A quoi que tu penses, . . .*; *Où que tu ailles, . . .*; *Quoi que tu dises, . . .* (although not **Quand que tu viennes*, **Comment que tu agisses*) was noted to follow from the formulation of DONT-FORM, on the assumption that *à quoi*, *où*, *quoi*, cited here, are not dominated by COMP. That assumption is reinforced by the existence of sentences such as:

(89) De quelque coté que tu te mettes, . . .

(perhaps also *Toute petite qu'elle soit, . . .*) which do not display a WH-word, yet which seem to be part of the same construction.[33] The non-WH-word makes it unlikely that (89) has an initial PP dominated by COMP.

The nondomination by COMP of *quoi* in *Quoi que tu fasses, . . .* will, along with the absence of an antecedent, insure that Rel-NP-Del is not applicable to that construction. Furthermore, the fact that *quoi* is not in COMP will allow an account of the contrast between that construction and ordinary relatives and interrogatives, with respect to the appearance of *que*:

(90) Où que tu ailles, . . .
*Où tu ailles, . . .

(91) *l'endroit où que tu demeures (Like (21))
l'endroit où tu demeures

The appearance of *que* in Standard French is prohibited when it would immediately follow a WH-phrase which is in COMP.

There is a variety of popular French that lacks such a prohibition; there, interrogatives such as Où que tu vas?, Je me demande comment qu'elle a pu faire ça are possible, as are relatives containing both complementizer que and an overt WH-phrase:

(92) la fille à qui que j'ai parlé

Significantly, the nonprepositional object counterpart to (92) is impossible even then:

(93) *la fille qui que j'ai vu

Instead of (93) is found:

(94) la fille que j'ai vu

with que alone. The contrast between (92) and (93) can be accounted for quite simply: This variety of popular French contains, like Standard French, the obligatory rule Rel-NP-Del, which, although inapplicable to (92), applies obligatorily in a structure corresponding to (93), deleting qui, with the result seen in (94).

The rule of Rel-NP-Del will likewise account for the absence of a subject counterpart to (92):

(95) *la fille qui qui t'aime bien
*la fille qui que t'aime bien

It will apply in such a case to delete the WH-NP (corresponding to the first qui of (95)), with the result:

(96) la fille qui t'aime bien

Although (95) and (93) are not possible, their interrogative counterparts are:

(97) Qui que tu as vu?
(98) Qui qui t'a dit ça?

since Rel-NP-Del is inapplicable in interrogatives just as in Standard French.[34]

3.3 QUE-DELetion and QUE-INSertion. Having considered the formulation of the rule of Rel-NP-Del (and found further evidence for it in popular French), I now turn to the rule or rules necessary to account for the behavior of que. We recall the generalization noted

at the beginning of this paper, namely, that embedded tensed S's in French are introduced by que. That generalization had one productive exception: constructions introduced by a WH-word (see the discussion centered on (21)), where the WH-word is in COMP (as indicated by (90)). This fact about que and WH-words can be incorporated into the grammar via the following rule (QUE-DELetion): $_{\text{COMP}}[\text{A} \ \text{que}]$ --> 1 ∅,
1 2
where A (which can stand for any category) is nonnull. It is clear that QUE-DEL must be ordered after Rel-NP-Del.[35]

Typical subderivations are: la fille qui que tu vois --> Rel-NP-Del --> la fille que tu vois --> QUE-DEL (inapplicable); and la fille à qui que tu parlais --> Rel-NP-Del (inapplicable) --> QUE-DEL --> la fille à qui tu parlais.

The preceding subderivations contain a que at the point of application of Rel-NP-Del. In that case,[36] given the formulation on p. 272 of Rel-NP-Del, if que is dominated by COMP (see note 35), then que must be analysable as -WH. One should therefore broach the question of how que is introduced into embedded tensed S's.

It can be noted immediately that, although all embedded tensed S's other than those affected by QUE-DEL are introduced by que, the converse is not true. More precisely, not all (embedded) S's introduced by que are tensed, at least in surface structure. This observation bears on the desirability of a rule such as the following (QUE-INSertion; cf., for English, Chomsky 1973): $\underline{+}$WH --> que / ___ NP V_T, where V_T is a tensed verb.

Consider, for example, sentences such as:

(99) Je crois que si.
Elle prétend que non.
Il est probable que oui.

The aforementioned rule QUE-INS, which inserts que into tensed S's, will not account for the que of (99), unless the sentences of (99) contained an embedded tensed verb at the point of application of QUE-INS. If they do not, then the que of (99) will have a different origin from those of Je crois que Jean partira, Elle prétend que Jean n'est pas malade, and Il est probable que Jean reviendra demain, which do come from QUE-INS.

A similar point can be made on the basis of:

(100) Il n'est pas si malin que ça.
Elle a d'autres amis que Jean et Georges.

where it is difficult to reconstruct a tensed S source for 'que NP' (cf. Bresnan 1973). Yet one would normally want to attribute to the que of (100) the same origin as one would assign to those of:

(101) Il n'est pas si malin que tu le crois.
Elle est autre qu'elle n' était il y a deux ans.

which, since they introduce tensed S's, could be attributed to QUE-INS.

A third case is that of echo, or incredulity, questions. In response to Elle prétend que Jean est malade, Elle est partie avant qu'il lui pose la question, one can have:

(102) Elle prétend que quoi?
Elle est partie avant que quoi?

where there is no overt embedded tensed verb.

The problem for QUE-INS posed by (102) might disappear in the context of a broader study of echo questions. For instance, if the quoi of (102) is rather freely inserted by some rule applying after all transformations,[37] as suggested by Sandfeld's (1965:I, 324) examples: Je les avale. Vous les quoi?; De l'endocardite. De l'endo quoi?, then (102) could well contain a tensed verb which would enable QUE-INS to apply.

The problem for QUE-INS posed by (100) could be eliminated by denying that the que of comparatives and related structures is due to exactly the same rule as the que of relatives and sentences acting as subject or object. That is, the que of (100) and (101), along with those of (7), could be assigned a somewhat different status from that assigned to the que of (102) and (1)-(6), (19), (26), (29), etc. In particular, it might be that the latter are derived through QUE-INS, and the former through a rule specifying -WH as que in comparative and related structures.[38]

The separation of comparative que from the domain of QUE-INS is supported by the observation that, unlike the que of QUE-INS, which are totally impossible with infinitives ((34) and (37)), comparative que can occur with an infinitive in the literary construction:[39]

(103) Elle n'est pas si naïve que de croire cela.

I therefore tentatively take the following stand: que is inserted in COMP, in the ±WH position, either when the SD of QUE-INS is met, i.e. whenever the main verb is tensed, or when the S in question is associated with a 'comparative' structure. Put another way, a complementizer que can have been inserted either by QUE-INS or by a rule (perhaps partially collapsible with QUE-INS) sensitive to 'comparative' structures.[40]

As stated, QUE-INS distinguishes sharply between tensed verbs (indicative, subjunctive) and infinitives, and in particular applies only with the former. Consider now the case of present participles, which are usually incompatible with _que_:

(104) (*Que) Jean l'ayant possédé, Georges s'est mis à hurler.
(*Que) En travaillant dur, tu pourras y réussir.
Je l'ai rencontré (*que) sortant du cinéma.
Tout homme (*que) désirant s'inscrire . . .

but not always:[41]

(105) Bien que pesant 100 kilos, Jean est très agile.
Quoique ressemblant à son père, . . .

The _que_ of (105) could in principle be accounted for by extending the domain of QUE-INS to certain present participles. Alternatively (note that present participles are more like tensed verbs than like infinitives with respect to adverb placement, e.g. _Jean ne ressemble pas à son pere_, _Il affirme ne pas ressembler à son pere_; _Bien que ne ressemblant pas . . ._, *_Bien que ne pas ressemblant . . ._), it might be that the verb of (105), but not (104), is tensed at the point of application of QUE-INS (there are other reductions: _Bien que très jolie, Marie . . ._). Or one might claim that the _que_ of (105) is not due to QUE-INS, but is rather part of the 'compound' subordinating conjunctions _bien que_, _quoique_.

This last possibility can be envisaged insofar as the reasons for treating other subordinating conjunctions such as _avant que_, _pour que_, _sans que_ as composed of two independent elements (cf. note 2) do not carry over to _bien que_, _quoique_. In fact, the latter never occur with an infinitive as main verb:

(106) *Bien (que) peser 100 kilos, Jean est très agile.
*Quoi(que) ressembler à son frère, Jean ne parle pas comme lui.

Nor can they lose their _que_ via the replacement of their S by a NP:

(107) Bien qu'il soit parti, . . . Quoiqu'il soit parti, . . .
*Bien son départ, . . . *Quoi son départ, . . .

Thus, no argument can be made for them comparable to one based on:

(108) avant son départ, pour son départ, sans son départ

in favor of the independence of que from the element preceding it. For the que of (105) to therefore be analyzed, as not due to QUE-INS, but as part of a 'compound' conjunction would require, however, that such compounds be, on occasion, separable:

(109) ?Bien, évidemment, que Jean soit revenu, . . .

(impossible with quoique).[42]

The last aspect of QUE-INS I am going to comment on is its sensitivity to the notion 'embedded S'. Thus, whereas QUE-INS applies in sentences like Jean croit que Marie est partie, it does not do so in:

(110) Marie est partie.

(cf. *Que Marie est partie.). Certain relevant cases have been mentioned earlier in note 4. Consider now:

(111) Heureusement qu'elle est repartie.
Sans doute que tu as réussi.
Peut-être qu'elle est malade.

In (111), the tensed strings elle est repartie, tu as réussi, elle est malade have apparently given rise to QUE-INS, despite their being 'embedded' only with respect to an adverbial element. Interestingly, (111) also displays 'embedded S' behavior with respect to the transformation SUBJ-CL-INV (Kayne 1972) operative in sentences such as: Où vas-tu?, Pourquoi Marie part-elle?. SUBJ-CL-INV, which is in general impossible in embedded S's: Je sais où tu vas, Je sais pourquoi Marie part, is likewise impossible in (111):

(112) *Sans doute qu'as-tu réussi.
*Peut-être qu'est-elle malade.

despite the grammaticality, without que, of:

(113) Sans doute as-tu réussi.
Peut-être est-elle malade.

On the other hand, (111) differs from clear cases of 'embedded S's, in that (111) does not allow the use of the subjunctive:

(114) *Heureusement qu'elle soit repartie.
*Sans doute que tu ais réussi.
*Peut-être qu'elle soit malade.

This is especially striking with heureusement and peut-être, for which there exist (near-) paraphrases containing a subjunctive:

(115) C'est heureux qu'elle soit repartie.
Il est possible qu'elle soit malade.
Il se peut qu'elle soit malade.

In fact, with respect to the subjunctive, (111)/(114) has the same behavior as sentences with no embedding at all:

(116) Elle est heureusement repartie.
Elle est peut-être malade.

(117) *Elle soit heureusement repartie.
*Elle soit peut-être malade.

The similarity in mood between (111) and (116), as opposed to (115), would be accounted for, on the assumption that subjunctive in modern French is excluded from S's not dominated by at least one other S,[43] if (111) did not have the structure: $_S[\ldots{}_S[\ldots]\ldots]$ (which is the structure of (115)). There would be (at least) two possibilities: either (111) would lack the inner S node, and have the structure $_S$[Adv COMP S'], as in Schlyter (1974), or (111) would lack the outer S node, and have the structure $_E$[Adv S], E a nonrecursive initial symbol, along the lines of Banfield (1973), Emonds (1974). Both hypotheses would predict the following to be ungrammatical:

(118) *?Heureusement que sans doute que tu as réussi.
*?Jean dira à ta mère que sans doute que tu as réussi.
*?Tout le monde croit qu'heureusement qu'elle est repartie.

the one because E is nonrecursive, the other because there can only be one $_{COMP}$[que] per S. The prediction is correct for many speakers, but some accept (118), especially with a popular flavor.[44]

If the absence of subjunctive in (111) is correctly accounted for by denying to (111) a $_S[\ldots{}_S[\ldots]\ldots]$ structure, then how is one to account for the incompatibility of (111) with SUBJ-CL-INV, as shown by (112) (vs. (113))? The problem is that whereas (119) could be attributed to Emonds' (1969a; to appear) theory restricting certain ('root') transformations to nonembedded S's:

(119) *Je sais où vas-tu.
*Je sais pourquoi Marie part-elle.

with SUBJ-CL-INV a root T, the superficially comparable ungrammaticality of (112) could not, since (111) would not then contain any embedded S (by Emonds' definitions, in particular).

The ungrammaticality of (112) follows, however, from the structural description of SUBJ-CL-INV as (cf. Kayne 1972):

X $_{NP}$[Y SCL]V --> 1 2 4+3, where X is either '+Q',
1 2 3 4

i.e. an interrogative element, or else one of a certain small class of adverbs (cf. Le Bidois 1952:88ff.), since SUBJ-CL-INV then makes no provision for a que intervening between terms 1 and 2.[45]

Similar to the ungrammaticality of (112) is that of:

(120) *Où que vas-tu?

which is rejected both by those who accept Où vas-tu? and by those who accept Où que tu vas? (cf. (97), (98)). If (120) is inconceivable, as I suspect, and not only a stylistic clash between inversion (Standard French) and unembedded que in interrogatives (Popular French), then it must, on the (reasonable) assumption that it contains no embedded S, be excludable by means other than Emonds' constraints. Again, the desired result is achieved by the above formulation of SUBJ-CL-INV.

A third case of subject-clitic inversion being blocked by que is the following:

(121) Jean est malade, a-t-elle dit.
(122) Jean est malade, qu'elle a dit.
*Jean est malade, qu'a-t-elle dit.

As with (120), the lack of inversion in (122) might be attributed to a stylistic clash, since (122) belongs to a style generally lacking inversions. One can wonder, however, if (122) could exist even in the absence of such stylistic incompatibilities. If it could not, then a solution akin to the preceding suggests itself: The inversion in (121) is due to a rule (perhaps SUBJ-CL-INV) requiring contiguity between the triggering element X and the NP containing the subject clitic.[46]

The blocking of SUBJ-CL-INV via an intervening que might well extend to (119), despite there being no que there in surface structure. This will be so, given the analysis of que I am proposing, if the following three rules are strictly ordered: QUE-INS before

SUBJ-CL-INV before QUE-DEL, in which case there will be a que in (119) at the point of application of SUBJ-CL-INV. This means of ruling out (119), which is essentially equivalent to that proposed for similar phenomena in English by Klima (1969:232), would appear to eliminate the necessity of invoking Emonds' constraints with SUBJ-CL-INV. However, the que-blocking solution and those constraints are not mutually exclusive, and there is in fact one kind of restriction on SUBJ-CL-INV which provides motivation for the latter:

(123) La fille à laquelle sans doute tu aurais dû parler s'appelle Marie.
Elle est plus intelligente que peut-être tu ne le croyais.

(124) *La fille à laquelle sans doute aurais-tu dû parler s'appelle Marie.
*Elle est plus intelligente que peut-être ne le croyais-tu.

The clear contrast between (123) and (124), indicating the inapplicability of SUBJ-CL-INV, cannot derive from any intervening que, since sans doute, peut-être are to the right of COMP, but can be ascribed to the inapplicability of root transformations, e.g. SUBJ-CL-INV, in (certain) embedded S's.[47]

If it is true that the que of (122), (120), (111) do not introduce embedded S's, then those are instances of que not immediately attributable to QUE-INS, since QUE-INS must usually be prohibited from applying in nonembedded S's:

(125) Marie est revenue.
*Que Marie est revenue.

One possible approach would be simply to allow QUE-INS to apply in certain nonembedded S's or, more likely, to have QUE-INS apply in all (tensed) S's, and then to delete it in nonembedded S's except in certain cases where it is not in initial position.

Such a deletion rule would be a 'root' deletion in Emonds' (forthcoming) sense, i.e. via an extension of the notion of root transformation to deletions. Now in French, unlike English, this kind of deletion of que (which is distinct from the rule QUE-DEL discussed earlier) is in general limited to nonembedded S's--compare (125) with (8). There is, however, one exception, where this deletion of que in fact takes place in an embedded S. In Emonds' framework, one is led to say that that embedded S has been idiosyncratically marked as a root S, whence the interesting expectation that it will act as a root S with respect to SUBJ-CL-INV. The relevant construction is:

(126) Si intelligente qu'elle soit, Marie ne trouvera pas la solution.

In (126), elle soit is clearly embedded, as indicated by the parallelism with (89), the appearance of que, the right-left pronominalization, and the subjunctive. The optional deletion of que does not affect either the pronominalization or the subjunctive,[48] but does result in the application of subject-clitic inversion:

(127) Si intelligente soit-elle, Marie ne trouvera pas la solution.

which inversion would, of course, have been impossible in the presence of que:

(128) *Si intelligente que soit-elle, Marie ne trouvera pas la solution.

I conclude that the generalization of QUE-INS to all tensed S's,[49] combined with a subsequent root deletion of que, is a promising way of treating the absence of que from (125), and the appearance of que in (122), (120), (111).

3.4 Introduction of A in INFinitival relatives. In section 1.4, I commented on the derivation of infinitival relatives in which the relativized element is an object NP. The infinitival character of the relative implies, of course, that QUE-INS is inapplicable. The obligatory application of Rel-NP-Del, along with EQUI, appears to lead to an ungrammatical output, as in (38): *Elle cherche quelqu'un photographier, etc. A grammatical output can be achieved, however, if structures such as (38) are obligatorily subject to a rule inserting à, to yield (39): Elle cherche quelqu'un à photographier, etc.

The ungrammaticality of (38) is in a sense not surprising. The impossibility of $*_{NP}$[quelqu'un photographier] would seem to be related to the fact that adnominal infinitival complements in French always require a linking preposition:

(129) *La volonté gagner est très forte chez lui.
*Sa facilité parler allemand est étonnante.
*L'idée repartir lui est venue hier.

(cf. La volonté de gagner, Sa facilité à parler allemand, L'idée de repartir). Consequently, the ungrammaticality of (38) could in principle be attributed to some surface constraint excluding structures like (129).[50]

A more interesting possibility, given the existence of (39), would be to say that the derivation leading to (38) continues on to yield (39), via some rule inserting à. One might then think of that rule as having the absence of (129) as its raison d'être, although the appearance of à might also be aligned with other, non-NP, phenomena, as will be be seen hereafter.

The derivation of (39) from the infinitival relative structure of (38) amounts to the claim that the derivation of (39) involves the transformation WH-movement, and in particular assigns to (39) a deep structure essentially the same as that of (32): Elle cherche quelqu'un avec qui parler, etc. None of this, on the other hand, obliges one to attribute a relative clause derivation to all adnominal à-infinitive complements. For example, a relative clause derivation, while not inconceivable, would be much less easily justifiable for Ce fer à repasser est très cher (cf. Cette boîte aux lettres est très grande) than for (39). The fer à repasser construction and that of (39) sometimes intersect to give an ambiguous sentence, e.g.:

(130) J'ai trouvé une machine à laver.

In the reading which is like fer à repasser, and for which I am not making any claims, (130) means 'I found a washing machine'. In the reading parallel to (39), to which I am attributing a relative clause derivation, (130) means 'I found a machine to wash', with 'I' the understood subject of 'wash'.[51]

The analysis of (39) as an infinitival relative is supported by a certain restriction common to (39) and (32). Thus, while both are possible with verbs like chercher, trouver, dénicher, they become difficult if the higher verb is changed, in sentences like:

(131) *Elle a dénoncé quelqu'un à photographier.
*Elle a abimé quelque chose à photographier.

(132) *Elle a dénoncé quelqu'un avec qui parler.
*Elle a abimé quelque chose sur quoi s'asseoir.

With elle interpreted as the subject of the infinitive, both (131) and (132) are decidedly better with trouver, chercher, dénicher than with dénoncer, abimer.

An additional similarity between the constructions of (39) and (32) is their sensitivity to depth of embedding:[52]

(133) *Elle cherche quelqu'un à lui dire de photographier.
*Elle a trouvé quelque chose à forcer Jean à lire.

(134) *Elle cherche quelqu'un sur qui dire à Jean de tirer.
*Elle a trouvé quelque chose sur quoi lui dire de s'asseoir.

This sensitivity is not found either in normal tensed relatives, nor in infinitival interrogatives:

(135) Je ne sais pas du tout lequel dire à Jean de photographier.
Elle m'a demandé sur quoi lui dire de s'asseoir.

Nor is it found in adnominal infinitives of the following type (which may or may not ultimately be derived as relatives; if so, then it would be the subject NP to be WH-moved, whereas in (39), (131), (133) it is the object NP):

(136) C'est un homme à voler sa grand'mère.
C'est un homme à dire à ses amis de voler sa grand'mère.

Assuming, then, that it is desirable to have the structure '. . . chercher $_{NP}$[quelqu'un photographier]' transformed into '. . . chercher $_{NP}$[quelqu'un à photographier]', the question arises as to the formulation of the rule. Consider the following statement:
$_{NP}$[NP $_{S}$[PRO V X]] --→ 1 2 à 3 4, where V is an infinitive (and
1 2 3 4
PRO its EQUI subject). The foregoing rule (A-INFinitive) will apply to '$_{NP}$[quelqu'un $_{S}$[PRO photographier]]', with *quelqu'un* satisfying term 1, and *photographier* term 3. The *à* will be inserted directly to the left of the infinitive.[53]

The postulation of a rule A-INF will receive further support if that rule can be shown to be applicable in constructions other than the infinitival relatives under discussion. There are two (mutually exclusive) extensions one might consider. First, there are sentences like:

(137) Le seul garçon à avoir réussi s'appelle Pierre.
La plus belle femme à être venue, c'est Marie.
Le dernier à s'être rendu, c'est lui.

where the *à*-infinitive phrases have much in common with the relatives of:[54]

(138) Le seul garçon qui ait réussi s'appelle Pierre.
La plus belle femme qui soit venue, c'est Marie.
?Le dernier qui se soit rendu, c'est lui.

Now if (137) is analyzed as containing infinitival relatives of the form

$_S[_{COMP}[_{NP}$ -WH] avoir réussi], where the subject NP has been moved into COMP by WH-movement (unlike (39), in which the object NP is moved), such that it will subsequently be deleted by Rel-NP-Del (as is the COMP-dominated (object) NP in (39)), yielding $_S$[avoir reussi], then A-INF will apply, with the desired result.[55]

The formulation of A-INF needed to cover both (137) and (39) must specify V as 'infinitive' to exclude from its domain:

(139) Tout homme ayant réussi sera félicité.

which does not receive an <u>à</u>:

(140) *Tout homme à ayant réussi sera félicité.

Furthermore, it must, unless the <u>de</u> is already present at the point of application of A-INF, distinguish (137) and (39) from <u>le fait d'être parti, le désir de Jean de faire cela</u> (cf. (129)), since one does not have:

(141) *le fait à être parti
*le désir de Jean à faire cela

It must also distinguish them from such appositive infinitives as: <u>mon jeu favori, danser en ronde; son plus grand désir, partir en Asie</u>, since <u>à</u> does not appear there either:

(142) *mon jeu favori, à danser en ronde
*son plus grand désir, à partir en Asie

The need to specify V as 'infinitive' might turn out to be unnecessary, and the potential problems caused by (141) and (142)[56] would disappear if the <u>à</u> of (137) and that of (39) were not attributed to the same rule, and if the latter were aligned instead with other instances of infinitives whose object NP has been removed:

(143) Marie est impossible à photographier.
Ce livre est difficile à lire.
Marie est jolie à regarder.
Ce travail est à refaire.

If the <u>à</u> of (39), repeated here as (144):

(144) Elle a trouvé quelqu'un à photographier.

is considered identical to those of (143), such that A-INF is restated to make reference to a 'missing object', then A-INF will not apply in

(141) or (142) since those have not had their object removed, and the same holds for (140). The à of (137) would then be attributed to some other rule.[57]

The reinterpretation of A-INF as a rule inserting à before infinitives that have lost their object would require the use of formal mechanisms beyond those found in Chomsky (1961, 1965, 1970a), and could be achieved through the use of 'traces', in the sense of Chomsky (1973). The validity of A-INF as evidence for such an increase in formal power will depend on the intertwined considerations of whether (143) and (144) really represent a linguistically significant generalization, and whether a rule using traces can be stated so as to distinguish naturally (143) and (144) from the numerous cases in which the removal of an object does not lead to the appearance of à.

The second consideration, more readily approachable than the first, leads to the discovery of contrasts such as the following:

(145) Cette revue est difficile à lire.
*Cette revue est difficile de lire.

(146) Quelle revue est-il difficile de lire?
*Quelle revue est-il difficile à lire?

In both (145) and (146), the object has been removed, but only in the former does à appear; in (146), de appears, just as if the object had remained:

(147) Il est difficile de lire cette revue.
*Il est difficile à lire cette revue.

Examples (145) and (146) differ, of course, with respect to the transformations moving the object NP ('Tough Movement' in the former),[58] but that could not be the determining factor, since the same transformation, WH-movement, is at work in (146) and (144), which two sets differ in de vs. à. Moreover, even if à were triggered by only certain transformations, one would need to ask why it was those, and not the others.

Other object movements that do not trigger à are SE-PLacement, CL-PLacement, and Leftward-TOUS-movement:[59]

(148) Il est difficile de se dénoncer.
Il est difficile de les dénoncer.
Il n'a rien été possible de faire.

(149) *Il est difficile à se dénoncer.
*Il est difficile à les dénoncer.
*Il n'a rien été possible à faire.

and Passive:

(150) Il est impossible d'être apprécié par tout le monde.
(151) *Il est impossible à être apprécié par tout le monde.

Leaving L-TOUS aside for the moment, it is noted that the other transformations of (148)-(151) differ from those of (143) in that the latter, but not the former, involve the crossing of a S-boundary. Our revised *à*-insertion rule, to be called A-INF-T (T for trace), can therefore be written as follows:

$$\underset{1}{NP_i}\ \underset{2}{X}\ {}_S[\underset{3}{PRO}\ \underset{4}{V}\ \underset{5}{Y}\ \underset{6}{trace_i}\ \underset{7}{Z}] \longrightarrow$$

1 2 3 à 4 5 6 7.[60] An *à* will be inserted before a V preceding a moved or deleted NP, if the position to which that NP was moved, or the controlling NP, in the case of deletion,[61] is situated outside the S containing that V.

The inclusion of a variable at term 5 of A-INF-T means that the moved or controller-deleted NP does not need to be the direct object of the verb immediately before which *à* is inserted. There are three cases: First, term 6 might be a prepositional object of that verb, but then there can be no conclusive examples, since French does not allow any of the relevant rules to strand prepositions (cf. notes 29, 28):

(152) *Jean est impossible à/de/Ø parler avec.
*Elle cherche quelqu'un à/de/Ø voter pour.

Second, term 6 might be the object of some other verb embedded with respect to the V of term 4. Although the constructions in question do not tolerate much embedding (cf. (133)-(134) and note 52), there are relevant examples:

(153) ?(Pour moi), ce livre serait impossible à commencer à lire aujourd'hui.
Ce plat serait facile à faire manger aux enfants.

(154) ?Elle a trouvé une maison à commencer à repeindre.
Elle a trouvé quelque chose à faire manger aux enfants.

Here *à* has been inserted before *commencer*, *faire* even though the moved NP did not directly follow them. Furthermore, the contrast between (153) and:

(155) *(Pour moi), ce livre serait impossible de commencer à lire aujourd'hui.
*Ce plat serait facile de faire manger aux enfants.

(cf. Pour moi, il serait impossible de commencer à lire ce livre aujourd'hui, Il serait facile de faire manger ce plat aux enfants --with de) shows that A-INF-T has to apply. Consequently, we would not want to eliminate term 5.[62]

The third case related to term 5 is that of a trace corresponding to the subject of some verb embedded below the verb of term 4. Consider:

(156) Jean a avoué avoir déclaré détester les pommes de terre au lard.

with the structure 'Jean a avoué $_S$[PRO_1 avoir déclaré $_S$[PRO_2 détester. . .]]'. Now this will meet the SD of A-INF-T if Jean is taken as term 1 and PRO_2 as term 6, with the incorrect result:

(157) *Jean a avoué à avoir déclaré détester . . .

Comparing (156) with the joli sentence of (143) and note 61, we see that it is unlikely that the solution lies in saying that 'PRO' cannot count as '$trace_i$'. However, one could attribute the inapplicability of A-INF-T in (156) to the fact that PRO_2 is not directly controlled by Jean. In other words, one could say that NP_i and $trace_i$ must be in a direct controlling relation, and that the required relation between the two is not transitive (so that the fact that PRO_2 is controlled by PRO_1, which is controlled by Jean, is irrelevant).[63]

The nontransitivity of the trace relation required for A-INF-T would also account for:

(158) Jean semble être difficile à photographier.
*Jean semble à être difficile à photographier.
Jean est susceptible d'être difficile à photographier.
*Jean est susceptible à être difficile à photographier.

For example: △ semble $_S$[△ être difficile $_S$[PRO de photographier Jean]] --➝ Tough-Movement --➝ △ semble $_S$[$Jean_i$ être difficile $_S$[PRO de photographier $trace_i$]] --➝ Raising --➝ $Jean_j$ semble $_S$[$trace_{j,i}$ être difficile $_S$[PRO de photographier $trace_i$]], and A-INF-T is applicable only in the lowest S.[64]

Similarly:

(159) Il serait impossible pour Jean d'être arrêté par la police.
*Il serait impossible pour Jean à être arrêté par la police.

Given: Il serait impossible pour Jean $_S$[la police de arrêter PRO] --> Passive --> Il serait impossible pour Jean $_S$[PRO$_i$ de être arrêté trace$_i$ par la police], where in addition there is a control relation between the object of pour and the subject of the embedded S: . . . Jean$_j$ $_S$[PRO$_{j,i}$ . . .], A-INF-T will be inapplicable since there is no direct link between 'Jean$_j$' and 'trace$_i$'.[65]

Returning to the inapplicability of A-INF-T in (146), one notes that it could be accounted for, given the PS-rule S --> COMP S', by requiring that NP$_i$ not be separated from V (term 4) by more than two S-type nodes, where S-type means either S or S'. Such a requirement would at the same time serve to distinguish between:

(160) *Jean serait difficile à leur dire d'embrasser. (Like (133))
(161) **Jean serait difficile à (or 'de') leur dire à embrasser.

where no à is inserted before embrasser, despite its having lost its object (Jean) to Tough-Movement. That requirement would not interfere with the generation of (144): '. . . $_{NP}$[quelqu'un] $_S$[$_{S'}$[photographier]]'.[66]

Alternatively, (146) could be handled by nontransitivity, if WH-movement were successive cyclic (see note 29), and if it applied in two steps in (146), but only in one step in (144), (154), with its one step in the latter pair then counted as the reason for the ungrammaticality of (133), (134).

The first step of a successive cyclic derivation of (146) would not trigger A-INF-T, since the displaced WH-element would not be outside the requisite S-boundary. The incorporation into A-INF-T of S, rather than S', essential for the successive cyclicity solution, has the consequence that in (144), NP$_i$ must be quelqu'un, and not the ultimately deleted relative pronoun, which in turn implies, given nontransitivity, that quelqu'un originates in the embedded S, as in Vergnaud (1974), and that it is moved directly into the head NP position, contrary to Vergnaud (1974), but compatible with his primary claim.[67]

If S is replaced by S' (and successive cyclicity dropped), then the relative pronoun could trigger A-INF-T, in which case the following:

(162) *Je ne sais pas lequel à choisir.

would be excluded parallel to the last example of note 35: *Je lui ai dit à qui de s'adresser, and subsequent to Rel-NP-Del.

As a final remark concerning the formalization of A-INF-T, consider the following possible convention: If some element is moved into a position vacated previously by another, then the trace left by the first movement is obliterated. If that is true, then one can conclude from:

(163) Jean est aussi difficile à photographier que Marie

that if 'comparative extraposition' precedes A-INF-T, then it does not have as target the position in which Jean originated, and similarly for:

(164) ?Il semble difficile à affirmer que Jean a fait cela.

Here, the extraposed (derived) subject S is probably attached not even as a sister to affirmer, but higher up in the tree, as suggested by:

(165) *Il embête Jean que tu sois comme ça.
(166) ?Il semble embêter Jean que tu sois comme ça.

a contrast expressible if (166) is derived from Que tu sois comme ça semble embêter Jean via an extraposition attaching the S as a sister to sembler, thereby avoiding the prohibition at work in (165).[68]

To the extent that A-INF-T successfully covers the range of data considered, and in the absence of a better alternative that does so, the claim that (143) and (144) constitute a linguistically significant generalization will be supported, as will the introduction of traces into linguistic theory. If the attempt to make A-INF-T precise, and therefore accountable, meets too many obstacles, one might conclude that the less ambitious A-INF is a superior way of introducing à into the infinitival relative of (144).

Conclusions. Either à-introducing rule will complement the analysis of relative que proposed earlier. The rules Rel-NP-Del, que/qui, DONT-FORM, QUE-DEL, and QUE-INS combine to provide a foundation for the claim that the que found in relative clauses does not have the status of relative pronoun, but is rather to be identified with the complementizer que that widely introduces tensed S's in French.

NOTES

1. A long list is given in Grevisse (1964:971).

2. The possibility shown in (12) of having simply *que* in the second half of such a coordination seems to be a general fact about subordinating conjunctions: *Pendant que Jean chantait et que Paul jouait de la batterie . . .*, *Bien qu'elle soit là et qu'elle désire lui parler . . .*, *Après que Jean ait chanté et que Marie ait dansé . . .*, which could be interpreted, following Klima (1965), as the result of a deletion rule: X - subord. conj.$_i$ - (que) - S et subord. conj.$_i$ - que - S
1 2 3 4 5 6 7 8
- Y ---- 1 2 3 4 5 ∅ 7 8 9 (blocked if X=X'-et; cf. the semantic con-
9
straints noted by Lerch (1925:172-3)).

This treats *après que*, *pour que*, *pendant que*, etc. as consisting of two distinct elements, the subordinating conjunction per se: *après*, *pour*, *bien*, etc. (often a prepositional or adverbial element), and *que*, whose presence is due to the tensed subordinate clause. This distinctness correlates with the separability found in: *avant même que*, *sans même que*, *pour ne pas que*, and more importantly, with the systematic absence of *que* when the subordinate clause is untensed: *après (*que) être parti*, *pour (*que) faire cela*, *sans (*que) aller là-bas*, *au lieu (*que) de faire cela*, *afin (*que) de mentir*, (*avant que de partir*, *à moins que de partir* are archaic--see note 39).

3. Perhaps linked with the relatedness of the *quand*, *comme* of (11) to the WH-words *quand*, *comment*. *Si* also occurs in WH-constructions: *Je ne sais pas si elle est là*.

4. I assume that the fact that direct quotes do not act as embedded S's with respect to *que*: *Jean a dit: je veux m'en aller* is a consequence of their more general behavior as nonembedded S's, e.g. they freely allow the application of root transformations (Emonds 1969a). Similarly, for the second half of a coordinate structure: *Jean est parti et (*que) Marie est restée*. (although an embedded tensed coordinate structure with overt subjects requires *que* there: *Elle croit que Jean est parti et que Marie est restée*), and for other 'coordinating conjunctions': *Jean est parti; pourtant (*que) Marie est restée*. Note that the distinction between subordinating and coordinating conjunctions is not based solely on the *que* data--the latter do not prepose (cf. Klima 1965): *Tandis que Marie est restée, Jean est parti* vs. **Pourtant Marie est restée, Jean est parti*. Unclear is the status of: *Plus elle lit, plus elle apprend*, without *que* in either half; cf. *Elle m'aurait dit cela, je l'aurais aidée*.

5. Since the rule deleting *lequel* is not applicable in (15), (16), (18), those relatives (and interrogatives) will continue to have a WH-word present, and so will not receive a *que* (21) (if the deletion were applicable there, and if *que* were then inserted, the ungrammatical (20) would be the output).

6. Whose presence is necessary (the same can be said of (19)): *Le garçon Marie préfère s'appelle Georges, *La fille Jean photographiera est là, exactly as in (8), (10).

7. It is not clear whether the deep structure of relatives with object qui is the same as for lequel. Perhaps qui and lequel differ simply in the particular element, within the relativized NP, to which the WH-marker is attached. On lequel, see the following.

8. This is like (21): *Ce à quoi que Marie pense, c'est au cinéma, and this is like (20): *Je cherche quelque chose sur que je pourrais m'asseoir, etc., cf. note 5. Unlike qui, lequel is the behavior of quoi in interrogatives; while Elle se demande à quoi Marie pense resembles (23) and (16), the following: *Dites-moi quoi Jean fera contrasts with (22) and (15). On interrogative quoi, see Obenauer (in preparation).

9. In other words, (31) represents a violation of the obligatory character of the deletion. The sharp difference between (30) and (31) contrasts with the duller contrast between the corresponding interrogatives: ?Je sais très bien avec la femme de qui/duquel tu t'es disputé vs. ??Je sais très bien la femme de qui/duquel tu as insultée; an explanation for the latter would therefore be unlikely to account fully for the status of (31). (Unembedded La femme de qui Jean a-t-il insultée? is acceptable, especially with stress on qui.)

10. This property of obligatoriness can also be demonstrated for clitic placement in French (cf. Kayne 1975).

11. Although not terribly plausible, since the only morphological case alternations in French are within the clitic system (cf. Kayne 1975).

12. In Quel est votre roman favori?, quel is probably not a (subject) NP, but a predicate (adjective). On *ce auquel, see Kayne (1975).

13. This process is obligatory. (One could conceivably consider it optional, if one were willing to introduce a (redundant) output constraint excluding relatives beginning with a WH-moved NP; I see no advantage to such a modification (and the disadvantage of extra machinery), while noting that it would have no effect on the (non-NP) complementizer status of relative que.)

14. Similarly, (*Que) Dire cela serait absurde, Il me plaît (*que) de faire cela, cf. note 2.

15. I am assuming here that que is inserted as a complementizer in tensed sentences; alternatively, one might have a rule (as in Gross 1968:123) deleting que before infinitives and present participles. The empirical differences between the two approaches are unclear; both are compatible with my analysis of relatives.

16. Note that, for those willing to choose, (34) is judged to be further from the realm of grammaticality than (33). Similarly, in

English one finds: 'I'm looking for someone *who/**that to talk to about linguistics', where the extra * for 'that' can be attributed to its complementizer status and taken to indicate that any explanation for *who (see Emonds 1969a and Huddleston 1971) is unlikely to be transposable into an alternative full account for **que. That relative 'that' is a complementizer was proposed by Klima (1969, 1965); that que is not a relative pronoun has similarly been held, within a non-generative framework, by Lerch (1925) and Jensen (1973).

17. Since the sequence 'object clitic + verb' is dominated by V; see Kayne (1975). It is noted that the surface structure attachment of subject clitic to verb will not interfere with the generation of (49), (51) (where qui is not introduced--see (54)), if that attachment rule (SUBJ-CL-ADJ) is ordered after the que-qui rule. It is of interest that the required ordering correlates with the ordering of SUBJ-CL-ADJ after STYL-INV (see Kayne 1972), insofar as the latter also needs to be ordered after the que-qui rule, because of ce que fait Jean vs. *ce qui fait Jean (see Moreau 1971 for discussion). A comparable ordering solution seems natural also for ?Combien crois-tu que (*qui) viendront de gens, if derived from ?Combien crois-tu que de gens viendront? via a postposition rule significantly similar to STYL-INV (see Obenauer 1974, and in preparation, for discussion).

18. Discounting adverbials and other parenthetical elements: la fille qui, vraisemblablement, sera là. Additional considerations bearing on the formulation of the rule are taken up later (see also note 17).

19. Yet to be explained is why the extraction of the embedded subject is impossible in *la fille que je tiens à ce qui/que l'épouse (vs. ??la fille que je tiens à ce qu'il epouse), *la fille qu'il est évident qui/que t'admire (vs. la fille qu'il est évident que tu admires). Opinions differ on ?la fille que je suis sûr qui arrivera la première (cf. Bourciez 1967a:743). The latter contrasts nonetheless with *la fille que je suis sûr être arrivée la première (cf. la fille que je crois être arrivée la première), which suggests that the construction of (58) not be treated as a 'raising' (cf. Postal 1974) construction such as 'I believed (*was sure) that girl to have arrived first'.

20. Deletion of an object is impossible: *Je l'ai rencontré que Marie engueulait, a contrast attributable to Chomsky's (1973) Specified Subject Condition.

21. Both Moreau (1971) and Gross (1968) assume that the que/qui alternation extends to relatives, although neither takes the step of identifying relative que with complementizer que.

22. Similarly: ??Cet homme, lequel marin est très intelligent, . . .; ???Cet homme, lequel marin Marie aime beaucoup, . . . Also, for some, with a nonrestrictive type pause: ??Je cherche un

homme, lequel photographier (but not: *. . . un homme, *qui/**que photographier*). This partially loosened obligatoriness might be compared to the fact that the English equivalent of Rel-NP-Del is inapplicable in nonrestrictives.

23. It is noted that the *que*'s of (75)-(77) introduce nontensed S's, and so might seem to clash with the latter part of note 2; I return to this point in section 3.3. The text solution would require that *voici* in: *l'homme que (*qui) voici* (example due to D. Perlmutter) be neither indicative nor subjunctive, which seems reasonable.

24. The extension of such a solution to *plus que chanté* (cf. Eng. 'He as much as confessed') is less than straightforward. On the relation between *ne . . . que* and comparatives, especially *autre que*, see Kayne (1975:section 2.17). This solution requires that *voici* have a deleted (syntactically nonplural: **Voici tous Jean*) subject.

25. '+WH' might also be found in exclamatory sentences (embedded or not); see Milner (1974).

26. Perhaps term 1 (and term 2) should be replaced by N^y, *y* a variable over the number of bars in Chomsky's (1970a) notation, and an optional Determiner allowed: $_{NP}[(Det)N^y \ _{COMP}[$ . . . . For relevant discussion concerning the internal structure of NP's containing relatives, see Vergnaud (1974). Recall that in French the problem is more complicated than in English, since Rel-NP-Del applies in both restrictives and nonrestrictives (see note 22). How to treat the split antecedent relatives of Perlmutter and Ross (1970) is unclear. The text formulation requires that Rel-NP-Del be ordered before any rule of 'extraposition of relative clause from NP'. The status of '3' also needs to be made more precise.

27. If Rel-NP-Del applies to NP's already pronominal, the same conclusion must hold. Recall that nondistinctness is not met by: 'l'homme $_{S}[_{COMP}[_{NP}[$la femme de qui] -WH] S']'--see the discussion of (47), (48). Note that no rule like Rel-NP-Del exists with interrogatives, this related to the fact that in interrogatives, there is in general no antecedent which could serve as an erasing term.

28. Because of the deletion of the preposition. Relevant here may be the deletion in popular French of certain *de* and *à*, e.g. *ce que j'ai besoin*, although the deletion may not be in COMP; it may rather apply to: **Ce que j'ai besoin de*--cf. Guiraud (1966:41) and note 34.

29. For French, (81) might also be excludable parallel to: **Cette table a été tombée sur/dessus (par Marie)*, etc., i.e. where certain rules cannot strand prepositions, if it could be distinguished from: *Elle est tombée dessus*, *J'ai voté pour*. In any case, such an approach would be inadequate for English, which can strand prepositions, but which still has: **The table on I was seated was beautiful*. This English sentence recalls **the table (which) I thought on he was*

seated; if both are part of the same phenomenon, then the latter need not be accounted for by requiring that WH-movement apply in one (long) step (since that solution does not carry over to the former), whence a severe weakening of Postal's (1972a) 'preposition dangle' argument (note that this conclusion depends on if . . . same . . ., and not directly on Chomsky's interpretive proposal).

30. The use of 'PRO' allows, given the ordering 'CL-PL (obligatory) before WH-movement' (see Kayne 1975: sections 2.16, 2.17, 4.3), an account of the contrast Ces chaises-là, dont deux sont belles, . . . vs. *Ces chaises-là, dont j'aime bien deux, although a problem remains with quelques'uns : Ces chaises-là, dont j'aime bien quelques'unes . . . despite *J'aime bien quelques-unes.

31. In Je me demande ce dont elle peut bien parler, the embedded S is a relative (-WH) structure. See Obenauer (in preparation).

32. Similarly, *dont et avec laquelle (vs. ?de qui et avec laquelle). Like dont in being a monomorphemic PP is où: la ville où elle est née (cf. Elle est née dans cette ville), even in le jour où elle est arrivée (see Ruwet 1969 and cf. 'She arrived (on) that day'). On the (English equivalent of) the archaic un jour que j'étais là (cf. Martinon 1927:227; also 217ff. on dont), see Klima (1965). The adverbial le long de NP must likewise not be a NP: la rivière le long de laquelle elle se promenait (vs. (47)); cf. *La rivière dont elle se promenait le long (like (84)), *Elle s'en est promenée le long--unless: $_{PP}[P\ _{NP}[$le long de NP$]]$, with P deleted after Rel-NP-Del.

33. In addition to similarities in mood, and meaning, compare (cf. Grevisse 1964:370-2) *Quoi qui t'ennuie with *Quelque livre qui t'intéresse (vs. Quelque vin que tu boives).

34. The qui of (96) and the second qui of (98) are due to the que/qui rule discussed earlier. In the popular French having la fille que je lui ai parlé, la fille que tu es sorti avec (cf. Tu es sorti avec), WH-movement will not have applied at all (hence there will be no Rel-NP-Del there), and complementizer que will introduce the clause alone.

35. Otherwise: la fille qui que tu vois --> QUE-DEL --> la fille qui tu vois --> Rel-NP-Del --> *la fille tu vois. If que were not in COMP (I assume that it is), QUE-DEL could be restated '$_{COMP}[$A$]$que'. In the French of (92), (97-8), QUE-DEL does not exist. One might try to extend QUE-DEL to: A qui lui as-tu dit de s'adresser? vs. Je lui ai dit à qui (*de) s'adresser, especially if the latter were possible with de in the French of (92), (97-8) (see note 39 and example (162)).

36. A perhaps conceivable alternative, which I shall not pursue, would be to claim that que-insertion is ordered after Rel-NP-Del (see note 40).

37. On 'rather', consider, e.g. Bien qu'elle soit partie. Bien que quoi? *Bien quoi?; Elle tient à ce que tu le fasses. Elle tient à ce que quoi? *Elle tient à ce quoi?.

38. Compare English 'than/as' vs. 'that'. Similarly, the implausibility of deriving the que of (99) other than via QUE-INS is reduced by a comparison with Italian: Credo che venga subito but Credo di si. Unclear is the import of *Que oui est probable. Many reject ?C'est probable que oui, recalling detachment: *Cela est probable, que oui.

39. See Grevisse (1964:1065). Like (101) is the last parenthesis of note 2, with avant taking comparative que in a way recalling pareil que (cf. 'different than'). Note that que de here makes de look like English 'to' rather than like complementizer 'for' (cf. note 35). The obscure que of C'est une erreur que de dire cela seems closer to that of C'est un salaud que ton ami than to that of (101); a deletion of (tensed) être would need restrictions: *C'est bête que de dire cela/ que ton ami.

40. No comparative que is subject to que/qui, which could suggest that comparative que be introduced after that rule, or perhaps that the order be: 'comparative' que, then que/qui restated as ±WH --→ qui/___V_T, then QUE-INS (recalling Moreau 1971); either ordering would provide another solution to (75). The relative order of application of QUE-INS and Rel-NP-Del is unclear; if QUE-INS applies first, certain derivations will need minor and irrelevant changes.

41. In the 17th century, one had (Haase 1969:81): Ce que le roi ayant su, . . . (cf. (77)).

42. On the possible 'compound' status of bien que, quoique, compare Lerch's (1925:174) citing from popular French of lorsque que S (usual: lorsque S), and the prepositional quoique ça (popular--Sandfeld 1965:II, 394).

43. The only productive counterexample to such an assumption would be Qu'elle parte tout de suite (cf. Grevisse:1964:667ff.), unless that construction (cf. the German verb-final exclamative noted by Milner 1974:85) contained a (deleted) higher verb, as in Ross's (1970) performative analysis.

44. Perhaps relatable, within Schlyter's framework, to Lerch's (1925) Elle dit que, s'il vient, que . . . . An additional difficulty for 'E' might be Dommage qu'elle soit partie, whose subjunctive suggests $_S[. . . _S[. . .] . . .]$, as in C'est dommage qu'elle soit partie; but then *Je crois que dommage qu'elle soit repartie couldn't be excluded parallel to (118).

45. And neither is que an adverbial or parenthetical element (cf. note 18 and Kayne 1972:note 76).

46. What X is here is unclear. Note Jean est malade, qu'a dit Marie-Claire (cf. Le Bidois 1952:202), suggesting that the inversion

of (121) and that of Jean est malade, a dit Marie-Claire are not due to the same rule (cf. Kayne 1972:note 27).

47. Better than (124) is ?Elle est si bête que sans doute n'a-t-elle rien compris; see Le Bidois (1952:120ff.) and Hooper and Thompson (1973).

48. That deletion seems to be possible only with a subject clitic, and then only if the entire construction is nonembedded: *Le fait que, si intelligente soit-elle, . . . vs. Le fait que, si intelligente qu'elle soit, ...

49. The fact that que blocks SUBJ-CL-INV in (122), (120), (112), but does not block STYL-INV in la table qu'a cassée Jean (from *la table laquelle . . .), see also note 46, could well be interpreted as meaning that STYL-INV, unlike SUBJ-CL-INV, can precede QUE-INS (which correlates with the ordering: STYL-INV before SUBJ-CL-INV proposed in Kayne 1972; cf. also notes 17, 40).

50. Which constraint might then be related to the impossibility of *N-NP (e.g. *la destruction la ville), as suggested by Jensen (1973).

51. It may be possible for the subject to be indefinite, but the same would be true of the clearest cases of infinitival relatives: C'est une chaise sur laquelle s'asseoir que j'ai trouvé.

52. This behavior is shared, however, by the facile-construction discussed below; see Kayne (1975:section 4.10). On both that construction and infinitival relatives, in English, see Berman (1974b).

53. The appearance of PRO in A-INF (unnecessary if A-INF follows the deletion of PRO) suggests the possibility of inserting à to the left of PRO, an analysis plausible if à is in COMP--but see note 39.

54. See Perlmutter (1970:245) and Barbaud (1974).

55. QUE-INS is rendered inapplicable by the infinitive. If A-INF does not follow PRO-deletion (see note 53), then term 2 will need to be optional, unless WH-movement leaves a trace analyzable as PRO (cf. Chomsky 1973).

56. Whether A-INF as stated previously could be made to exclude them in a natural way would depend on the precise dominance configurations of the various infinitives internal to NP's; for some relevant discussion, see Vergnaud (1974). On appositives, see Delorme and Dougherty (1972).

57. On the vast range of à in French, see Sandfeld (1965:III). On French vs. Italian, see de Boer (1926) and Jensen (1973). The linking of the Italian equivalents of (143) and (144) via the notion 'missing object' is proposed by Napoli (this volume).

58. See Postal (1971) and Berman (1974b).

59. These transformations are discussed in Kayne (1975). The L-TOUS sentence bears on the point of formulation mentioned in Kayne (ibid., chap. 1, note 28), and in addition suggests that L-TOUS can apply to the output of 'extraposition'.

60. If the de of (147) is present at the point of application of A-INF-T, then one can write: . . . PRO (de) V . . . --> . . . 3 à 5 . . .; see note 53.
3 4 5

61. Because of the third S of (143), and *Il est joli de regarder Marie. If the actual deletion does not precede A-INF-T, the controlled PRO must be analyzable as 'trace'; cf. note 55.

62. The insertion of à before manger: *Ce plat serait facile à/de/∅ faire à manger aux enfants will be excluded both by the absence of PRO before manger and by the absence of a S-boundary between faire and manger, if the faire-rule raises the embedded infinitive out of the embedded S, as suggested in Kayne (1975:section 4.9).

63. If 'super-EQUI' (see Grinder 1970) sentences like: '*Jean m'a reproché d'avoir déclaré que _se tuer t'ennuierait' were possible in French, A-INF-T would have to be appropriately restrained from inserting à in place of de. It is noted that nontransitivity for (the foregoing formulation of) A-INF-T is incompatible with Chomsky's (1973) suggestion that Tough-Movement apply stepwise.

64. If A-INF-T could not precede Raising (a rule discussed in Postal 1974), the 'trace' would have to be analyzable as NP, given our formulation of A-INF-T.

65. Assuming, of course, that trace indices and coreference indices are distinct. (On coreference transitivity, see Wasow 1972). One speaker, years ago, accepted: *Jean serait impossible à être arrêté, with A-INF-T, and the Italian equivalent seems to be grammatical. The contrast between such a sentence and (159) would appear to be statable only if Jean is moved directly from post-arrêté position to before serait.

66. And should be compared with Chomsky's (1973) subjacency condition, with which one might try to collapse it. It will not rule out the L-TOUS sentence of (149), which could be handled by ordering L-TOUS after A-INF-T, or by denying to L-TOUS the ability to leave a trace, that linked to its not applying to a major category.

67. In which case, A-INF-T should never apply in nonrestrictives: *J'ai trouvé Jean, à photographier. In Je n'ai trouvé que Jean à photographier (better than ??J'ai trouvé seulement Jean à photographier), the relative à photographier may well be on the head of ne . . . que, i.e. personne (d')autre, and not on Jean (see note 24).

68. It is not clear how one could distinguish (165) and (166) in an extrapositionless (Emonds 1969a) framework; cf. Higgins (1973a).

INFINITIVAL RELATIVES IN ITALIAN

DONNA JO NAPOLI

Georgetown University

0. This paper is a study of the syntax of infinitival relatives in Italian. In the first section it will be established that strings of NP+Infinitival Relative constitute a noun phrase. In section 2 it is argued that infinitival relatives are reduced relative clauses, i.e. they are full sentences in deep structure. In section 3, I consider the mood of the underlying clauses. Finally, the reduction rules for deriving infinitival relatives are examined in section 4, and a parallel with English infinitival relatives is drawn in the last section, which closes with a suggestion for a similar analysis in English.

1. Constituency. The following sentences illustrate the infinitival clauses under consideration:

(1) Cerco una ragazza con cui ballare.
'I'm looking for a girl with whom to dance.'
(2) Cerco una ragazza da baciare.
'I'm looking for a girl to kiss.'

There is abundant evidence from the syntactic behavior of these clauses that they form a NP constituent with the preceding NP, as shown in (3),

(3)

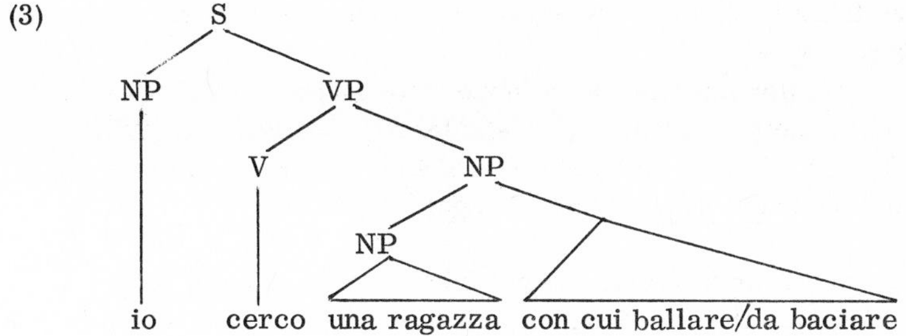

and that these infinitival clauses are not directly dominated by the VP of the main sentence in a structure such as the following:

(4)

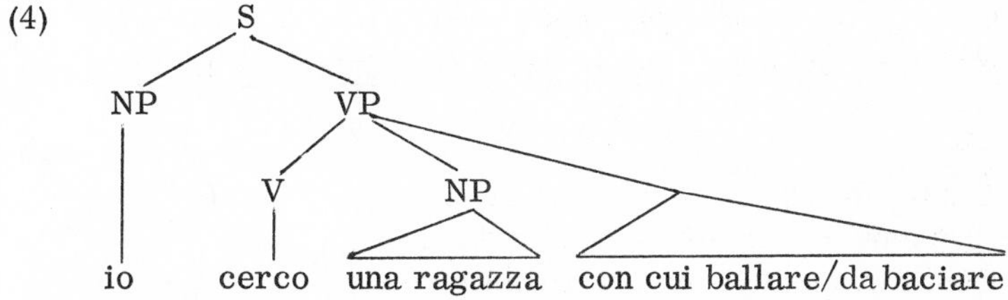

The evidence for (3) and against (4) comes from sentences that have undergone movement transformations, and from the distributional facts about infinitival relatives.

1.1 Movement transformations. There are a number of transformations which move NP's and are subject to Chomsky's (1964b) A-over-A principle (cf. Ross's (1967) Complex NP Constraint). These transformations may move only the circled NP in a structure like the following, where A is any node:

(5) (NP)

NP A

Thus, for instance, PASSIVE may move a NP+PrepP string provided it forms a NP:

(6) Le ciambelle nel frigo sono state mangiate da Claudio.
'The doughnuts in the refrigerator were eaten by Claudio.'

But it cannot move a similar string when it does not constitute a NP:

(7) *Le ciambelle nel frigo sono state messe da Claudio.
'The doughnuts in the refrigerator were put by Claudio.'

Clearly, facts of this sort constitute evidence in establishing constituent structure.

Other transformations which move a NP and are subject to the A-over-A principle are SUBJECT-RAISING, OBJECT-RAISING, and OBJECT-PREPOSING. SUBJECT-RAISING is observed in sentences with the verbs sembrare 'seem' and parere 'appear':

(8) Sembra che le ciambelle nel frigo siano ancora fresche.
'It seems that the doughnuts in the refrigerator are still fresh.'

(9) Le ciambelle nel frigo sembrano essere ancora fresche.
'The doughnuts in the refrigerator still seem to be fresh.'

OBJECT-RAISING (or TOUGH-MOVEMENT in Postal 1971) relates pairs of sentences whose predicates contain Cop+Adj, with adjectives such as difficile 'difficult', facile 'easy', and interessante 'interesting':

(10) È difficile leggere quel libro sulla guerra.
'It's hard to read that book on the war.'

(11) Quel libro sulla guerra è difficile da leggere.
'That book on the war is hard to read.'

OBJECT-PREPOSING (cf. Napoli, in preparation), on the other hand, is a transformation which fronts a direct object NP in indefinite-si constructions, relating pairs of sentences such as:

(12) Si vendono tutti i tipi di pesce nel mercato.
'They sell all kinds of fish in the market.'

(13) Tutti i tipi di pesce si vendono nel mercato.
'All types of fish are sold in the market.'

These transformations, like PASSIVE, observe the A-Over-A principle, as illustrated by the ungrammatical sentences that follow.

(14) *Le ciambelle sembrano nel frigo essere ancora fresche. (S-R)
'The doughnuts seem in the refrigerator to be still fresh.'

(15) *Quel libro è difficile da leggere sulla guerra. (O-R)
'That book is hard to read on the war.'

(16) *Tutti i tipi si vendono di pesce nel mercato. (O-P)
'All types are sold of fish in the market.'

I now examine the behavior of the infinitival relatives with respect to the four transformations cited.

PASSIVE:

(17a) Ogni sera Enzo cerca una ragazza con cui ballare/da baciare.
'Every night Enzo looks for a girl to dance with/to kiss.'
(17b) Ogni sera una ragazza con cui ballare/da baciare è cercata da Enzo.
(17c) *Ogni sera una ragazza è cercata con cui ballare/da baciare da Enzo.

SUBJECT-RAISING:

(18a) Sembra che una ragazza con cui ballare/da baciare è la perfetta soluzione.
'It seems that a girl to dance with/to kiss is the perfect solution.'
(18b) Una ragazza con cui ballare/da baciare sembra essere la perfetta soluzione.
(18c) *Una ragazza sembra con cui ballare/da baciare essere la perfetta soluzione.

OBJECT-RAISING:

(19a) È difficile trovare una ragazza con cui ballare/da baciare.
'It's difficult to find a girl to dance with/to kiss.'
(19b) Una ragazza con cui ballare/da baciare è difficile da trovare.
(19c) *Una ragazza è difficile da trovare con cui ballare/da baciare.

OBJECT-PREPOSING:

(20a) Si può trovare una ragazza con cui ballare/da baciare.
'One can find a girl to dance with/to kiss.'
(20b) Una ragazza con cui ballare/da baciare si può trovare.
(20c) *Una ragazza si può trovare con cui ballare/da baciare.

As can be observed in the foregoing (c) sentences, the noun phrase una ragazza cannot be moved and separated from the infinitival relatives by any of these movement transformations. Rather, una ragazza con cui ballare/da baciare is always treated as a NP constituent.

Since these transformations are all subject to the A-over-A principle, these data clearly indicate that the constituent structure of una ragazza con cui ballare/da baciare cannot be that shown in (4). Rather, they constitute convincing evidence supporting the structure postulated in (3), where the infinitival relative forms a NP with the noun phrase it follows:

(21)

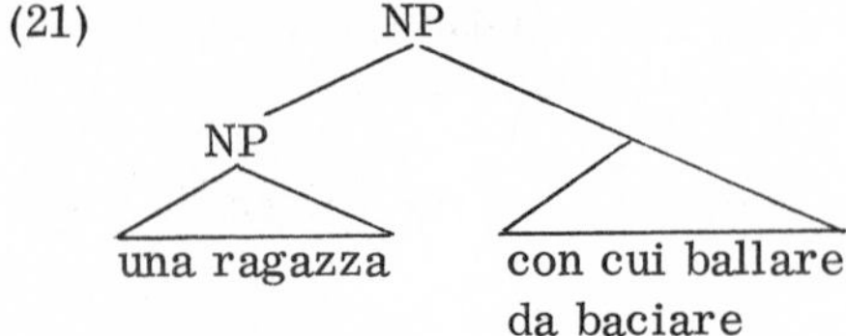

1.2 Distribution. Infinitival relatives may follow a noun phrase appearing in any position in a sentence. That is, they may be constructed with a subject NP, a direct object NP, an indirect object NP, an NP object of a preposition, and so forth:

(22) Una ragazza con cui ballare è appena entrata.
'A girl to dance with just entered.'

(23) Cerco una ragazza con cui ballare.
'I'm looking for a girl to dance with.'

(24) Parlavo alla perfetta ragazza con cui ballare.
'I was speaking to the perfect girl to dance with.'

(25) Camminavo dietro della perfetta ragazza con cui ballare.
'I was walking behind the perfect girl to dance with.'

But their position is fixed with respect to that noun phrase: they must always follow it. In fact, infinitival relatives cannot occur unless they are constructed with a preceding noun phrase.

If it is assumed that these infinitival phrases form a constituent with their preceding noun phrase, these distributional facts are all an automatic consequence of the distribution of that preceding noun phrase. If this constituent structure is not assumed, then their distribution will have to be defined separately by each phrase structure rule that puts out a NP. Every such rule would have to generate optionally an infinitival phrase after a NP. Assuming for the moment that infinitival phrases originate as S, the rules needed, for instance, to describe the structure of sentences (22)-(25) would be as follows:

(26) S → NP (S) VP
VP → V NP (S)
PrepP → Prep NP (S)

But there is no evidence, apart from the sentences bearing infinitival relatives, to support such rules. Clearly, they would be ad hoc, and would completely miss the generalization underlying the distributional facts previously noted.

In short, unless it is assumed that these infinitival phrases are part of a complex NP structure, as in (21), there is no satisfactory way to explain why they do not appear without a preceding NP, and why they may occur after a noun phrase in any position that such noun phrase may assume in a sentence.

2. Deep structure. I have so far established that (3) is the proper underlying constituent structure of sentences (1) and (2) at some stage in their derivation. One question to be examined now is whether the node dominating the infinitival phrase is a VP in deep structure, as shown in (27), or whether it is an S, as shown in (28).

(27)

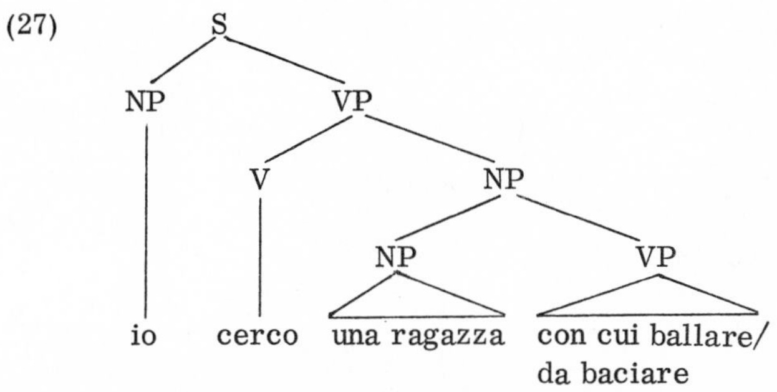

(28)

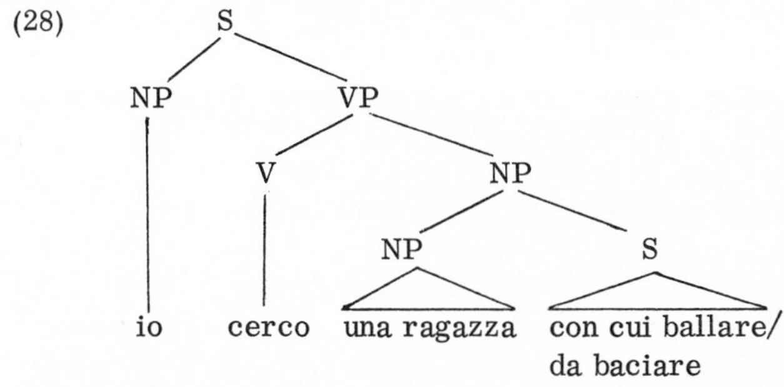

In this section I argue that the operations of Equi-NP DELETION and Fare-ATTRACTION show that (28) is the proper deep structure of sentences (1) and (2). Then I present facts concerning relative pronouns, coreference, and pied-piping, which support the contention that the infinitival phrases under consideration are reduced relative clauses; that is, they have the deep structure of a full relative clause, namely, an underlying S.

2.1 An underlying S. EQUI-NP DELETION is the rule that deletes the subject of a complement sentence when it is coreferential with a noun phrase in the next higher sentence. It can be shown that EQUI is cyclic and that it applies to the structure underlying the infinitival phrases. Then, for EQUI to be operative on these phrases, they must be dominated by an underlying S node rather than by a VP node.

One may begin by considering a sentence like the following:

(29) Gianni vuole sembrare amare (di) studiare.
'John wants to seem to love to study.'

This sentence has roughly the following underlying structure:[1]

(30)

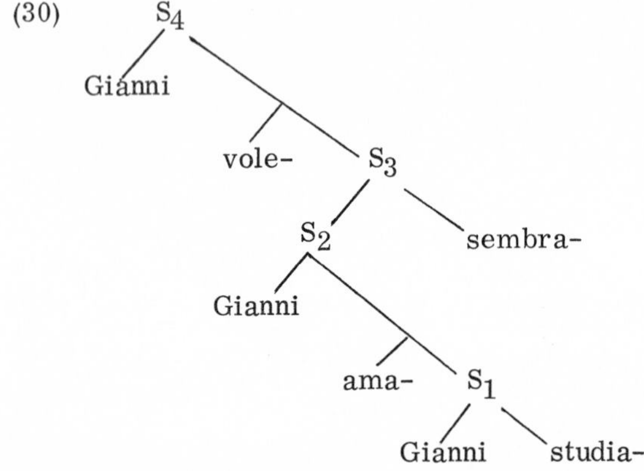

Its surface form is derived through applications of EQUI and SUBJECT-RAISING in the following way. In the second cycle, EQUI applies to yield:

(31) $[_{S_2}$ Gianni ama- (di) studiare $]_{S_2}$

In the third cycle, SUBJECT-RAISING applies and gives:

(32) $[_{S_3}$ Gianni sembra- amare (di) studiare $]_{S_3}$

Then, in the fourth and final cycle, EQUI applies again, yielding:

(33) $[_{S_4}$ Gianni vole- sembrare amare (di) studiare $]_{S_4}$

In the derivation of (29) two rules were applied in the order that follows:

(34) EQUI
SUBJECT-RAISING
EQUI

This ordering is the only one possible in this derivation. EQUI must apply in S_2 before SUBJECT-RAISING raises its subject to S_3. Then, EQUI must apply again in S_4 to erase the derived subject of S_3. But unless SUBJECT-RAISING applies in S_3 there is no environment for EQUI in S_4. Thus, (34) is the proper ordering of the rules in the derivation of (29).

Given a theory of rule application in which rules are ordered, the only way to solve the ordering paradox of (34) is to assume that these rules apply in a cyclic fashion, so that each of the two applications of EQUI is on a different cycle.

Given a theory of rule application in which rules are not ordered, but rather apply whenever their structural description is met, the cycle is still needed. Otherwise, there is no way to explain why certain rules must apply before others in a derivation. Within such a theory the ordering in (34) is a natural outcome as long as EQUI and SUBJECT-RAISING are cyclic. If they were not cyclic, there would be no way to prevent SUBJECT-RAISING from applying in S_3 before EQUI applied in S_2, to generate *<u>Gianni vuole sembrare amare che Gianni studi(a)</u> 'John wants to seem to love that John studies'. Thus, even within this theory EQUI must be a cyclic rule (cf. Perlmutter 1973, and in preparation, for arguments for the cycle).

Consider now sentences bearing infinitival relatives. It may be observed that EQUI applies in these phrases, as illustrated here:

(35) Cerco una ragazza con cui provare a ballare.
'I'm looking for a girl to try to dance with.'
(36) Cerco una ragazza da provare a baciare.
'I'm looking for a girl to try to kiss.'
(37) Cerco una ragazza con cui cominciare a ballare.
'I'm looking for a girl to begin to dance with.'
(38) Cerco una ragazza con cui fingere di ballare.[2]
'I'm looking for a girl to pretend to dance with.'

In all these sentences EQUI takes place between the subjects of the two infinitives. Thus, the infinitival phrases beginning with <u>con cui</u> and <u>da</u> must be dominated by an S node. Furthermore, EQUI was shown to be cyclic; therefore, the node dominating the infinitival phrases, again, must be a cyclic node, in this case, an S node.

I now turn to another rule, <u>Fare</u>-ATTRACTION, which furnishes another argument that the infinitival relatives are dominated by an underlying S node. <u>Fare</u>-ATTRACTION is the rule that derives sentences in which the verb fare 'make' (also lasciare 'let', and verbs of perception, such as vedere 'see', and sentire 'hear') is followed immediately by an infinitive, e.g.

(39a) Faccio piangere.
'I make people cry.'
(39b) Faccio andare Martina.
'I make Martina go.'
(39c) Faccio mangiare la pasta a Martina.
'I make Martina eat the pasta.'
(39d) Faccio leggere la lettera a Silvia da Martina.
'I make Martina read the letter to Silvia.'

To show that Fare-ATTRACTION is cyclic, it is sufficient to show that it is neither precyclic nor postcyclic.

Fare-ATTRACTION is not precyclic for it must apply after SUBJECT-RAISING, which is cyclic. The evidence that it must apply after SUBJECT-RAISING comes from sentences like:

(40) Quello sbaglio ha fatto sembrare (?essere) stupido Pinco.

The underlying structure of such a sentence is roughly the following:[3]

(41)

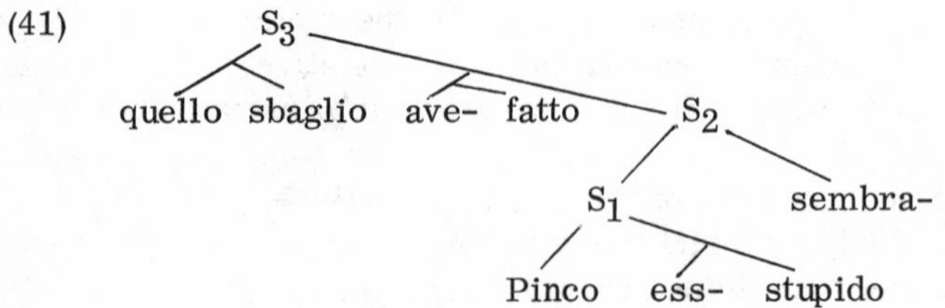

Its surface form is derived by application of SUBJECT-RAISING in the second cycle, yielding:

(42) $[_{S_2}$ Pinco sembra- (essere) stupido $]_{S_2}$

and application of Fare-ATTRACTION in the final cycle, yielding:

(43) $[_{S_3}$ quello sbaglio ave-fatto sembrare (essere) stupido Pinco $]_{S_3}$

In the operation of Fare-ATTRACTION, S_2 is pruned. This must be so because REFLEXIVE, which applies within S boundaries, may apply between the subject of fare and some object of the verb in the complement of fare, e.g.

(44) Gianni si è fatto tagliare i capelli dal barbiere.
John to-himself had cut the hair by the barber
'John had his hair cut by the barber.'

If Fare-ATTRACTION applied before SUBJECT-RAISING instead of after it in the derivation of (40), then the environment for the latter rule would be destroyed, since S_2 would be pruned. Then, the fact that Fare-ATTRACTION must here apply after SUBJECT-RAISING, which is cyclic, indicates that Fare-ATTRACTION cannot be precyclic.

Fare-ATTRACTION can apply before REFLEXIVE. This can be seen in the derivation of a sentence like the following:

(45) Carlo si è fatto tagliare i capelli da Maria.
'Carlo had his hair cut by Maria.'

The underlying structure of such a sentence being roughly as follows:

(46)

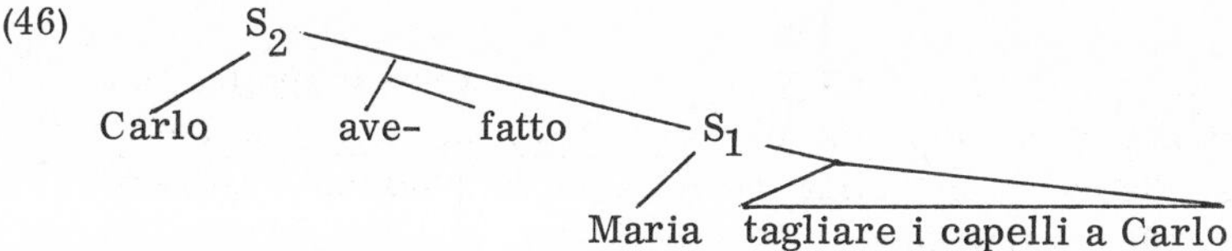

Fare-ATTRACTION applies in the second cycle, yielding:

(47) $[_{S_2}$ Carlo ave-fatto tagliare i capelli a Carlo da Maria $]_{S_2}$

Then, REFLEXIVE applies in the same cycle (since the previous operation of Fare-ATTRACTION causes S_1 to prune), yielding the surface structure of sentence (45). If Fare-ATTRACTION were not to precede REFLEXIVE, there would be no way to derive the reflexive pronoun in that sentence. Thus, Fare-ATTRACTION must precede REFLEXIVE in this derivation.

Now, REFLEXIVE, which is an obligatory rule, must be able to operate before EQUI, which was shown earlier to be a cyclic rule. Evidence that REFLEXIVE must apply before EQUI comes from sentences like the following:

(48a) Giorgio vuole pettinarsi.
George wants to comb-the-hair to himself
'George wants to comb his hair.'

(48b) *Giorgio$_i$ vuole pettinarlo$_i$.
George wants to comb-the-hair to him

If REFLEXIVE can apply before the cyclic rule EQUI, then REFLEXIVE must not be postcyclic. Further, since *Fare*-ATTRACTION was shown to be able to precede REFLEXIVE, *Fare*-ATTRACTION also cannot be postcyclic. Since it has been seen that *Fare*-ATTRACTION cannot be precyclic either, it must be concluded that *Fare*-ATTRACTION is a cyclic rule.

Let us now examine the following sentences in whose derivation *Fare*-ATTRACTION has applied in the infinitival phrases concerned:

(49) Cerco una ragazza da fare cantare.
'I'm looking for a girl to make sing.'

(50) Cerco una ragazza a cui fare cantare la canzone.
'I'm looking for a girl to make sing the song.'

(51) Cerco una ragazza da cui farmi tagliare i capelli.
'I'm looking for a girl to make cut my hair.'

Since *Fare*-ATTRACTION is cyclic, and since it applies in the infinitival phrases introduced by *da*, *a cui*, and *da cui* in these sentences, the node dominating these infinitival phrases must be a cyclic node, in this case, an S node.

2.2 A relative clause. It is clear, then, that the underlying structure of NP+Infinitival phrase is a complex noun phrase:

(52)

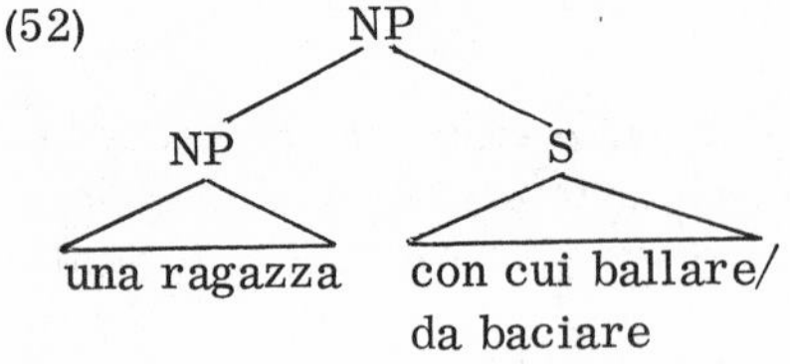

This structure is common to two well-known types of complex noun phrase in Italian, namely, a complex NP with a sentential complement, as in (53),

(53) Il fatto che Giorgio non può venire mi fa piangere.
'The fact that George cannot come makes me cry.'

and a complex NP with a relative clause, as in (54).

(54) Cerco una ragazza con cui io possa ballare.
'I'm looking for a girl with whom I can dance.'

A natural question is whether the complex NP structure in (52) is one of these two kinds of structure, or whether it is a third kind, to be distinguished from the others.

There is abundant and convincing evidence that the complex NP structure underlying the infinitival phrases under consideration is the same as underlies relative clauses. That is, these infinitival phrases are not different in deep structure from the commonest relative clause.

First, there is the matter of relative pronouns. Relative clauses may be introduced by che 'that', by a form of the relative pronoun il quale, or, when preceded by a preposition, by cui or a form of il quale, e.g.[4]

(55a) Cerco una ragazza che posso baciare.
'I'm looking for a girl that I can kiss.'
(55b) (*)Cerco una ragazza la quale posso baciare.
'I'm looking for a girl whom I can kiss.'
(55c) Cerco una ragazza con cui posso ballare.
'I'm looking for a girl with whom I can dance.'
(55d) Cerco una ragazza con la quale posso ballare.
'I'm looking for a girl with whom I can dance.'

Complex noun phrases like the one in (53) never employ a form of il quale:

(56) *Il fatto il quale Giorgio non può venire mi fa piangere.
'The fact which George cannot come makes me cry.'

These facts, together with the fact that il quale cannot appear in any other complement construction, as illustrated here:

(57a) *Il quale Carlo l'ha fatto è triste ma vero.
'Which Carlo did it is sad but true.'
(57b) *Ho detto il quale Sandro veniva.
'I said which Sandro was coming.'
(57c) *Volevo il quale Romolo restasse.
'I wanted which Romolo would stay.'

indicate that the relative pronoun il quale may not occur in structures other than relative clauses. But the infinitival phrases under consideration may bear cui or any form of il quale when introduced by a preposition,

(58a) Cerco una ragazza con cui/la quale ballare.
'I'm looking for a girl with whom to dance.'
(58b) Cerco una ragazza a cui/la quale dare l'anello.
'I'm looking for a girl to whom to give the ring.'

Moreover, relative clauses in which the NP coreferential with the head NP is possessive may be introduced by cui preceded by the definite article and followed by the possessed noun. In many dialects this type of relative clause is well formed provided the possessed noun is not accusative, e.g.

(59a) Conosco l'uomo la cui figlia è bella.
'I know the man whose daughter is pretty.'
(59b) Conosco l'uomo alla cui figlia Giorgio parla.
'I know the man whose daughter George is speaking to.'
(59c) ??Conosco l'uomo la cui figlia Giorgio ama.
'I know the man whose daughter George loves.'

Likewise, infinitival phrases may be introduced in a similar fashion, and with the same restriction:

(60a) Cerco un uomo ricco colla cui figlia ballare.
'I'm looking for a rich man with whose daughter to dance.'
(60b) ??Cerco un uomo ricco la cui figlia (da) sposare.
'I'm looking for a rich man whose daughter to marry.'

Clearly, the occurrence of relative pronouns and their behavior in these constructions must be taken as evidence that these infinitival phrases are relative clauses.

Consider now the question of coreference in relative clauses. A relative clause must contain in underlying structure a noun phrase which is coreferential with its head noun phrase. The relative pronoun is derived from this coreferential noun phrase in the clause. The fact that it has the same gender and number as the head noun phrase indicates that at some point in its derivation there was a coreferential noun phrase in its place.

Not all embedded clauses must have a coreferential noun phrase. For instance, complements of noun phrases like il fatto 'the fact' do not. Other complements may have a coreferential noun phrase, but, unlike relative clauses, there is no trace of such noun phrases in these embedded clauses. Consider, for instance, the following sentences which illustrate complements that require coreference:[5]

(61a) Le ragazze cercano di venire.
'The girls try to come.'

(61b) *Le ragazze cercano che vengano.
'The girls try that they come.'

(61c) Maria è bella da guardare.
'Mary is pretty to look at.'

(61d) *Maria è bella da guardare Maria.
'Mary is pretty to look at Mary.'

(61e) *Maria è bella da guardarla.
'Mary is pretty to look at her.'

The infinitival phrases under consideration may be introduced by relative pronouns, and, as in relative clauses, these pronouns must have a head coreferential noun phrase. Witness the ungrammaticality of the following examples:

(62a) *Cerco una ragazza da baciare Maria.
'I'm looking for a girl to kiss Mary.'

(62b) *Cerco una ragazza con il quale ballare.
'I'm looking for a girl with whom (masc. sg.) to dance.'

(62c) *Cerco una ragazza alle quali dare l'anello.
'I'm looking for a girl to whom (fem. pl.) to give the ring.'

If the infinitival phrases under discussion are derived from relative clauses, the fact that their coreferential noun phrase may leave a trace (i.e. the relative pronoun) is thereby explained.

In short, then, the fact that these infinitival phrases require coreference, and that the coreferential noun phrase may appear in the surface as a relative pronoun, is evidence that these infinitival phrases are reduced versions of relative clauses.

I now turn to another aspect of relative clauses, namely, the fronting of prepositions and case markers, commonly referred to as Pied-Piping. When the object of a preposition is relativized, the preposition must be fronted along with its object:[6]

(63a) Cerco una ragazza con $\left\{\begin{matrix}\text{cui} \\ \text{la quale}\end{matrix}\right\}$ io possa ballare.

(63b) *Cerco una ragazza $\left\{\begin{matrix}\text{cui} \\ \text{la quale}\end{matrix}\right\}$ io possa ballare con.

Likewise, in the infinitival phrases under consideration, prepositions must be pied-piped:

(64a) Cerco una ragazza con $\left\{\begin{matrix}\text{cui} \\ \text{la quale}\end{matrix}\right\}$ ballare.

(64b) *Cerco una ragazza {cui / la quale} ballare con.

If the subject of a verb embedded in the complement of <u>fare</u> is relativized, the case marker of that subject must be pied-piped:

(65a) La ragazza a cui faccio cantare questo si chiama Pina.
'The girl I make sing this is named Pina.'

(65b) La ragazza dalla quale mi faccio tagliare i capelli si chiama Pina.
'The girl by whom I have my hair cut is named Pina.'

Likewise, in the cited infinitival phrases, case markers must be fronted:

(66a) Cerco una ragazza a {cui / la quale} fare cantare questo.

(66b) Cerco una ragazza da {cui / la quale} farmi tagliare i capelli.

Thus, with respect to prepositions and case markers, the infinitival phrases under discussion observe the same conditions on Pied-Piping as relative clauses. Moreover, their similarity is more striking when one considers pied-piping of noun phrases.

Consider the following sentence:

(67) Il governo stabilisce l'altezza dei caratteri sulla copertina dei libri.
'The government prescribes the height of the lettering on the cover of books.'

The structure of this sentence is roughly as in (68).

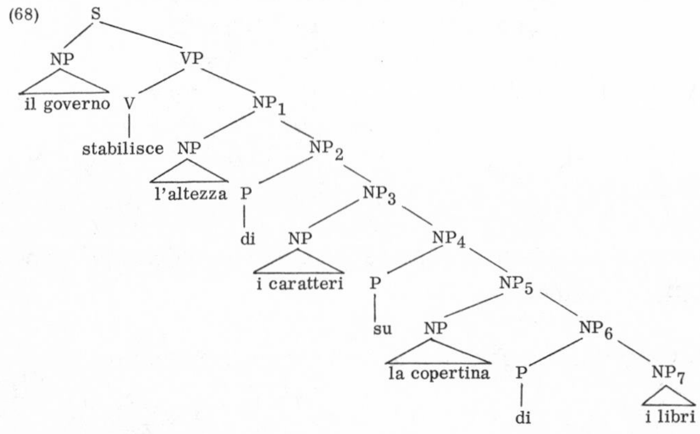

If NP_7 is relativized, NP_1 and everything dominated by it must be pied-piped (contrast to the facts on English given in Ross 1967):[7]

(69) i libri l'altezza dei caratteri sulla cui copertina/sulla copertina dei quali il governo stabilisce . . .
'the books the height of the lettering on whose cover/on the cover of which the government prescribes . . .'

(70) *i libri dei caratteri sulla cui copertina/sulla copertina dei quali il governo stabilisce l'altezza . . .

(71) *i libri sulla cui copertina/sulla copertina dei quali il governo stabilisce l'altezza dei caratteri . . .

(72) *i libri di cui/dei quali il governo stabilisce l'altezza dei caratteri sulla copertina . . .

Likewise, in the cited infinitival phrases when an NP in a similar structure is fronted, every NP dominating that NP must also be fronted:

(73) Cerco una ragazza nella tasca della cui blusa/della blusa della quale mettere il garofano.
'I'm looking for a girl in the pocket of whose blouse to put the carnation.'

(74) *Cerco una ragazza della cui blusa/della blusa della quale mettere il garofano nella tasca.

(75) *Cerco una ragazza della quale mettere il garofano nella tasca della blusa.

Thus, with respect to Pied-Piping of noun phrases, relative clauses and the infinitival phrases under discussion exhibit the same behavior. This fact is the more remarkable when one examines pied-piping in questions. In questions the fronting of prepositions and case markers is obligatory. However, questions do not require fronting of noun phrases; in fact, they do not even allow it:

(76) Di quali libri stabilisce l'altezza dei caratteri sulla copertina il governo?
'Of which books does the government prescribe the height of the lettering on the cover?'

(77) *Sulla copertina di quali libri stabilisce l'altezza dei caratteri il governo?

(78) *Dei caratteri sulla copertina di quali libri stabilisce l'altezza il governo?

(79) *L'altezza dei caratteri sulla copertina di quali libri stabilisce il governo?

The fact that the same conditions on Pied-Piping hold in relative clauses and in infinitival relatives, and are different from those observed by other structures (e.g. questions) follows from a theory in which the infinitival phrases are reduced forms of relative clauses. If they do not derive from relative clauses, this set of facts would seem purely accidental, and the grammar must duplicate the conditions on Pied-Piping in relative clauses for Pied-Piping in these infinitivals. Thus, the fact that these conditions are identical for both structures provides an argument in favor of relating these structures.

In short, it has been shown that the infinitival relatives under consideration behave like relative clauses in at least three important respects. First, they may be introduced by a relative pronoun; second, they require coreference, and, finally, they pied-pipe noun phrases. I submit that these infinitival phrases behave like relative clauses simply because they are relative clauses.

3. Mood. If infinitival relatives are reduced clauses, there are four logical possibilities as to their derivation. Either they derive from indicative clauses only, or from subjunctive clauses only, or from both indicative and subjunctive clauses, or from nontensed clauses. All these possibilities will be examined and the conclusion will be reached that infinitival relatives derive from both indicative and subjunctive clauses.

The mood of a relative clause is determined by the semantic nature of its head noun phrase. If this is specific or generic, the clause is in the indicative mood. If it is nonspecific or irrealis, the clause is in the subjunctive mood in many dialects. These facts are illustrated here. The indicative in (81) is accepted by some speakers.

(80) Cerco una ragazza con cui { posso (Ind.) / *possa (Subj.) } ballare--ma non ricordo il suo nome. 'I'm looking for a girl with whom I can dance--but I don't remember her name.'

(81) Cerco una ragazza con cui io { *posso / possa } ballare--ne conosci una? 'I'm looking for a girl with whom I may dance--do you know one?'

The fact that the speaker in (80) once knew but has forgotten the name of the girl he is looking for imposes the specific interpretation of <u>una ragazza</u>. Thus the subjunctive is rejected while the indicative is appropriate. In (81), on the other hand, the specific interpretation is ruled out by the fact that the speaker asks the listener if he knows any girl to dance with. Thus, the indicative is rejected while the subjunctive is preferred by many speakers.

It may be observed in the examples that follow that infinitival relatives may be constructed with specific head noun phrases, or with nonspecific ones. Again, notice that the indicative is allowed in (83) by some speakers.

(82) Ho trovato un uomo da cui ({posso / *possa}) comprare i biglietti.
'I found a man from whom I can/may buy the tickets.'

(83) Devo trovare la perfetta compagna da cui (io {*posso / possa}) dipendere.
'I must find the perfect companion I can/may depend on.'

These facts thus lead to the rejection of the proposals that infinitival relatives derive from indicative clauses only, or from subjunctive clauses only.

However, there is a fact which leaves one puzzled. On looking at (80) and (81), one finds that there is no corresponding sentence with an infinitival relative for the former, while there is for the latter:

(84) *Cerco una ragazza con cui ballare--ma non ricordo il suo nome.

(85) Cerco una ragazza con cui ballare--ne conosci una?

These sentences are not isolated examples. Many indicative clauses, in contrast to subjunctive clauses, do not have corresponding infinitival relatives. Furthermore, proper nouns may not be constructed with infinitival relatives, just as they may not be constructed with subjunctive relative clauses.[8]

(86) *Cerco Maria con cui ballare.
'I'm looking for Mary with whom to dance.'

(87) Ho trovato l'impiegato (*Rossi) da cui comprare i biglieti.
'I found the employee (Rossi) from whom to buy the tickets.'

However, proper nouns in the non . . . che construction may appear with an infinitival relative.[9]

(88) Non ho trovato che Maria con cui ballare.
'I found only Mary to dance with.'

I have no explanation for these facts. However, they suggest that if infinitival relatives derive from tensed clauses, then the reduction of subjunctive clauses may be more general and less restricted than the reduction of indicative clauses.

All full relative clauses in Italian are either indicative or subjunctive. There are no nontensed full relative clauses. The hypothesis that infinitival relatives derive from nontensed clauses requires an obligatory reduction rule that goes along with the assumption that these relatives constitute the only type that must undergo reduction. This consequence makes the hypothesis very unappealing.

Since every infinitival relative has a corresponding full relative that is either indicative or subjunctive, it seems preferable to propose an optional reduction rule for these attested relatives rather than an obligatory reduction rule for hypothetical nontensed relatives.

Various linguists have proposed tenseless sentences as the source for infinitives (cf. Chomsky 1973), despite the fact that such sentences never occur. For instance, Bordelois (1972) has proposed that many (perhaps all) infinitives have such a source. She refutes Kiparsky and Kiparsky (1970), who proposed that infinitives arise when their subject is removed, by citing Spanish infinitives which appear with nominative pronouns. In Italian, however, no such examples exist. No infinitive retains its subject. Infinitive constructions in the complement of verbs of perception cannot be considered counterexamples, for the NP subject of the infinitive is never nominative and is, in fact, treated as a direct object by PASSIVE.

(89a) Ho visto il ladro scappare. 'I saw the thief escape.'
(89b) L'ho visto scappare. 'I saw him escape.'
(89c) Il ladro è stato visto scappare. 'The thief was seen to escape.'

But there are also gerunds and participles whose subjects may have been removed, e.g.[10]

(90a) Camminando per la strada, ho visto Giorgio.
'Walking down the street, I saw George.'
(90b) Arrivata in fretta, Carla apparve affannata.
'Having arrived in a hurry, Carla appeared out of breath.'

Thus, it cannot be claimed that the loss of the subject automatically makes a verb an infinitive. Either the complement is already marked as to which form of the verb appears after deletion, or there are several subject-deletion rules which determine the form of the verb. The latter possibility would require at least two additional, distinct rules to produce gerunds and participles. This proposal, however, may well find support if one considers sentences like the ones cited, which suggest that deletion conditions and results are distinct. Therefore, it is not unreasonable to assume that the reduction rule producing infinitival relatives determines the form of the verb.

The main reason why Bordelois proposes tenseless sentences as the source for infinitives is that the understood tense of the infinitive is dependent upon and predictable from the tense and aspect of the main clause. But in Italian the tense of a subjunctive verb also depends on the tense and aspect of the main clause, and is thereby predictable.

In order to account for the sequence of tenses with subjunctive clauses, Bordelois proposes that subjunctive clauses derive from tenseless clauses by a 'Subjunctive Projection Transformation'. As far as I can see, there are no arguments which require that tenseless verbs be mapped onto subjunctive ones rather than vice versa. Thus, the facts about temporal features of tenseless clauses and subjunctive clauses could follow just as well from a hypothesis that infinitives come from subjunctives.

In addition, when one moves away from purely mechanical considerations of rules for sequences of tenses, one finds that in many instances the tense of indicative verbs must be concordant with the tense in the main clause, just as the temporal features of an infinitive depend on its main clause:

(91a) Finalmente, ho trovato un uomo da cui comprare i biglietti. Cosí li ho comprati subito. 'Finally, I found a man from whom to buy the tickets. So I bought them immediately.'

(91b) Finalmente ho trovato un uomo da cui potevo/ho potuto comprare i biglietti. Cosí li ho comprati subito. 'Finally I found a man from whom I was able to buy the tickets. So I bought them immediately.'

(91c) *Finalmente ho trovato un uomo da cui avevo potuto/posso/potei/ebbi potuto/potrò/potrei/avrò potuto/avrei potuto comprare i biglietti. Cosí li ho comprati subito. 'Finally, I found a man from whom I had been able/can/was able/was able/will be able/would be able/will have been able to buy the tickets. So I bought them immediately.'

The infinitive in (91a) has the reading corresponding to an imperfect or present perfect verb. Likewise, the indicative relatives in the subsequent examples are limited to these two sentences. Thus, temporal features of verbs in the indicative mood are also determined to varying degrees by the context in which they occur. Any argument based on the interpretation of the temporal features of infinitives, therefore, cannot provide conclusive evidence for underlying tenseless sentences.

To sum up, it has been argued that infinitival relatives cannot be reduced exclusively from indicative relatives, nor exclusively from subjunctive relatives. Since no good motivation for underlying tenseless relatives was found, and there are full indicative or subjunctive relatives corresponding to infinitival relatives, I conclude that infinitival relatives must be reductions from both indicative and subjunctive relatives.

4. Rules. I have proposed that infinitival relatives are derived from subjunctive and indicative relatives. In this section the rules responsible for the reduction of such clauses are examined. First, I consider the conditions that control the deletion of the subject of an infinitival relative. Second, I propose that infinitival relatives come from relatives containing a modal, and that the modal is optionally deleted. Third, I argue that relative pronouns must be deleted when not preceded by a preposition. Finally, I argue that the complementizer da is inserted initially in any clause whose direct object is deleted.

I am going to begin by considering the subject of the infinitives. In sentences (1) and (2) (Cerco una ragazza con cui ballare/da baciare) the subject of the infinitive is coreferential with the subject of the matrix sentence. However, this is not always the case. In other instances the subject of the infinitive has no antecedent in the immediate linguistic context, and must be interpreted according to the immediate situation. To illustrate this point, consider (92b) in the following dialogue.

(92a) Cerco una ragazza con cui ballare, ma non ci riesco. 'I'm looking for a girl to dance with, but I'm not succeeding.'

(92b) Che dici? La perfetta ragazza con cui ballare è là, vicino alla fontana. 'What are you saying? The perfect girl to dance with is over there, by the fountain.'

The subject of the infinitive in (92b) is coreferential with the listener. In fact, the antecedent of the subject of the infinitive is not present in that sentence.

In other cases, the subject of an infinitive is not a specific person but rather anyone, in which case there is no antecedent NP, e.g.

(93a) La perfetta ragazza con cui ballare fa sentire importante il suo compagno. 'The perfect girl to dance with makes her partner feel important.'

If a full relative is used, the subject of the relative is the indefinite si:

(93b) La perfetta ragazza con cui si possa ballare fa sentire importante il suo compagno.

Green (1972) has studied the conditions on subject deletion in English relatives. She argues that this deletion rule cannot be the same as Super Equi, and points out that it violates the Complex NP Constraint and the Coordinate Structure Constraint (Ross 1967). In Green (1973) she points out further problems of the controller-to-delete relationship.

Since the subject of the infinitive in a sentence like (93) has no antecedent, it seems that the safest generalization one could make about a rule that deletes such a subject is that the discourse information must make it possible to recover it.

The same facts might lead to a different proposal, namely, that the relative clauses underlying these infinitives have a dummy PRO subject in deep structure which receives its interpretation at surface level by interpretive semantic rules. The fact still remains that such interpretive rules would need to account for all the various ways in which the subject of an infinitival relative may be understood, as illustrated in (92) and (93). The interpretive approach has one advantage, however; it presents no violation of Ross's constraints.

Moreover, regardless of whether the subject of these relatives is deleted or interpreted, one important fact to be accounted for is that the subject of the infinitive cannot be understood as coreferential with the head NP of the infinitival relative.

Consider now the modal interpretation of infinitival relatives. Infinitival relatives may appear with the modal potere 'can' with basically the same meaning as without it.[11]

(94a) Cerco una ragazza con cui poter ballare.
(94b) Cerco una ragazza da poter baciare.
'I'm looking for a girl with whom to be able to dance/ to be able to kiss.'

The corresponding sentences with full relatives, on the other hand, must have the modal potere:

(95a) Cerco una ragazza con cui io possa ballare.
(95b) *Cerco una ragazza con cui io balli.
(95c) Cerco una ragazza che io possa baciare.
(95d) *Cerco una ragazza che io baci.

I propose that the modal of these relatives optionally deletes in the infinitival relatives.[12]

Many people have argued that infinitival phrases often receive a modal interpretation despite the fact that no modal is present.[13] But not all infinitivals are thus understood. Consider, for instance, the following examples:

(96a) Ho detto di averlo fatto. 'I said that I did it.'
(96b) Ho detto di poter averlo fatto/di aver potuto farlo.
'I said that I could have done it/I was able to do it.'
(96c) Ho detto di *dover averlo fatto/di aver dovuto farlo.
'I said that it should have been that I did it/I had to do it.'

Clearly, these sentences are not synonymous. Likewise, the sentences that follow are not equivalent in meaning:

(97a) Ho dimenticato di farlo. 'I forgot to do it.'
(97b) Ho dimenticato di poter farlo. 'I forgot that I could do it.'
(97c) Ho dimenticato di dover farlo. 'I forgot that I had to do it.'

Any account which tries to avoid deleting a modal from infinitival relatives must explain why they have a modal interpretation while many other infinitival phrases do not. A theory which allows modal deletion, on the other hand, has a natural explanation for the lack of modal interpretation in infinitival phrases such as (96a) and (97a), namely, no modal is present in their deep structure.

Modal deletion, just like copula deletion, seems to be common to various structures in Italian. For instance, there is good reason to suppose that infinitival embedded questions, as in (98a), are derived from full questions. The full questions, however, must have a modal, as shown in (98b), for one notes that (98c) without a modal is not synonymous with (98a). So the derivation of infinitival questions must also involve modal deletion.

(98a) Non so dove andare. 'I don't know where to go.'
(98b) Non so dove posso/potrei/devo/dovrei andare. 'I don't know where I can/could/must/might go.'
(98c) Non so dove vado. 'I don't know where I'm going.'

Given these facts, a rule of modal deletion seems well motivated, independent of infinitival relatives. This rule operates only on clauses whose subject has been deleted, and may well be restricted to structures containing a WH-question or relative word.

I now turn to the occurrence of the relative pronoun in infinitival relatives. The relative pronoun <u>il quale</u> may show up in infinitival relatives if and only if a preposition or a case marker precedes it:[14]

(99a) Cerco una ragazza con la quale ballare.
(99b) Cerco una ragazza da baciare.
(99c) *Cerco una ragazza la quale baciare.
(99d) *Cerco una ragazza dalla quale baciare.

Da in the last three sentences is a complementizer. Notice that il quale occurs with da, when it is a locative preposition, or when it is the agentive marker, as illustrated in (100a) and (100b), respectively:

(100a) Cerco una ragazza dalla quale andare. 'I'm looking for a girl whose house to go to.'
(100b) Cerco una ragazza dalla quale farmi tagliare i capelli. 'I'm looking for a girl by whom to have my hair cut.'

Very similar facts appear in both English and French. In English one can say I'm looking for a girl with whom to speak, but never *I'm looking for a girl who(m) to photograph. In French one can say Je cherche une fille avec laquelle parler, but never *Je cherche une fille laquelle photographier. Emonds (1969a) proposes that since infinitival relatives in English can be introduced by for followed by the subject of the relative clause (e.g. I'm looking for a girl for Jack to photograph), the complementizer position, if filled, must be filled by a prepositional phrase. Thus, if no for introduces the infinitival relative, only WH-fronted PPs can move into COMP position, but NPs cannot. (This proposal accounts for the difference between infinitival relatives and infinitival indirect questions, the second of which never have for followed by the subject and accordingly always keep the WH-word.) Unfortunately, Emonds' proposal cannot account for the Italian or French facts, since neither of these languages allows the subject of the infinitival relative to appear in a prepositional phrase:

(101a) Cerco una ragazza per Gianni da fotografare.
(101b) *Je cherche une fille pour Jean photographier.

In the Italian example, per Gianni does not form a constituent with da fotografare. Rather, it is a matrix dative. Moreover, the sentence is ambiguous. The subject of fotografare may be interpreted to be coreferential with the matrix subject, or with the matrix dative, or with neither. Thus, the subject of fotografare has not been moved into COMP position in a prepositional phrase.

Kayne, in this volume, proposes that since full relative clauses in French cannot be introduced by lequel unless it is preceded by a preposition, lequel cannot introduce infinitival relatives either. Again, unfortunately, Kayne's proposal cannot account for the Italian and English facts, since in both these languages the direct object relative pronoun may introduce full relative clauses:[15]

(102a) (*)Il ragazzo il quale Maria preferisce si chiama Al.
(102b) The boy who(m) Mary prefers is named Al.

To my knowledge, no one has offered an explanation for the nonoccurrence of direct object relative pronouns in infinitival relatives that will account for the facts in all three languages. Furthermore, no one has offered an explanation that will work for Italian alone. And once more, unfortunately, I have no explanation to offer.

In full relative clauses either il quale, cui, or che must occur.

(103a) Cerco una ragazza la quale/che io possa baciare.
(103b) *Cerco una ragazza io possa baciare.

Kayne (ibid.) proposes that the complementizer que in French is inserted if lequel is deleted, but that que can introduce tensed clauses only. Thus, it cannot occur in infinitival relatives. A similar explanation would rule out che in Italian and that in English infinitival relatives, respectively.[16] Thus one needs to account only for the nonoccurrence of il quale.

In all sentences in Italian in which the relative pronoun of an infinitival relative is not preceded by a preposition, the complementizer da is present. Thus, one may say that the relative pronoun deletes after da in infinitival relatives. Assuming that infinitives arise only when their subjects are removed, the rule that deletes the relative pronoun must operate after the subject of the relative has been deleted. I assume, then, that the rule RELATIVE PRONOUN DELETION has the following form:

(104) il quale ⟶ ∅ / da [+complementizer] ___ V [+infinitive]

Next, I consider the insertion of da. It was seen that complementizer da introduces infinitival relatives only when the direct object of the infinitival is coreferential with the head of the infinitival relative:

(105a) Cerco una ragazza da baciare.
'I'm looking for a girl to kiss.'
(105b) *Cerco una ragazza da ballare.
'I'm looking for a girl to dance.'
(105c) *Cerco una ragazza da dare l'anello.
'I'm looking for a girl to give the ring.'

If one turns to other infinitival phrases whose direct object has been moved or deleted, one finds that da shows up:

(106a) Maria è difficile da capire.
'Mary is hard to understand.'
(106b) *Maria è difficile da parlare.
'Mary is hard to talk to.'
(106c) *Maria è difficile da ballare (con).
'Mary is hard to dance with.'

(107a) Maria è bella da guardare.
'Mary is pretty to look at.'
(107b) *Maria è bella da parlare.
'Mary is pretty to talk to.'
(107c) *Maria è bella da ballare (con).
'Mary is pretty to dance with.'

(108a) La Turchia è un paese da scoprire.
'Turkey is a country to discover.'
(108b) *La Turchia è un paese da far visita.
'Turkey is a country to pay a visit to.'
(108c) *La Turchia è un paese da dipendere.
'Turkey is a country to depend on.'

(109a) Ho molto da fare.
'I have a lot to do.'
(109b) *Ho molto da fare attenzione.
'I have a lot to pay attention to.'
(109c) *Ho molto da pentirmi.
'I have a lot to regret about.'

The infinitival phrases in these examples are not infinitival relatives; the relative pronoun cannot occur in any of them. In the grammatical sentences, where da occurs, the direct object of the infinitive has been moved or deleted. In the ungrammatical sentences, an oblique object has been moved or deleted.

I propose that da is inserted in complementizer position whenever any rule deletes or moves a direct object out of the 'S proper' in an infinitival clause. In relative clauses, the direct object is placed in complementizer position. The complementizer is considered to be outside the S proper (inside the S proper are NP and VP, cf. Chomsky 1970a). Da shows up in the surface, however, without a relative pronoun, WH-question word, or noun phrase following it. RELATIVE PRONOUN DELETION (see (104)) deletes relative pronouns after da.

Thus, what is to be accounted for is the nonoccurrence of da before a WH-question word and before a noun phrase, as illustrated here.

(110a) Non so (*da) chi baciare.
'I don't know who to kiss.'
(110b) Cerco un uomo ricco (*dal)la cui figlia sposare.
'I'm looking for a rich man whose daughter to marry.'

To account for the facts illustrated in (105)-(110), I propose the following rules:

(111) Da-INSERTION:
Insert da in complementizer position in an infinitival clause whose direct object has been deleted or moved out of the S proper.[17]

(112) Da-DELETION

$$\text{da} \longrightarrow \emptyset \;/\; \underline{\qquad} \begin{Bmatrix} \text{WH-question word} \\ \text{NP} \end{Bmatrix}$$

The rules proposed so far to derive infinitival relatives describe the facts observed, but they are certainly not the only rules that might be proposed. For example, one might wish to claim that da is inserted into empty complementizer position before infinitives. This approach would avoid the question of deleting da before a NP or a WH-question word, since the COMP would not be empty in such cases. The problem of the nonoccurrence of direct object relative pronouns still remains for this analysis, and must be handled by some relative pronoun deletion rule--not unlike mine--or by an interpretive rule stating that da plus a relative pronoun must be interpreted as a prepositional phrase. One unsurmountable problem this analysis faces, however, is how to prevent da from being inserted before some infinitives that should not have it, as shown here.

(113a) Voglio (*da) andare. 'I want to go.'
(113b) Faccio (*da) andare Carlo. 'I make Carlo go.'

Alternatively, one might propose that da is inserted before infinitival relatives. Then a rule could delete da before prepositional phrases. This analysis, however, makes the explicit claim that the da of infinitival relatives is not the same as the one in infinitival phrases like those in (106)-(109). Also, the fact that da, in all these cases, occurs only when the direct object has been removed from its clause is purely accidental in this analysis. This undesirable consequence springs from a failure to recognize an important generalization that the rule of DA-INSERTION in (111) does capture.

The arguments for deriving infinitival relatives from relative clauses are sound. Therefore, while the rules needed for the reduction process may not be as I have proposed, there is little doubt that some such rules exist. Thus, despite the unwieldiness of the rules sketched in (104), (111), and (112), they must stand until a better analysis is proposed.

5. Implications. The analysis of infinitivals presented in this study may be duplicated for many languages other than Italian--including, of course, other Romance languages. This analysis, however, may not be duplicated point by point for English, since part of the crucial evidence is not available in English. Still, the Italian data may help to shed light on the English construction.

If one goes through the arguments, one finds that many of them are applicable to English, while others are simply inapplicable because of the lack of corresponding data in English. However, no data in English seem to conflict with the Italian data. Moreover, the differences between English and Italian infinitival relatives parallel differences between English and Italian full relative clauses. Thus, while English can extrapose both full and infinitival relatives, Italian extraposes neither. While English can optionally pied-pipe prepositions, Italian must pied-pipe them. While English can optionally pied-pipe NPs in relatives but never in questions, Italian must pied-pipe them in relatives but never in questions.

Although these facts are less than conclusive with respect to the analysis of English infinitival relatives, they become more important when viewed in comparison with the Italian facts. Why should Italian and English infinitival relatives be so similar syntactically, and why should their few differences parallel their differences between full relatives if these infinitivals are not reduced from full relatives in both languages? Furthermore, if an analysis of a given construction is well motivated in one language, and if that same analysis works for another language in which it might be less well motivated but in which no data are inconsistent with the given analysis, it is reasonable to think that the analysis may be valid for both languages.

In conclusion, it has been seen that infinitival relatives in Italian are reduced from full relative clauses. I have suggested that English infinitival relatives, as well, derive from full relatives. Major questions left unanswered in this study are why the relative pronoun cannot appear unless preceded by a preposition, and why subjunctive relatives in Italian lend themselves to this reduction process much more frequently than indicative ones. Both questions await further study.

NOTES

Many thanks go to Dave Perlmutter and Avery Andrews for their suggestions and criticisms. I benefited also from discussions with Arlene Berman, Michael Szamosi, Susumo Kuno, Bob Faraci, and John Goldsmith. Special thanks go to Marta Luján for her generous help in editing. All errors are unmistakably my own.

1. That an infinitive in an Equi construction occurs in an S in deep structure is clear from the fact the PASSIVE may apply in that S:

(i) Fingo di esser stato ferito.
'I pretend to have been wounded.'

(ii) Amo di essere considerato intelligente.
'I love to be considered intelligent.'

Thus S_1 in (30) is justified.

2. Notice that if da is used in a sentence like (38), we get an ungrammatical sentence:

(i) *Cerco una ragazza da fingere di baciare.
'I'm looking for a girl to pretend to kiss.'

Many speakers reject these infinitivals when da precedes one infinitive and di precedes the next, regardless of structure. I have no explanations for these facts.

3. The arguments given by Kayne (1975) for such deep structures with faire in French are applicable to the Italian parallel constructions.

4. (55b) is marked with an asterisk in parentheses because for some speakers il quale cannot function as direct object.

5. In poetic style, a sentence like the following is acceptable:

(i) Maria è bella da guardarsi.
'Mary is pretty to look at.'

See Napoli (in preparation) for evidence that this si is not a reflexive pronoun coreferential with Maria, but rather the indefinite si.

6. There are some prepositions that may be used without objects as adverbials. These prepositions need not be pied-piped when their object is relativized:

(i)a. Stavo davanti alla ragazza.
'I was standing in front of the girl.'

(i)b. la ragazza davanti a cui stavo . . .
'the girl in front of whom I was standing . . .'

(i)c. la ragazza a cui stavo davanti . . .

However, all prepositions that cannot be used without an object as an adverbial must be pied-piped. Thus con, senza, and di, etc. must be pied-piped. For further discussion, see Napoli (1974a).

7. Many speakers do not agree with the judgments given in (69)-(72). Such speakers accept (71) and reject (69), (70), and (72).

However, no one I know of disagrees with the grammaticality assigned to the sentences in (73)-(75) and (76)-(79).

8. Example (87) is due to Mario Saltarelli.

9. Example (88) is due to Richard Kayne.

10. For a discussion of the deletion rule that is operative in a sentence like (90a), see Napoli and Nespor (1976), and Napoli (in preparation).

11. The glosses might mislead the reader as to the interpretation of the infinitival relatives in Italian. In English the equivalent construction may be ambiguous. Thus (i) has two paraphrases:

(i) I'm looking for a girl to dance with.

(ii) I'm looking for a girl so that I can dance with her.

(iii) I'm looking for a girl who I can dance with.

Italian infinitival relatives are not ambiguous. They do not have a purpose interpretation. To say (ii) in Italian one must use per 'for':

(iv) Cerco una ragazza per ballare con lei.

12. The modal that is deleted need not be potere; it could also be dovere 'must'. This is suggested by examples like the following:

(i) Ho qualcosa da fare.
'I have something to do.'

(ii) Ho qualcosa che devo/dovrei fare.
'I have something that I must/should do.'

13. Bordelois (1972) gives a history of the dispute over modal deletion versus modal interpretation.

14. (99d) is grammatical in the reading 'I'm looking for a girl at whose house to kiss', but not with the reading of (99b).

15. (102a) is ungrammatical for some speakers.

16. There is at least one instance in which che occurs with an infinitive:

(i) Non ho niente che fare con lui.
'I have nothing to do with him.'

However, in general one can say that che introduces tensed complements only.

17. This condition on the insertion of da is global. That is, it must have access to an earlier stage in the derivation in which the direct object of an S is moved or deleted. As an alternative to the global rule, one might have da-insertion as part of any rule involving movement or deletion of a direct object. However, this alternative seems to miss the generalization that da is inserted always in the same environment regardless of which rule produces the environment.

THEME AND RHEME IN SPANISH SYNTAX

HELES CONTRERAS

University of Washington

The analysis of sentences into theme and rheme, roughly old and new information, respectively,[1] has been the subject of numerous papers by Prague school pioneers like Vilém Mathesius and contemporary Czech linguists like Jan Firbas and František Daneš. In this country, with the exception of a few scholars like Anna Granville Hatcher (1956a, 1956b) and Dwight Bolinger (1952, 1954, 1954-5, 1972), and more recently, Wallace L. Chafe (1970) and Susumo Kuno (1972), these ideas have been generally ignored or discarded, in the words of Nelson Francis (1966:149), as 'impressionistic ventures into stylistics, marked by a good deal of arbitrary statement.'

There is, in fact, much arbitrariness and vagueness in the writings of the Czech linguists mentioned, but there is also an intuitively recognizable ring of truth to them.

My purpose in this paper is to present some evidence in support of the relevance of the notions of theme and rheme to the grammar. More specifically, I intend to show that the theme/rheme organization of the sentence is not merely a peripheral stylistic matter but it affects semantic interpretation in a rather central way and it also conditions the application of certain syntactic rules. My examples are primarily from Spanish, but some of the points illustrated undoubtedly apply to other languages as well.

First, in order to show the semantic relevance of the notions of theme and rheme, let us consider sentences like (1) and (2).

(1) Juan viene.
(2) Viene Juan.
'John is coming.'

In a standard transformational grammar, for instance Hadlich (1971:108), these sentences would be considered to be synonymous and would be generated from a deep structure resembling (1), to which an optional rule of SUBJECT-VERB INVERSION could apply, thus generating (2). These sentences, however, are not synonymous, as can be seen from the following examples:

(3a) A. Creo que Juan VIENE.[2] 'I believe John is COMING.'
B. No, se queda. 'No, he's staying.'
(3b) A. Creo que Juan VIENE. 'I believe John is COMING.'
B. *No, Pedro. 'No, Peter is.'

(4a) A. Creo que viene JUAN. 'I believe JOHN is coming.'
B. *No, se queda. 'No, he's staying.'
(4b) A. Creo que viene JUAN. 'I believe JOHN is coming.'
B. No, Pedro. 'No, Peter is.'

The appropriateness of the response by B depends on the message conveyed by A. If, as in (3), he is communicating that John is coming, as opposed to staying, B can contradict him only by negating the verb, not by negating the subject. If, as in (4), A is stating that the one who is coming is John, B can contradict him by negating the subject, not the verb. Quite clearly, Juan viene and Viene Juan have different semantic contents, and the choice between them is not merely a matter of stylistic preference. In order to express this difference, the sentence constituents must be identified as either theme or rheme, where the latter carries the main sentential stress and normally appears in final position.[3]

As additional evidence for the semantic relevance of the categories of theme and rheme, consider the following sentences:

(5a) Prefiero que venga JUAN, no PEDRO.
'I prefer for JOHN to come, not PETER.'
(5b) *Prefiero que venga JUAN, no que se QUEDE.
'I prefer for JOHN to come, not for him to STAY.'

(6a) Prefiero que Juan VENGA, no que se QUEDE.
'I prefer for John to COME, not for him to STAY.'
(6b) *Prefiero que Juan VENGA, no PEDRO.
'I prefer for John to COME, not PETER.'

The semantic anomaly of the (b) sentences is easily explainable in terms of a theme/rheme analysis: their two rhematic elements, in contrast with those of the (a) sentences, come from different nodes, one from the subject, one from the verb. Presumably, this constitutes violation of a principle of semantic well-formedness which could not, of course, be formulated without recourse to the notions of theme and rheme.

I am now going to present some evidence in support of the relevance of the theme/rheme organization of the sentence to the applicability of certain syntactic transformations.

First, there is CONJUNCTION-REDUCTION, the rule which relates sentences (7) and (8).

(7) Pedro llegó ayer, y Juan llegó ayer.
'Peter arrived yesterday, and John arrived yesterday.'

(8) Pedro y Juan llegaron ayer.
'Peter and John arrived yesterday.'

With normal intonation, Pedro and Juan are thematic, and the verb phrase is rhematic. If it is assumed that CONJUNCTION-REDUCTION applies regardless of the theme/rheme structure of the sentence, one has to admit (9) as another possible source of (8).

(9) Pedro llegó AYER, y ayer llegó JUAN.
'Peter arrived YESTERDAY, and JOHN arrived yesterday.'

But this is wrong, because (8) can only be interpreted as equivalent to (7), not to (9). Clearly, CONJUNCTION-REDUCTION must be sensitive to the theme/rheme structure of the input conjuncts.

The theme/rheme structure of the sentence may also explain sentences like (10).

(10) PRESENTÍ y empezó a MORTIFICARME el desairado papel . . . (J. Valera, Pepita Jiménez.)
'I SENSED--and it began to BOTHER me--the sad role . . .'

Notice that the appropriate reading of this sentence is as indicated, that is, with the verbs as rheme and the noun phrase el desairado papel as (postposed) theme. What is strange about this sentence is that, even though the NP has different grammatical functions in the two conjuncts--direct object in the first, and subject in the second--its two occurrences are still treated as instances of the same NP for the purposes of CONJUNCTION-REDUCTION. But this disregard for the syntactic function of the constituents involved is only possible under the condition that they have the same thematic function. CONJUNCTION-REDUCTION does not apply if the NP in question is theme in one conjunct and rheme in the other. Thus, (10) is not the output of (11),

(11) Presentí el desairado PAPEL, y empezó a MORTIFICARME el desairado papel.
'I sensed the sad ROLE, and the sad role started to BOTHER me.'

but that of (12).

(12) PRESENTÍ el desairado papel, y empezó a MORTIFICARME el desairado papel.
'I sensed the sad role, and the sad role started to BOTHER me.'

Dougherty (1971) has argued against the existence of the rule of CONJUNCTION-REDUCTION, and has proposed instead a lexicalist hypothesis according to which coordinate structures are generated in the base. If this theory is correct, my argument based on the existence of CONJUNCTION-REDUCTION is, of course, invalid. There is, however, strong evidence in favor of the existence of such a rule, provided by sentences like (13).

(13) Mi padre y mi madre son español y griega respectivamente.
'My father and my mother are Spanish (masc.) and Greek (fem.), respectively.'

If sentences like this are generated directly in the base, a complicated rule of semantic interpretation will be needed to pair up the adjectives in the predicate with the nouns in the subject. The fact that in surface structure there may be other nouns intervening between the agreeing pairs, as in (14),

(14) Su padre y su madre le dijeron a María y Juan que eran español y griega respectivamente.
'Their father and mother told Mary and John that they were Spanish and Greek, respectively.'

indicates some of the difficulties in formulating such a rule. In a transformational approach, on the other hand, agreement takes place by rather simple rules, before the application of CONJUNCTION-REDUCTION.

Another rule which is sensitive to the theme/rheme organization of the sentence is GAPPING.

Consider the following sentences:

(15a) Transilvania eligió presidente a KOSTERLITZ, y Argentina eligió presidente a PERÓN.

'Transylvania elected KOSTERLITZ President, and Argentina elected PERÓN President.'

(15b) Transilvania eligió presidente a KOSTERLITZ, y Argentina a PERÓN.
'Transylvania elected KOSTERLITZ President, and Argentina PERÓN.'

where (b) is obtained from (a) through GAPPING. Now consider the following anomalous sentences:

(16) *Transilvania eligió presidente a KOSTERLITZ, y Argentina SENADOR.
'Transylvania elected KOSTERLITZ President, and Argentina SENATOR.'

(17) *Transilvania eligió a Kosterlitz de PRESIDENTE, y Argentina a PERÓN.
'Transylvania elected Kosterlitz PRESIDENT, and Argentina PERÓN.

Clearly, the gapped material cannot include any element which is rhematic in the leftmost conjunct. Or, conversely, the element gapped must be thematic in the left conjunct. Huckin (1973) has formulated this principle as follows:

(18) THE VARIABLE-DELETION HYPOTHESIS (VDH):
Variable constituents not represented in the sentence in a fixed position can be deleted only under identity to a controlling element bearing the feature [+theme].

This principle gives a more adequate account of variable deletion phenomena than other alternatives which do not take into account the theme/rheme structure of the sentence. One such alternative has been proposed by Hankamer (1973).

To account for the fact that a sentence like (19) is not ambiguous,

(19) Jack wants Mike to wash himself, and Arnie to shave himself.

since it can only be interpreted as (20)

(20) . . ., and Jack wants Arnie to shave himself.

and not as (21),

(21) . . ., and Arnie wants Mike to shave himself.

although the grammar provides for both derivations, Hankamer (1973: 29) proposes a No-Ambiguity Condition (NAC):

(22) Any application of Gapping which would yield an output structure identical to a structure derivable by Gapping from another source, but with the 'gap' at the left extremity, is disallowed.

However, the readings disallowed by Hankamer's NAC are quite acceptable with the right kind of intonation; thus, for example, (23) has precisely the interpretation disallowed by Hankamer's NAC,

(23) JACK wants Mike to WASH himself, and ARNIE to SHAVE himself.

namely (24), especially with a pause after ARNIE, while the reading

(24) Jack wants Mike to wash himself, and Arnie wants Mike to shave himself.

predicted by his condition is not possible at all.

Huckin's VDH, on the other hand, accounts for this case as well as for (19) read with normal intonation, that is, with peaks on wash and shave, since what these sentences have in common is that the gapped material is thematic in the first conjunct.

Huckin's hypothesis also accounts for cases like the following, which Hankamer himself presents as counterexamples to his NAC:

(25) Jack likes Sally more than Susan.

According to Hankamer's NAC, this sentence should be interpreted only as (26),

(26) Jack likes Sally more than Jack likes Susan.

not as (27):

(27) Jack likes Sally more than Susan likes Sally.

In fact, (25) is ambiguous between the senses of (26) and (27). This ambiguity poses no problem for Huckin's VDH, since both Jack likes and likes Sally are thematic.

Huckin's VDH also accounts for the otherwise mysterious difference in grammaticality noted by Jackendoff (1971:27) between the two sentences of (28):

(28a) Either Bill ate the peaches, or Harry.
(28b) *Bill didn't eat the peaches, nor Harry.

In (28a), Bill is the rheme of the first conjunct, whereas in (28b) the rheme is the verb phrase, since normally a negated verb phrase constitutes new information. Since the gapping in (28b) would involve material which is rhematic in the first conjunct, the sentence is ungrammatical. If instead of the verb, the subject is negated, it is possible to gap the verb phrase, as in (29):

(29) Neither BILL ate the peaches, nor (did) HARRY.

So far, it has been seen that theme and rheme are relevant to the application of CONJUNCTION-REDUCTION and GAPPING. I now present some evidence pointing out the relevance of these notions to the application of a movement rule which I call MAIN-CLAUSE POSTPOSITION. This rule, which is discussed in Hooper and Thompson (1973) under the name of Complement Preposing, may be illustrated by sentence (30):

(30) It's just started to rain, he said.

Hooper and Thompson note the ungrammaticality of a sentence similar to (30) but with a negated main clause:

(31) *It's just started to rain, he didn't say.

Within a theme/rheme framework, this fact can be accounted for by restricting the rule to main clauses which are thematic. Since, normally, a negated clause is rhematic, the ungrammaticality of (31) follows from this formulation, which explains in addition the behavior of the following sentences:

(32a) He SAID it's just started to rain. (He didn't WRITE it.)
(Main clause is rhematic; postposition not allowed.)
(32b) He DIDN'T say it's just started to RAIN. (He said something else.)
(Main clause is rhematic; postposition not allowed.)
(32c) He didn't say it's just started to RAIN. (In answer to 'What was it he didn't say?')
(Main clause is thematic; postposition allowed.)

These sentences indicate that Hooper and Thompson are not entirely correct in starring (31), since that sentence is ungrammatical only if its main clause is rhematic.

Let us now consider some Spanish examples of MAIN CLAUSE POSTPOSITION:

(33a) Creo que va a LLOVER. 'I think it's going to rain.'
(33b) Va a LLOVER, creo. 'It's going to rain, I think.'

(34a) No CREO que vaya a llover. 'I don't THINK it's going to rain.'
(34b) *Va(ya) a llover, no CREO. 'It's going to rain, I don't THINK.'

The ungrammaticality of (34b) is due to the rhematic nature of the main clause, not just to the presence of the negative. In fact, it is possible to construct a version of (34a) where the main clause is thematic, and that version is subject to MAIN-CLAUSE POSTPOSITION:

(35a) No creo que vaya a LLOVER. (In answer to ¿Qué es lo que no crees? 'What is it you don't believe?')
(35b) Que va(ya) a LLOVER no creo.

Another indication that it is the theme/rheme distinction which is relevant to the application of this rule, and not just the presence of the negative, is found in sentences where the rhematic function is associated with elements other than the negative, for instance, the adverb sólo 'only':

(36) Sólo SOSPECHO que va a llover. (No tengo certeza).
'I only SUSPECT it's going to rain.' (I'm not certain.)

Predictably, according to my analysis, the inverted position is ungrammatical:

(37) *Va a llover, sólo SOSPECHO.

although the verb sospechar 'suspect' does undergo postposition when it is thematic, as in (38):

(38a) Sospecho que va a LLOVER.
'I suspect it's going to RAIN.'
(38b) Va a LLOVER, sospecho.
'It's going to RAIN, I suspect.'

Theme/rheme considerations are also relevant to the distribution of adverbs. Jackendoff (1972) has distinguished a class of subject-oriented adverbs (e.g. cleverly) from a class of sentence adverbs (e.g. evidently). Notice the following sentences:

(39a) Por supuesto, Juan llegó ATRASADO.
'Of course, John came LATE.'
(39b) Por supuesto, llegó JUAN.
'Of course, JOHN came.'

(40a) Astutamente, Juan llegó ATRASADO.
'Cleverly, John came LATE.'
(40b) *Astutamente, llegó JUAN.
'Cleverly, JOHN came.'

Por supuesto 'of course', a sentence adverb, cooccurs both with a clause where Juan is theme and with one where it is rheme. Astutamente 'cleverly', which Jackendoff would classify as subject-oriented, cooccurs only with a clause where Juan is theme. It would seem more adequate, then, to call such adverbs theme-oriented rather than subject-oriented.

Up to this point, I have been assuming that there is a basic underlying order determined by phrase structure rules, which can be altered by transformational rules, sensitive, among other things, to the theme/rheme organization of the sentence. But I think a stronger claim can be made for Spanish, and presumably for most languages which, unlike English, have relatively 'free' word order; namely, that the semantic structure--which is, of course, not linear--becomes 'linearized' by reference to theme and rheme, rather than by reference to subject, verb, and object. Thus, a rule assigning an unmarked order of theme-rheme seems to account for Spanish word order more adequately than a rule which generates an unmarked sequence of subject-verb-object.

Consider again sentence (33a):

(33a) Creo que va a LLOVER. 'I think it's going to RAIN.'

and compare it with sentence (41):

(41) Me parece que va a LLOVER. 'It seems to me it's going to RAIN.'

In a standard transformational grammar, (41) derives from a remote structure like (42),

(42) Que va a llover me parece.

which in turn may derive, depending on the abstractness of the analysis proposed, from something like (43)

(43) *Yo parecer que va a llover. 'I seem that it's going to rain.'

via a PSYCH-MOVEMENT rule. Sentence (33a), on the other hand, has not undergone any reordering. It would be expected that this difference in the derivational history of the two sentences under discussion would correspond to different judgments on the part of the fluent speaker, as in the case of (44a) and (44b).

(44a) Quiero manzanas. 'I want apples.'
(44b) Manzanas quiero. 'Apples I want.'

where (44b), which has undergone reordering, is felt to be 'emphatic' as opposed to (44a), which has not undergone reordering and which is considered normal. But this is not the case with sentences (33a) and (41). Even though (41) has undergone one or two reordering rules, it is not felt to be different from (33a), which has not undergone any. Thus, either sentence can answer question (45) appropriately.

(45) ¿Qué crees? 'What do you think?'

If order is determined by the theme/rheme organization of the sentence, with the theme normally preceding the rheme, the intuitive similarity between (33a) and (41) can be accounted for by stating that verbs which express opinions, like creer 'believe' and parecer 'seem' are normally thematic; consequently, no reordering has taken place in either sentence.

This thesis is also supported by sentences like (46) and (47).

(46) Salió el SOL. 'The SUN came out.'
(47) El sol EXPLOTÓ. 'The sun EXPLODED.'

A classical transformational analysis would derive (46) from (48)

(48) El sol salió.

by a SUBJECT-VERB INVERSION rule. However, it is (46), not (48), which is normal (or unmarked), for instance, in the sense that, the same as (47), it can answer a question like (49).

(49) ¿Qué sucedió? 'What happened?'

This artificial difference between (46), derived from (48), and (47), with a deep structure similar to its surface structure, need not be created in a grammar where order is determined by the theme/rheme organization of the sentence. The order of (46) and (47) is specified by a rule that says that verbs of existence or appearance (salir 'come out', but not explotar 'explode') are normally thematic (see Hatcher 1956b).

Further support for this theory comes from the behavior of negative sentences. Thus, the normal negative sentence corresponding to (46) is (50),

(50) El sol no SALIÓ. 'The sun didn't come OUT.'

which would be hard to explain without recourse to the notions of theme and rheme, since reordering would be obligatory for the affirmative but not for the negative, at best a very strange rule. In theme/rheme terms, the explanation is simply that the negative is normally rhematic, and that this rule overrides the one that assigns thematic status to verbs of existence or appearance.

As a final piece of evidence for the crucial role of theme and rheme in determining word order in Spanish, consider Emonds' (1969a) Root Transformations, which, as Hooper and Thompson (1973) have shown, apply only to assertive sentences, both embedded and nonembedded. This is illustrated in the following sentences:

(51) Never have I seen such a mess.
(52) I insist that never have I seen such a mess.
(53) *I am happy that never have I seen such a mess.

where NEGATIVE-CONSTITUENT PREPOSING, a root transformation, produces grammatical sentences in (51) and (52) because the clauses in question are both assertions, but when applied to the complement of (53), which is not an assertion, it produces an ungrammatical string.

As Terrell shows elsewhere in this volume, many of these root transformations which produce 'emphatic' sentences in English do not have that effect in Spanish. Consider, for instance, the following sentences:

(54) Over the trees flew many birds.
(55) He said that over the trees flew many birds.
(56) *I'm happy that over the trees flew many birds.

which show that DIRECTIONAL-ADVERB PREPOSING, a root transformation, may apply to (54) and the complement of (55) because they are both assertions, but not to the complement of (56) because it is not an assertion.

In Spanish, however, all of the following are grammatical:

(57) Sobre los árboles volaban muchos pájaros.
(58) Dijo que sobre los árboles volaban muchos pájaros.
(59) Me alegro de que sobre los árboles volaran muchos pájaros.

Notice that from a theme/rheme point of view, these Spanish sentences are not emphatic: they all show the unmarked order theme-rheme. If this order is altered, however, one gets emphatic sentences which are subject to the restrictions posited by Hooper and Thompson, i.e. they can only be assertive. This is illustrated by the following examples:

(60) MAÑANA lo operan. 'They operate on him TOMORROW.'
(61) Dice que MAÑANA lo operan. 'He says that they operate on him TOMORROW.'
(62) *Siento que MAÑANA lo operen. 'I'm sorry they operate on him TOMORROW.'

This set of sentences is directly comparable to the set (54), (55), (56), which indicates that if the Hooper-Thompson hypothesis is correct, root transformations must be defined for Spanish as transformations which alter the unmarked theme-rheme order, and not as transformations which operate on syntactically defined constituents.

Notice, furthermore, that the only way to relate the oddity of (62) to that of (63)

(63) *Siento que JUAN venga. 'I'm sorry that JOHN is coming.'

is to define root transformations in terms of theme and rheme for Spanish, since under that definition, the complement of (63) has, in fact, undergone a root transformation reversing the order of theme and rheme, whereas if root transformations are defined in the usual way, the complement of (63) cannot be said to have undergone a root transformation, since it shows the 'unmarked' order subject-verb, and its oddity will have to be explained independently from that of (62) by some additional criterion of 'emphasis'. The unified explanation made possible by our definition of root transformation in terms of theme and rheme is clearly preferable.

In conclusion, there seems to be abundant evidence that the notions of theme and rheme occupy a central position in the structure of sentences, since they determine not only semantic interpretation but also the operation of certain syntactic rules, especially rules of deletion and movement.

In view of the arguments presented here, a reexamination of the problem of word order seems to be necessary. The implications of such a study are far-reaching, since several important theoretical proposals, e.g. Greenberg's (1966) word-order universals and Ross's (1967) correlation between GAPPING and underlying word order, are based on a nonthematic view of word order which is certainly not adequate for all languages.

NOTES

1. For a refinement of this rough definition, see Firbas (1964).

2. Capital letters signal the location of the main sentential stress.

3. The order, but not the location of the main stress, may be reversed in certain cases. Although I have not examined this problem in detail, I would guess that only presupposed themes can be postposed. Thus, (i)

(i) Quiere DORMIR mi hermano. 'He wants to SLEEP, my brother.'

with postposed theme mi hermano, is acceptable as an answer to (ii),

(ii) ¿Qué quiere tu hermano? 'What does your brother want?'

but not as an answer to (iii).

(iii) ¿Qué pasa? 'What's happening?'

This last question can, of course, be answered by (iv),

(iv) Mi hermano quiere DORMIR. 'My brother wants to SLEEP.'

with the theme in the normal initial position.

THE SEMANTICS OF COPULATIVE CONSTRUCTIONS IN PORTUGUESE

ANTONIO A. M. QUERIDO

1. Introduction. By copulative constructions are meant clauses where the complement (in the algebraic sense) of the verb in the VP has the syntactic function 'predicate'. This term has been successively used by Chomsky to denote a syntactic function (1965) and to denote a syntactic category ('Pred') (1970a).

So the underlying structure of copulative sentences like John felt angry or His hair turned gray would be NP-V-Pred. Since the variable 'Pred' may have as its value an adjective phrase, a prepositional phrase, or noun phrase (cf. sentence (1a), (1b), and (1c), respectively), rule (2) must be treated more as a 'categorial rule scheme' than as a categorial rule proper.

(1a) Ela $\left\{\begin{array}{l}\text{é}\\\text{está}\end{array}\right\}$ alegre 'She is happy'

(1b) Ela está no Algarve 'She is in the Algarve'

(1c) Ela é a minha melhor amiga 'She is my best friend'

(2) VP → V Pred

If 'Pred' were to be interpreted in the metalanguage of syntax strictly as a categorial symbol, the grammar of Portuguese would contain a categorial rule like (3):[1]

(3) Pred → $\left\{\begin{array}{c}\text{A}\\\text{P}\\\text{N}\end{array}\right\}$ (Comp)

Rule (3) has two major drawbacks: (a) sequences 'N Comp' and 'P Comp' would be categorized by other rules in the base as 'noun phrases and 'prepositional phrases', respectively, and (b) it would not conform to the rule scheme (4), proposed by Chomsky (1970a), 'where in place of . . . there appears the full range of structures that serve as complements and X can be any one of N, A, or V' (I have added P).

(4) $\bar{X} \rightarrow X \ldots$

Of course, NP, for example, is an adequate equivalent symbol for $\bar{N}$, but 'Pred' is not.

I therefore consider (2) as a rule scheme where the variable 'Pred' stands for AP, NP, or PP.

A nineteenth century Portuguese grammarian, Barbosa (1822), proposed a more abstract underlying structure. Copulative verbs in his conception are the 'analogatum princeps' of the verbal category: he calls them 'substantive verbs'. Ordinary verbs, the ones which take 'Comp' instead of 'Pred', become 'adjective verbs', by analogy with the classical partition of nouns into substantives and adjectives. As adjective nouns depend on substantive nouns, so adjective verbs are under substantive verbs at least in the underlying structure.

From this it follows that every sentence in Portuguese would have a substantive verb, but the choice of an adjective verb, i. e. of a VP predicate, would only be an alternative to other kinds of predicates: AP, PP, or NP.

One could modify the proposal by Chomsky (1970a) for the initial rule of the base grammar according to Barbosa's suggested underlying structure.

Instead of rule (5)--rule (48) in Chomsky (1970a)--there would be rule (6), where V_A stands for the lexical category of adjective verbs and V_S for the grammatical category of substantive verbs:

(5) $S \rightarrow \bar{\bar{\bar{N}}}\ \bar{\bar{\bar{V}}}$

(6) $S \rightarrow \bar{\bar{\bar{N}}}\ V_S \begin{Bmatrix} \bar{\bar{\bar{V}}}_A \\ \bar{\bar{\bar{A}}} \\ \bar{\bar{\bar{P}}} \\ \bar{\bar{\bar{N}}} \end{Bmatrix}$

The function of copulative verbs (V_S) in this perspective is to make sentences out of pairs (NP, NP), (NP, AP), (NP, PP), and even (NP, VP). They are 'sententializers'.

This 'deep structure' seems a little bit artificial only in the case of sentences which have a 'predicate' VP. In this case the realization of the copula on the surface obliges the adjective verb to take a participial form. This explains why it seemed more natural for the analysis of Greek and Latin, languages with rich participial paradigms.

But even in languages like English and Portuguese it would represent quite naturally the underlying structure of passive and progressive constructions.

(7a) Maria está admirando Paulo 'Mary is admiring Paul'
(7b) Maria admira Paulo 'Mary admires Paul'

(8) Maria é uma admiradora de Paulo 'Mary is one of Paul's admirers'

Note that simple tenses, like the present in (7b), have two readings in Portuguese: the 'progressive' reading would correspond to an underlying structure like (7a), while the 'habitual' reading would perhaps correspond to an underlying structure like (8) (see section 4 for the semantic analysis of *ser* and *estar*).

One could, of course, retain from Barbosa's underlying structure only the distinction V_S vs. V_A and adopt a Chomsky-like configuration for rule (6):

(6'a) $S \rightarrow \bar{\bar{N}}\ \bar{\bar{V}}$

(6'b) $\bar{\bar{V}} \rightarrow V_S \begin{Bmatrix} \bar{\bar{V}}_A \\ \bar{\bar{A}} \\ \bar{\bar{P}} \\ \bar{\bar{N}} \end{Bmatrix}$

Empirical evidence will decide which configuration is to be retained. In the sentences where the substantive verb (V_S) is not realized, a rule would be necessary to erase or 'incorporate' it into the adjective verb.

The situation presents a certain analogy with the ellipsis of substantive nouns before adjective nouns. In this case, in Portuguese, the substantive nominal position is 'incorporated' into the adjective noun: *os (homens) fracos* 'the weak men' becomes *os fracos* 'the weak ones'.

2. The class of substantive or copulative verbs. The distributional criterion to determine the class of copulative verbs is, as I have mentioned in section 1, the cooccurrence with supercategory 'Pred'.

Luján (1972) gives five syntactic properties that 'clearly differentiate predicate attributes from verbal complements: (i) the head of a predicate attribute agrees with the subject in number and gender, (ii) a predicate attribute is never preceded by a case-marking preposition, (iii) predicate attributes pronominalize differently than object noun phrases, (iv) sentences bearing predicate attributes cannot be topicalized or pseudo-cleft, (v) there are restrictions on the fronting of a predicate attribute NP in relative clauses.'

Note that Luján restricts the supercategory 'Pred' (she marks it by means of a constituent feature [+pred] following Emonds (1970) to NPs and APs. If one includes PPs (cf. example (1b), section 1), properties (i), (ii), and (iii) will not apply.

This could be an indication to treat estar in Ela está no Algarve 'She is in the Algarve' or ser in Ela é do Algarve 'She is from Algarve' as adjective verbs, as opposed to the ser in Ela é algarvia 'She is Algarvian'. But what about properties (iv) and (v) that still differentiate these PPs from complement PPs?

Consider also predicate NPs introduced by the preposition como, which, of course, do not agree with the subject and violate also condition (ii):

(9) Ela é (como) uma avestruz 'She is (like) an ostrich'

This preposition must play an important role in the underlying syntax of predicate APs, since the interrogative pro-form of adjective predicates is como too:

(10a) Como é ela? 'What is she like?'
(10b) Como está ela? 'How is she?'

(11a) Ela é ruiva 'She is a redhead'
(11b) Ela está desmaiada 'She is unconscious'

Compare the sentences in (10) and (11). Since como is probably an intransitive preposition (call it an adverb, if you like) and since, according to Luján, PPs are not predicates, it follows that ser and estar in (10) are not copulative but adjective verbs and como is a verbal complement. But since (11a) is an answer to (10a) and (11b) an answer to (10b), and since como is a pro-form both for the predicate ruiva and the predicate desmaiada, the analysis must be wrong.

Chomsky (1970a) presented some empirical arguments to show that verbs like feel are sometimes adjective (John felt that he was *angry*) and sometimes substantive (*John felt angry*). In the second usage the equivalent verb in Portuguese is *sentir-se*. About *parecer*, Quicoli (1972) presented some data to show that the adjective verb of (12a) is not to be confused with the substantive verb of (12b):

(12a) Ela parece {ser / que é} asiática, mas não é
'She seems to be Asiatic, but she isn't'

(12b) Ela parece asiática, mas não é
'She looks Asiatic, but she isn't'

Note that (12a) is contradictory where (12b) is not. This fact stands against the derivation of (12b) from the same underlying structure as (12a). If that were the case, the derivation would use the rule of COPULA ELLIPSIS, which seems to be necessary anyway in Portuguese to derive sentences like (13b) from underlying markers like (14):

(13a) Todos julgam {que éla é / ela ser} asiática
'Everybody believes {that she is / her to be} Asiatic'

(13b) Todos a julgam asiática
'Everybody takes her for an Asiatic'

(14)

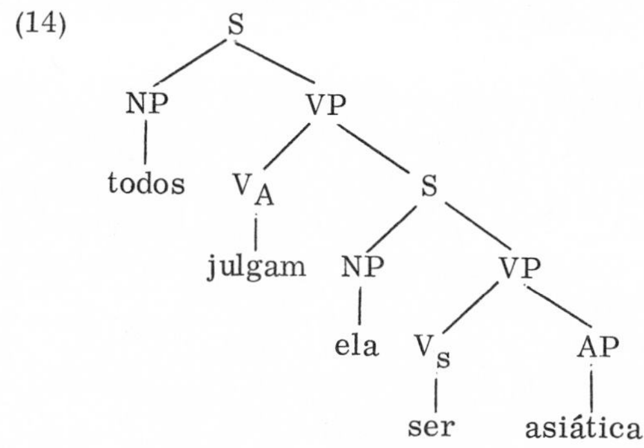

Since the ordinary *julgar* 'judge' is an adjective verb which takes NPs, tensed and untensed Ss as complements, it would be necessary to find some empirical evidence to introduce a homonym substantive verb. But the verbs of (13a) and (13b) do not seem to be differentiated by semantic features like the ones which were apparent in the case of the two *sentir* 'feel' and the two *parecer* 'seem'.

One could consider, therefore, that there is a class of pseudo-copulative verbs like *julgar* in Portuguese. To the same class belong verbs like _achar_ 'find', _crer_ 'believe', _imaginar_ 'imagine', _querer_ 'want', etc.

(15a) Nem todos a acharam simpática
'Not everybody finds her pleasant'
(15b) Creio-a capaz de tudo
'I consider her capable of everything'
(15c) Imaginava-a loura e frágil
'I imagined her blonde and fragile'
(15d) Quero-a perto de nós 'I want her close to us'

The class of true copulative verbs includes, besides _ser_ and _estar_, _ficar_ 'stay', _permanecer_ 'stay', _tornar-se_ 'become', _parecer_ 'seem', _sentir-se_ 'feel', etc.

3. The diachrony of the opposition _estar/ser_. Copceag and Escudero (1966) tried to develop a diachronic explanation of the use of _estar_ in Romance languages. Initially, _estar_ expresses a locative relation and _ser_ a pure copulative relation (i.e. 'independently of the nature of the attribute', p. 342):

(16a) Alegre era el Campeador (cf. _Poema de Mio Cid_ (1218))
'The Campeador was joyful'
(16b) El Campeador estava en su palacio
'The Campeador was in his palace'

Now suppose that one wants to conjoin the two attributes:

(17) El Campeador era alegre y el Campeador estaba en su palacio
'The Campeador was joyful and the Campeador was in his palace'

GAPPING would turn (17) into:

(18) El Campeador era alegre y estaba en su palacio
'El Campeador was joyful and was in his palace'

Then the two attributes would combine into one (deletion of _y_) and the copula retained would necessarily be _estar_ because of the initial rule:

ser → _estar_ / locative attribute

(19) El Campeador estaba alegre en su palacio
'The Campeador was joyful in his palace'

This extension of the use of estar (observable also in Rumanian) would continue in Castilian in contexts where, according to Hanssen, there is no explicit locative attribute but a kind of metaphoric spatiality. So, in Libro de la Caza by Juan Manuel, one finds systematically es dicho 'is said' but está escrito 'was written'.

From modern Rumanian Copceag and Escudero (1966) give the following examples where the adjectives trist, îngîndurat, and nemiscat may take estar because they connote spatiality:

(20a) Bietul om statea trist şi nu scotea o vorba
'The poor man was sad without saying a word'
(20b) Statea îngîndurat şi nu vorbea cu nimeni
'He was thinking and would not speak with anybody'
(20c) Statea nemiscat cu privirea pierduta în gol
'He was still with his eyes lost in the vacuum'

Of course, the expansionism of estar was not carried out in the other Romance languages as completely as in Castilian. Even in Portuguese, as observed by Ribeiro (1959), the use of estar is more restricted than in Castilian:

(21a) Claro está que tengo razón 'It is clear that I am right'
(21b) É claro que tenho razão 'It is clear that I am right'

In Italian, even locative predicates select essere. Stare is used systematically only in progressive and future-like constructions:

(22a) Sto cantando 'I am singing'
(22b) Sta per piovere 'It is about to rain'
(22c) Stanno per suonare le due e mezza 'It's about to strike half past two'

In Neapolitan, the use of stare is closer to the use in Spanish and Portuguese, as can be seen by the following examples from Italian and Neapolitan:

(23a) Era tutta nuda
Steva a 'nnura
'She was completely naked'
(23b) Dov'è il nostro amico?
Addò sta 'o nostro amico?
'Where is our friend?'
(23c) Io sonno qui
I' stongo ccà
'I am here'

(23d) Chi non è per me, è contro di me
Chi no sta co me, sta contra a me
'Whoever is not with me, is against me'

Another interesting diachronic phenomenon is that even French, which did not elaborate an equivalent of the substantive verb estar, has built the paradigm of être by borrowing forms from Latin paradigms stare and perhaps even sedere (cf. Ribeiro 1959). Synchronically speaking, the only form of this paradigm estar in French is the nominal form état:

(24a) Dans quel état est-elle? 'In what state is she?'
(24b) Elle est évanouie 'She is unconscious'

(25a) {*Dans quel état / Comment} est-elle? {'In what state / 'How} is she?'
(25b) Elle est petite et fragile 'She is small and fragile'

The main differences in the distribution of estar in Spanish and Portuguese, as far as my observation goes, are in the environment of locative PPs (see section 4) and in the environment of past participles (see section 5). In both these environments the use of estar is more restricted in Portuguese.

In the following discussion I am not going to presume anything about the applicability of rules designed for Portuguese to Spanish.

4. Environments where ser and estar alternate. Classical 'theories' of the distribution of copulative verbs have almost always assumed that there is a general semantic explanation for this distribution. Some grammarians (see, for example, Gili y Gaya (1969)), have even assumed that a unique semantic general principle should also explain the occurrences of ser and estar as auxiliaries.

As for Barbosa (1822), he clearly separates copulative or substantive verbs from auxiliary verbs.

The semantic difference between ser and estar should appear in environments where they truly alternate. They are in complementary distribution as auxiliaries and before predicate PPs. Before predicate NPs only ser may consistently occur. As for adjectives, they are divided, according to Luján (1972), into three groups:

--intrinsically stative,[2] the ones which select estar exclusively, marked [+state] in the lexicon
--intrinsically nonstative, the ones which select ser exclusively, marked [-state] in the lexicon
--unmarked.

I am therefore going to look first for the semantic difference between ser and estar before unmarked adjectives like alegre, feliz, triste, doente, pálido, amarelo, livre, calmo, tranquilo, etc.

In Portuguese, at least in my dialect, it is quite difficult to delimit the three classes proposed by Luján for Spanish. I start, therefore, with a small subset of true members of the class of unmarked adjectives:

(26) Maria é triste 'Mary is sad'

(27) Esta canção {é / *está} triste 'This song is sad'

(28) Maria {é / está} pálida 'Mary is pale'

(29) As folhas desta árvore {são / estão} amarelas
'The leaves of this tree are yellow'

(30) Maria {é / está} mais pálida do que ontem
'Mary is paler than she was yesterday'

The semantic explanations of this alternation that have been proposed by classical grammarians are summarized by Luján, who proposes that 'the use of estar with an adjective indicates a state or condition'. Then she goes on to say that besides temporal states, or, in the words of Keniston, states 'which result . . . from an action', there are spatial states. This would explain the use of estar with locative PPs.

On the contrary, 'a predicate with ser asserts of an individual that it is a member of a certain class; for instance, es mortal means "is a member of the set of mortal things"' (see also Stockwell et al. 1965).

This would explain that common nouns, which are natural classifiers, are systematically constructed with ser.

Note that this explanation is not distinct from the Aristotelian one, according to which 'it (estar) is used to indicate that the quality involved is regarded as accidental rather than essential' (quoted by Luján from Keniston).

It is well known that what can be expressed in terms of predicate calculus can be expressed in terms of the logic of classes, and vice-versa. So suppose that 't' stands for the predicate triste 'sad' and T stands for the class of sad things, i.e. to the set $\{x : tx\}$.

(31a) tx

(31b) $x \in T$

Expressions (31a) and (31b) can be interpreted as stating, respectively, 'that t is truly predicated of x' and 'that x belongs to the class of individuals of whom t is truly predicated.'

All predicates being potential classifiers, to call some predicates 'states' does not make them a disjoint set with respect to the set of classifiers. It is not difficult to conceive the class of things which are in a state of sadness or the class of things which are in a state of paleness or yellowness (cf. examples (26), (28), and (29) with estar).

This means that when one opposes 'states' to 'classes', one implicitly restrains the term 'class' to mean 'essential class'. In other words, to say that the predicate pálida stands for a state in Maria está pálida and for a class (the class of pale things) only in Maria é palida, is to decide arbitrarily that classes made up by 'accidental' predicates, whatever that means, are not interesting.

To recapitulate, the semantic explanation proposed by Luján is ultimately based on the Aristotelian dichotomy, essential vs. accidental.

One could try the definition of 'state' given also by Keniston: what 'results from an action'. I would like to unrestrain this definition by replacing 'action' by 'change'. States are semantically correlated with 'verbs of change' (it will be seen in section 6 that 'agentive verbs' are only a subset of 'verbs of change'). [3]

This correlation can be formalized in the lexicon of a generative grammar by means of meaning postulates that would account for deductions like (32), assuming that they represent the meaning of stative adjectives:

(32) Maria está triste therefore Maria entristeceu
'Mary is sad' 'Mary became sad'

It can be said that for any stative adjective A there is a meaning postulate (33), [4] where V_A is a verb of change (change into the state A), [5] and t_i and t_j are arbitrary instants of time such that t_i is past with respect to t_j ($t_i < t_j$).

(33) x está A at time $t_j \supset$ x V_A at time t_i

Note that for (33) to hold, sentences in (34) must be contradictory, which they are.

(34a) Maria está triste apesar de não ter entristecido
'Mary is sad despite her not having become sad'

(34b) Maria está pálida apesar de não ter empalidecido
'Mary is pale despite her not having become pale'

(34c) As folhas desta árvore estão amarelas apesar de não terem amarelecido
'The leaves of this tree are yellow despite their not having become yellow'

The difference between <u>ser</u> and <u>estar</u> seems to be well established, since if <u>estar</u> is replaced by <u>ser</u>, the contradiction disappears:

(35a) Maria não entristeceu, é triste
'Mary didn't become sad, she is sad'

(35b) Maria não empalideceu, é pálida
'Mary didn't turn pale, she is pale'

(35c) As folhas desta árvore não amareleceram, são amarelas
'The leaves on this tree didn't turn yellow, they are yellow'

But this test is not enough to establish the adequacy of meaning postulates like (33) to represent the meaning of <u>estar</u>.

Let 'p' stand for the antecedent in formula (33), and 'q' for the consequent. For '$p \supset q$' to be true, '$p \wedge \sim q$' must be contradictory, which it is, as shown by sentences (34). But by the rule of 'modus ponens', since '$p \supset q$', if the speaker knows that 'p', he should also know that 'q'. Therefore, scheme (33) predicts that sentences (36) are contradictory. But they are not:

(36a) Não sei se Maria entristeceu, sei que está triste
'I don't know if Mary became sad, I know she is sad'

(36b) Não sei se Maria empalideceu, sei que está pálida
'I don't know if Mary turned pale, I know she is pale'

(36c) Não sei se as folhas desta árvore amareleceram, sei que estão amarelas
'I don't know if the leaves of this tree became yellow, I know they are yellow'

Therefore scheme (33) must not be adequate to represent the semantics of <u>estar</u>.

One could imagine a special situation where sentences like (29b) or (36c) may be uttered by a speaker of Portuguese.

Suppose a Brazilian botanist is participating in the opening of the trans-Amazonic highway. He finds a new species of tree with yellow leaves and wants to report his finding. The sentence he is about to write is a copulative sentence. He has scheme (37) in his mind:

(37) As folhas desta árvore PRES COPULA amarelas.

Must he select ser or estar? If scheme (33) was adequate to govern the use of estar, then he should not select this verb, since there is no evidence that the leaves are yellow due to a change in color: he does not know if As folhas desta árvore amareleceram. But of course, the same lack of evidence should prevent his using ser. He would risk a tremendous 'fiasco' by writing in his report:

(38) As folhas desta árvore são amarelas
'The leaves of this tree are yellow'

Suppose that (38) is possibly true, from a biological point of view. He must then write something that does not imply the falsity of (38).

If he had to make observations over the full vegetal cycle of the tree before deciding what copulative verb he should have used in the circumstances, one would have an astounding counterexample to Frege's (1963) 'principle of effability':

(39) 'A thought grasped by a human being for the first time can be put into a form of words which will be understood by someone to whom the thought is entirely new'

In fact, if I were the botanist I would write (40):

(40) As folhas desta árvore estão amarelas
'The leaves of this tree are yellow'

This shows that estar is the appropriate copula to report a first sensorial experience by means of a predicate AP, without making any induction or generalization.

I claim that this is the basic meaning of 'stative adjectives'.

States are therefore empirical predicates and estar, not ser, is the basic copulative verb (for Barbosa (1822) the basic substantive verb is ser).

Sentence (38) would be appropriately used if the botanist had the required evidence to make a generalization about the species or the genus of the newly found tree (in Aristotelian words, about its essence). So estar before adjectives is used to make empirical predications while ser is used to make metaphysical predications.

One can now explain the noncontradictoriness of sentences like (36c). Of course, this sentence becomes contradictory if estão is replaced by são:

(41) Não sei se as folhas desta árvore amareleceram, sei que são amarelas 'I don't know if the leaves of this tree became yellow, I know that they are yellow'

I am going to resort now to modal logic to make more precise the semantics of ser AP predications. Note that (41) is contradictory because, if the speaker knows that As folhas desta árvore são amarelas, then he also knows that at no moment past or future can it be the case that As folhas desta árvore não são amarelas.

What that means is that the speaker, by using ser in any predication 'p', is in fact saying that 'It is impossible that ~p' or '~ ◇ p' or '□p'.

And therefore the semantic difference of ser with respect to estar may be translated by the modal operator of necessity.

This claim predicts that if there is in Portuguese an equivalent of '□', for example, the adverb necessáriamente in one of its readings, it must be compatible with ser and incompatible with estar. This prediction is apparently confirmed by examples (42). Sentence (42a) is ungrammatical or at least contradictory, and sentence (42b) is even tautological:

(42a) *As folhas desta árvore estão necessáriamente amarelas
(42b) As folhas desta árvore são necessáriamente amarelas
'The leaves of this tree are necessarily yellow'

Note that formula '□ p', taken as the semantic representation of sentences like (42b), has perhaps a slightly different interpretation from modal logic: 'it is necessary that p' is what the use of ser says. Perhaps a performative analysis of declaratives, as proposed by Ross (1970), would solve this problem.

What about the meaning of estar in terms of modal logic? By eliminating meaning postulate (33), we have excluded the hypothesis of assigning to estar the operator of contingency: the example of the botanist shows that at least in certain cases the user of ser is precisely restraining from taking a position about the necessity or the contingency of the predication. By writing (40), the botanist does not exclude the truth of (38). This confirms my claim that estar is the basic copula.

When used before past participles (which I call deverbal adjectives in section 5), the meaning of estar is perhaps best represented by meaning postulate (33).

When used before locative PPs, meaning postulate (33) becomes inadequate.

(43a) Maria está em Brasília 'Mary is in Brasilia'
(43b) Paulo está para o Algarve 'Paul is for the Algarve'

Note that (43a) does not imply that Maria went to Brasilia, or in other words, does not imply a previous change in location as

(43b) does. To represent the meaning of (43a) I suggest something like (44):

(44) Maria is in Brasilia but not necessarily.

This is to mark the opposition with the use of *ser* in sentences like (45):

(45a) O palácio da Alvorada é em Brasília
'The palace of Alvorada is in Brasilia'
(45b) O Algarve é no sul de Portugal
'The Algarve is in the south of Portugal'

By selecting *ser* or *estar* before locative PPs, the speaker is expressing his beliefs about the movability of the individual denoted by the subject NP. For me, sentences like (46), where Itamarati would refer to a building,[6] are semantic jokes based precisely on the rules I am suggesting:

(46a) O Itamarati está {em / para} Brasília
'The Itamarati is {in / for} Brasilia'
(46b) A ponte de Londres está {no / para o} Arizona
'London Bridge is {in / for} Arizona'

5. Deverbal adjectives. I am now going to discuss the semantics of *estar* before adjectives like *desmaiado* in sentences like (47a):

(47a) Maria estava desmaiada 'Mary was unconscious'
(47b) *Maria era desmaiada

Adjectives of this kind have been traditionally called 'past participles' or 'passive participles'.[7] I contend that they are not intrinsically 'past' (they may take any tense), that they are not more 'passive' than active, and that they are not even 'participles', since they do not belong to the verbal paradigm. They are, for the most part, homonyms with true past participles, i.e. with the form of the verb which enters the formation of some perfect past tenses:

(48a) Ela tem desmaiado com freqüência
'She has fainted frequently'

(48b) Ela {tinha / terá / teria} desmaiado à saída do teatro

'She {had / will have / would have} fainted on leaving the theater'

They are also sometimes homonyms with true passive participles, i.e. with the verbal form which enters the formation of passives:

(49) Maria foi {visitada / beijada / empurrada} (furtivamente) por Paulo

'Mary was {visited / kissed / pushed} (furtively) by Paul'

Note that there is no transitive homonym of desmaiar 'faint', and therefore there is no passive participle desmaiado 'fainted'.

Nobody, perhaps, doubts that true past participles belong in the verbal paradigm: verbs are not subcategorized by their having or lacking perfect past tenses.

As for the true passive participles, I am going to assume that the PASSIVE transformation is a necessary rule in the grammar of Portuguese; this transformation will derive passive participles from the basic active form of the verb. Of course, in shallow syntax passive participles behave like adjectives, but this is different from saying that they are adjectives in deep structure, or that they have the semantic properties of adjectives, as it is contended that deverbal adjectives do. Suppose that past participles and passive participles in Portuguese are derived basically in the same way as in English, by the interplay of PASSIVE and AFFIX-HOPPING rules.

How are stative constructions like (47) derived? Since transformational grammarians have not, to my knowledge, seen a problem there,[8] I guess they would have derived them from passive constructions. I am going to show that this derivation is out of the question.

The first problem with the transformational derivation from passives is the replacement of ser by estar. In Portuguese, one cannot replace ser by estar without violating syntactic restrictions or changing the meaning of the sentence (see section 4).

The second problem with this hypothetical derivation (and this one goes for French, too) is how to derive stative constructions from passive constructions which do not exist. There is no passive construction for desmaiar (cf. (47b)) or for s'évanouir. And still there is a stative construction:

(50) Elle était évanouie (*par Paul) ‘She had fainted (by Paul)’

The third problem would be to prevent the derivation of stative constructions in cases like (49), where the verb allows passive but not stative constructions:

(51) *Maria esteve {visitada / beijada / empurrada} ‘Mary got {visited’ / kissed’ / pushed’}

Of course, this argument could not have been made in French or in English where the copulas for passive and stative constructions are homonyms:

(52) Marie a été {visitée / embrassée / poussée} ‘Mary has been {visited’ / hugged’ / pushed’}

(53) Mary has been {visited / kissed / pushed}

The fourth problem would be that since stative constructions may not cooccur with an agent PP, they could be derived only from passives without an explicit agent:

(54) Essa âmfora esteve quebrada (*pelos bárbaros)
‘That urn was broken (by the barbarians)’

The fifth argument against the derivation from passives can only be made for English, where a few stative adjectives are not homonyms with passive participles,[9] e.g. ‘open’, ‘opened’.

(55a) The door was open {*by John / from 7 to 9 P.M.}

(55b) The door was opened {by John / *from 7 to 9 P.M.}

In Portuguese there are also long and short versions of verbal forms in -do, but they are not used systematically to oppose stative to passive constructions (see Barbosa 1822).

We infer that stative adjectives with -do endings, like desmaiado, quebrado, lembrado, are basic adjectives: they cannot be derived by a syntactic transformation from passive participles. We are going to assume that they are derived from verbs of change by a lexical rule.

There are, of course, still two alternatives to derive syntactically forms like desmaiado from basic verbs like desmaiar. The first is to derive them from true past participles (see (48)) by a transformation which would be the syntactic counterpart of the meaning postulate (33) in section 4. The second is to introduce them directly in the base, under the constituent Aux, estar + -do (see note 8 and Chomsky (1957)).

The first alternative could be based on the hypothesis that sentences in (57) are paraphrases of sentences in (56):

(56a) Maria desmaiara 'Mary has fainted'
(56b) Maria desmaiou 'Mary fainted'
(56c) Maria desmaia 'Mary faints'

(57a) Maria estava desmaiada 'Mary was unconscious'
(57b) Maria está desmaiada 'Mary is unconscious'
(57c) Maria estará desmaiada 'Mary will be unconscious'

But this hypothesis proves to be false: (57a) implies (56a), according to meaning postulate (33) in section 4, but (56a) does not imply (57a), and therefore the two propositions are not equivalent. If a STATIVE transformation were to be meaning-preserving, it would not be right to make (57a) a transform of (56a).

Another problem with this hypothetical transformation would be that it would have to convert the tenses of the input structure: 'plus-que-parfait' would be converted into imperfect, (56a) and (57a); perfect into present, (56b) and (57b); and present into future, (56c) and (57c).

Observe now examples (58) and (59):

(58a) Maria tinha sido distraida por Paulo
'Mary had been distracted by Paul'
(58b) Maria tinha-se distraido 'Mary had become distracted'
(58c) Maria estava distraida 'Mary was distracted'

(59a) A carta tinha sido escrita por Paulo
'The letter had been written by Paul'
(59b) *A carta tinha-se escrito 'The letter had become written'
(59c) A carta estava escrita 'The letter was written'

It has been assumed that the STATIVE transformation would apply to intransitive constructions like (56a) to derive (57a). Therefore, (58c) would be derived from the intransitive construction (58b), and not from the transitive passive construction (58a). (It has already been demonstrated that stative constructions cannot be derived from passive constructions.) But then how does one get rid of the expletive se, Maria estava-se distraida being ungrammatical?

And what about verbs like escrever 'write', which do not have an intransitive homonym? Since (59b) does not exist, it would be impossible to derive (59c) by the transformation STATIVE.

There is also the inverse situation where an intransitive construction is available but the stative construction is ungrammatical:

(60a) Maria tinha sorrido 'Mary had smiled'
(60b) *Maria estava sorrida 'Mary was smiled'

The transformation STATIVE would, therefore, have to be constrained to apply only to verbs of change: sorrir obviously does not belong in this class.

The second alternative must also be rejected. If estar + -do were just another tense (stative tense?) in the paradigm of the intransitive verb distrair-se, how could we explain that it alone lacks the expletive pronoun se?

Moreover, no tense subcategorizes the verb which the stative construction does.

And finally, stative estar has to be a copulative verb (not an auxiliary) since it is incompatible with the class of copulative verbs:

(61a) *Maria está sida linda
(61b) *Maria está ficada pálida

Note that the progressive estar, on the contrary, is not incompatible with copulative verbs. Therefore, it is not a copulative verb:

(62a) Maria está sendo indulgente 'Mary is being indulgent'
(62b) Maria está ficando pálida 'Mary is becoming pale'

Besides the large class of deverbal adjectives which are intrinsically stative (e.g. desmaiada in sentence (47a)), there is a small class whose members are unmarked (they perhaps prefer even ser to estar):

(63) agradecido 'grateful', atrevido 'daring', arrufado 'angry', calado 'silent', comedido 'courteous', desconfiado 'distrustful', despachado 'granted', dissimulado 'sly', distraído 'distracted', encolhido 'shrunk', engraçado 'pleasant', entendido 'skillful', fingido 'feigned', lido 'read', moderado 'moderate', ousado 'daring', parecido 'alike', presumido 'presumptuous', sabido 'known', viajado 'traveled', etc.

According to Barbosa (1822),[10] 'participles' of this type may be distinguished from passive participles by the fact that they take only human subjects and by the fact that they are intransitive (remember that stative deverbal adjectives may take human or nonhuman subjects, and that they are intransitive too).

A few of these adjectives are derived from verbs of change (distrair-se 'become distracted', calar-se 'shut up'), but the majority are derived from nonchange verbs. Almost the same arguments that have been developed for stative deverbal adjectives may be used to demonstrate that adjectives in (63) are derived from intransitive verbs by a lexical rule, i.e. that they are basic adjectives (they are, in fact, recorded as such by the dictionaries).

6. The semantic classification of adjectives and verbs. In a generative grammar of Portuguese the class of intrinsically stative deverbal adjectives like desmaiado must be tied to the class of verbs of change like desmaiar both semantically, by meaning postulate (33) in section 4, and morphologically, by a lexical derivational rule.

In the same way, the stative occurrences of unmarked adjectives like amarelo are tied to deadjectival verbs of change like amarelecer.

The semantic tie is not exactly identical in both cases. It has been shown, in section 4, that As folhas estão amarelas 'The leaves are yellow' does not imply As folhas amareleceram 'The leaves yellowed'. One can only say that if the speaker selected estar instead of ser, it is because he does not want to exclude the possibility of As folhas amareleceram being true.

The semantic difference between As folhas estão amarelas and As folhas estão amarelecidas can therefore be shown by meaning postulates.

I have suggested that deverbal adjectives of the desmaiado kind were lexically derived from intransitive verbs of change (some of which, like distrair-se, are pseudoreflexive). But if for transitive distrair there is an intransitive distrair-se, or for transitive mudar 'change' there are two intransitives mudar and mudar-se, from which to derive stative adjectives, there is no intransitive escrever-se for escrever 'write' (see section 5, example (59b)). Stative adjectives, in this case, must be derived from transitive verbs of change: note that the lexical derivation of an 'intransitive' adjective from a transitive verb does not constitute a problem like the syntactic derivation would (see section 5).

I want to extend the class of verbs of change to include also what Gruber (1970) called 'positional verbs'. Instead of a change away from or into an internal state, these verbs denote a spatial change (movement) 'from' or 'to' a given location.

The morphological tie here is less obvious: we are tying verbs to prepositions. But cases of morphological resemblance exist nevertheless:

(64a) Maria está dentro de casa 'Mary is inside the house'
(64b) Maria entrou em casa 'Mary entered the house'

The semantic tie in this case cannot be exclusively a meaning postulate like (33) in section 4: (64a) does not imply (64b) because Maria could have been always inside the house. What (64a) implies is that Maria is not necessarily inside the house: even if she never entered it, she can leave it (she is movable). We can use modal operators or meaning postulates according to the locative preposition selected by the speaker.[11] So (65a) does not imply (66), but (65b) does.

(65a) Paulo está no Algarve 'Paul is in the Algarve'
(65b) Paulo está para o Algarve 'Paul is for the Algarve'

(66) Paulo foi para o Algarve 'Paul went to the Algarve'

The meaning of sentence (65a) can be represented by means of the necessity operator: 'Paulo is in Algarve but not necessarily (since) he is movable.' Compare with (67), where it means 'is necessarily':

(67) Sagres é no Algarve 'Sagres is in the Algarve'

The semantic tie of verbs of change with stative adjectives and prepositions is obviously more systematic than the morphological tie: the lexical derivational rules must account for the accidental gaps in the lexicon of a particular language. Still, this double tie seems to me a very important feature in the theory of generative grammar.

By observing the paradigms of primitive verbs[12] and isolating those which have a stative (i.e. an adjective which selects exclusively estar), we get a subset of the class of verbs of change. Another subset is derived from primitive adjectives like entristecer 'sadden' and desentristecer 'cause not to be sad' (from triste).

I claim that this is a natural semantic class because its membership can be established by means of an empirical test. It is also obvious that it is a large class and that its role is central for the classification of verbs and adjectives.

Lakoff's (1966) dichotomy (stative vs. active) is syntactic, not semantic, as I have already mentioned (section 4). Moreover, it is not exhaustive: the imperative, the 'do-something', the 'persuade', and, of course, the 'enthusiastically' criteria, are satisfied only by human-agentive verbs. The only criterion general enough to find the complement of the class of states is apparently the progressive criterion. But even this one fails, as Vendler's taxonomy shows.

I have proposed, in section 4, to subdivide adjectives into pure states (the ones which occur before estar) and generalized or necessary states (the ones which occur before ser). Now what about Lakoff's dichotomy of 'active' vs. 'stative' adjectives? It does not, of course, coincide with my semantic dichotomy (see also Luján 1972). 'Active' adjectives may have some correlation with the class of agent-oriented adverbs. So prudente corresponds to the adverb prudentemente. I think that it is pure nonsense to class adjectives like prudente as active. They do not denote actions: they denote properties (in my terminology, 'states' or 'generalized states') predicable of agents.

Vendler (1967) proposes an interesting taxonomy for verbs based on what he calls 'time schemata' (duration complements).

The first partition is operated by the test of the continuous or progressive tenses. Vendler notes that verbs which can normally take continuous tenses, like smoke or run, may also occur in noncontinuous (stative?) constructions, when they denote 'habits' (including 'occupations', 'dispositions', 'abilities', etc.). This fact reinforces Gruber's (1967) observation that 'the progressive possibility [and I would say every other aspectual feature] depends to a large extent on the structure of the sentence as a whole, not only on the verb.'

Verbs which take continuous tenses are subdivided into two classes. The first class is based on the fractionability of the process into as many fragments as there are segments of time in its duration, e.g. verbs like run, play, etc. (if someone plays for five minutes you can say that he has already played even if he continues to play). Fractionable processes are indivisible, like 'running a mile', 'drawing a circle', etc. These are 'accomplishments'.

Accomplishments in Portuguese take duration complements introduced by preposition em (e.g. em cinco minutos) while activities take durante-complements (e.g. durante cinco minutos). The examples I have given illustrate Gruber's observation about how aspect is context dependent: verbs like correr 'run' may denote activities or accomplishments:

(68a) Paulo correu durante cinco minutos
'Paul ran for five minutes'

(68b) Paulo correu os cem metros em dez minutos
'Paul ran the hundred meters in ten minutes'

Verbs like percorrer 'run an allotted distance' are not so flexible:

(69) *Paulo percorreu durante cinco minutos
'Paul made the complete run for five minutes'

Among the verbs which do not take continuous tenses the opposition is between 'states' (e.g. 'Mary knows Paul') and processes with a climax (e.g. 'reached the top', 'spotted the plane'). Climactic processes are called 'achievements' by Vendler. They cannot cooccur with true duration complements, because the climax is a point in the time continuum.

On the contrary, states, even if they are not processes going on in time, may take duration complements introduced by durante:

(70a) Maria gostou de Paulo durante cinco anos
'Mary liked Paul for five years'

(70b) Maria esteve cega durante três meses
'Mary was blind for three months'

The semantic class of states, therefore, includes not only adjectives (see section 4), but also a few verbs.

The members of these four classes of verbs are cross-classified by the dichotomy agentive vs. nonagentive (cf. Gruber 1970 and Vendler 1967). Vendler proposes the test of the cooccurrence with adverbs like 'deliberately' or 'carefully'. I would add all the adverbials introduced in Portuguese by para (adverbials of purpose). According to Vendler, states are all nonagentive, accomplishments and activities all agentive, and achievements partly nonagentive (e.g. reconhecer, descobrir) and partly agentive (e.g. entrar, sair). I doubt that activities and accomplishments are all agentive; the test of the progressive tense and the test of the duration apply to verbs without a human agent. Following the criteria given by Vendler, Gruber, or Fillmore, however, these verbs are not agentive:

(71a) A cascata perforou (*deliberadamente) o rochedo en cinco milhões de anos
'The waterfall (deliberately) wore through the cliff'

(71b) O Stromboli esteve (*deliberadamente) vomitando lava durante meio sêculo
'Stromboli was (deliberately) spewing lava for half a century'

Even human activities, like crescer 'grow', and human accomplishments, like digerir duas dúzias de ostras 'to digest two dozen oysters', may be nonagentive:

(72a) Maria esteve crescendo (*deliberadamente) durante cinco anos
'Mary was (deliberately) growing up for five years'

(72b) Paul digeriu (*deliberadamente) duas dúzias de ostras em quatro horas
'Paul (deliberately) digested two dozen oysters in four hours'

The dichotomy agentive vs. nonagentive is, therefore, cross-classifying for all Vendler's aspectual classes except states.

What about the 'change-of-state' vs. 'nonchange' dichotomy? It has perhaps some correlation with accomplishment and achievement vs. activity. It is also perhaps correlated with the classical aspectual dichotomy perfective vs. imperfective (see Querido 1974).

NOTES

1. Again rule (3) would be a rule scheme since 'Comp' (not exactly a category) would have as its values sequences of constituents like NP, PP, NP PP, etc. I consider symbols like 'Pred' and 'Comp' supercategories (or are they functions?).

2. The term 'stative' here does not refer to a syntactic feature as in Lakoff (1966), but to a semantic feature. (See Luján 1972 for the difference between the two features.)

3. This semantic class has also been independently found by Fillmore (1970). But note that Fillmore has only considered a subset of concrete verbs, 'verbs of hitting and breaking'. My class includes change in the internal state (physical or psychological) and change of place, i.e. Gruber's class of positional verbs.

4. To be precise, (33) is not a meaning postulate but a scheme of meaning postulates to be derived for each stative adjective in the lexicon.

5. Besides the verbs which mean change into the state A, there are potential verbs which mean change away from the state A. For the A triste, we get, respectively, entristecer and desentristecer-se.

6. Itamarati was the name of the Ministry of External Affairs in Rio de Janeiro and is now the name of the Ministry of External Affairs in Brasilia (the stones of the Itamarati have not been removed).

7. Cf. Barbosa (1822). He classes them as both 'perfect' and 'passive'.

8. See, for example, Chomsky (1957), who introduces 'be + en' under the constituent 'Aux', in the first place, only to decide later that it must be introduced by transformation.

9. Jespersen (1924) quotes from Curme this example: 'When I came at five, the door was open but I do not know when it was opened.'

10. For Barbosa, who elaborated a very sophisticated theory of participles, adjectives like atrevido 'daring' or fingido 'phony' are perfect passive participles 'with . . . active meaning'.

11. Presumptions concerning movability which apparently play a role in the selection of ser or estar before locative prepositions are the expression of the speaker's beliefs.

12. Not only primitive verbs but also denominal verbs like deslocar, liquefazer, vaporizar, etc.

SPANISH BE PREDICATES AND THE FEATURE 'STATE' VS. 'ACTION'

MARK G. GOLDIN

Indiana University

1. The description of verbs of being, or copulas, presents problems in European languages because these items have syntactic characteristics very much like verbs, while at the same time they are like grammatical rather than lexical items since their presence often seems to be required by other elements in a sentence rather than by any elements of a situation (semantic elements). Descriptions of English be differ as to whether and when this item is basic or transformationally derived. Under the assumption, shared by the authors of descriptions summarized in (1), that transformations do not insert meaningful elements, a transformational derivation of be represents the claim that a verb of being has no semantic content but is predictable from features of its environment. A statement that a verb of being is basic claims that it contains semantic information.

(1)

	Early TG	Bach 1967	Jacobs & Rosenbaum 1968	Langendoen 1970
Predicate nominals	Basic	Derived	Basic	Derived
Adjectives	Basic	Derived	Derived	Derived
Locatives	Basic	Derived	Basic	Basic
Progressives	Basic	Derived	Derived	Derived
Passives	Derived	Derived	Derived	Derived

The array in (1) summarizes four descriptions of be in English. In early transformational grammars, as represented, for example, by Chomsky (1958), the passive be was treated as different from other occurrences of be, presumably since for every passive sentence with be there is a synonymous sentence without be. Bach (1967) observed that many languages have no overt form corresponding to be, and felt that to insert all cases of be by transformation would introduce more overall formal simplicity into the description. Jacobs and Rosenbaum (1968), following the work of Lakoff and Ross, observed that certain instances of be are predictable from features of neighboring elements. Langendoen (1970:79) included predicate nominals in that category, but he decided that locative be is different from other instances since it acts like a lexical rather than a grammatical item in analogies like the following:

John laid the magazine on the coffee table.
The magazine lay on the coffee table.
John put the car in the garage.
The car is in the garage.

If lie and lay are lexical items, then so are put and be.

In the remaining sections, this paper considers some empirical questions relating to be predication in Spanish: first, whether there are any rules applying to be predicates but not to other verbs; second, whether there are any rules that apply to certain instances of be predication but not to others. These questions will be considered as a basis for evaluating descriptions like those summarized in (1).

One can see that a description like Langendoen's, which differentiates locative be from all other types, is the most nearly appropriate for Spanish for two reasons. The rule of relative clause reduction applies differently to locative than to nonlocative be predications. Also, a principle of copula selection describes the choice of ser or estar in all but locative be predications.

2. Relative clause reduction is the rule that relates full relative clauses containing a copula to reduced forms of the same clauses containing neither the relative pronoun nor the copula. Both ser and estar participate in relative clause reduction, but the rule is not relevant to verbs which are not be predicates.

For most restrictive relative clauses containing be predicates in Spanish there are corresponding reduced forms.

Predicate nominals (noun predications)

(2) Tengo un hermano que es médico.
'I have a brother who is a doctor.'
Tengo un hermano médico.
'I have a doctor brother.'

Adjective predications

(3) Tengo un hermano que es guapo.
'I have a brother who is handsome.'
Tengo un hermano guapo.
'I have a handsome brother.'

(4) Tengo un hermano que está enfermo.
'I have a brother who is sick.'
Tengo un hermano enfermo.
'I have a sick brother.'

Passives and participles (verb predications)

(5) Carranza es un hombre que es querido por toda la gente.
'C. is a man who is loved by all the people.'
Carranza es un hombre querido por toda la gente.
'C. is a man loved by all the people.'

(6) Marbella es un pueblo que está ocupado por turistas.
'M. is a town that is occupied by tourists.'
Marbella es un pueblo ocupado por turistas.
'M. is a town occupied by tourists.'

Clauses with progressive constructions undergo reduction only under certain conditions which I do not fully understand, but which seem to have to do with the presence of additional material in the clause.

(7) La chica que está cantando es mi prima.
'The girl who is singing is my cousin.'
*La chica cantando es mi prima.
'The girl singing is my cousin.'

(8) La chica que está cantando en el coro es mi prima.
'The girl who is singing in the choir is my cousin.'
?La chica cantando en el coro es mi prima.
'The girl singing in the choir is my cousin.'

Clauses with prepositional predication reduce normally except in the case of locatives.

Nonlocative

(9) Aquí está el regalo que es para María.
'Here is the gift which is for M.'

Aquí está el regalo para María.
'Here is the gift for M.'

Locative

(10) Tráeme el libro que está en el estante.
'Bring me the book that is on the shelf.'
*Tráeme el libro en el estante.
'Bring me the book on the shelf.'

In one of its interpretations, (11) is the correct reduced form of (10):

(11) Tráeme el libro del estante.
'Bring me the book on the shelf.'

The basic locative preposition <u>en</u> does not appear in reduced restrictive relative clauses. Instead <u>de</u> appears.

Compound locative prepositions have a reduced form with an added <u>de</u>.

(12) el libro que está debajo de la mesa
'the book which is under the table'
el libro de debajo de la mesa
'the book under the table'

Locative 'adverbs'--identical to prepositions except that their objects are not expressed--require <u>de</u> in reduced relative clauses.

(13) Viven en la casa que está enfrente.
'They live in the house which is across the street.'
*Viven en la casa enfrente.
Viven en la casa de enfrente.
'They live in the house across the street.'

Other locative prepositions apparently do not permit relative clause reduction at all.

(14) Las niñas que están con Alicia son sus hijas.
'The girls that are with A. are her daughters.'
*Las niñas con Alicia son sus hijas.
'The girls with Alice are her daughters.'

Consider the preposition <u>sobre</u>, which has both locative and non-locative senses. When it occurs in the locative sense it does not appear in reduced relative clauses; rather, <u>de</u> appears. <u>Sobre</u>

in the nonlocative sense, however, occurs freely in reduced relative clauses.

(15) Léeme el libro que está sobre la cama.
'Read me the book which is on the bed.'
*Léeme el libro sobre la cama.[1]
'Read me the book above the bed.'
Léeme el libro de la cama.
'Read me the book above the bed.' (understood only in context)
(16) Léeme el libro que es sobre camas.
'Read me the book which is about beds.'
'Léeme el libro sobre camas.
'Read me the book about beds.'

In order to state correctly the rule of relative clause reduction in Spanish, it is necessary to refer to the feature Locative to describe the reduced clauses that contain de, and the failure of locative prepositions like en, con, and sobre to occur in reduced relative clauses. In other words, locative expressions with the equivalent of be are syntactically different from other expressions with be predication with respect to relative clause reduction.

3. Locatives also differ from nonlocative be predications in the question of the selection of copulas. While all the locative examples noted involved estar, there is another locative be predicate, haber; and it is possible that ser and some occurrences of tener, including possessives, are related to locatives along the lines suggested by Lyons (1967, 1968). Investigation of these matters would take us far afield, so I will not try to state any principles for the selection of locative copulas. There is a single selection principle, however, which appears to apply to all kinds of be predication except locatives, upholding the basic difference between locatives and all other be predications.

Consider these two sentences:

(17) La casa será de ladrillo.
'The house will be (made of) brick.'
(18) La casa estará hecha de ladrillo.
'The house will be made of brick.'

Both sentences describe the same objective reality, yet one requires será, the other estará. The conditioning factor is that in (18) the speaker has chosen to use a verb hecha. The verb conditions estar.

There is another sentence which is not synonymous with (17) or (18).

(19) La casa será hecha de ladrillo.
'The house will be built of brick.'

Sentence (19) describes an action to take place, while (17) and (18) do not. The alternation between <u>será</u> and <u>estará</u> in (18) and (19) corresponds to a semantic difference; the alternation in (17) and (18) to a grammatical difference. Both semantic and grammatical features are involved in the selection of <u>ser</u> or <u>estar</u>.

The nature of the relevant features is as follows. The values of some syntactic features are tied to individual lexical items. The feature Animate vs. Inanimate is an example of this; the noun <u>brother</u>, for example, is lexically animate. This means that a speaker knows he cannot use the word <u>brother</u> to refer to anything that is not animate. That is simply a property of the lexical item. The feature Singular vs. Plural, on the other hand, is not linked to particular lexical items. In general, any count noun can be singular or plural, and a speaker chooses the appropriate value based on the message he wants to express. Of course, there are exceptions, like <u>pants</u>, which is always plural; but the general nature of Singular vs. Plural is that it is independent of lexical items. Let us call features of the Animate vs. Inanimate type 'lexical features' and those of the Singular vs. Plural type 'focus features'.

Most relevant to the selection of nonlocative <u>ser</u> and <u>estar</u> is the concept State vs. Action. Lakoff (1971a:121-22), in justifying this feature in a grammar, implies that it is a lexical feature of verbs and adjectives: <u>look</u> and <u>noisy</u> are actions and have certain syntactic properties; <u>know</u> and <u>tall</u> are states and have other properties.

Certain observations about Spanish indicate that there is additionally a focus feature related to State vs. Action. Luján (1974:182) describes a number of properties dependent on such a feature, and describes it as a focus feature when she says: 'Most adjectives may refer to a state or to a property and this semantic difference is overtly marked by the use of different copulas', referring to the contrast between <u>ser</u> and <u>estar</u> with adjectives. Roca Pons (1958:26-28) also observes lexical and focus features in distinguishing <u>aspecto</u>, a property of all verbs, from <u>modo de acción</u>, a classifying feature of individual verbs.

In what follows I am going to discuss two distinct binary features in Spanish related to the concept State vs. Action: a lexical feature of verbs (other predicate types are redundantly lexical states), and a focus feature of all predicate types including nouns, verbs, and adjectives. In examining a variety of nonlocative <u>be</u> predications, I offer an explanatory principle for the choice of <u>ser</u> or <u>estar</u> based on the values of the two features. This principle can be stated as follows:

Copula selection. When a copula is called for, if the values of the lexical and focus features match, ser occurs; when they differ, estar occurs.

The following sentences are presented to exemplify the principle of copula selection.

		Predicate type:	Lexical feature:	Focus feature:
(17)	La casa será de ladrillo. 'The house will be (made of) brick.'	Preposition	State	State
(18)	La casa estará hecha de ladrillo. 'The house will be made of brick.'	Verb	Action	State
(19)	La casa será hecha de ladrillo. 'The house will be built of brick.'	Verb	Action	Action
(20)	Aquello es bien sabido. 'That is well known.'	Verb	State	State
(21)	*Aquello está bien sabido.	Verb	State	Action
(22)	Están haciendo la casa. 'They are building the house.'	Verb	Action	State
(23)	Es feliz. 'He is happy.'	Adjective	State	State
(24)	Está feliz. 'He is happy.'	Adjective	State	Action
(25)	*Es contento. 'He is happy.'	Adjective	State	State
(26)	Está contento. 'He is happy.'	Adjective	State	Action
(27)	Es carpintero. 'He is a carpenter.'	Noun	State	State
(28)	Está de carpintero. 'He is acting as a carpenter.'	Noun	State	Action

First contrast (18) and (19). Both contain the verb hecha whose lexical value is Action. Example (19) focuses on the action of building the house: the lexical and focus values agree, and ser is used.

Example (18) focuses on the 'resultant state'; the lexical and focus values differ, and estar occurs.

In (20) is found the verb sabido, whose lexical value is State. The focus value is also State, and the copula is ser. For some speakers it is impossible to add action focus to a state verb, so (21) is ungrammatical. For other speakers (21) means 'That has become well known'.

Another verbal construction is the progressive, whose function is to add state focus to an action verb--metaphorically, to stop an action in progress, as a photograph does. Verbs which are lexically stative have no progressive, a fact which Lakoff (loc. cit.) used as justification for the lexical feature State vs. Action. The principle of copula selection thus correctly predicts estar as the copula with action verbs, as in (22).

Verbs are the only class of predicates in Spanish which shows both values of the lexical feature State vs. Action. Nonverb predicates seem to be redundantly State. The focus values for nonverbs can, of course, be either state or action, where action focus refers to the speaker's belief that a property is changeable or has changed.[2] In this sense the principle of copula selection is a formalization of Bull's (1942:441) well known description of ser and estar: 'Ser expresses a first impression or a normal concept; estar, a change or deviation from the average or normal concept.' Examples (17) and (23) through (28) all show this. Observe in (25) that contento is an example of an adjective which exceptionally requires the focus feature to be Action--in other words, contento is viewed only as a changeable property.[3]

4. The focus feature which has been shown to operate in the selection of ser and estar is not an ad hoc feature introduced solely to describe be predication. It has already been seen that the combination of active lexical and state focus features is the conditioning environment for the progressive form of verbs (-ndo participle: examples (22) and (23)). That the progressive is a separate process from other be predication can be seen by observing that it produces a second copula with adjectives and verbs that need be independently. This construction allows speakers to focus on both state and action aspects.

(29) Está siendo agasajado.
'He is being entertained.'

(30) Está siendo injusto.
'He is being unfair.'

That both focus values are present in these progressive constructions can be seen from the fact that *está estando never occurs with verbs, where it would result from two be predications on state focus, nor with adjectives, where it would represent two on action focus.

The focus feature State vs. Action is also a determining factor of past aspect in Spanish (preterit vs. imperfect). Normally, the preterit corresponds to action focus in the past and the imperfect to state focus. That the same focus feature is operating in past aspect as in be predication can be seen from constructions with action verbs that also require be predication. Suppose there was an accident in which nobody was injured. With action focus the preterit of ser is used to describe the event:

(31) Nadie fue herido.
'No one was injured (during the accident).'

With state focus the imperfect of estar appears:

(32) Nadie estaba herido.
'No one was injured (after the accident).'

The other two logically possible combinations, the imperfect of ser and the preterit of estar, are not possible in this context.[4]

(33) *Nadie era herido.
(34) *Nadie estuvo herido.

Both the occurring and the nonoccurring combinations of past aspect and be predicates with action verbs are explained if the same feature conditions both past aspect and copula selection.

It was suggested earlier that the progressive in combination with another be predication is a construction in which both state and action focus may be expressed. If past aspect is conditioned by the same feature as copula selection, then one should find past progressives with either state focus alone or with both state and action focus. That contrast does exist:

(35) Anoche estaba estudiando cuando . . .
'Last night I was studying (when something else happened)'
(36) Anoche estuve estudiando hasta las doce.
'Last night I was studying until midnight.'

These data suggest that the focus feature State vs. Action is a conditioning factor not only for copula selection but for verbal aspect as well, which lends independent support to the statement of the principle of copula selection.

NOTES

1. This sentence is grammatical in either of these two senses:
(a) 'Read me the book about beds.'
(b) 'Read me the book (while you are) on the bed.'

2. Luján (1972, 1974) uses the name 'state' for changeable properties, where I use the name 'action'; and she uses 'property' for what I call 'states'. This difference is purely terminological, since we are discussing the same contrast.

3. Significant numbers of adjectives in Spanish have fixed values for the focus feature 'State' vs. 'Action'. Luján-Gough (1972: chapter 1) describes the syntactic behavior of these groups, which include adjectives with only action focus and adjectives with only state focus. Compare the focus feature 'Singular' vs. 'Plural', where mass nouns are only singular.

4. The imperfect of ser and preterit of estar with past participles describe complex situations with double focus involving the passage of relatively long periods of time. Compare Las cartas eran escritas a mano 'Letters used to be written by hand', and La ropa estuvo colgada toda la tarde, pero no se secó 'The clothes were hung out all afternoon, but they didn't get dry'.

THE ANALYSIS OF REFLEXIVE INCHOATIVES

MARTA LUJÁN

University of Texas at Austin

0. Introduction. Roldán (1971), following Lakoff (1971a), has proposed that reflexive inchoative verbs in Spanish derive transformationally from a complex deep structure. Napoli (1974b) argues against this analysis and proposes instead a simple-sentence source for such verbs in Italian and, possibly, other Romance languages.

It is argued here that the transformational analyses so far proposed are descriptively inadequate. Reflexive inchoatives cannot be appropriately derived from related nonreflexive verbs by the rule REFLEXIVE. The arguments adduced also apply to case grammar analyses in the current literature (cf. Langacker 1970).

1. A characterization. Inchoative verbs denote beginning of an action, state or process. Reflexive inchoatives characteristically denote inception with respect to states, which can be physical or mental (e.g. <u>enfermarse</u> 'to become ill', <u>resfriarse</u> 'to catch a cold', <u>ablandarse</u> 'to soften', <u>espesarse</u> 'to thicken', <u>enojarse</u> 'to become annoyed', <u>irritarse</u> 'to become irritated', and so on). These verbs typically mean 'to come to be in a certain state'. For every expression with a reflexive inchoative predicated of an individual (animate or inanimate) there exists a related stative expression with the copula <u>estar</u> that describes the resultant state the individual comes to be:

(1)	enfermarse	estar enfermo
	resfriarse	estar resfriado
	ablandarse	estar blando
	espesarse	estar espeso
	enojarse	estar enojado
	irritarse	estar irritado

Characteristic of a sentence with a reflexive inchoative as main verb is the fact that an animate subject is never understood to be an agent. Proof of this is the fact that instrumental phrases and purpose clauses cannot be constructed with reflexive inchoatives, for they imply the presence of an agent:

(2) *Se adormeció con una píldora. 'He dozed off with a pill.'
*Se murió con un veneno. 'He died with a poison.'

(3) *Se adormeció para descansar un rato. 'He fell asleep in order to rest for a while.'
*Se murió para no sufrir más. 'He died in order not to suffer anymore.'

If an instrumental or a purpose clause is acceptable with one of these reflexives, e.g.

(4) Se enfermó para faltar a clase. 'He fell ill in order to miss class.'

then the reflexive is no longer an inchoative but a causative with the meaning 'to cause to come to be in a certain state'. Some of these reflexive verbs lend themselves to this extended use as causatives (e.g. enfermarse, enojarse), but many others cannot be used as causatives because their intrinsic semantic nature precludes the possibility of an individual having any control or responsibility over the inception of the states denoted by such verbs (e.g. morirse 'to die', sorprenderse 'to be astonished', desmayarse 'to faint', adormecerse 'to fall asleep', among others).

It has been observed (Roldán 1971) that reflexive inchoatives in the simple present tense may have any of the meanings associated with this tense, except the meaning related to ahora 'now', which is one of the meanings of this tense in Spanish:

(5) Me caso. (future) 'I'm getting married.'
En ese momento se despierta. (historical present) 'In that moment he wakes up.'
Se resfría cada invierno. (habitual) 'He catches a cold every winter.'
*Me enfermo. 'I sicken.'

It is claimed that inchoation has no duration; thus, it 'is over as soon as it is begun' (ibid.). Indeed, most of these verbs are odd in this tense with the time adverb ahora 'now'.

(6) *Se enferma ahora. 'He sickens now.'
*Se resfría ahora. 'He catches a cold now.'
*Se irrita ahora. 'He becomes irritated now.'
*Se espesa ahora. 'It thickens now.'

Some of these examples may become acceptable only if ahora is understood to refer to the immediate future.

2.0 Current transformational analyses. For many years now the analyses of various reflexive verbs, most noticeably reflexive inchoatives, have remained a puzzle to students of the Romance languages. A decade ago G. Lakoff proposed that simple inchoative verbs in English (e.g. thicken, sicken, darken, and so on) derive from complex structures with an inchoative abstract verb. He further suggested that a similar analysis for languages like Spanish or Russian would explain the otherwise inexplicable occurrence of reflexive pronouns with inchoative verbs in such languages.

Roldán (1971) developed such an account for Spanish. According to this analysis the deep structure and derivation of a sentence like (6) are as sketched in (7):

(6) Juan se hirió. 'John got hurt.'

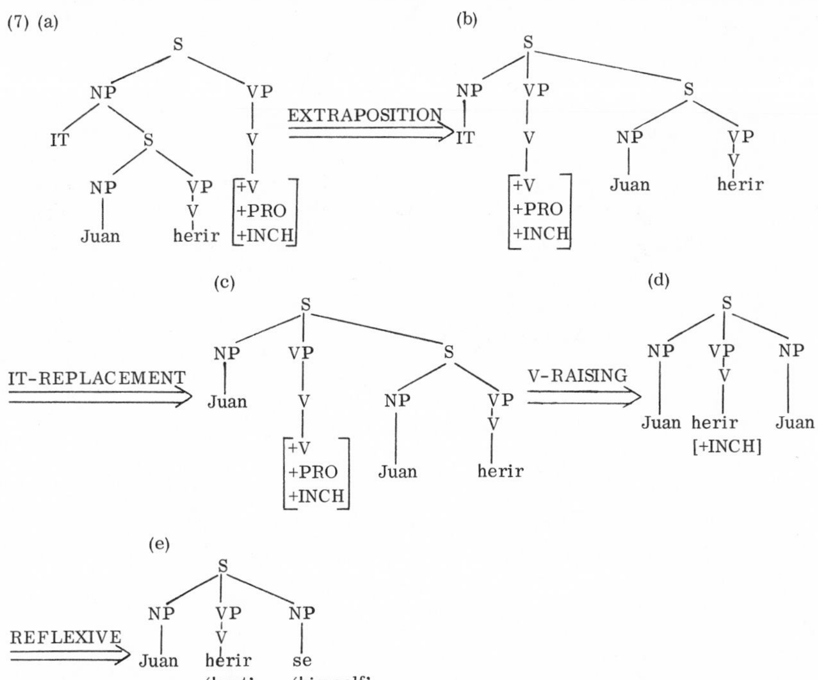

Following Lakoff's original suggestion, the difference with the analysis for English is that EQUI-NP DELETION does not apply after IT-REPLACEMENT in Spanish. Consequently, the structure that derives from application of the latter rule presents two occurrences of the same noun phrase, as seen in (7c), which will ultimately provide the structural description for the REFLEXIVE rule to apply, as shown in (7e).

Napoli (1974b) argues against this analysis and proposes instead a simple-sentence source for such verbs in Italian, an analysis which, she suggests, may be extended to other Romance languages. She attacks Roldán's (or Lakoff's) analysis on two grounds. First, she claims that there are no transformations which may apply in the embedded sentence, in which case V-RAISING must be precyclic. However, in the Lakoff analysis V-RAISING applies after two cyclic transformations; namely, EXTRAPOSITION and IT-REPLACEMENT.

Second, she argues that such a complex structure should admit two time adverbs, and she presents sentence (8) to show that reflexive inchoatives with two time adverbs are not possible:

(8) Alle otto il ghiaccio si è fuso per due ore. (ibid.)
'At eight o'clock the ice melted for two hours.'

Notice, however, that similar examples can be constructed that are not altogether unacceptable:

(9) Alle otto il ghiaccio si è fuso per un breve istante.
'At eight o'clock the ice melted for a brief instant.'

The simple-sentence source that Napoli postulates for Italian inchoatives, as in sentence (10), is sketched in (11) together with the corresponding derivation:

(10) Roberto si ammalò. (Italian) 'Robert got sick.'
Roberto se enfermó. (Spanish)

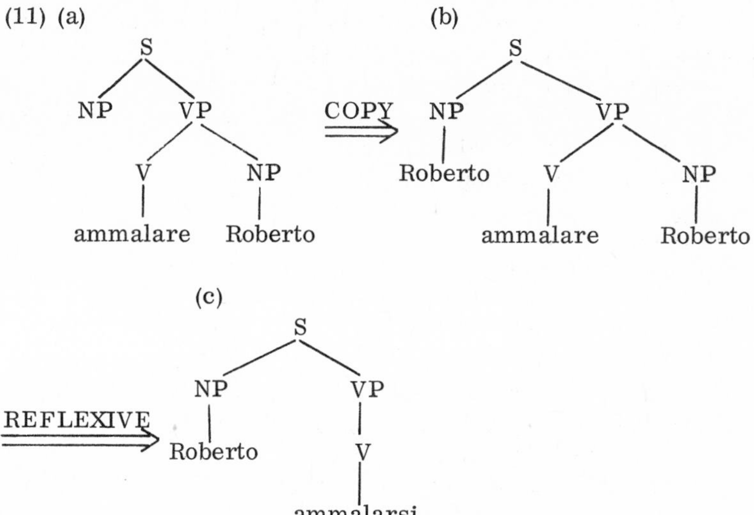

In Napoli's analysis the surface subject of an inchoative is an object in deep structure. This is argued on the basis that most inchoatives in Italian have nonreflexive counterparts that are transitive verbs, and the selectional restrictions of the objects of such verbs are the same as for the subjects of related inchoatives.

Furthermore, in Napoli's analysis inchoatives bear no subject in deep structure. This is argued on the basis that reflexive inchoatives cannot be constructed with manner adverbials and purpose clauses:

(12) *Il fieno si infiammò deliberatamente. (ibid.)
'The hay caught fire deliberately.'

(13) *Il fienno si infiammò per spaventare la mamma. (ibid.)
'The hay caught fire in order to scare mommy.'

Such adverbials and purpose clauses require underlying agentive subjects.

Moreover, she argues that some instrumental phrases cannot co-occur with agentive subjects, but they can be constructed with reflexive inchoatives:

(14) Il fieno si infiammò per el fulmine. (ibid.)
'The hay caught fire because of the lightning.'

It may be noticed in passing that these facts that Napoli cites in support of her analysis also follow from a complex-source analysis such as the one proposed by Lakoff, for in such analysis there is neither an agentive subject for the inchoative.

2.1 Arguments against current transformational analyses. There are three main syntactic arguments against a simple-sentence source, as proposed by Napoli, for Spanish or Italian inchoatives. To begin with, in Spanish many reflexive inchoatives do not have a transitive counterpart, hence no possible source in a simple-sentence analysis. Such verbs are, among many others:

(15) arrepentirse 'to repent'
ausentarse 'to become absent'
resfriarse 'to catch a cold'
acatarrarse 'to catch a head cold'
congestionarse 'to become congested'
afiebrarse 'to become feverish'
ensimismarse 'to become engrossed'
engolfarse 'to become engrossed'
acalambrarse 'to become cramped'
empeñarse 'to persist'
empecinarse 'to become persistent'
enfurruñarse 'to show annoyance'
agangrenarse 'to become gangrenous'
incautarse 'to attach'
injerirse 'to become involved'

It is not possible to construct any of these verbs transitively: *arrepentir a alguien, *ausentar a alguien, *resfriar a alguien, and so forth, are all unacceptable.

Inchoatives without nonreflexive counterparts are rather numerous in Spanish. In Italian, there are not as many. Still, a number of examples can be found:

(16) affebbrecitarsi 'to become feverish'
interiorizarsi 'to get acquainted'
impegnarsi 'to persist'

Furthermore, in Spanish there are some reflexive inchoatives that are related to intransitive verbs; for instance, caerse from caer 'to fall', and morirse from morir 'to die'. This fact is clearly incompatible with the hypothesis that reflexive inchoatives are transitive verbs in deep structure.

The verbs cited in (15) and (16) also constitute evidence against an analysis as proposed by Roldán, for in that analysis they must occur as simple nonreflexive main verbs of an embedded sentence. But these verbs do not occur as nonreflexive in any simple sentence:

(17) *arrepentir
*ausentar
*resfriar
*ensimismar
*congestionar, etc.

A second syntactic argument against Napoli's hypothesis is the fact that not all transitive verbs in the language have related reflexive inchoatives. However, her analysis predicts that they all have. If this were so, it should be possible to make reflexive inchoatives from verbs like *impelir* 'to impel', *impedir* 'to impede', *pintar* 'to paint', *escribir* 'to write', and many others in Spanish and Italian. But sentences bearing such verbs are ungrammatical.

(18) *Roberto se impelió. 'Robert got impelled.'
*Roberto se impidió. 'Robert got impeded.'
*La puerta se pintó. 'The door got painted.'
*La flor se cortó. 'The flower got cut.'
*El libro se compró. 'The book got bought.'
(19) *La finestra si lavò. 'The window got washed.'
*La fiore si tagliò. 'The flower got cut.'
*Il libro si comprò. 'The book got bought.'

Some of these sentences may be acceptable in the interpretation of impersonal sentences, that is, as sentences with implied unspecified agents. The fact that manner adverbials and purpose clauses may be added corroborates this interpretation:

(20) La puerta se pintó deliberadamente. 'The door was painted deliberately.'
(21) El libro se compró para que estudiaras. 'The book was bought to be studied.'

Now, to avoid generating ungrammatical strings like (18) and (19) in this analysis, one would have to constrain the proposed deep structure so that not all transitive verbs may appear in it. Or, alternatively, the COPY rule would have to be constrained so that it does not apply to all transitive verbs. It is not clear that the first alternative is plausible. For, supposing there is a semantic reason to prevent these verbs from occurring in the deep structure in question, for instance, the fact that they seem to require agentive subjects, it would still be difficult to explain on this account why two active verbs like *cerrar*/*abrir* 'to close'/'to open' can underlie reflexive inchoatives while the active verbs in (18) and (19) cannot. As for the second alternative, it amounts to marking all verbs that do not have a related reflexive inchoative as not allowing the operation of the COPY rule. The needed modification would be ad hoc and it belies the apparent generality Napoli's analysis originally offered.

The third syntactic argument against deriving reflexive inchoatives from underlying transitives is based on the fact that they behave differently from reflexive verbs that happen to have an underlying transitive structure. Such verbs may occur with the contrastive phrase a sí mismo (se stesso in Italian):

(22) Se vió a sí mismo. 'He saw himself.'
Me consideré a mí misma. 'I considered myself.'
Te examinarás a tí mismo. 'You will examine yourself.'
(23) Giovanni ha tagliato se stesso. 'John cut himself.'

But the contrastive phrase cannot be added to reflexive inchoatives. If these verbs are derived from an intermediate transitive structure by application of the rule REFLEXIVE, why are they ungrammatical with the contrastive phrase?

(24) *Se enfermó a si mismo.
*Me moriré a mí misma.
*Te adormeciste a tí mismo.
(25) *Roberto ammalò se stesso.
*La finestra ruppe se stesso.

This argument concerning the distribution of the contrastive phrase a sí mismo defies the two types of transformational analysis so far proposed. Whether the REFLEXIVE rule is to apply to a deep object (as in Napoli's analysis) or to a derived object (as in Roldán's), such object should be grammatical with the contrastive phrase. For both deep and derived objects behave alike in contrastive sentences, as may be observed in (26) and (27), respectively.

(26a) No la ví. 'I didn't see her.'
No la ví a ella. (Contrastive)
(26b) No te creo. 'I don't believe you.'
No te creo a tí. (Contrastive)

Consider now the derived objects in the following examples:

(27a) No la ví salir apurada.
No la ví a ella salir apurada. (Contrastive)
'I didn't see her leave in a hurry.'

(27b) No te creo capaz de engañar.
No te creo a tí capaz de engañar. (Contrastive)
'I don't believe you to be capable to deceive.'
(27c) No me considero capaz de hacerlo.
No me considero a mí misma capaz de hacerlo. (Contrastive)
'I don't consider myself to be capable to do it.'

2.2 Further inadequacies of the simple-sentence analysis. From the semantic point of view the simple-sentence analysis is totally inadequate, for it does not provide any structural basis for the inchoative interpretation of these reflexive verbs. This is bound to be a basic shortcoming of any simple-sentence analysis.

Furthermore, Napoli's simple-sentence analysis puts sentences with reflexive inchoatives almost on an equal footing with the so-called 'impersonal' sentences, such as:

(28) Se ven malos programas en la TV. 'Bad shows are seen on TV.'

Presumably, these impersonal sentences would have an unspecified animate subject in deep structure in contrast to reflexive inchoatives, which would have <u>no</u> subject in deep structure in her analysis.

Although inchoative and impersonal sentences share features of interpretation (e.g. their surface subject is never an agent but a patient), there are sufficient differences in syntactic behavior to warrant a structural difference more substantial than the mere occurrence of a subject in deep structure. For instance, Roldán (1971) has pointed out that stative verbs are not allowed as reflexive inchoatives:

(29) saber/*saberse 'to know'
ver/*verse 'to see'
oir/*oirse 'to hear'
entender/*entenderse 'to understand'
respetar/*respetarse 'to respect', etc.

But there are no restrictions on the occurrence of stative verbs in impersonal sentences. Consider the following examples:

(30) Se saben muchas cosas. 'Many things are known.'
Se oyen las campanas. 'The bells are heard.'
Se ven las ruinas. 'The ruins are seen.'

Moreover, impersonal sentences can be constructed with copulas, but a copula cannot be the basis for a reflexive inchoative:

(31) Se es obediente. 'One is obedient.'
(32) *Roberto se es.

Furthermore, Roldán has also observed that inchoatives in the simple present tense can only receive the interpretation of habitual, future, or historical present. In contrast, impersonal sentences in this tense may have the present time reference:

(33) *El hielo se derrite ahora. 'The ice melts now.'
(34) Ahora se oyen las campanas. 'The bells are heard now.'

3. Conclusions. The arguments presented above indicate that the two types of transformational analysis so far proposed to derive reflexive inchoatives are descriptively inadequate. Basically, these analyses make the wrong predictions with respect to which verbs may function as reflexive inchoatives, while they do not account for why these verbs behave as intransitive reflexives. These analyses share the presuppositions that these reflexive inchoatives derive from basic verbs, and that the reflexive clitic is the result of the operation of the rule REFLEXIVE. Insofar as a transformational analysis in the case grammar framework, such as Langacker's 1970, shares these presuppositions, it is apt to be target to the same criticisms. Langacker postulates an underlying simple-sentence structure and a copying process on which the application of the rule REFLEXIVE crucially depends. (He assumes that SUBJECT CHOICE has two parts, COPY and DELETION, the would-be reflexive inchoatives being exceptions to the second part.)

Despite the systematicity predicted by all these analyses, a quick scrutiny of the lexicon reveals quite a different state of affairs. First, there is a large class of causatives that have related reflexive inchoatives, e.g. enojar/enojarse 'to annoy'/'to become annoyed', enfurecer/enfurecerse 'to enfuriate'/'to become furious', asustar/asustarse 'to frighten'/'to become frightened', asombrar/asombrarse 'to amaze'/'to become amazed', etc. Along with these there is also a considerable number of reflexive inchoatives for which there are no basic verbs, e.g. *ausentar/ausentarse 'to become absent', *arrepentir/arrepentirse 'to repent', *resfriar/resfriarse 'to catch a cold', *ensimismar/ensimismarse 'to become engrossed', etc. There are, on the other hand, verbs that denote change of state that cannot appear as reflexive inchoatives, e.g. fallecer/*fallecerse 'to die', nacer/*nacerse 'to be born', surgir/*surgirse 'to appear', etc. Finally, there are other verbs denoting change of state for which the reflexive clitic is optional, e.g. enflaquecer(se) 'to become thin', engordar(se) 'to become fat', enfermar(se) 'to become sick', etc. Given the unsystematic distribution of these verbs in the lexicon, and the fact that they are semantically and syntactically different from other reflexive verbs, it seems rather hopeless to try to relate them to other verbs.

A reexamination of the facts about these verbs, as well as of the process of reflexivization, is clearly needed. Where the answer lies cannot be surmised, but it has now become obvious that any future proposal will have to avoid the pitfalls of the old ones if it is to achieve descriptive adequacy.

NOTE

This is a revised version of a paper presented at a meeting of the Linguistic Society of America, December, 1975.

REFERENCES

Anderson, S. and P. Kiparsky, eds. 1973. A festschrift for Morris Halle. New York, Holt, Rinehart and Winston.

Anttila, R. 1972. An introduction to historical and comparative linguistics. New York, Macmillan.

Bach, E. 1967. 'Have' and 'be' in English syntax. Lg. 43.462-85.

_____ and R. T. Harms, eds. 1968. Universals in linguistic theory. New York, Holt, Rinehart and Winston.

Baker, C. L. 1970. Note on the description of English questions: The role of an abstract question morpheme. Foundations of language. 6.197-219.

Banfield, A. 1973. Narrative style and the grammar of direct and indirect speech. Foundations of language. 10.1-39.

Barbaud, P. 1974. Constructions superlatives et structures apparentées. Thesis. Université de Paris VIII, France.

Barbosa, J. S. 1822. Gramática filosófica da língua portuguesa. Lisboa, Tipografía da Academia das Ciências.

Bennett, C. E. 1918. New Latin grammar. Boston, Allyn and Bacon.

Berman, A. 1973. Adjectives and adjective complement constructions. Unpublished doctoral dissertation. Harvard University. 1974 NSF Report No. 29.

_____. 1974a. On the VSO hypothesis. Linguistic inquiry. V.1-37.

_____. 1974b. Infinitival relative constructions. In: Papers from the tenth regional meeting of the Chicago Linguistic Society. 37-46.

Bierwisch, M. and K. E. Heidolph, eds. 1970. Progress in linguistics. The Hague, Mouton.

Bolinger, D. 1952. Linear modification. PMLA. 67.1117-44.

_____. 1954. English prosodic stress and Spanish sentence order. Hispania. 37.152-6.

_____. 1954-5. Meaningful word order in Spanish. Boletín de filología, Universidad de Chile. 7.45-6.

Bolinger, D. 1968. Postponed main phrases: An English rule for the Romance subjunctive. Canadian journal of linguistics. 14.3-30.

_____. 1972. Accent is predictable (if you're a mind reader). Lg. 48.633-44.

Boons, J. P. 1973. Acceptabilité, interprétation et connaissance du monde--A propos du verbe PLANTER. Rapport LADL.

Bordelois, I. 1972. Untitled unpublished mimeo on infinitives in Spanish, French, and English. MIT.

Borkin, A. 1973. To be or not to be. In: Papers from the ninth regional meeting of the Chicago Linguistic Society. 44-56.

Bourciez, E. E. J. 1967a. Eléments de linguistique romane. 5ème. ed. Paris, Klincksieck.

_____. 1967b. Phonétique française. Paris, Klincksieck.

Bourulot, H. 1966. Atlas linguistique et éthnologique de la Champagne et de la Brie. Paris, CNRS.

Brame, M. K. (to appear). Conjectures and refutations in syntax and semantics.

_____ and I. Bordelois. 1973. Vocalic alternations in Spanish. Linguistic inquiry. IV.111-68.

Bresnan, J. 1970. On complementizers: Towards a syntactic theory of complement types. Foundations of language. 6.297-321.

_____. 1971. Sentence stress and syntactic transformations. Lg. 47.257-81.

_____. 1972. The theory of complementation in English syntax. Unpublished doctoral dissertation. MIT.

_____. 1973. Syntax of the comparative clause construction in English. Linguistic inquiry. IV.275-343.

Browne, W. 1970a. Noun phrase definiteness in relatives and questions: Evidence from Macedonian. Linguistic inquiry. I.267-70.

_____. 1970b. More on definiteness markers: Interrogatives in Persian. Linguistic inquiry. I.359-63.

Bull, W. 1942. New principles for some Spanish equivalents of 'to be'. Hispania. 25.433-43.

Campbell, R. J., M. G. Goldin, and M. C. Wang, eds. 1974. Linguistic studies in Romance languages. Washington, D.C., Georgetown University Press.

Casagrande, J. and B. Saciuk, eds. 1972. Generative studies in Romance languages. Rowley, Mass., Newbury House.

Caton, C. E., ed. 1963. Philosophy and ordinary language. Urbana, University of Illinois Press.

Chafe, W. 1970. Meaning and the structure of language. Chicago, The University of Chicago Press.

Chomsky, N. 1957. Syntactic structures. The Hague, Mouton.

Chomsky, N. 1958. A transformational approach to syntax. In: Proceedings of the third Texas conference on problems of linguistic analysis in English. Ed. by A. A. Hill. Austin, The University of Texas Press. 124-58.

_____. 1961. On the notion rule of grammar. Proceedings of the twelfth symposium in applied mathematics. 12.6-24. Reprinted in J. A. Fodor and J. J. Katz. 119-36.

_____. 1964a. Current issues in linguistic theory. The Hague, Mouton.

_____. 1964b. The logical basis of linguistic theory. In: Proceedings of the ninth international congress of linguists. Ed. by H. Lunt. The Hague, Mouton.

_____. 1965. Aspects of the theory of syntax. Cambridge, Mass., The MIT Press.

_____. 1970a. Remarks on nominalization. In: Jacobs, R. and P. Rosenbaum, eds. 184-221.

_____. 1970b. Deep structure, surface structure, and semantic interpretation. In: Jakobson, R. and S. Kawamoto, eds. 52-91.

_____. 1973. Conditions on transformations. In: Anderson, S. and P. Kiparsky, eds. 232-86.

_____ and M. Halle. 1968. The sound pattern of English. New York, Harper and Row.

Copceag, D. and G. Escudero. 1966. 'Ser' y 'estar' en español y en rumano. Revue roumaine de linguistique. 11.339-49.

Cornulier, B. 1973. Considérations sur les incises en français contemporain. Thesis. Université de Provence.

D'Amourette, J. and E. Pichon. 1933. Des mots à la pensée: Essai de grammaire de la langue française. Vol. III. Morphologie du verbe; structure de la phrase verbale; infinitif. Paris, Collection de linguistes contemporains.

De Boer, C. 1926. Essai sur la syntaxe moderne des prépositions en français et en italien. Paris, Champion.

Delattre, P. 1966. Studies in French and comparative phonetics. Amsterdam, Mouton.

Dell, F. 1972. Une règle d'effacement de i en français. Recherches linguistiques. 1.63-87.

_____. 1973. Les règles et les sons. Paris, Herman.

Delorme, E. and R. C. Dougherty. 1972. Appositive NP constructions: We, the men; we men; I, a man; etc. Foundations of language. 8.2-29.

Densusianu, Ovid. 1901. Histoire de la langue roumaine. Vol. I. Paris, E. Leroux.

Detrich, E. E. (in preparation). Constraints on final consonant deletion in French.

Dimitrescu, Florica. 1967. Introducere în fonetica istorică a limbii române. Bucureşti.

Dougherty. R. 1971. A grammar of coordinate conjoined structures, II. Lg. 47.298-339.

Dworkin, S. N. 1974. Studies in the history of Latin primary -D- in Hispano-Romance. Unpublished doctoral dissertation in Romance philology. University of California, Berkeley.

Emonds, J. 1969a. Root and structure-preserving transformations. Unpublished doctoral dissertation. MIT. 1970. Mimeo. Bloomington, Indiana Linguistics Club. Revised version to appear, Cambridge, Mass., The MIT Press.

_____. 1969b. Constraints on transformations. Mimeo. Bloomington, Indiana University Linguistics Club.

_____. 1972. A reformulation of certain syntactic transformations. In: Peters, S., ed. 21-62.

_____. 1974. Parenthetical clauses. In: Rohrer, C. and N. Ruwet, eds. I. 192-205.

Ernout, A. and F. Thomas. 1951. Syntaxe latine. Paris, Klincksieck.

Fauconnier, G. 1974. La coréférence: Syntaxe ou sémantique? Paris, Seuil.

Fillmore, C. 1970. The grammar of 'hitting' and 'breaking'. In: Jacobs, R. and P. Rosenbaum, eds. 120-33.

_____ and T. Langendoen, eds. 1971. Studies in linguistic semantics. New York, Holt, Rinehart and Winston.

Firbas, J. 1964. On defining the theme in functional sentence analysis. Philologica praguensia. 8.170-6.

Fodor, J. A. and J. J. Katz, eds. 1964. The structure of language. Englewood Cliffs, N.J., Prentice-Hall.

Foley, J. 1965. Spanish morphology. Unpublished doctoral dissertation. MIT.

Fouché, P. 1956. Traité de prononciation française. Paris, Klincksieck.

_____. 1966. Phonétique historique du français. 3 vols. Paris, Klincksieck. 2nd ed.

Foulet, L. 1967. Petite syntaxe de l'ancien français. Paris, Champion.

Francis, N. 1966. Review of Brno studies in English. Vol. 4. Lg. 42.142-9.

Frege, G. 1963. Compound thoughts. Mind. 72.1-17.

Gaatone, D. 1970. La transformation impersonnelle en français. Le français moderne. 38.389-411.

Gamillscheg, E. 1957. Historische französische Syntax. Tübingen, Niemeyer.

Gili y Gaya, S. 1969. Curso superior de sintaxis española. Barcelona, Bibliograf. 9a. ed.

Gilliéron, J. and E. Edmont. 1902-1910. Atlas linguistique de la France. Paris, Champion.

Gouet, M. 1971. Lexical problems raised by some of the 'foutre'-constructions. Studies out in left field. Chicago, The University of Chicago Press. 79-85.

Green, G. M. 1972. On the derivation of a relative infinitive construction. Presented at a meeting of the Linguistic Society of America.

_____. 1973. Some remarks on split controller phenomena. In: Papers from the ninth regional meeting of the Chicago Linguistic Society. 123-38.

Greenberg, J. 1966. Universals of language. Cambridge, Mass., The MIT Press.

Grevisse, M. 1964. Le bon usage. 8ème. ed. Gembloux, J. Duculot.

Grinder, J. 1970. Super Equi-NP deletion. In: Papers from the sixth regional meeting of the Chicago Linguistic Society. 297-317.

Gross, M. 1967. Analyse formelle comparée des complétives en anglais et en français. Rapport LADL.

_____. 1968. Grammaire transformationnelle du français: Syntaxe du verbe. Paris, Larousse.

_____. 1969. Lexique des constructions complétives. Ms.

_____. 1975. Méthodes en syntaxe. Paris, Herman.

_____, M. Halle, and M. P. Schützenberger, eds. 1973. The formal analysis of natural languages. The Hague, Mouton.

Gruber, J. S. 1967. Look and see. Lg. 43.937-47.

_____. 1970. Studies in lexical relations. Mimeo. Bloomington, Indiana University Linguistic Club.

Guiraud, P. 1966. Le système du relatif en français populaire. Langages. 3.40-48.

Haase, A. 1969. Syntaxe française du XVIIème siècle. Paris, Delagrave.

Hadlich, R. 1971. A transformational grammar of Spanish. Englewood Cliffs, N.J., Prentice-Hall.

Hankamer, J. 1973. Unacceptable ambiguity. Linguistic inquiry. IV. 17-68.

Hanssen, F. 1913. Gramática histórica de la lengua castellana. Halle, Max Niemeyer.

Harris, J. W. 1969. Spanish phonology. Cambridge, Mass., The MIT Press.

_____. 1972. Five classes of irregular verbs in Spanish. In: Casagrande, J. and B. Saciuk, eds. 247-71.

Harris, J. W. 1974. Las formas verbales de segunda persona plural y otras cuestiones de fonología y morfología. Revista de lingüística aplicada y teórica. Universidad de Concepción, Chile.

_____. 1975. Stress assignment rules in Spanish. In: Milan, W. G., J. J. Staczek, and J. C. Zamora, eds. 56-83.

Hatcher, A. G. 1956a. Syntax and the sentence. Word. 12.17-68.

_____. 1956b. Theme and underlying question: Two studies of Spanish word order. Word. Vol. 12, supplement No. 3.

Helke, M. 1971. The grammar of English reflexives. Unpublished doctoral dissertation. MIT.

Hensey, F. G. 1972. Portuguese vowel alternation. In: Casagrande, J. and B. Saciuk, eds. 285-92.

Higgins, F. R. 1973a. On J. Emonds's analysis of extraposition. In: Kimball, J., ed. Vol. 2. 149-95.

_____. 1973b. The pseudo-cleft construction in English. Unpublished doctoral dissertation. MIT.

Hintikka, J. 1972. Different constructions in terms of the basic epistemological terms: A survey of some problems and proposals. In: Olson, R. E. and A. M. Paul, eds. 105-22.

Hochester, A. 1973a. Subordinate clause raising and lexical gap. Mimeo. Bloomington, Indiana University Linguistics Club.

_____. 1973b. Is the Like-subject constraint necessary? Presented at a meeting of the Linguistic Society of America.

Hooper, J. 1973. Aspects of natural generative phonology. Unpublished doctoral dissertation. UCLA.

_____. 1974. On assertive predicates. Syntax and semantics IV. New York, Seminar Press.

_____ and T. Terrell. 1974. A semantically based analysis of mood in Spanish. Hispania. 57.484-494.

_____ and S. A. Thompson. 1973. On the applicability of root transformations. Linguistic inquiry. IV. 465-98.

Householder, F. 1973. On arguments from asterisks. Foundations of language. 10.365-76.

Huckin, T. 1973. The variable-deletion hypothesis. Unpublished paper.

Huddleston, R. 1971. A problem in relative clause reduction. Linguistic inquiry. II.115-16.

Hyart, C., ed. 1969. Mélanges Fohalle. Université de Liège.

Hyman, L. 1973. The feature 'grave' in phonological theory. Journal of phonetics. 1.329-37.

Jackendoff, R. S. 1969. Some rules of semantic interpretation for English. Doctoral dissertation. MIT.

_____. 1971. Gapping and related rules. Linguistic inquiry. 2.21-36.

_____. 1972. Semantic interpretation in generative grammar. Cambridge, Mass., The MIT Press.

Jacobs, R. and P. Rosenbaum. 1968. English transformational grammar. Waltham, Mass., Blaisdell.

_____, eds. 1970. Readings in English transformational grammar. Waltham, Mass., Ginn.

Jakobson, R., G. Fant, and M. Halle. 1951. Preliminaries to speech analysis. 1963 printing. Cambridge, Mass., The MIT Press.

Jakobson, R. and S. Kawamoto, eds. 1970. Studies in general and Oriental linguistics. Tokyo, TEC.

Jensen, J. S. 1973. L'infinitif et la construction relative en français et en italien contemporains. Revue romane. VIII. 122-32.

Jespersen, O. 1924. The philosophy of grammar. London, George Allen and Unwin.

Kajita, M. 1966. A generative-transformational study of semi-auxiliaries in present-day American English. Tokyo, Sanseido.

Karttunen, L. 1971a. Implicative verbs. Lg. 47.340-58.

_____. 1971b. Some observations on factivity. Papers in linguistics. 4.55-69.

Kaye, J. 1973. Rule mitosis: The historical development of Algonquian palatalization. To appear in: Linguistic studies of native Canada. Ed. by E. Cook and J. Kaye.

Kayne, R. S. 1969. On the inappropriateness of rule features. QPR. RLE, MIT. No. 95.

_____. 1972. Subject inversion in French interrogatives. In: Casagrande, J. and B. Saciuk, eds. 70-126. French version: 1973. Le français moderne. 41.1. 10-42 and 41.2. 131-51.

_____. 1975. French syntax: The transformational cycle. Cambridge, Mass., The MIT Press.

Keenan, E. L. 1971. Two kinds of presuppositions in natural language. In: Fillmore, C. and T. Langendoen, eds. 45-52.

Keniston, H. 1937. The syntax of Castillian prose. Chicago, The University of Chicago Press.

Kenstowicz, M. and C. Kisseberth. 1973. Issues in phonological theory. The Hague, Mouton.

Kimball, J., ed. 1973. Syntax and semantics. New York, Seminar Press.

King, R. 1973. Rule insertion. Lg. 49.551-78.

Kiparsky, P. 1968. Linguistic universals and linguistic change. In: Bach, E. and R. T. Harms, eds. 171-202.

_____. 1972. Explanation in phonology. In: Peters, S., ed. 189-227.

_____. 1973. Abstractness, opacity, and global rules. Mimeo. Bloomington, Indiana University Linguistics Club.

Kiparsky, P. and C. Kiparsky. 1970. Fact. In: Bierwisch, M. and K. E. Heidolph, eds. 143-73.

Kisseberth, C. 1970. On the functional unity of phonological rules. Linguistic inquiry. I. 291-306.

_____. 1973. On the alternation of vowel length in Klamath: A global rule. In: Kenstowicz, M. and C. Kisseberth, eds. 9-25.

Klima, E. S. 1965. Studies in diachronical transformational syntax. Unpublished doctoral dissertation. Harvard University.

_____. 1969. Relatedness between grammatical systems. In: Reibel, D. A. and S. A. Schane, eds. 227-46.

Kuno, S. 1972. Functional sentence perspective. Linguistic inquiry. 3.269-320.

Kuroda, S. Y. 1969. English relativization and certain related problems. In: Reibel, D. A. and S. A. Schane, eds. 264-87.

Lakoff, G. 1966. Stative adjectives and verbs in English. In: Mathematical linguistics and automatic translation. NSF Report No. 17. Harvard University Computational Laboratory.

_____. 1971a. Irregularity in syntax. New York, Holt, Rinehart and Winston.

_____. 1971b. The role of deduction in grammar. In: Fillmore, C. and T. Langendoen, eds. 63-70.

Lakoff, R. 1968. Abstract syntax and Latin complementation. Cambridge, Mass., The MIT Press.

_____. 1973. Review of Progress in linguistics by Bierwisch and Heidolph, eds. Lg. 49.685-96.

Landreau, G. 1927. La phonétique française. Montréal, Bibliothèque de l'Action française.

Langacker, R. W. 1966. A transformational syntax of French. Unpublished doctoral dissertation. Urbana, University of Illinois.

_____. 1970. Review of Spanish case and function by Mark Goldin. Lg. 46.167-85.

Langendoen, D. T. 1970. Essentials of English grammar. New York, Holt, Rinehart and Winston.

_____. 1973. Review of From deep to surface structure by Burt. Lg. 49.714-25.

Lausberg, H. 1965. Lingüística románica. Vol. I. Madrid, Gredos.

Le Bidois, R. 1952. L'inversion du sujet dans la prose contemporaine. Paris, Editions d'Artrey.

Lehmann, W. P. and Y. Malkiel, eds. 1968. Directions for historical linguistics: A symposium. Austin, The University of Texas Press.

Lerch, E. 1925. Historische französische Syntax, I. Leipzig, Reisland.

Lightner, T. 1970. Why and how does vowel nasalization take place? Papers in linguistics. 2.179-226.

Littré, Emile. 1873. Dictionnaire de la langue française. Paris, Hachette.

Long, M. 1974. Prepositions and propositions: Some remarks on French infinitives. In: Campbell, R. J. et al., eds. 237-53.

Luján, M. 1974. Prenominal adjectives in Spanish predicates. In: Campbell, R. J. et al., eds. 178-88.

Luján Gough, M. 1972. Adjectives in Spanish. Unpublished doctoral dissertation. The University of Texas at Austin.

Lyons, J. 1967. A note on possessive, existential, and locative sentences. Foundations of language. 3.390-96.

_____. 1968. Introduction to theoretical linguistics. Cambridge, Cambridge University Press.

Malkiel, Y. 1968. The inflectional paradigm as an occasional determinant of sound change. In: Lehmann, W. P. and Y. Malkiel, eds. 23-64.

_____. 1974a. New problems in Romance interfixation (I): The velar insert in the present tense (with an excursus on -zer/-zir verbs). Romance philology. 27.304-55.

_____. 1974b. Etiological studies in Romance diachronic phonology. Acta linguistica hafniensia. 14.2.201-42.

_____. 1974c. Pre-classical French une (un) image 'likeness, statue', Old Portuguese um (uma) viage (m) 'journey': A study of parallelism in reverse. Romance philology. 28.1.20-27.

Martin, R. 1970. La transformation impersonnelle. Revue de linguistique romane. 34.377-94.

_____. (to appear). Trois aspects de la syntaxe de C'EST. Genève, Droz.

Martinet, A. 1971. La prononciation du français contemporain. Genève, Droz. 2nd edition.

Martinon, P. 1927. Comment on parle en français. Paris, Larousse.

Mateus, M. H. M. 1973. Aspectos de fonología portuguesa. Thesis. Universidade de Lisboa, Portugal.

Meillet, A. 1964. Introduction à l'étude comparative des langues indo-européennes. University of Alabama Press.

_____ and J. Vendryes. 1968. Traité de grammaire comparée des langues classiques. Paris, Champion.

Menéndez Pidal, R. 1926. Orígenes del español. Madrid, Hernando. 1950, 3ra ed. Madrid, Espasa-Calpe.

Meyer-Lübke, W. 1922. Palatalizarea labialelor. Dacoromania. II.1-19.

_____. 1911. Romanisches-Etymologisches Wörterbuch. Heidelberg, C. Winter.

Milan, W. G., J. J. Staczek, and J. C. Zamora, eds. 1975. 1974 colloquium on Spanish and Portuguese linguistics. Washington, D.C., Georgetown University Press.

Milner, J. C. 1974. Les exclamatives et le complementizer. In: Rohrer, C. and N. Ruwet, eds. I. 78-121.

Moreau, M. L. 1971. L'homme que je crois que est venu; qui, que: Relatifs et conjonctions. Langue française. 11. 77-90.

Morin, Y. 1974. Régles phonologiques à domaine indéterminé: Chute du cheva en français. Les cahiers de linguistique de l'Université du Québec. 4. 69-88.

Napoli, D. J. 1974a. Reflexivization across S boundaries in Italian. Presented at a meeting of the Linguistic Society of America.

_____. 1974b. In chaos or inchoative? An analysis of inchoatives in Modern Standard Italian. In: Campbell, R. J. et al., eds. 219-36.

_____. (in preparation). Indefinite subject sentences in Italian.

_____ and M. Nespor. 1976. Negatives in comparatives. To appear in Language, December, 1976.

Navarro, T. 1946. Estudios de fonología española. Syracuse, N. Y., Syracuse University Press.

Niedermann, M. 1953. Historische Lautlehre des Lateinischen. Heidelberg, C. Winter.

Obenauer, H. G. 1974. Combien je suppose qu'il faut de règles pour isoler 'combien'. Deux aspects de la syntaxe du 'combien'. In: Rohrer, C. and N. Ruwet, eds. I. 164-81.

_____. (in preparation). Recherches sur la structure interne de NP et AP en français: les quantifieurs. WH. Thesis. Université de Stuttgart. (To appear, Tübingen, Niemeyer.)

Olson, R. E. and A. M. Paul, eds. 1972. Contemporary philosophy in Scandinavia. Baltimore, The Johns Hopkins Press.

Pardal, E. A. 1974. Aspects de la phonologie générative du portugais. Thesis. Université de Paris VIII, France.

Perlmutter, D. 1970. On the article in English. In: Bierwisch, M. and K. E. Heidolph, eds. 233-48.

_____. 1971. Deep and surface structure constraints in syntax. New York, Holt, Rinehart and Winston.

_____. 1973. Evidence for the cycle in Japanese. Bulletin of the Research Institute of Logopedics and Phoniatrics, University of Tokyo. 6.

_____. (in preparation). The cyclical theory of grammar.

_____ and J. R. Ross. 1970. Relative clauses with split antecedents. Linguistic inquiry. I. 350.

Peters, S., ed. 1972. Goals of linguistic theory. Englewood Cliffs, N. J., Prentice-Hall.

Petrovici, E. 1936. Băn. u > W, V, B, P. Dacoromania. VIII. 180-81.

Postal, P. M. 1968. Coreferentiality and sentence formation. Unpublished.

Postal, P. M. 1969. Review of Patterns of language--Papers in general, descriptive, and applied linguistics by A. McIntosh and M. A. K. Halliday. Foundations of language. 5.409-26.

Postal, P. M. 1970a. On coreferential complement subject deletion. Linguistic inquiry. I.439-500.

_____. 1970b. On the surface verb 'remind'. Linguistic inquiry. I.37-120.

_____. 1971. Cross-over phenomena. New York, Holt, Rinehart and Winston.

_____. 1972a. On some rules that are not successive cyclic. Linguistic inquiry. III.211-22.

_____. 1972b. A global constraint on pronominalization. Linguistic inquiry. III.35-59.

_____. 1974. On raising. Cambridge, Mass., The MIT Press.

Procopovici, A. 1931. Review of Recherches sur la phonétique du roumain au XVIe. siècle by A. Rosetti. Dacoromania. VI. 395-419.

Querido, A. A. 1974. Structures lexicales du français. Analyse componentielle des verbes et adjectifs. Travaux du laboratoire de recherches sur le langage, Université de Montréal.

Quicoli, A. C. 1972. Aspects of Portuguese complementation. Unpublished doctoral dissertation. Buffalo, State University of New York.

_____. (to appear). On Portuguese impersonal verbs. In: Schmidt-Radefeldt, J., ed.

Rankin, R. L. 1973a. Yod increment in Romanian dialects. Presented at the Kentucky Foreign Language Conference, Lexington.

_____. 1973b. Palatalization as a phonetic process. To appear in the Clarence Parmenter festschrift.

Redenbarger, W. (to appear). Vocalic evolution in Proto-Romance.

Reibel, D. A. and S. A. Schane, eds. 1969. Modern studies in English. Englewood Cliffs, N.J., Prentice-Hall.

Ribeiro, J. A. 1959. 'Essere', 'sedere' e 'stare' nas línguas românicas. Boletim de filologia. 17.147-76.

Richardson, H. B. 1930. An etymological vocabulary to the 'Libro de buen amor' of Juan Ruiz. New Haven, Yale University Press.

Rivero, M. L. 1971. Mood and presupposition in Spanish. Foundations of language. 7.305-36.

Roca Pons, J. 1958. Estudios sobre perífrasis verbales del español. Revista de filología española. Anejo 67. Madrid.

Rohlfs, G. 1949. Historische Grammatik der Italienischen Sprache und ihrer Mundarten. Vol. I. Bern, A. Francke.

Rohrer, C. and N. Ruwet, eds. 1974. Actes du colloque franco-allemand de grammaire transformationnelle. 2 vols. Tübingen, Niemeyer.

Roldán, M. 1971. Spanish constructions with se. Language Sciences 18.15-29.

Ronat, M. 1974. Echelles de base et mutations en syntaxe française. Thesis. Université de Paris VIII, France.

Ronconi, A. 1946. Il verbo latino. Principi di sintassi storica. Bologna, Zanicelli.

Rosenbaum, P. S. 1965. A principle governing deletion in English sentential complementation. In: RC 1519, Thomas J. Watson Research Center, IBM Corporation, Yorktown Heights, N.Y.

_____. 1967. The grammar of English predicate complement constructions. Cambridge, Mass., The MIT Press.

Rosetti, A. 1932. Despre palatalizarea labialelor. Grai şi Suflet. V. 351-58.

_____. 1966. Istoria limbii române. Vols. I, IV, V, and VI. Bucureşti, Minerva.

Ross, J. 1967. Constraints on variables in syntax. Unpublished doctoral dissertation. MIT.

_____. 1970. On declarative sentences. In: Jacobs, R. and P. Rosenbaum, eds. 222-72.

_____. 1973. Slifting. In: Gross, M., M. Halle, and M. P. Schützenberger, eds. 133-69.

Ruwet, N. 1968. Introduction à la grammaire générative. Paris, Plon.

_____. 1969. A propos des prépositions de lieu en français. In: Hyart, C., ed.

_____. 1972. Théorie syntaxique et syntaxe du français. Paris, Seuil. (English translation to appear. London, Longmans).

Saltarelli, M. 1973. Periphrastic causatives and functional squish. Presented at a meeting of the Linguistic Society of America.

_____. (in preparation). Functional constraints in syntax.

Sanders, G. 1970. Some general grammatical processes in English. Unpublished doctoral dissertation. Bloomington, Indiana University.

Sandfeld, K. 1965. Syntaxe du français contemporain. Vol. I: Les pronoms. Paris, Champion. Vol. II: Les propositions subordonnées. Vol. III: L'infinitif. Paris, Droz.

Schane, S. A. 1968. French phonology and morphology. Cambridge, Mass., The MIT Press.

_____. 1971. The phoneme revisited. Lg. 47.503-21.

_____. 1974. There is no 'French Truncation rule.' In: Campbell, R. J., et al., eds. 89-99.

Schlyter, S. 1974. Une hiérarchie d'adverbes et leurs distributions, par quelles transformations? In: Rohrer, C. and N. Ruwet, eds. II. 76-86.

Schmidt-Radefeldt, J., ed. (to appear). Studies in Portuguese linguistics. The Hague, Mouton.

Shibatani, M. 1973. The role of surface phonetic constraints in generative phonology. Lg. 49.87-106.

Shopen, T. 1972. A generative theory of ellipsis. Mimeo. Bloomington, Indiana University Linguistics Club.

Solta, G. R. 1966. Palatalisierung und labialisierung. Indogermanische Forschungen. 70.276-315.

Sonnenschein, E. A. 1914. A new Latin grammar. Oxford, Clarendon Press.

Stockwell, R. P., J. D. Bowen, and J. W. Martin. 1965. The grammatical structures of English and Spanish. Chicago, The University of Chicago Press.

Tobler, A. 1886. Vermischte Beiträge zur französischen Grammatik. 2nd ed. Vol. I. Leipzig, S. Hirzel.

UESP [UCLA English syntax project]. 1968. Integration of transformational theories on English syntax. UCLA.

Urmson, J. O. 1963. Parenthetical verbs. In: Caton, C. E., ed. 220-40.

Vago, R. 1972. On the universality of subject pronoun deletion. Harvard University. Unpublished paper.

Vendler, Z. 1967. Linguistics in philosophy. Ithaca, Cornell University Press.

Vennemann, T. 1972. Phonetic detail in assimilation: Problems in Germanic phonology. Lg. 48.863-92.

Vergnaud, J. R. 1974. French relative clauses. Unpublished doctoral dissertation. MIT.

Wasow, T. 1972. Anaphoric relations in English. Unpublished doctoral dissertation. MIT.

Williams, E. B. 1962. From Latin to Portuguese. 2nd ed. Philadelphia, University of Pennsylvania Press.